D1411515

Quest for the Jade Sea

Quest for the Jade Sea

Colonial Competition Around an East African Lake

Pascal James Imperato

Westview Press
A Division of HarperCollinsPublishers

Copyright © 1998 by Pascal James Imperato.

Published in 1998 in the United States of America by Westview Press, 5500 Central Avenue, Boulder, Colorado 80301-2877, and in the United Kingdom by Westview Press, 12 Hid's Copse Road, Cumnor Hill, Oxford OX2 9JJ

Library of Congress Cataloging-in-Publication Data
Imperato, Pascal James
  Quest for the Jade Sea : colonial competition around an East African lake / Pascal James Imperato.
    p. cm.
  Includes bibliographical references and index.
  ISBN 0-8133-2791-1
  1. Rudolf, Lake, Region (Kenya and Ethiopia)—Discovery and exploration—European.   2. Rudolf, Lake, Region (Kenya and Ethiopia)—Politics and government.   3. Great Britain—Foreign relations—Ethiopia.   4. Ethiopia—Foreign relations—Great Britain.
  I. Title.
  DT434.R75I47   1998
  967.62'7—dc21   98-4983
                                                                           CIP

Text design by Heather Hutchison

The paper used in this publication meets the requirements of the American National Standard for Permanence of Paper for Printed Library Materials Z39.48-1984.

10   9   8   7   6   5   4   3   2   1

*Dedicated with admiration and affection to
the Reverend Paolo Tablino,
who has given a lifetime of service
to the peoples of the lake*

Contents

Contents

Illustrations

Center Photograph Section

Acknowledgments

$\mathcal{M}$any people and institutions provided me with valuable assistance over the years that this work was in progress. I want to thank my wife, Eleanor, and my children, Alison, Gavin, and Austin, for their constant support and encouragement and their remarkable understanding and patience. I want to especially thank the Reverend Paolo Tablino of Marsabit, Kenya, an internationally respected authority on the peoples and history of northern Kenya, for his many years of friendship and for helping me with my research.

Several leading Africanists gave me advice and encouragement, for which I wish to express my sincere gratitude. They include: Karl W. Butzer, Ph.D., Dickson Centennial Professor of Liberal Arts in the Department of Geography at the University of Texas at Austin; Robert O. Collins, Ph.D., professor of history, University of California at Santa Barbara; Professor David Turton, formerly of the Department of Social Anthropology at the University of Manchester and currently director of the Refugee Programme at the University of Oxford, England; and Professor Paul T.W. Baxter of the Department of Social Anthropology at the University of Manchester.

The research effort for this book engaged me for many years and required my studying primary source documents and published works in several languages: English, French, German, Hungarian, and Italian. My own fluency in the first two and passable knowledge of the last greatly facilitated my research. My wife assisted me with the Italian-language publications, and André Szabo of Raanana, Israel, a friend and colleague from my years in Africa, translated a large number of Hungarian-language documents into French. Professor Frederick E. Hueppe of Saint John's University, Jamaica, New York, translated a number of German-language documents for me over several years.

My research would not have been successful without the help of some of the descendants and relatives of the travelers described here, the assistance of other scholars and writers, and the cooperation of institutions that hold various archival materials. Geza Teleki gave me access to Count Samuel Teleki's diaries, spent many patient hours over the years providing me with important information about the count and his family, and carefully critiqued the chapter on his relative's epic journey; Lajos Erdélyi of Budapest, Hungary, Count Teleki's biographer, shared with me his knowledge of Teleki and the world in which he lived in Transylvania; David Bresch, M.D., assisted me by conducting field inquiries in Romania in early 1997 and during my lengthy 1997 meeting in New York with Lajos Erdélyi; Elisabeth Mauthner of the Hungarian Human Rights Foundation graciously served as a translator during my meeting with Lajos Erdélyi; John Winthrop Aldrich, William Astor Chanler's grandnephew, gave me complete access to the extensive Chanler Family archives, read drafts of the Chanler chapter, and was an enthusiastic supporter of this project over many years; Maddie De Mott, Chanler's niece, made very helpful suggestions about the manuscript and facilitated my research; Chanler's sons, William Astor Chanler Jr. and the late Ashley Chanler, were always the willing subjects of interviews and helped me to delve into family documents; George E. Galvin Jr. allowed me to examine archival materials concerning his father; the late H. Spencer Potter, Ph.D., Arthur Donaldson Smith's grandnephew, and his wife, Margaret, provided valuable assistance; and Simon F. Austin, Herbert Henry Austin's grandson, sent me copies of important primary source documents and read drafts of the relevant chapters.

Monty Brown, Arthur Neumann's biographer, shared with me his vast knowledge of Lake Rudolf and northern Kenya and facilitated my contacts with some of the descendants and relatives of the travelers covered in this book; the late Elspeth Huxley, Lord Delamere's biographer, gave me much encouragement and help; Errol Trzebinski, a leading authority on early travelers and settlers in Kenya, and her husband, Sbish, have been faithful friends and supporters for many years; Edward Rodwell not only assisted me with my field research in Kenya but also made suggestions about the manuscript; Manlio Bonati, Vittorio Bottego's biographer, furnished me with valuable resource documents and publications and made suggestions about the Bottego chapter; Richard Seltzer, a leading authority on Alexander Bulatovich and the translator of two of his books of African travel, provided me with English-language copies of his unpublished manuscripts and read a draft of the chapter on this traveler; and Prince André Orbeliani, Bulatovich's nephew, and his wife, Princess Irene Orbeliani, were very generous with their assistance, provided me with important information about their uncle, and made helpful suggestions about the manuscript.

Richard Pankhurst provided valuable suggestions about the chapter on the Ethiopian and Russian travelers to Lake Rudolf; Nancy Marples, Montagu Sinclair Wellby's niece, encouraged me in my research quest and critiqued the chapter on her uncle's journey; Nigel Evans, Wellby's second cousin, and his wife, Marion, shared with me important family background information and made suggestions about the manuscript; William Fitzhugh Whitehouse Jr., the son of William Fitzhugh Whitehouse, has been an enthusiastic supporter of this project and reviewed the chapter on the Harrison-Whitehouse Expedition; Dr. Jane Mee, curator of the Wood End Museum of Natural History in Scarborough, York, England, assisted me with the James Jonathan Harrison archives; Keith Nicklin, former curator of the Powell-Cotton Museum in Birchington, England, sent me important materials about the museum and Major Percy Horace Gordon Powell-Cotton; John Butter provided important information about his father, Archibald Butter; and Amanda Hill, archivist of Rhodes House Library, University of Oxford, England, helped me examine the Lord Delamere materials.

Maggie Magnuson, assistant librarian, Royal Engineers Library, Chatham, Kent, England, located documents concerning Charles William Gwynn and Philip Maud; Christine Kelly, former archivist, and Paula Lucas, archivist, the Royal Geographical Society, London, accessed and photocopied letters and a large number of documents related to several travelers; Katharine Turok, executive editor, Holmes & Meier Publishers, made useful research suggestions; Colin Legum and Oliver Hoare helped me obtain copies of Foreign Office documents from the Public Record Office, Richmond, England; Ronald E. Coons, Ph.D., professor of history, University of Connecticut, and my colleague and collaborator on a project to prepare Ludwig von Höhnel's English-language autobiography for publication, ran down items for me in the Austrian State Archives in Vienna and provided much encouragement; the Reverend W. Robert Griffin greatly assisted me in researching Arthur Donaldson Smith's later years; the late D. Strother Pope, M.D., provided me with useful insights based on his own extensive travels in Africa; Gerald Rilling tracked down a number of books and documents and helped me in analyzing some based on his own extensive knowledge of East Africa; Lois Hahn patiently and expertly prepared numerous drafts of the manuscript and made many helpful suggestions about revisions; Barbara Ellington and Laura Parsons, my editors at Westview Press, provided enthusiasm, suggestions, and guidance; Joan Sherman edited the manuscript with care; and Lynn Arts expertly supervised the book's production.

I also want to thank the following individuals and institutions for their help and apologize for any names I have overlooked: Ella Abney, librarian, Albion D. Bernstein Library, Medical Society of the State of New York; the Austrian State Archives, Vienna; Robert Baker; the late

Sister Antoinette Casertano; the late Sister Martha Casertano; Coudersport Public Library; William G. Dixson; Cynthia Downey; the late Sydney Downey; the late Henry Evans; Dr. Lidia Ferenczy, National Szchenyi Library, Budapest; John T. Flynn, M.D.; Free Library of Philadelphia; Jan Hemsing; Gerard A. Imperato; Maryellen C. Kaminsky, archival specialist, University of Pennsylvania Archives; Margaret Kummerfeldt; Joseph J. Lauer, Africana bibliographer, Michigan State University Libraries; Library of the American Museum of Natural History; Library of Congress; Library of the Department of State; Library of the New York Academy of Medicine; Library of the New York Historical Society; Library of the State University of New York, Health Science Center at Brooklyn; Manhasset Public Library; Professor Harold G. Marcus; McBlain Books; National Council for Science and Technology, Nairobi, Kenya; Stephen Pern; the late Lady Alys Reece; Lord Rennell of Rodd; Professor G.N. Sanderson; Barnett Serchuk, librarian, IPRO Library; Carol M. Spawn, manuscript/archives librarian, Academy of Natural Sciences of Philadelphia; Janet L. Stanley, librarian, Warren M. Robbins Library, National Museum of African Art; Grayel Tauscher; Barbara Wilson, archivist, University of Pennsylvania Museum; and Arthur H. Wolintz, M.D., Distinguished Teaching Professor and Chairman Emeritus, Department of Ophthalmology, State University of New York, Health Science Center at Brooklyn.

Pascal James Imperato

Introduction

The first published illustration of Lake Rudolf, drawn from a photograph taken by Count Samuel Teleki (from Discovery of Lakes Rudolf and Stefanie, *1894).*

I n 1961, I traveled into the hot desert wastes of what was then the Northern Frontier District of Kenya Colony and Protectorate and saw a great salt lake called Rudolf. It lay in a wild and remote corner of Africa frequented only by pastoral nomads, small bands of El Molo fishermen, colonial administrators, and occasional visitors. There were no roads leading to the lake, and one had to reach it over trails worn deep into the volcanic slag and sand by generations of wildlife and cattle. A first glimpse of the jade green waters was scarce reward for the grueling trip entailed in reaching them. There were no creature comforts or any sense of ease near the lake, as one had to be continuously on alert for life-threatening dangers that lurked in the waters and on the land nearby. Enormous, aggressive crocodiles patrolled the shallows along the lake's shores, and warring pastoralists and armed poachers roamed the rocky hills. Lions roared at night from the cover of dry riverbeds, scorpions and poisonous snakes frequented the rocky lake shore, and hyenas seemed to dance at midday in mirages on the horizon.

Although I did not realize it then, I had been privileged to see this lake much as late-nineteenth-century travelers had, before a paved road was put through to its western shore and lodges and landing strips were set up for fishermen and tourists. The area was so inaccessible, in fact, that the colonial authorities used it as a place to detain Kenya's nationalist leaders, including Jomo Kenyatta. Even if they had managed to escape from their detention camps at Lokitaung and Lodwar, the detainees could never have survived the numbing heat and desert wastes.

My early travels through the Northern Frontier District stirred my interest in its peoples and their history, as well as in the story of first European contact. These interests eventually led me to an in-depth study of late-nineteenth-century travelers to the lake and the broader issue of colonial competition for this part of Africa. What struck me from the outset was the sheer number and diversity of well-outfitted European expeditions that headed for the lake in the last decade of the nineteenth century. Close to a dozen of them arrived there between 1888 and 1901, led by Americans, Austro-Hungarians, Britons, Frenchmen, Italians, and Russians. To them must be added a number of Ethiopian military expeditions, about which there is no known documentation. That so remote and desolate a lake received such extraordinary attention reflected misguided colonial judgments about its economic and strategic importance and its presumed relationship to the Nile.

For a period of fifteen years, I carefully studied the published writings of these colonial travelers. I also quarried numerous repositories of primary source materials for letters, diaries, diplomatic dispatches, and confidential reports. In order to provide a fuller portrait of these travelers, I sought out and interviewed their direct descendants and other relatives. Their recollections of family stories, anecdotes, and opinions have enabled me to complement and balance the information available in published writings, letters, and diaries. A number of these relatives also gave me access to family documents not otherwise available. Drawing on all this information and the writings of others, I have tried to reconstruct a comprehensive account of the adventures and experiences of these travelers while analyzing the broader political issues that lay at the heart of colonial interest in this corner of Africa.

Lake Rudolf, which is also known as Lake Turkana, lies in the eastern arm of the great Rift Valley. It is primarily fed by the Omo River, which flows south from the Ethiopian highlands and sits in an inhospitable landscape of dormant volcanoes, wind-driven semidesert, and old lava flows. During the morning hours, strong gusts of wind usually blow from the east down the slopes of Mount Kulal and across the surface of the lake. This unrelenting wind creates large, white-capped waves on the lake's surface and makes navigation almost impossible. It also gives the lake a beautiful bluish color, reflecting the clear sky above. However, when the wind dies down in the afternoon, the lake takes on the color of green jade, due to algae that rise to the surface when the waters are calm. It is because of this afternoon and evening color that the lake has long been known as the Jade Sea.

Prior to the Pleistocene epoch, the lake was much larger than it is today, and it drained into the Nile through the Sobat River. It was then situated in a lush tropical environment that supported abundant wildlife and early hominids. Today, Rudolf is very much a desert lake, surrounded by volcanic slag in the south and east and sand dunes and mudflats in the north and west. Three islands—North, Center, and South—attest to the volcanic origins of the lake bed and the surrounding countryside.

The absence of an outlet has long made Rudolf's waters brackish. Yet they support large populations of fish, crocodiles, and hippopotamuses and many species of birds, including pelicans, flamingos, kingfishers, and cormorants. For most of the twentieth century, the crocodiles of the lake and the Omo River were renowned for both their enormous size and their ferocity. But extensive hunting over the years has resulted in the disappearance of most of the larger crocodiles and the extinction of the elephant herds that once frequented the lake's eastern shore.

Although Lake Rudolf primarily lies in Kenya, a portion of its northern end stretches across the border into Ethiopia. The amount of the lake on the Ethiopian side has progressively shrunk during the past several decades as the water levels have fallen. This in turn has altered the configuration of the Omo River delta at the northern end of the lake, especially in periods of drought when virtually none of the lake lies on the Ethiopian side of the border. The lake is currently 155 miles long and from 10 to 20 miles wide. Although it is a Rift Valley lake, it is relatively shallow in most places but has occasional depths of up to 250 feet.

By the mid-nineteenth century, there were several reports from missionaries and travelers far to the north, in the lush cool highlands of Ethiopia, about a great lake to the south. However, their information was based on the often conflicting accounts of African traders and travelers. In 1859, Léon des Avanchers, a Capuchin missionary living in Ethiopia, published a detailed map of the area using information he had obtained from African and European travelers. He called this great lake El Boo and made the startling claim that it was a source of the Nile. At the same time, Johann Ludwig Krapf, a German missionary who had lived in both Ethiopia and what is now Kenya, published a map of the East African interior on which he placed a large lake called Zamburu at the site of Lake Rudolf. Although these two reports corroborated one another, neither Avanchers nor Krapf had actually seen the lake themselves. As a result, influential armchair geographers in Europe initially paid scant attention to their reports. In addition, the Avanchers and Krapf lake struck them as probably fictitious since it did not fit in with the puzzle of the Nile sources that they had pieced together in London.

John Hanning Speke's visit to Lake Victoria in 1862 and his subsequent claim that it was the source of the Nile not only captured the world's attention but also ushered in an era of accelerated exploration of central Africa. Speke's claim was promptly challenged by his former expedition leader, Richard Burton, and doubted by powerful armchair geographers who encouraged others to unravel the mystery of the sources of the Nile. Throughout the 1860s and 1870s, several expeditions traveled into Central Africa in order to resolve what Europeans considered to be the greatest geographic challenge of their time. These expeditions laid open a complex world of magnificent lakes, interlacing rivers, swamps, and snow-covered mountains, all of which constituted the source of the Nile.

In 1883–1884, Joseph Thomson successfully traveled from coastal Mombasa across Maasai land to the northern end of Lake Victoria and back. In so doing, he came to within 150 miles of Lake Rudolf. Africans who had been there told him that it was called Samburu and that its salt waters contained large populations of crocodiles, fish, and hippopotamuses. Eventually, the British became very interested in this large lake because it was possibly another source of the Nile, whose entire course they were determined to control. However, other Europeans were also intrigued by this lake, among them Crown Prince Rudolf of Austria-Hungary, who encouraged Count Samuel Teleki to find it. Teleki's 1887–1888 expedition not only resulted in a wealth of geographic information but also drew the attention of European colonial powers to the lake, which was then perceived as a possible source of the Nile.

European colonial interest in Lake Rudolf developed at a time when Ethiopia was emerging as a powerful military state engaged in imperial expansion. Although the French, Italians, and Russians initially harbored ambitions in this part of Africa, Britain eventually became the dominant colonial power and, as a result, found itself competing with Ethiopia for control of the lake. In furthering its colonial aims, Ethiopia used French and Russian proxies, military force, and shrewd diplomacy that exploited European rivalries. This volume examines this unique African colonialism, its impact on the peoples of the lake, and its interactions with its European analogs.[1]

A number of recent authors have carefully studied nineteenth-century travel accounts, often from a postmodern perspective. They make a number of cogent observations about these writings, including their quest romance character and their infusion with European ideals and values.[2] The sense of European superiority frequently expressed in these accounts usually reaffirmed national values and served as a justification for Eurocolonialism. In addition, the realities presented by these travelers were often textured by race attitudes, religious beliefs, social values, and economic and political self-interest.[3] Although these characteristics of nineteenth-century travel writing may have nuanced field observations to some degree, they also serve to better inform us of the cultural and social references of the authors themselves and permit a better understanding of their motives. Thus, the activities and accomplishments of these travelers must be judged within the framework of their times, not according to latter-day cultural and social norms. Wherever relevant, I have drawn attention to these issues, especially in the context of colonial expansion.

There has been a tendency for some modern writers to characterize the geographic accomplishments of nineteenth-century travelers to Africa as a process of "converting local knowledges (discourses) into European national and continental knowledges associated with European forms and relations to power."[4] Although there is some obvious merit to such statements, one should not forget that local knowledge bases were frequently fragmented and imprecise and usually not set in larger geographic contexts. European travelers did not, as these writers imply, simply translate local knowledge into their own. Rather, they used local knowledge bases as points of departure and greatly augmented them through the application of scientific techniques by which topographic features were situated, quantified, and contextualized. In addition, European travelers communicated their knowledge to wide audiences of Europeans and Africans. The latter often used the received knowledge to open up new trade routes and markets that greatly benefited them and local populations.

The systematizing of nature was a powerful force in the nineteenth century, and in Africa, it often represented the projection of European power and control onto the untamed wilderness. Not surprisingly, most of the men who traveled to Lake Rudolf devoted significant time and effort to measuring topographic features and collecting natural history specimens. These activities, even when modest, as in the case of some sportsmen, tended to valorize expeditions and justify the slaughter of wildlife. The shooting of elephants on a large scale was more difficult to justify, and as a consequence, some travelers chose not to mention the extent of their killing. Though sport and adventure played a role in drawing them to elephant hunting, the prospect of collecting enough ivory to offset the costs of an expedition was often the more powerful incentive. Yet one must not lose sight of the fact that this killing of wildlife took place in an era when African animal herds seemed inexhaustible. Whatever the propensities of a given traveler, they all returned home with sizable collections of bones, hides, horns, insects, plants, seeds, geologic specimens, and ethnographic objects, which became grist for the curators' mills in major museums.

Most late-nineteenth-century curators were skilled at taxonomy, but they and some of their successors were not always adept at keeping records. During my years of research, I found that many of the natural history collections had lost their identities in larger holdings, had deteriorated, or had been dispersed. Ethnographic collections fared far better, and some, such as Arthur Donaldson Smith's at the University of Pennsylvania Museum, have been well cared for and are easily identifiable and accessible. Private trophy collections did not, for the most part, survive the ravages of moths and time. Many descendants disposed of them for a variety of reasons, including disinterest, a lack of space, or the need to raise money.

All of the travelers to Lake Rudolf were bold, resourceful, and unorthodox men well endowed with originality and eccentricity. They were adventurers and risk-takers at heart, men whose courage and daring enabled them to overcome the enormous obstacles presented by climate, geography, and disease. Whether as the willing agents of larger colonial designs, soldiers intent on advancing their military careers, hunters out for sport, or explorers devoted to advancing science, they all left behind a legacy of fascinating adventure stories and tales of the unknown. This book is about them, their travels, and the complex story of colonial competition for a far-off lake called the Jade Sea.

1

The Sources of the Nile

Johann Ludwig Krapf (from Travels, Researches, and Missionary Labours, *1860).*

*A*round 140 A.D., Claudius Ptolemaeus (Ptolemy), the renowned Alexandrian astronomer and geographer, produced a map of the world. On it, he showed the Nile arising from two large lakes below the equator. These in turn were fed by streams flowing down the slopes of the snow-covered Lunae Montes (Mountains of the Moon). Ptolemy had never been to equatorial Africa but based his map and *Guide to Geography* on a variety of recorded sources. Among these was an account by a Syrian geographer of the first century named Marinus of Tyre. Marinus had recorded the voyage of a Greek merchant, Diogenes, who claimed to have traveled inland from the coast of East Africa for twenty-five days.

Diogenes left the coast from an emporium called Rhapta and eventually came to two lakes and a snowy range of mountains, which he said were the source of the Nile. The actual location of Rhapta is currently debatable. However, it may have been on the Pangani River or

7

farther south in the Rufiji River delta. In either case, it appears to have been on the coast of present-day Tanzania. Given the regularity of Greco-Roman trading along the East African coast and in the Indian Ocean, it is not at all inconceivable that Diogenes had traveled inland as Marinus of Tyre claimed. There is also the possibility that the information presented by Marinus was relayed to him by Greco-Roman traders who had obtained it from their counterparts on the East African coast.[1]

Whatever the origins of the information contained on Ptolemy's maps and in his *Guide to Geography*, it came to represent most of what was known in Europe about the source of the Nile for the next 1,700 years. It was not until around 1835 that theoretical scholars based in Great Britain began their intense studies of East Africa. These "armchair geographers," as they are sometimes called, heavily relied on the formalistic methods of medieval scholasticism. They applied these methods to Arab, classical, medieval, and Portuguese texts in an attempt to deduce the precise geography of places they had never seen. This painstaking pursuit of geographic truth through meticulous logic was soon to come into direct conflict with the findings of those who had seen the equatorial snow-covered mountains and lakes of East Africa. Yet the armchair geographers never retreated from their deduced assertions, even when faced with overwhelming evidence gathered in the field. To have done so would have eroded the power of their established authority. However, they were quite adept at reinforcing the validity of their conclusions by claiming that certain discoveries in Africa clearly confirmed their own carefully reasoned opinions. In so doing, they did not cite the numerous instances where field observations contradicted their strongly held contentions.

British armchair geographers received their first serious challenge in 1849 when a German missionary named Johann Rebmann, working in the service of the Church Missionary Society (CMS) in East Africa, reported that he had visited Mount Kilimanjaro three times in 1848 and 1849 and had seen its snow-covered peaks.[2] This was threat enough to armchair theories about East African geography. However, Rebmann's assertion was strengthened by the report of his senior colleague, Johann Ludwig Krapf, who had also journeyed into the interior from their coastal mission station at Rabai, near Mombasa. He not only corroborated Rebmann's observations of Kilimanjaro but also reported seeing another snow-covered mountain, Mount Kenya, to the north.

The Krapf and Rebmann reports were not received by an unbiased and uninformed audience. Their chief critic was William Desborough Cooley, a prominent member of the Royal Geographical Society, who had never been to Africa. Yet at the time, he was recognized and respected as a leading authority on African geography. His authority derived from numerous publications in which he diligently analyzed the previous writings of classical, medieval, Arab, and Portuguese authors.

As Cooley saw it, Ptolemy's Mountains of the Moon were not in East Africa and Kilimanjaro and Kenya were only a fifth the height claimed by Rebmann and Krapf. It was even suggested that Rebmann and Krapf had merely seen white rocks gleaming in the sun atop relatively small mountains.

Cooley's views may not have been convincing enough to completely sway the leaders of the Royal Geographical Society. However, they had the effect of sowing doubt about Krapf and Rebmann's claims. Those claims, based as they were on what Cooley characterized as "ocular testimony," were made in an era when the society placed great store in scientific determinations of altitude, distance, latitude, and longitude. David Livingstone, who worked farther south in Africa, shared Krapf and Rebmann's view of using geographic exploration in the interests of missionary goals. However, he employed a variety of observing and measuring instruments that gave his findings a credibility that pundits like Cooley could scarcely challenge.

Krapf did indeed possess a range of scientific instruments, given to him by the Bombay Geographical Society. But it is doubtful that he knew how to use them, and even if he did, he reported that it was impossible to do so in the presence of curious African crowds. As a result, his estimations of distances and directions fell wide of the mark and made them and his visual discoveries an easy target for Cooley's pen.

Cooley was unrelenting in his criticisms of Krapf and Rebmann's reports, pouring acidic comments about them onto the pages of prominent periodicals and eventually into a book entitled *Inner Africa Laid Open*. In this book, he characterized Krapf and Rebmann's snow-covered mountains as myths: "With respect to those eternal snows on the discovery of which Messrs. Krapf and Rebmann have set their hearts, they have so little shape or substance, and appear so severed from realities that they take quite a spectral character."[3]

Two other powerful armchair geographers entered the fray. James MacQueen was an opinionated Scotsman who had once been the manager of a sugar plantation in the West Indies.[4] There, he came into contact with slaves from West Africa, from whom he learned a great deal about the geographic features of the continent's interior. It was through their accounts and a trenchant analysis of the available literature that he correctly deduced the location of the Niger River delta in 1816.[5] However, it was his experience as editor of the *Glasgow Courier* and his part ownership of the Colonial Bank and the Royal

Mail Steam Packet Company that gave him a power base from which to project his views.

MacQueen was fairly gentle with Krapf and Rebmann. He had, in fact, previously contributed a geographic memoir to a book about Krapf's six years as a missionary in Ethiopia.[6] Nevertheless, Mac-Queen had very strong views about the source of the Nile, which he vigorously presented in a number of publications. He was convinced that the Nile issued from two large lakes in East Africa, an assumption that was closer to the truth than Cooley's belief in only one.

The third member of the armchair triumvirate was Charles Tilstone Beke. Unlike Cooley and MacQueen, he had actually traveled in Africa. Primarily a businessman with international mercantile interests, he went to Abyssinia in 1840. The threefold purpose of this trip was to open up commercial links with Abyssinia, to abolish the slave trade, and to discover the sources of the Nile. Over a period of three years, Beke surveyed some 70,000 square miles of country but had little success in setting up trade with Abyssinia or in stamping out the slave trade. Beke's scientific accomplishments in Abyssinia were truly substantial. In addition to mapping the watershed between the Nile and Awash Rivers, he meticulously collected the vocabularies of fourteen languages and dialects, as well as a number of natural history specimens.

After his return to London in 1843, Beke was awarded the gold medal of the Royal Geographical Society. He once again took up his commercial pursuits and also authored many publications dealing with his scientific explorations in Abyssinia.[7]

Beke was no stranger to Krapf since the two had met in Abyssinia. He respected Krapf and his intellectual integrity and opined that Kilimanjaro and Kenya were part of Ptolemy's Mountains of the Moon. He also claimed that the rivers that fed the Nile flowed from the slopes of these mountains. It was not merely friendship for Krapf that drove Beke to these conclusions; it was also a certain amount of self-interest. Based on his own survey work in Abyssinia, he had concluded that Africa had a principal mountain system running from north to south on the eastern side of the continent. He viewed the Mountains of the Moon as part of this range, the northern extent of which he claimed to have fully explored in Abyssinia. So convinced was Beke of the validity of this theory that he organized an expedition in 1849 to prove it. Queen Victoria's husband, Prince Albert, and other prominent individuals gave the expedition their patronage. Unfortunately, Beke recruited a Dr. Bialloblotsky from Hanover to lead it. Bialloblotsky was a bizarre and unsuitable character who made a very bad impression on Lieutenant-Colonel Atkins Hamerton, the British agent in Zanzibar.

After consulting with Krapf, Hamerton effectively sabotaged the Beke expedition by recommending that the sultan of Zanzibar not give Bialloblotsky letters requesting the assistance of local governors.[8]

Krapf, who had been at the Rabai mission station since 1843, regularly obtained information about the interior from Arab and Swahili traders. These men often traveled inland along well-established caravan routes to the great East African lakes. Since they dealt in slaves and ivory, they were often vague about their routes and important geographic landmarks. However, over several years of interviewing these traders, Krapf had concluded that there were probably three large lakes in the interior, Nyasa, Tanganyika, and Ukerewe. Despite these conclusions, he reluctantly accepted the erroneous interpretations of a junior missionary colleague, Jacob J. Erhardt, who had arrived at Rabai in 1849. Thirteen years younger than Krapf, Erhardt quickly proved to be a valuable addition to the mission team, especially because he had some medical knowledge. But he soon voiced firm views on a number of issues that were sometimes in conflict with Krapf's opinions. Krapf and Rebmann also had frictions of their own over the direction of their missionary endeavors, which eventually led to a permanent estrangement. Krapf left Rabai in September 1853, and after a return visit to Abyssinia in 1854, he retired to his native Württemberg.

Meanwhile, Erhardt traveled to Tanga farther down on the East African coast in March 1854. It was his hope to strike inland to the Usambara Mountains, where he planned to establish a mission station. However, the Arab traders along this coast, protective of their slave trading, proved so hostile that Erhardt was unable to travel inland. He finally left Tanga in October 1854 and, after a brief stay at Rabai, permanently departed from East Africa in 1855. Only Rebmann remained at Rabai, where he was to labor for another twenty years before returning to Württemberg a blind and broken man.[9]

Erhardt's 1854 stay at Tanga would have lasting consequences for the geographic reputations of all three missionaries. While there, he collected as much information as he could about the interior. From what he heard, it seemed that all caravan routes terminated at great waters to the west. Based on this information, he wrongly concluded that there was an enormous inland sea in the heart of East Africa, and back at Rabai, he easily convinced Rebmann of this as well. Erhardt's conclusion did not square at all with Krapf's opinion that there were at least three large interior lakes. Yet Krapf reluctantly acquiesced to Erhardt's view, perhaps because he did not wish to further exacerbate their very strained relations, and never publicly presented his own correct opinion that there were, in fact, three lakes.

Erhardt called the enormous body of water Lake Uniamesi and drew up a map depicting it at the center of East Africa. He published his map in a Württemberg missionary magazine, *Das Calwer Mission-blatt*, in 1855. Its appearance in such a limited-circulation publication drew little attention. However, the renowned Africa explorer Dr. Heinrich Barth sent the map, along with three letters by Rebmann, to the German geographic scholar August Petermann, who in turn submitted a report on the letters to the widely read *Athenaeum*, published in London.[10] Meanwhile, the CMS sent the map to the Royal Geographical Society, where it was hotly debated at a November 1855 meeting. Its publication in the society's proceedings early in 1856 caused both an uproar and an outpouring of ink from the pens of the armchair geographers.[11]

Cooley, MacQueen, and Beke lost no time rushing into print. They wrote passionate letters to the *Athenaeum* in which they both criticized the map and once again expounded on their long-held theories about the geography of the East African interior.

In the ensuing debates, Erhardt's creation was pejoratively referred to as the "slug map" because of the peculiar shape given to Lake Uniamesi. It was not only the lake's shape that drew comment but also the fact that it was said to cover much territory previously thought to be dry. Even Richard Burton, the famous explorer, could not resist throwing critical barbs:

> In 1855, Mr. Erhardt, an energetic member of the hapless "Mombas Mission," had on his return to London offered to explore a vast mass of water, about the size of the Caspian Sea, which, from information of divers "natives," he had deposited in slug or leech shape in the heart of intertropical Africa . . . thus bringing a second deluge upon sundry provinces and kingdoms thoroughly well known for the last half century.[12]

Fortunately, cooler heads prevailed. Francis Galton of the Royal Geographical Society summed up the then current state of "exceeding ignorance" of the region when he drew attention to the obvious differences between the maps of Cooley, MacQueen, and Erhardt.

The near hysterical debate about the source of the Nile focused the attention of geographers on Lake Uniamesi, and no one took time to comment on a much smaller lake depicted in Erhardt's map. It lay to the northeast at three degrees north latitude and thirty-nine degrees east longitude in the arid lands of the Rendille and Boran peoples and was called Lake Zamburu. To its southwest was Lake Baringo, and to its east the great Juba (Giuba) River. Except for the longitude, which is off by two degrees, the placement of this lake and the surrounding geographic and ethnographic names leave little doubt but that it is Lake

Rudolf. Neither Krapf, Rebmann, nor Erhardt had ever seen Lake Baringo or Lake Rudolf; their information about these distant lakes came from Arab and Swahili traders, who knew of them as good sources of ivory.

Lake Zamburu drew little interest in the swirl of the slug map debate because it was thought to lie well outside the Nile watershed. Almost three decades would go by before that perception would change. By that time, European interest in the Nile and its sources was no longer being driven by the intellectual curiosity of the 1840s and 1850s but by fierce colonial competition for the river. Every possible Nile source became the focus of rival European powers, for whoever possessed the Nile and its sources controlled the heart of Africa and the fate of Egypt.

Erhardt's map made it clear to the leadership of the Royal Geographical Society that the riddle of the Nile's watershed could never be deduced either from London or from the East African coast. What was needed was a well-equipped scientific expedition that would make for the interior and accurately replace the fanciful features that had for so long cluttered the map of Africa. They chose for this expedition thirty-five-year-old Captain Richard Francis Burton. He was an officer in the Indian army, a highly respected Arabic scholar, and an experienced traveler who had once made a daring dash into Mecca in disguise. He had proven his mettle under fire, had great leadership abilities, and was fluent in Arabic—a great asset in dealing with the Arab-speaking traders who controlled the East African coast and interior trade routes. But Burton was also domineering, eccentric, opinionated, and intolerant of those who did not measure up to his intellectual standards. It puzzled many that he chose as his traveling companion John Hanning Speke, a rather bland fellow army officer and avid sportsman who had little to show for his ten years in India apart from the usual collection of heads, skulls, and skins. But Burton assessed Speke as the ideal subaltern since he presented an exterior that was modest, quiet, methodical, and self-effacing. What was not so apparent to Burton was Speke's enormous need to distinguish himself, a need that would eventually transform him from a loyal disciple into a fierce rival.

With a grant of £1,000 from the Foreign Office and the patronage of the Royal Geographical Society, Burton and Speke set out in 1856 to investigate the Rabai missionaries' 300-mile-wide and 800-mile-long Lake Uniamesi. They arrived in Zanzibar in December and left for the interior in June 1857. A violent antipathy eventually developed between the two men, kept in check in large measure by frequent incapacitating bouts of illness. Finally, after many difficulties, they came within sight of Lake Tanganyika on February 13, 1858. They learned from Arab traders what Krapf had known all along: There were, indeed, three separate lakes—Nyasa, Tanganyika, and Ukerewe (or Nyanza)—all separated by appreciable distances. Because he was temporarily blinded by illness, Speke could not at first see the lake. Burton was so ill that he eventually led their caravan back to the Arab center of Tabora so that they could recuperate.

Speke quickly recovered, whereupon, according to Burton, he became antagonistic, restless, and patronizing with the Arab traders with whom he was unable to converse. He finally asked Burton if he could go a short distance to the north and look for Ukerewe Lake. Burton was quite willing to let him go, not least of all because Speke was causing so much trouble with their Arab hosts in Tabora. Burton, though, had other motives, motives that would eventually prove to be his own undoing. He had little regard for Speke's abilities and was certain he would fail. More importantly, he had concluded that Ukerewe Lake, if such a place really existed, was not a source of the Nile. He was wrong on both counts.

It was a relatively easy, two-week walk of 180 miles from Tabora to the lake. On August 3, 1858, Speke stood on its southern shore, convinced that it was the source of the Nile. But this powerful conviction was not substantiated by any scientific facts. Elated with his discovery, he named the lake Victoria Nyanza (Lake Victoria) in honor of Queen Victoria and later wrote: "The pale blue waters of the Nyanza burst suddenly upon my gaze. . . . I no longer felt any doubt that the lake at my feet gave birth to that interesting river [the Nile], the source of which has been the subject of so much speculation and the object of so many explorers."[13]

Such sentiments made little impression on Burton when Speke returned to Tabora: "At length my companion had been successful, his 'flying trip' had led him to the northern waters. . . . We had scarcely, however, breakfasted, before he announced to me the startling fact that he had discovered the source of the White Nile. . . . The fortunate discoverer's conviction was strong; his reasons were weak."[14]

Burton was fairly convinced at this time that the true source of the Nile lay to the east, near Mount Kenya and Mount Kilimanjaro. Although he allowed for the possibility that Lake Tanganyika was also a source, he viewed Lake Victoria as perhaps a series of lakes that fed into the Upper Nile. He reasonably argued that he and Speke should report to the Royal Geographical Society on their findings regarding Lake Tanganyika. Speke clearly had other plans. Convinced that he had discovered the source of the Nile, he fully intended to claim the glory that he thought was justly his. Burton was a man who achieved fame by distinguishing himself in many endeavors. But for a man of

Speke's limited abilities, fame could only come through a singular chance accomplishment. Seeing Lake Victoria and claiming it as the source of the Nile was that chance.

The return trip to the coast was unpleasant for both men. Their arguments over the sources of the Nile and Lake Victoria grew so acrimonious that they agreed not to discuss the subject further. Worse still, they were both extremely ill, Speke more so than Burton. It was during his febrile deliriums that Speke expressed his strong resentments against Burton, who was nursing him. Each man had helped the other through illness and adversity on this journey, and this should have forged a strong and lasting friendship between them. But as the journey drew to a close, it was clear to both of them that Lake Victoria and Speke's personal need for it to be the source of the Nile made a future friendship impossible.

Burton was quite ill when they arrived at Aden, where the civil surgeon, Dr. John Steinhauser, advised him to rest. Speke, however, had fully recovered and was anxious to go home. He left aboard the *Furious*, after bidding Burton a polite farewell. Burton later claimed that Speke had assured him that he would not go to the Royal Geographical Society until Burton's return. If Speke had given such reassurances, he quickly changed his mind after meeting Laurence Oliphant, the eccentric and wealthy travel writer, aboard the *Furious*. On hearing Speke's story, Oliphant advised him not to wait for Burton but rather to put forth his views to the Royal Geographical Society at once.[15]

The reporting of the findings of an expedition by a subaltern before the leader's return was clearly a breach of accepted Victorian conduct. As an army officer, Speke knew this only too well. But Oliphant was persuasive, preying on Speke's sense of self-righteousness and vanity and stirring up not only his greed, ambition, and desire for recognition but also his resentments against Burton. Even in the absence of Oliphant's influence, it is likely that Speke would have behaved much the same anyway. He wrongly viewed his discovery of Lake Victoria as something of a personal accomplishment and not as part of the official expedition. Thus, he felt fully justified in presenting this finding and his theory about the lake being the source of the Nile to the Royal Geographical Society.

Speke privately approached Sir Roderick Murchison, the president of the society.[16] He and the society's other leaders must have known that Speke's attempt to present a portion of the expedition's findings in the absence of Burton was unscrupulous, if not unethical. Yet they were swept up by the excitement of Speke's discovery and by a powerful self-interest in associating themselves with it. They seem to have bought into Speke's theory that Lake Victoria was the source of the

Nile and had no wish to wait for Burton, who would have dismissed the claim. In allowing Speke to present his findings, they denied Burton any role in the discovery of Lake Victoria.

Speke seized his chance, but in so doing, he trampled Burton underfoot. He quickly became Britain's hero of the hour, hailed as the discoverer of the source of the Nile. The Royal Geographical Society actively promoted Speke's theory, and by late May, before Burton returned to London, the society had helped to raise £2,500 to send Speke back to Africa. In the process, the society and Speke foreclosed any possibility of Burton sowing seeds of doubt among the proposed expedition's financial sponsors.

When Burton finally reached London on May 21, 1859, twelve days after Speke's address before the society, he found that there was little interest in his Lake Tanganyika.[17] More troubling was the harsh realization that he had greatly misjudged the man who had been his traveling companion and that he had been betrayed by those in whom he had placed so much trust.

It was inevitable that the Speke-Burton conflict would become public. The insecure Speke, surrounded by allies and friends, went on the offensive against the one man who could demolish his claim. He viciously attacked Burton in print, exaggerated his own modest accomplishments, and trivialized Burton's. He published two articles in *Blackwood's Magazine* about the expedition, replete with errors, and had the temerity to claim that without him the expedition would have failed. At first, Burton remained silent, partly because he was still racked by malaria but more because he was very depressed by this ugly turn of events. His friends rallied to his support, and eventually, in 1860, he published his book *The Lake Regions of Central Africa*, in which he made known his true assessment of Speke:

> I could not expect much from his assistance; he was not a linguist . . . nor a man of science, nor an accurate astronomical observer. . . . During the exploration he acted in a subordinate capacity. Can I then feel otherwise than indignant, when I find that, after preceding me from Aden to England, with the spontaneous offer, on his part, of not appearing before the society that originated the expedition until my return, he had lost no time in taking measures to secure for himself the right of working the field I had opened . . . ?[18]

Speke, the man of the hour, was sent back to Africa to definitively resolve the issue of the source of the Nile. He was a poor choice for this job for many reasons. He lacked Burton's thoroughness, had no real interest in science, and was deficient in his knowledge of the instruments used for determining latitude, longitude, and altitude. He was also strongly biased in that he was not so much seeking the source of the Nile as attempting to prove his earlier claim about Lake Victoria. He chose as his traveling companion James Augustus Grant, a handsome fellow army officer who was a talented artist and botanist. Grant was unassuming and obedient, and as such, he was not apt to challenge Speke's supremacy either during or after the expedition.

Speke and Grant arrived in Zanzibar in 1860, and by late 1861, they were in Tabora. From there, they moved north into the country surrounding Lake Victoria. This was a part of Africa ruled by several politically volatile kingdoms, including Karagwe, Buganda, and Bunyoro. Delayed in Buganda for months by King Mutesa, Speke was finally able to leave in 1862. On July 21, he stood where the lake emptied into a river, which he called the Somerset Nile. He stood there alone, without Grant, whom he had sent off to the neighboring kingdom of Bunyoro. Although both men later claimed that this was a mutual decision, many suspected that Speke had taken advantage of Grant's modest and malleable nature so that he could reserve the glory of discovery for himself.

By November 1862, Speke and Grant were in the kingdom of Bunyoro. While there, they heard of a large lake, the Luta Nzigé (Dead Locust), that lay to the west. It was obvious to them that it might be yet another source of the Nile. But debilitated by malaria and short of supplies, they could not visit it even though it was but a short distance away. They headed down the Nile and struck for Gondokoro, where John Petherick, the British vice consul at Khartoum, was to meet them as prearranged by the Royal Geographical Society. The society had given Petherick £1,000 to purchase boats and supplies for the explorers. Drained by fever, emaciated from a meager food supply, and with their clothes in tatters, they pushed on toward Gondokoro with the expectation of being relieved by Petherick.[19]

When Speke and Grant struggled into Gondokoro on February 13, 1863, two and a half years had elapsed since the start of the expedition. They were pleasantly surprised to find Speke's old sportsman friend Samuel Baker and his future wife, Florence, there to meet them. Baker was a widely traveled man who, almost on a whim, decided to go to Gondokoro when he and Florence first reached Khartoum in June 1862. They finally arrived in Gondokoro on February 2, eleven days before Speke and Grant, only to find that Petherick had gone on a short ivory-collecting trip west of the Nile.

Speke was delighted to see Baker, who fed and clothed them and supplied them with all the news of the past two and a half years. But he was furious with Petherick, who arrived a week later. As Speke saw it, Petherick had put his personal trading interests ahead of the expedition's welfare and thus been derelict in his responsibilities to him and the Royal Geographical Society. Actually, Petherick and his wife had nearly died trying to get to Gondokoro. But this was of no concern to Speke. Well fed and supported by Baker and with Baker's boats at his disposal to continue on to Cairo, he had no need of Petherick and his supplies. Petherick's wife, who was emaciated from the nearly fatal trip to Gondokoro, pleaded with Speke to accept her husband's help. But Speke showed the revengeful side of his character by refusing to "recognize the succour dodge." That was not all. He and Grant defamed Petherick far and wide when they returned to England, going so far as to allege that he had been involved in the slave trade. As a result, Petherick lost his post as British vice consul at Khartoum and was almost made penurious. But he was not without friends, who were augmented by Speke's enemies, including the armchair geographer James MacQueen.[20] Still, it required many years for Petherick to rehabilitate his reputation and to clear himself of Speke's reckless charges.[21]

As Speke and Grant traveled down the Nile and back to London in triumph, Baker headed for the Luta Nzigé. For the next two years, he and Florence traveled through what is now northern Uganda. On March 14, 1864, they reached the Luta Nzigé, which they renamed Lake Albert in honor of the recently deceased prince consort. Equally important, they determined that the Somerset Nile that flowed out of Lake Victoria emptied into Lake Albert after crashing over the Murchison Falls (now Kabalega Falls). Another river, the Albert Nile, then flowed out of Lake Albert to form the White Nile.[22]

A year before, Speke's presumptuous telegram from Egypt—"The Nile is settled"—had been greeted with near hysteria in Great Britain. However, during the ensuing year, Speke had clearly shown that he was a man who could not shoulder fame and glory modestly or tolerate even minimal questioning of his findings. And increasingly, there were many questions put to him. He had not circumnavigated Lake Victoria or traced the Somerset Nile from the lake to the Nile. Baker would later show that Speke's river actually flowed into Lake Albert and that another river, the Albert Nile, flowed out of this lake to form the White Nile. But even without Baker's information, newspaper and magazine editorialists grew more and more skeptical of Speke's claims.

Comfortable with his hero's laurels and sensing he was invulnerable, Speke became reckless and began to attack his rivals in public. Petherick, who became a special object of his scorn, was finally forced to file a libel suit against him. Even Sir Roderick Murchison, once his arch supporter, now saw him as aberrant. Just as Speke had dismissed

Burton as irrelevant to his discovery of Lake Victoria, he now similarly viewed the Royal Geographical Society, which had obtained the funds for him to find the source of the Nile. He went so far as to refuse to write a report for the society's journal, as he feared it would endanger the profits from his soon to be published *Journal of the Discovery of the Source of the Nile*.[23] Murchison viewed Speke's refusal as representing both ingratitude and treachery. But he had only himself to blame. He had behaved treacherously against Burton in his rush to support Speke in the first place and had refused to give credence to Burton's accurate assessments of him.

Speke's book was published in December 1863 and became a bestseller. However, by spring 1864, public and scientific opinion was openly against him. Murchison was shocked by the grossly inferior quality of the scientific paper Speke eventually submitted for publication in the society's journal. It was so poorly written that Murchison felt compelled to write a preamble criticizing its weaknesses. Much to his chagrin, Murchison was discovering that everything Burton had said in 1860 about this man was true. He was also squirming because Speke had put the society and the Foreign Office in an awkward situation by convincing them that Petherick was a slave trader. They had rushed to judgment against Petherick and were now seeing Speke's reckless allegations proven false in the public press.

If Speke had lied about Petherick, could he have been telling the truth about the source of the Nile? Murchison was a shrewd political operative who recognized the danger posed to the society and himself personally by their continued support of an increasingly discredited Speke. In an attempt to shift public scrutiny away from the Speke-Petherick controversy and all that it implied for the society, Murchison supported Oliphant's brilliant scheme of arranging a debate between Speke and Burton. He knew that Burton would relish the opportunity and that as an army officer and a man of honor, Speke could not refuse.[24] The debate was scheduled to take place in September 1864 during a meeting of the British Association for the Advancement of Science. The topic was to be the sources of the Nile. In matching Burton against Speke, Oliphant was staging a journalistic spectacular. He must have known that in any debate between these two men, the odds were not in favor of Speke. Burton was a polished and experienced speaker, with one of the finest minds in the country. Speke was fumbling and inarticulate and partially deaf, all of which put him at a clear disadvantage.

Burton and the eighty-five-year-old but vigorous MacQueen had recently joined in common cause against Speke. They were brought together by a strong belief in alternate lake sources for the Nile and by

MacQueen's outrage against Speke for what he had done to Petherick. In addition, MacQueen had an intense revulsion to Speke's philandering at the court of King Mutesa of Buganda.[25]

Burton was prepared to propose that the Nile issued from Lake Tanganyika and Lake Baringo to the east. Lake Baringo, he said, was fed by the snows of Mount Kilimanjaro and Mount Kenya, which he now claimed were really Ptolemy's Mountains of the Moon. This theory, for such it was, appealed to MacQueen, who had long postulated a two-lake source for the Nile linked to the Mountains of the Moon.

The Burton-Speke debate never took place as planned on September 16, 1864. As Burton waited on the platform for the "Nile Duel" to begin, a note was passed around informing those present that Speke had been killed the previous afternoon while out shooting, with relatives nearby. He was found shot in the chest. The coroner determined the fatal injury had occurred when Speke's gun accidentally fired as he climbed over a stone wall. Burton fell back into his chair on hearing the news and exclaimed, "By God, he's killed himself." Many others were of the same opinion.

Speke was an experienced sportsman who had never had an accident with firearms. Yet he may have been understandably anxious and distracted because of the upcoming debate with a man who was clearly his intellectual superior and an accomplished speaker. He was also worried that his partial deafness would place him at a disadvantage with his rival and the audience. Distracted by these worries, he could easily have been careless as he climbed over the wall and pulled the gun up after himself.

Speke's enemies, and he had many at this point, were inclined to think that he had committed suicide. His allegations against Petherick were crumbling, thus opening to question his integrity and the veracity of his geographic claims. And now he was grandiosely speaking of making a trip across Africa, claiming that if he did not do it, no one could. In brief, he had made a successful grab for glory and fame and had just as quickly self-destructed because of his serious character flaws.

Burton and MacQueen preferred to interpret Speke's death as a suicide. Such an interpretation validated their conclusion that his discoveries were so faulty that he could not successfully defend them in public. Yet Burton was truly saddened by Speke's tragic death.[26] Also, he eventually came to realize that Speke had, in fact, made an important contribution to solving the mystery of the sources of the Nile.

Another thirteen years elapsed before all the details of the Nile watershed were elucidated. By this time, Beke and MacQueen were dead, and Burton's interests had taken him far away from the Nile source controversy to Brazil, India, the Middle East, and Trieste. It displeased many in class-conscious Great Britain that the honor of definitively resolving the riddle of the Nile sources fell to an American-raised Welsh orphan, Henry Morton Stanley.

A journalist for the *New York Herald*, Stanley became famous in 1871 when he "found" Livingstone at Ujiji on Lake Tanganyika. Livingstone had been in the interior since 1866, searching for the source of the Nile in the regions of Lake Tanganyika and Lake Bangweulu. Because of his strong efforts to end slavery, no caravan leaders were willing to carry his letters back to Zanzibar for fear that they contained information about their own slaving activities. Since he had not been heard from in several years, many assumed he was lost somewhere in Central Africa. Stanley's 1871 trip to find Livingstone was conceived of by James Gordon Bennett, the son of the publisher of the *New York Herald*.[27] More lasting for Stanley than the newspaper publicity created by his meeting with Livingstone was his desire to finish the work of Speke, Burton, Baker, and Livingstone.

In 1874, the British *Daily Telegraph* and the *New York Herald* sent an expedition into Africa, led by Stanley, to definitively resolve the issue of the sources of the Nile.[28] During this three-year expedition, Stanley circumnavigated Lake Tanganyika and, finding no northern outlet, proved that it was not connected to Lake Albert and was therefore not a source of the Nile. He also circumnavigated Lake Victoria, thus confirming Speke's claim that it was one lake, and found that it was the largest lake in Central Africa, not a series of lakes as Burton had claimed. He found only one river flowing out of the lake, Speke's Somerset Nile. The features of the Nile watershed north of this area were fully explored by Lieutenant Colonel Charles Chaillé-Long, an American, and Romolo Gessi, an Italian. Both were in the service of General Charles Gordon, who was then the governor of Egypt's Equatoria Province in the Sudan. In 1876, Gessi was the first to completely circumnavigate Lake Albert. He and Chaillé-Long eventually verified all of the geographic findings of Speke, Grant, and Baker in this region.[29]

Stanley proved that the Lualaba River, which Livingstone had hoped was the Nile, actually joined the Congo and flowed west into the Atlantic. When Stanley arrived back in Zanzibar in 1877 after navigating the Congo to its mouth on the Atlantic, the mystery of the Nile sources in Central Africa was resolved. By that time, it was known that the White Nile originated in Lake Victoria, which in turn was fed by the Kagera River on its western shore and by rainfall. It was also known that Speke's Somerset Nile, later called the Victoria Nile, flowed out of the northern end of Lake Victoria into spider-shaped Lake Kyoga, which was first seen by Chaillé-Long. It then coursed into the northeast corner of Lake Albert. The Albert Nile flowed out of the extreme northern end of Lake Albert for some 200 miles to Nimule in the Sudan, where it formed the White Nile. The White Nile flowed for almost 1,000 miles north to Khartoum, where it was joined by the Blue Nile coursing down from the highlands of Ethiopia. The source and path of the Blue Nile had long been known through the seventeenth-century explorations of Portuguese Jesuit missionaries in Ethiopia.[30] But between 1770 and 1773, James Bruce, the British traveler, definitively traced the river's course from Lake Tana in the Ethiopian highlands to its confluence with the White Nile.[31]

This remarkable charting of Africa's lake and river systems was not driven solely by scientific interest in the source of the Nile. These waterways also comprised a vital transportation network that gave access to the continent's resources and provided a means of eventually imposing political control. As European competition for possession of the Nile and its sources intensified, attention shifted to other lakes that might feed into the watershed. Among these was Lake Zamburu, which had first appeared on Erhardt's slug map of 1855 but which no European had ever seen.

2

A Whispered Reality

Charles Tilstone Beke, a leading armchair geographer (from The Nile Quest, *1903).*

*A*fter Krapf returned to Württemberg in 1855, he began work on a two-volume book describing his experiences in Ethiopia and East Africa. This book essentially consisted of his journal entries, many of which had been previously published in the *Church Missionary Record* and the *Church Missionary Intelligencer*. When *Reisen in Ost-Afrika* was self-published by Krapf in Kornthal in 1858, it attracted little attention in geographic circles.[1] Most of its content was well known to geographers through Krapf's periodical publications, and the slug map he included was no longer of much interest.

Since Krapf had left the East African coast in 1855, the Royal Geographical Society had sent Burton and Speke into the interior to settle the issue of the Nile watershed. Their return was anticipated in a matter of months. In addition, geographers now attached less importance to information gathered on the coast. They firmly believed that Africa's true physical features could only be determined by direct scientific observation. Thus,

Krapf's book, with its older and less convincing account of Africa's inland waterways, held little interest for them.

Krapf's inclusion of Lake Zamburu on his map served to affirm his
strong belief in a large lake that lay to the south of the Ethiopian highlands. Yet this also attracted little notice because it was so intimately
associated with Erhardt's largely discredited Lake Uniamesi.

Shortly after the appearance of Krapf's book, Léon des Avanchers, a
Capuchin missionary from Savoy, published an important paper and
map detailing the geography and ethnography of the East African interior. He did so in the form of a lengthy letter addressed to the eminent
French geographer Antoine Thomson d'Abbadie, which was published
in the March 1859 issue of the *Bulletin de la Société de Géographie.*[2]
Avanchers had gathered his information while on the Somali coast.
There, he interviewed many caravan leaders, some of whom actually
drew maps for him. One informant who proved to be especially reliable was Hadji Abd-el-Nour, the sheikh of Brava, who drew up a detailed map marked by the courses of rivers, the locations of mountains, and the distributions of various ethnic groups.

What separated Avanchers's publication from those of many of his
contemporaries was the degree of effort he devoted to giving credit to
African collaborators for the information he presented. He obviously
was successful in establishing a close and trusting relationship with
these men, who in turn provided him with accounts that were both reliable and accurate. Even a century and a half later, one cannot but be
impressed by the wealth of new and valid information contained in
Avanchers's report. Yet at the time, it was hardly noticed because its
focus was on the East African coast and the vast area covering what is
now southern Ethiopia and northern Kenya. This region was of little
interest to a world obsessed with the sources of the Nile that lay to
the west.

A dominant feature on Avanchers's map was a large lake that he
called El Boo. Draining out of it to the northwest was a river marked
"Affluent that the Soomali say is the Nile." The placement of El Boo
between thirty-five and thirty-six degrees east longitude and at one degree north latitude put it in the general vicinity of Lake Rudolf. What
was more convincing, however, was the strong ethnographic and geographic contextual evidence Avanchers presented for the lake. The
Rendille people were correctly depicted as living to its south and east,
the Boran to the northeast, and the Konso to the north. The lake was
shown as being south of the Tertala Plateau and to the northeast of
Lake Baringo, features that accurately defined Lake Rudolf's location.

In his text, Avanchers provided other important observations made
by his African collaborators:

Several days south of the lake, is a chain of mountains called *Obada* . . . south of the mountains is the Baharingo country, near which there is a large lake.

To the south of the mountains is an active volcano, and at the extremity of the chain, hot springs.

All of the country south of Lake El Boo is inhabited by the Wa-Kuafi (*wa* signifying people).[3]

This information was remarkable for its accuracy. The volcano was probably Mount Teleki, which was extremely active then, and the Wa-Kuafi were the Samburu people, who still live south of the lake. Nonetheless, there were a number of inaccuracies on Avanchers's map. These related not so much to the existence of the topographic features depicted as to their spatial and positional relationships to one another. For example, the Lorian Swamp was shown to the southwest of the lake although it actually lay to the southeast.

Avanchers was clearly familiar with the work of Krapf, Rebmann, and Erhardt and also with the writings of the armchair geographer James MacQueen. As Avanchers wrote: "I put myself in contact with all the caravan leaders who had penetrated the interior of the continent. Several among them drew some maps which had all the same form and which, with a few corrections, had a great resemblance to those of the Protestant missionaries and to that of Mr. MacQueen."[4]

Avanchers may also have had access to the slug map. Even if he did, however, it had no influence on his own map, which bore little resemblance to it. The shape and position of his lake El Boo were quite different from Krapf's Lake Zamburu. Yet it is clear that both maps depicted Lake Rudolf, albeit by two different names.

It was reasonable for Avanchers to send his draft report and map to Antoine Thomson d'Abbadie for correction and corroboration. Both Antoine and his brother Arnaud Michel were among France's best-known geographers and were also leading authorities on Ethiopia. In 1838, the French Academy had sent the brothers to Ethiopia on a scientific and geographic expedition that was to last for a dozen years. They surveyed most of the central and northern areas of the country and made important observations on the southern province of Kaffa, about which little was then known in Europe. They studied the fauna, flora, local languages, and customs and amassed a large collection of manuscripts, which they subsequently took back to Paris.

The d'Abbadie brothers were especially recognized for their knowledge of the geography of southern Ethiopia, the area adjacent to that described by Avanchers. In 1843, they conducted explorations of the upper Omo River, the principal affluent of Lake Rudolf. This region, comprising the upper Lake Rudolf basin, was first visited by two Por-

tuguese diplomatic emissaries, António Fernandes and Fequr Egzi'e,
in the late sixteenth century. The record of their observations of the
upper Omo River system was preserved in the 1646 descriptions of the
Portuguese Jesuit Manoel de Almeidea.[5] The d'Abbadies were the first
Europeans to visit the upper basin of Lake Rudolf since the Portuguese
two hundred years earlier. Thus, they were ideally qualified to comment on Avanchers's findings, especially his descriptions of Lake El
Boo.

In 1849, Antoine d'Abbadie entered the Nile source controversy
with the publication of his book _Note sur le Haut Fleuve Blanc_, in
which he incorrectly claimed that Ethiopia's Blue Nile was the river's
principal headstream. Not only did he make this claim, he also further
stated that, based on his travels in Kaffa and other areas of southern
Ethiopia, the White Nile was not a major source.[6] These views quickly
brought him into conflict with Charles Tilstone Beke, who, despite
his own geographic work in Ethiopia, was fast becoming one of London's leading armchair geographers.

Beke had arrived in Ethiopia in 1840, two years after the d'Abbadie
brothers, and left in 1843. Some of his own geographic work in central
Ethiopia had overlapped with that of the d'Abbadies. Thus, from this
perspective alone, they were rivals. Still, this did not fully explain the
viciousness of his attack on Antoine d'Abbadie's views on the Nile
sources. Beke was a strong proponent of the idea that the White Nile
was the river's main source, an opinion later strengthened by Speke's
report to the Royal Geographical Society in May 1859 on finding Lake
Victoria. But he was confronted by Antoine d'Abbadie, who, in refut-
ing this and stating that the Blue Nile was the principal source, had
the authority of firsthand observation on his side. In order to promote
his views and discredit d'Abbadie's, Beke recklessly resorted to character assassination. He alleged that d'Abbadie had never actually traveled in southern Ethiopia and stated that the information from this
"pretended journey" was therefore meaningless.[7]

Beke had the temerity to bring these charges before the Geographical Society of Paris in hopes that that organization would publicly
censure Antoine d'Abbadie and strip him of his membership. Blinded
by jealous rivalry and obsessive opinion, Beke did not foresee the society's response to his charges or d'Abbadie's convincing rebuttal. After
listening to both men, the society wisely decided to take no action.
Beke was furious with this outcome. He promptly resigned from the
society and returned the gold medal awarded to him in 1846. Unable
to obtain satisfaction through the society, he then went on to publish
a small inquisitorial booklet in which he attempted to thoroughly discredit d'Abbadie and his thesis about the Blue Nile.[8] This action and

the charges of fraud that he had brought before the Geographical Society of Paris successfully placed a cloud of suspicion over the veracity of d'Abbadie's travels and discoveries for many years to come. Fortunately, Antoine d'Abbadie lived to see his reputation restored when later travelers confirmed his discoveries.[9]

Antoine d'Abbadie's overt support of Avanchers's speculation that Lake El Boo fed into the Nile represented an accommodation on his part to Beke's original theory. Yet by the time Avanchers's paper appeared, Speke's report of seeing Lake Victoria was but two months off. The debate would quickly shift from the views of coast-based missionaries, Beke and d'Abbadie, to those of Burton and Speke. Still, a lasting effect of Avanchers's paper and d'Abbadie's support of it was new credence given to Krapf's original claim about a large lake south of the Ethiopian highlands. The slug map's Lake Uniamesi may have been a fiction, but Lake Zamburu was still a challenge waiting to be explored.

In 1860, Krapf published an English-language version of his 1858 book. Entitled *Travels, Researches, and Missionary Labours During an Eighteen Years' Residence in Eastern Africa*, it was an abbreviated version of his original German publication.[10] In an attempt to make the geographic information current, Krapf enlisted the help of Ernst Georg Ravenstein, a German cartographer from Frankfurt who had begun working for the British War Office Topographical Department in 1855. Since he had participated in the debates about East African geography, he was intimately familiar with the findings of Burton and Speke, as well as the opinions of Beke, Cooley, and MacQueen.[11] He provided Krapf's book with both an introduction and a new map, which reflected a reasonable opinion about the East African interior as of 1860. Significantly, the map erroneously showed Lake Baringo as the principal source of the White Nile and reflected Beke's assumption that the Mountains of the Moon were to the north of Mount Kenya. Lake Zamburu was not shown on this map. Had it been, Ravenstein would have been hard-pressed to link it to the source of the White Nile, given its large size and proximity to Lake Baringo. Because of the excitement so recently produced by the findings of Burton and Speke, it is not surprising that Krapf's book elicited so little interest.

Since leaving East Africa, Krapf had kept alive his hope of bringing Christianity to the Galla people. It was this continuing interest that brought him into contact with the Missionary Committee of the United Methodist Free Churches. Krapf met with this group in Manchester in November 1860 and agreed to spend two years in East Africa helping them establish a mission station. In January 1862, he arrived in Zanzibar with Thomas Wakefield and J. Woolner. By April, they were at Ribe, some fifteen miles north of Mombasa and a short distance from Rabai, where Krapf had worked for so many years. They began the construction of a mission station at Ribe, but by October, Krapf had to leave because of spinal problems. Woolner also left because of illness, and eventually, Wakefield joined Rebmann at Rabai for a short while.[12]

The United Methodist Free Churches soon sent out a replacement for Krapf and Woolner. The man they chose was Charles New, the twenty-three-year-old son of a Berkshire carter. New, who had worked as a bootmaker for several years before entering the Methodist ministry in 1860, was healthy, enthusiastic, and intelligent. He arrived in Mombasa in June 1863, and he and Wakefield reopened the Ribe mission station, where they hoped to launch their effort to bring Christianity to the Galla. This of necessity focused their attention on the vast area that lay to the north and northwest of Ribe. Although New was doubtful about this mission to convert the Galla, Wakefield would pursue it for almost thirty-five years.[13]

New and Wakefield were to work together for the next decade, and unlike Krapf and Rebmann, they had an extremely harmonious relationship. Their partnership extended not only to their missionary activities but also to their geographic and ethnographic studies. They gave form to some of the whispered realities of the interior, such as Lake Zamburu. But more important, they both traveled beyond the coast and substantially added to what was known about East Africa's rivers and mountains.

Prior to New's arrival in East Africa, Baron Carl Claus von der Decken, a Hanoverian naturalist, and Richard Thornton, a British geologist who had worked for David Livingstone on his Zambezi expedition, tried to scale Mount Kilimanjaro. They made their attempt in 1861 but only reached a height of 5,200 feet. In 1862, von der Decken was back, this time with Otto Kersten, a young German scientist. They hoped to climb Mount Kilimanjaro and then travel on to Lake Victoria. They managed to climb 14,200 of the mountain's 19,340 feet but were unable to proceed to Lake Victoria because of the alleged opposition of the Maasai at Arusha. Von der Decken had hoped to make a third try on Mount Kilimanjaro and also climb Mount Kenya. However, he was killed in Somaliland in 1865.[14]

On his return from the second attempt on Mount Kilimanjaro, von der Decken met Charles New and encouraged him to try to climb the mountain. Eight years were to elapse before New followed this advice. In July 1871, he set out from Ribe on a three-month trip that would take him to Taveta, Moshi, and finally up the mountain to a height of some 15,000 feet. He and two African assistants succeeded in reaching the snow line. This great accomplishment was in no small measure due to the assistance he received from the local Chagga chief, Manga Rindi (Mandara). But Mandara's hospitality did not come cheap for either New or other explorers who followed him: Mandara also succeeded in duping them into believing that his chiefdom was the most powerful one on the southern side of the mountain. In reality, Mandara ruled over a relatively small and weak chiefdom. However, he was able to hide this fact from a number of travelers and benefit from their gifts and tributes by being a gracious but exploitative host.

New safely arrived back at Ribe on October 10, 1871, where he found an invitation to return to England on leave. However, Sir John Kirk, the acting British consul in Zanzibar, was organizing an expedition to rescue Livingstone, and he invited New to join it. This expedition, though, was soon abandoned when Stanley reappeared on the coast with the news that he had met Livingstone at Ujiji. New arrived in London in July 1872, where he wrote his book *Life, Wanderings, and Labours in Eastern Africa*, which was published in 1874.[15] He returned to East Africa that same year, determined to continue the work of missionary exploration in the Mount Kilimanjaro region. With this in mind, he set out for Kilimanjaro on December 3, 1874, and by January 14, 1875, was in Moshi. On his arrival there, he found that Mandara was preparing to attack the neighboring chiefdom of Marangu. Some 2,000 excited warriors had even been assembled by Mandara for this purpose. The threat of imminent warfare alone made it impossible for New to continue his explorations. However, worse was to come. Mandara proved hostile and effectively plundered New's modest caravan under the guise of receiving gifts. He confiscated New's most valuable possessions, including his silver aneroid barometer and his gold watch and chain. To complicate matters, most of New's twenty-three porters deserted, and he himself came down with dysentery.

Mandara's hostility toward New was in response to the latter's stated intentions of pushing farther west to the neighboring chiefdom of Machame and the frontiers of Maasai country. Mandara wanted to prevent this at all costs. Had New gone on to Machame, he would have quickly discovered that it was a much more powerful chiefdom than Mandara's own. Future European travelers would then have bypassed Mandara, thus depriving him of access to tribute.

In plundering and sabotaging New's expedition, Mandara may have had an accomplice in Sadi bin Ahedi. He was an Arabic-speaking trader, about forty-five years of age at the time, who was New's chief guide. Sadi was an experienced caravan leader who had traveled through the interior on numerous occasions and who fluently spoke

Maa, the language of the Maasai. Sadi's wonderful linguistic abilities, vast knowledge of the interior, and skills as a leader and guide were offset, in New's opinion, by a number of defects, which he described in detail:

> Makes a good appearance for a headman . . . at heart he is a coward. . . . [He] begs hard, and when begging fails him, he resorts to scheming. As a guide, he is a man of great experience, and knows the Masai country and language better, it is said, than any other man upon the coast; yet as a guide he has long been discarded, all his caravans having failed to bring back anything like an adequate return. . . . A timid, craven soul . . . he would rather give away his last scrap of clothing rather than incur a chief's frown. He was engaged by the Baron von der Decken for a journey to the Masai country, but the undertaking failed, and the failure is attributed by the Wasuahili to Sadi's overcautious tactics. He was the only guide available . . . otherwise I might not have employed him. I thought . . . I could control his evil propensities; and in taking him I had this advantage, I knew him. I took him in hand, therefor, under bit and curb; with what success will be seen.[16]

New's assessment was written after his first trip to Mount Kilimanjaro in 1871. Sadi's motives in sabotaging New's second expedition probably related to a desire to keep Europeans from penetrating too far into the interior. Coastal traders were extremely protective of their ivory-trading monopoly and feared that Europeans would take control of it. As part of their effort to keep Europeans out of the interior, they greatly exaggerated the threat posed by the Maasai, whom they characterized as warlike and bloodthirsty. It was not beyond people of Sadi's ilk to sabotage expeditions like New's once the Europeans tried to push on beyond Mount Kilimanjaro. However, protection of his fellow traders' commercial interests may not have been Sadi's only motive. He may also have been fearful of so small an expedition approaching Maasai country, and perhaps he personally benefited from Mandara's plundering of New.

Europeans on the coast had, for a number of years, suspected Sadi of sabotaging von der Decken's 1862 attempts to cross Maasai country. New alluded to this, and Joseph Thomson, a later traveler, was quite explicit about it: "Their caravan leader was one Sadi-bin-Ahedi. . . . I have every reason to believe that von der Decken's failure was mainly due to the machinations of Sadi, whose little ways in that direction, I have much reason to know."[17]

New was now so weakened by dysentery that he, Sadi, and a couple of the remaining members of the expedition were forced to retreat to the coast. Riding a donkey at first, he eventually had to be carried on a stretcher. On February 13, 1875, he sent an urgent plea for help to the Church Missionary Society station at Rabai. Although help was sent, it arrived too late. On February 14, New's faithful assistants carried his body into Rabai.

New's death on the road back to the coast came as a shock to Wakefield, for New had been physically fit and full of enthusiasm when he left a few months before. In all probability, he died from either acute bacillary dysentery or typhoid fever. There is really no evidence to support Mandara's later allegations (made to Thomson) that Sadi had poisoned New. As Thomson himself said, "That part of the story I can hardly believe; Sadi could have no motive for anything of the sort."[18]

As much as Thomson came to dislike Sadi, he spoke highly of his positive attributes when he first met him in Taveta in 1883, eight years after New's death: "He had a commanding and venerable presence, a not unimportant qualification in the Masai country, and . . . without exception he had the most thorough knowledge of the Masai language of any man on the coast. Even the Masai had to admit they were no match for him in power of talking out a subject. I never knew anyone with such a singular 'gift of the gab.'"[19]

New's geographic accomplishments were significant. He was the first to reach the snow line of Mount Kilimanjaro; he collected many new specimens of flora from the mountain's alpine region; he identified Mount Kenya as the source of the Tana River; and he refuted some of the more absurd speculations of armchair geographer William Desborough Cooley, who still maintained that Mount Kenya and Mount Kilimanjaro were not snow-covered. In addition, New and Wakefield had identified some of the principal features of East Africa, based on their travels and those of caravan leaders such as Sadi. These included several lakes—Baringo, Naivasha, and Nakuru—Mount Kenya, Mount Kilimanjaro, and the Tana River.[20]

In 1870, Wakefield published a lengthy article describing the caravan routes from the coast into the interior, based on information provided by Sadi. With this article, he also published an important map reflecting information he and New had gathered on their travels, as well as the accounts of Sadi and other caravan leaders. But it was primarily because of Sadi's recollections of his travels that Wakefield and New were able to fix the position of the large northern lake that traders called Samburu. Wakefield showed it on the map as lying between thirty-eight and thirty-nine degrees east longitude and one and two degrees north latitude. Although the lake's position was somewhat off the mark for Lake Rudolf, its position relative to Lake Baringo was accurate.[21]

According to Wakefield, Sadi had some interesting things to say about the lake:

> This is the limit of Sadi's journey from Sigirari. He did not really enter Samburu, but only reached the southern frontier. He states that he saw the northern [southern?] end of the Samburu Lake, which appeared two days off, and described it as being in length from station at Ribe to Kipumbui (128 miles); breadth from Ribe to Gasi (37 miles); bearing N.N.E., S.S.W.[22]

Sadi's description of the lake was of great significance because it included measurements that later proved to be accurate to within a few miles. The lake's incorrect orientation can be explained by the fact that Sadi had not personally traveled up along its shores and therefore could not verify its true geographic position.

In view of Sadi's eyewitness testimony, it was difficult for geographers to ignore this large northern lake called Samburu. By the mid-1870s, it regularly appeared on maps produced by other explorers who had traveled through adjacent areas. An example of this is the map that accompanied the book of the German botanist George Schweinfurth, who had spent three years traveling through the Upper Nile, the Bahr el Ghazal River, and the upper reaches of the Uele River in what is now the northeastern Congo. He showed Lake Zambu007 as feeding into the Upper Nile.

New and Wakefield's discoveries had, for the most part, consolidated geographic opinion in favor of a great northern lake. Their Lake Samburu gave tangible form to the whispered reality that had been Krapf's Lake Zamburu and Avanchers's Lake El Boo. They had also filled in the interior map of East Africa with some precise geographic features determined through their own travels and those of their African colleagues. In so doing, they had responded to Jonathan Swift's satirical challenge of almost a century and a half before:

> *So geographers on Afric-maps,*
> *with savage-pictures fill their gaps,*
> *and o'er uninhabitable downs*
> *place elephants for want of towns.*[23]

New and Wakefield succeeded in replacing some of the elephants with rivers, lakes, mountains, and streams. They had also set the stage for yet another generation of travelers who would come and replace even more.

3

A Race Across Maasai Land

Joseph Thomson and two of his African companions, James Livingstone Chuma and Makatubu (from Through Masai Land, *1885).*

By the late 1870s, the principal geographic features of the East African interior had been documented. Travelers and explorers had triangulated Mount Kilimanjaro, circumnavigated the large central African lakes, and charted the courses of the major rivers. The great era of European exploration of Africa had been largely driven by the desire to pursue geographic knowledge, suppress the slave trade, and promote missionary endeavors. Burton, Speke, Krapf, Rebmann, New, Wakefield, Stanley, and Livingstone had all been part of it.

This era symbolically ended when two men, Verney Lovett Cameron and Henry Morton Stanley, succeeded in crossing the continent from east to west. Cameron crossed Africa on foot in 1873–1875, and Henry Morton Stanley sailed down the Congo River in 1876–1877.[1] Although there were still many blank spaces on the map, they were not suffi-

ciently important to draw financial support solely in the interests of
geographic exploration. The decades-long era of geographic inquisi-
tiveness was slowly but inexorably giving way to one in which commercial and political interests were to determine how and when the
blank spaces would be explored. Reflective of this change was the formation of the African Exploration Fund in 1877 by the Royal Geographical Society. Its patron was the Prince of Wales, and its executive
committee was composed of several eminent scientists and explorers,
including James Augustus Grant, who had traveled with Speke in
Africa. In reality, the fund represented a British foil to the International African Association established in 1876 by King Leopold II of
Belgium as a lofty-sounding cover for his own colonial ambitions.[2]

The society's African Exploration Fund was, in many ways, a necessary British response to emerging European challengers in East Africa.
The British had, in fact, taken the lead in the exploration of East
Africa, but they had done so in an era when political and commercial
considerations were not paramount. Now they were faced with the
prospect that the lands they had opened through scientific, geographic
inquiry would be commercially and politically claimed by other European powers. It was this specter of interlopers seizing for profit what
the Royal Geographical Society had opened for science and religion
that forced the society's hand.

For many society members, the African Exploration Fund's economic and political focus represented an uncomfortable departure
from their organization's previous direction. However, the society's
leaders successfully muted most of the dissension so as to improve
their ability to raise money for the fund. This they did by appealing to
dissenting members with a fund prospectus that emphasized geographic and scientific objectives, in addition to the economic ones
bound to be of interest to industrialists and men of commerce. This
compromise also sustained the flame of evangelization that had for so
long been at the heart of British exploratory efforts in Africa. The link-
age between missionary endeavors and commerce was not new, for it
had always been a part of the work of Livingstone and others. Yet the
balance had shifted, if not in the text of the prospectus then certainly
in the minds of its authors.[3]

The African Exploration Fund Committee set forth seven routes in
Africa that it viewed as of the utmost importance in promoting science, geography, religion, and, above all, commerce. These included:
the route from Witwatersrand in southern Africa to Lake Tanganyika;
the route along the eastern side of the mountains from the Zambezi
River to the equator; the route from the East African coast to the
northern end of Lake Nyasa; the area from Lake Nyasa to Lake Tan-

ganyika; the route from Bagamoyo on the East African coast to Lake Victoria and Lake Tanganyika; the route from the East African coast at Mombasa to Mount Kilimanjaro and Lake Victoria; and the route from Formosa Bay on the East African coast up the Tana River to Mount Kenya and Lake Victoria.[4] As some saw it, there would soon be roads and telegraph wires running along these routes to support rich commercial prospects that only Arab and Swahili traders had previously exploited.

In April 1878, soon after the committee had published its prospectus, Alexander Keith Johnston Jr. volunteered to explore the route from Mombasa to Mount Kilimanjaro and Lake Victoria. However, the committee denied his request on the grounds that the Maasai had recently prevented the German explorer Dr. Johann Maria Hildebrandt from crossing their lands.[5] Fearing certain failure for a similar, fund-supported expedition, they suggested that he instead try to explore the more southerly route from Dar es Salaam on the coast to Lake Nyasa. They viewed this as a modest and relatively inexpensive trip devoid of major risks. Yet they also knew that it was one whose results would appeal to their several constituencies, including scientists, churchpeople, and industrialists. In brief, the Lake Nyasa expedition could give the fund the quick and certain success it needed to carry on its future programs.

Johnston, who was the thirty-three-year-old son of an eminent Scottish geographer, had impeccable credentials. He had trained under the highly respected cartographer Edward Stanford and with Dr. August Petermann, the finest geographer in continental Europe. He had also acquired significant field experience in India and Paraguay and had served during the previous two years as the Royal Geographical Society's assistant map curator.[6] The selection of Johnston by the African Exploration Fund Committee pleased many in the society's old guard because they were sure that, as a scientist and geographer, he would return with a wealth of information covering geography, natural history, ethnology, and climate.

In June 1878, after the committee had approved of Johnston's expedition to Lake Nyasa, another Scotsman read of it in the *Dumfries and Galloway Standard & Advertiser*. Joseph Thomson, the twenty-year-old son of a successful stonemason and quarry owner, had recently completed his studies in geology and natural history at the University of Edinburgh. He was an excellent student, winning medals in both subjects and high praise from Professor Archibald Geikie, who lectured on geology. Like many young men of his age, Thomson was faced with the difficult decision of choosing a future career. He could have worked with his father and brothers managing the quarry. However, such an ordinary career held little interest for him. A romantic by nature, he had avidly read the travelogues of Burton, Speke, Livingstone, and Stanley and was fascinated by them. These books had so fired his imagination that his fondest hope was to travel one day into Africa with an expedition such as Johnston was about to lead.

Romantic that he was, Thomson was also bold and at times excessively self-confident. He immediately wrote to Johnston, volunteering to serve without pay in any capacity. An enthusiastic letter of recommendation from Professor Geikie attesting to Thomson's geologic and natural history knowledge resulted in his plea receiving special consideration. Johnston needed a subaltern who could assist him in the geologic, natural history, and collecting aspects of the expedition. However, he also wanted someone who, by reason of his limited geographic skills, could not challenge his authority and supremacy either during or after the trip, as Speke had done with Burton. Thomson filled these needs since he was young, inexperienced, superficially knowledgeable about geology and natural history, but unable to use a sextant or take other important geographic measurements. The committee liked Thomson not only because of his educational credentials but equally because he agreed to serve as geologist and naturalist for so little pay.[7]

Johnston and Thomson arrived in Zanzibar on January 6, 1879, where they met Dr. John Kirk, the British consul general who had previously traveled with Livingstone on his Zambezi expedition. Kirk told them that it would be impossible to strike for Lake Nyasa until May since the "long rains" that had begun in November were the heaviest in years. In order to fill their time and gain some practical safari experience, he suggested that they make a brief visit to the Usambara Mountains, which by then were frequently visited by Europeans.[8] On their return from this uneventful trip, they began recruiting porters in Zanzibar with Kirk's assistance. They eventually engaged 125 men to carry their food, supplies, guns, ammunition, and bundles of beads, wire, and cloth. Johnston was fortunate that James Livingstone Chuma, Livingstone's former caravan leader, was available. He agreed to serve as the expedition's headman and helped to recruit several reliable assistant headmen. Chuma had been with Livingstone when he died and had carried his body back to the coast. This remarkable act of loyalty and devotion had won him wide admiration in Great Britain. He also spoke several African languages and possessed superior skills in resolving problems among the porters and in negotiating with local chiefs.

The expedition finally set off for Lake Nyasa on May 20, 1879, following the well-used Arab trading route west. Prior to leaving Zanzibar, Johnston had written to the African Exploration Fund Committee requesting that Thomson be recalled and sent back to Scotland. During the Usambara journey, he had found him insufferably conceited and extremely superficial in his scientific work. Thomson's almost adolescent enthusiasm had proven to be no substitute for a diligent and meticulous approach to scientific inquiry.

Thomson had tried hard to please Johnston and to socialize his relationship with him, even before they left London, but to no avail. Johnston, the sophisticated, well-bred, and well-educated scientist, found little in common with this rough-hewn country boy from the Scottish lowlands. Yet he was always civil to Thomson and at no point let him know that he had requested his recall.[9]

The committee reluctantly agreed to Johnston's request and sent Thomson a recall letter via Kirk in Zanzibar. However, the letter arrived after the two men had left for the interior, and Kirk wisely decided not to forward it.[10] Such a letter, when read in the interior, would have created an open breach between the two and perhaps led to the collapse of the expedition. In addition, Kirk feared that Thomson's dismissal from London while in the interior held the seeds for a very embarrassing public quarrel that could have rivaled the Burton-Speke dispute in its notoriety. The last thing that the fund needed, he reasoned, was a messy conflict that might jeopardize its future plans.

The expedition was in the field for little more than a month when Johnston became seriously ill with dysentery. His condition rapidly deteriorated to the point where he could not stand. Finally, on June 26, he lapsed into a coma, and he died the following afternoon at Behobeho.[11] Thomson, who was only twenty-one years old, was now in charge of the Royal Geographical Society's East African Expedition. Kirk promptly supported Thomson's decision to continue the trip, even though he knew that, without Johnston, the principal objectives set out by the committee would not be achieved. He had taken a reasonable measure of Thomson when he was in Zanzibar. Although he found him ignorant in the use of the sextant and a far second to Johnston in his scientific abilities, he was optimistic that he had the resourcefulness, tenacity, and stamina to successfully lead the expedition. At the same time, he did not believe that a Thomson-led caravan would produce much in the way of useful scientific results,[12] for Thomson was really a dilettante at science, an adventurer who enjoyed the excitement and challenge of travel in Africa, and a man whose mind was both disorganized and unfocused. Still, he had his positive points, among which were his patience and ability to successfully oversee the infinite logistical details of a large caravan. These were considerable assets: In fact, the most scientifically proficient expeditions had sometimes collapsed because their European leaders had little patience and few skills in handling porters and the recurrent, nagging details of caravan life. More an efficient quartermaster than an expedition leader, Thomson stood a better chance than some experienced explorers of reaching his destination and returning alive, albeit with little in the way of meaningful results to show for the effort.[13]

With Kirk's blessing, Thomson and the expedition traveled to the northern end of Lake Nyasa and then on to Lake Tanganyika. Returning by a more northerly route, Thomson visited Lake Rukwa, which had not been previously seen by European travelers. After spending fourteen months in the interior and walking 3,000 miles, he arrived at Bagamoyo on the coast in June 1880.[14] Thanks to Thomson's skills and those of Chuma, no porters had deserted and no armed conflicts had erupted between the caravan and local peoples. Only two men on the expedition had died, Johnston and a porter. This remarkable record of survival and peaceful transit more than compensated, in Kirk's view, for the expedition's cartographic and geologic failures, which were significant. But Thomson was a keen observer and recorded many useful descriptions of the areas he had visited. In addition, scientists were pleased with the plant and shell collections he took back to London.[15]

Few could find fault with the man who had rescued the African Exploration Fund Committee's East African Expedition from certain failure. Yet despite his boundless enthusiasm, excessive confidence, and ability to get a job done efficiently and quickly, some found him scientifically superficial, imprecise in his observations, and endowed with an inclination to exaggerate and overdramatize events. However, their reservations about him were scarcely heard above the chorus of praise for what was hailed as one of the most successful British expeditions ever to venture into the East African interior.

When Thomson returned to London, he was thrust before a public long accustomed to the accounts of eminent travelers and explorers. Although the newspapers hailed his personal triumph and armchair travelers took vicarious pleasure in his adventures, many others made the inevitable comparisons between Thomson and Burton, Baker, Livingstone, and Stanley.[16] The flush of admiration for a young man who had successfully surmounted so many dangers in the African interior soon gave way to a realization that his voyage was of little lasting value. The governing council of the Royal Geographical Society did not rush to summon him, fully aware that the expedition had fallen terribly short of its geographic and scientific objectives. It was only after writing several letters that Thomson finally obtained an audience with Lord Henry Austin Bruce Aberdare, the society's president. He and others had praised Thomson for his accomplishment; to have done otherwise would have been an admission that the society's expedition had failed. Yet Thomson was disappointed that Lord Aberdare did not respond to his request to lead further expeditions or financially compensate him for the one he had just rescued.[17] In part, this was due to his own lack of insight. The press and his friends and relatives may have lionized him as a hero, but privately, some in the society saw him as little more than a pure adventurer. After all, these were men who had known Livingstone and Speke and who counted Burton, Baker, and Stanley among their friends. Thomson clearly did not measure up to these explorers, and as they saw it, his personal triumph came by chance and at the expense of sacrificing the scientific objectives of their expedition.

After waiting for almost five months at the society's door, Thomson was finally invited to speak to a packed assembly hall. He gave a factual account of his fourteen months in the interior and ended by saying, "I never once was required to fire a gun for either offensive or defensive purposes," thus evoking empathy from the missionary supporters and liberals in the audience. The society's officers did their public duty by praising him, but Lord Aberdare clearly overdid it when he said, "None of the expeditions in which this Society has borne a part . . . had been marked by . . . greater success than this."[18]

The society, not wanting a complaining Thomson going before the public, gave him £250 and had suitable medals made for the African members of the expedition. At last sensing his own deficiencies, Thomson announced that he was going to use the society's financial gift to further his education in science. There was a taint of self-interest in this announcement since he wanted to lead future society-sponsored expeditions to Africa.[19]

In reality, the prospects for this were rather dim at the time for reasons unrelated to his qualifications. By 1880, public interest in and support for expeditions to Africa had dramatically declined in Great Britain. The society's African Exploration Fund was so unsuccessful in raising money that it was terminated, with its remaining bank balance being used to pay Thomson and produce medals for his men.[20] Still, Thomson was hopeful as he set out on speaking engagements and began writing a book based on his journals.

Thomson's two-volume book, *To the Central African Lakes and Back*, was published in the summer of 1881 by Sampson Low, Marston, Searle, and Rivington in London and later that year by Houghton Mifflin in New York.[21] It received good reviews in newspapers and magazines, but it disappointed those accustomed to the writings of Thomson's heroes. What came across was the author's tact, tenacity, and logistical genius, which were no substitutes for the vision, vitality, and purpose that characterized the writings of Burton, Livingstone, and Stanley.[22] In a sense, Thomson's book was a forerunner of a genre of adventure story that would be popularized a few years later by H. Rider Haggard, creator of the fictional hero Allan Quartermain. But Great Britain of the early 1880s was not quite ready for either Allan Quartermain or Indiana Jones, for whom Thomson could have served as the real-life paradigm. It is of more than passing interest that the Allan Quartermain of Haggard's 1885 book *King Solomon's Mines* is so similar to Thomson. Like him, Quartermain is courageous, sportsmanlike, respectful of nature, and endowed with endurance, resourcefulness, and physical strength.[23] Thomson's exploits were at first measured against those of Burton, Baker, Livingstone, and Stanley and found wanting. However, later generations of Victorian and Edwardian boys would be mesmerized by both Thomson and Quartermain.

After his African triumph, Thomson was not about to return to Scotland and help manage the family quarry. He felt that his future lay in Africa and continued to hope that a proposal to return there would soon come his way. He did not have to wait very long. In early 1881, while still basking in the glory of his Lake Nyasa expedition, he received an offer from Sultan Seyid Barghash of Zanzibar to explore possible mineral deposits in his dominions along the East African coast. Thomson immediately accepted and set out on a trek covering several hundred miles along the Rovuma River, where coal deposits were thought to exist. After two brief months in the interior, he returned to the coast in early September with the unpleasant news that there was no coal to be found.[24]

This quick trip helped to bolster Thomson's reputation as an explorer in Great Britain, even though the Sultan was displeased with its results. His next opportunity to show his mettle as an explorer came from an unexpected source. In 1881, as Thomson was winding up his Rovuma River expedition, the British Association for the Advancement of Science was holding its annual meeting in York. Although the Royal Geographical Society had grown somewhat cool toward exploration in Africa, the association had not. Its council passed a resolution calling for the scientific exploration of the snowy mountains of East Africa. Implicit in this was the obvious assumption that someone had to cross Maasai land to achieve this goal.

The association formally asked the Royal Geographical Society to sponsor an expedition, for which the former would provide financial support.[25] In a sense, the society's hand was forced because if it refused the request, it ran the risk of the association undertaking the expedition itself or else seeking a rival sponsor. Still, the society moved slowly, and it was not until June 1882 that its Expedition Committee passed a resolution endorsing the association's proposal. The resolution also added another objective, namely, the exploration of the area between the snowy mountains and Lake Victoria.[26] This was one of the last great parcels of East African land that had not yet been visited by Europeans. It was viewed as having potential commercial importance as it contained the shortest route to the wealthy kingdoms around Lake Victoria and the sources of the Victoria Nile.

Most in London saw this as a daunting undertaking, primarily because it required crossing Maasai country. By this time, the Maasais' two-decade-old reputation in Europe as violent savages was accepted as fact. Arab and Swahili traders described them as warlike and fierce, both because they believed this to be the case and also because they wanted to keep Europeans out of their rich ivory-trading fields. Missionaries on the coast added their opinions on this side of the equation, as did explorers such as Grant and Stanley, who had never visited the Maasai.[27] These mistaken perceptions were reinforced by Dr. Johann Maria Hildebrandt's failure to enter the area in 1877 because of threats by Maasai warriors.

Thus, by 1882, as the society was resolving to send an expedition across Maasai country, these pastoral people were perceived in Europe as fierce, bloodthirsty warriors. In reality, even if this characterization had once been true, it was clearly dated by the 1880s. The Maasai were certainly a powerful force on the East African steppes and plateaus by the middle of the century. But about that time, a series of widespread civil wars greatly decimated both their numbers and their power. Refugees from these wars sought haven in places like Taveta, a caravan staging point, or began raiding neighboring peoples in order to survive. The latter action, instead of being interpreted as a sign of social disintegration, was viewed by missionaries and travelers as evidence of the Maasais' continued ferocity and power. Disease had also taken a heavy toll on these people and their herds.[28] A serious cholera epidemic in 1869 killed many, and their herds were soon decimated by outbreaks of pleuropneumonia.[29] Finally, a serious smallpox epidemic further reduced their strength in 1883–1884.

It is no surprise, then, that Zanzibar-based Arab and Swahili traders began penetrating this region with great frequency by the early 1880s, by which time Maasai political and military power had significantly declined. One of the few who sensed this change was the Venerable J.P. Farler, archdeacon of the Universities' Mission Station at Magila, near Maasai country. Based on information he had obtained about trading routes from coastal merchants, he concluded that a well-armed caravan could successfully cross the Maasais' high plateaus.[30]

Thomson was the obvious person to lead this expedition, given his previous exploratory successes. Although the Royal Geographical Society laid out laudable scientific objectives, all that it really wanted was for Thomson to explore the two snowy mountains and open a route to Lake Victoria through the country of the Maasai. This would provide confirmation of Mount Kenya's existence and lay open the shortest route to the headwaters of the Nile and the lake kingdoms of Central Africa. Thomson agreed to serve without pay and volunteered to study the use of instruments for taking astronomical observations, under the guidance of the society's cartographer, John Coles.[31]

Thomson left London on December 13, 1882, and on arriving in Zanzibar, he began recruiting 113 porters, most of whom were armed with Snider rifles. Showing good judgment, he engaged a number of men who had reliably served with him or other explorers before. Chuma was dead, and in his place, Thomson hired as headman Muinyi Sera, who had worked in that capacity on Stanley's cross-Africa trip in 1874–1877. For assistant headman, Thomson hired Makatubu, who had traveled with him to Lake Nyasa and along the Rovuma River. He took on another of Stanley's former employees, a man named Kacheche, to serve as quartermaster.[32]

Although Thomson had not intended to take another European along with him, he changed his mind when he met James Martin in Zanzibar. Martin, whose real name was Antonio Martini, was a year older than Thomson, having been born in Malta in 1857. A sailmaker by profession, he had arrived in Zanzibar from India on an American ship a few years before. Because the crew was drunk, the ship ran aground, and only the sober Martin was able to give credible testimony in the naval court hearing that would follow. This clearly put him in jeopardy with the rest of the crew, so the authorities found a place for him at Frere Town, near Mombasa, where he was employed at the headquarters of the Church Missionary Society. Martin was very highly thought of by all the Europeans with whom he had worked. This, coupled with his organizational abilities, dependability, and fluency in Swahili, persuaded Thomson to make him his second in command.

Unfortunately for posterity, Martin was illiterate, and thus the journeys he made with Thomson and others in subsequent years went unrecorded. He was clearly a man of exceptional abilities, who made important contributions to the success of Thomson's trip.[33] Thomson admitted as much when the expedition ended, but he defined Martin as the perfect, unquestioning subordinate: "I cannot speak in too high terms of this young sailor, who was ever prompt to do whatever was required, always cheerful, and, though uneducated, an intelligent companion. He never presumed upon the favour with which I regarded him, and he had no opinions of his own—an admirable quality for a subordinate in an African expedition."[34] Even a quarter of a century later, Speke's successful challenge of Burton's leadership was a lesson not lost on expedition leaders. Martin's personality and illiteracy ensured that there would be no challenges of that kind to Thomson.

Thomson headed for the interior on March 6, 1883, after visiting Thomas Wakefield, the Methodist missionary who had recorded much of what was then known about the interior. He proceeded with considerable haste, not to avoid the rains that would soon begin but to overtake a German naturalist, Dr. Gustav A. Fischer, who had set out in December from Pangani, on the coast, on what was clearly a rival expedition across Maasai land. Fischer had made good progress through the initial stretches of the Maasai steppe. He visited the soda lake Magadi and was the first European to see the Rift Valley. Descending its eastern escarpment, he traveled on to Lake Naivasha, where he soon encountered stiff opposition from large numbers of Maasai warriors. Fischer's caravan included an assortment of ivory merchants, whose dishonest dealings probably led to problems with the Maasai. In retaliation, the warriors threatened the porters and demanded huge quantities of tribute, which Fischer could not pay. Forced to retreat, he moved south to Lake Natron, another soda lake, then passed Mount Meru and made for Pangani, where he arrived in August 1883, eight months after setting out.[35]

As Thomson headed for Taveta, the caravan staging point southeast of Mount Kilimanjaro, he had no way of knowing that Fischer's expedition would fail. It was in Taveta that he met the famous ivory trader Sadi bin Ahedi, who had traveled with New and von der Decken and who had provided Wakefield with detailed geographic information about the interior. Sadi had fallen into debt to a number of coastal merchants and had, as Thomson said, "fled to Taveta to escape imprisonment." Thomson hired Sadi as a second guide, though he later regretted this move when he realized Sadi's cowardice and treachery.[36]

While in Taveta, Thomson opened negotiations with Mandara, the Chagga chief of Moshi. On April 18, he set off for Moshi, and on arrival there, he was impressed by Mandara's hospitality and kindness. However, Mandara's cupidity soon became apparent. Through tact and patience, Thomson was able to fend off the chief's shakedown and in the process retrieve New's gold watch and chain. He also raced up the slopes of Mount Kilimanjaro, reaching a height of 8,700 feet in seven hours. Just as quickly, he rushed down, gathering up a small collection of botanical specimens on his way. Had he really tried, given himself enough time, and taken sufficient supplies and equipment, he probably would have reached the summit.

Taking his leave of Mandara, Thomson moved west toward the border of Maasai country. There, he learned that Fischer's caravan had come to blows with the Maasai and that as a result, the local warriors were on a war footing. This called for a change of plans, and so he wisely retreated to Taveta, where he arrived on May 12, 1883. He now realized that, contrary to the advice Grant had given him in London, his best chance for getting across Maasai land was by joining forces with a large trading caravan. Meanwhile, he made a speedy trip to Mombasa for additional supplies and returned to Taveta on July 2, 1883. There, a stroke of luck in the form of a large caravan led by Jumbe (Chief) Kimemeta from Pangani and heading for Maasai land changed his fortunes. Kimemeta was an experienced ivory trader and traveler who, had he been literate in any language, would have gone down in history as the "discoverer" of many East African landmarks for which Europeans later received credit.[37] But Kimemeta's interest was principally ivory. With the greater protection afforded by this caravan, plus Kimemeta's knowledge of the country and its peoples, Thomson once again set off, moving around the northern flank of Kilimanjaro and up to Ngongo Bagas, near modern-day Nairobi. He found the Maasai arrogant and intrusive, but he managed to deal with them diplomatically, passing himself off as a *laibon* (medicine man) by popping out his false teeth and putting effervescent salts in water. The two caravans moved on north through the Rift Valley to Lake Naivasha and up along the Nyandarua Mountains, which Thomson named the Aberdares in honor of the president of the Royal Geographical Society. He paid a hasty visit to the slopes of Mount Kenya but did not attempt to climb it as he had Kilimanjaro. Yet he was the first European to confirm Mount Kenya's existence since Krapf had seen it thirty-five years before. He then rejoined the main part of the caravan, which had gone on to Lake Baringo. From there, Kimemeta went north to trade for ivory among the Turkana, and Thomson headed for the village of Nyemps at Lake Baringo. After a short stay at Nyemps, Thomson set off in a rush to Lake Victoria, a relatively short distance away, which he reached on December 11, 1883. He visited 14,178-foot-high Mount Elgon but did not attempt to reach its peak. He then charged back to Lake Baringo, enjoying considerable sport along the way.

For all intents and purposes, Thomson had achieved his objectives at this point, less than a year after leaving the coast for the first time. He had visited the snowy ranges of East Africa, had crossed Maasai land to Lake Victoria, and had even attempted to climb Kilimanjaro. Yet had it not been for Martin's competence as the expedition's second in command, Thomson might have died, for shortly after returning to Lake Baringo and until he regained the coast, he suffered from severe dysentery and was virtually incapacitated. He left the Lake Baringo area on February 22, 1884, and for most of the way to Ngongo Bagas was accompanied by Jumbe Kimemeta. It was largely thanks to Kimemeta that he had safely crossed Maasai country and achieved some of the other goals of his expedition. But Thomson disregarded Kimemeta's advice about traveling together to Pangani and was carried down to the coast via a parallel route through Kamba country, reaching the mission station at Rabai in late May. He was greeted by Mrs. Thomas Wakefield. She later described his arrival in her diary entry of June 2:

> Mr. Thomson has returned! On Saturday afternoon, he came here with his caravan. . . . He is very unwell, and is anxious to obtain a doctor's advice. He is worn very thin, but says he is very much stouter than he was some months ago. Mr. Wakefield was at Ribe when Mr. Thomson arrived. . . . Mr. Thomson put his hand into his pocket and said, "Here is something Mr. Wakefield will have seen before!" And he drew out a gold watch and chain and seal. "These," he said, "were Mr. New's. Mandara, the Chief of the Chagga, who took them from Mr. New in such a heartless manner, has restored them to me to be taken to England and given to Mr. New's friends."[38]

This gesture was reflective of Thomson's determination and sense of duty. He had been carried on a litter for almost three months, and yet, hardly able to stand, he presented Mrs. Wakefield with the watch and chain Mandara had seized from New over a decade before.

The other heroes of this journey were James Martin, Makatubu, and the African staff who devotedly cared for Thomson when he was ill. Martin virtually took charge of the expedition on the return to the coast and proved himself to be skilled, trustworthy, and loyal. Finally, Thomson owed a great debt to Jumbe Kimemeta, who provided the expedition with guidance and protection. Thompson would later praise Kimemeta while at the same time revealing some of the prejudices of his own culture: "A more thoroughly good fellow than Jumba Kimameta never lived (though he possessed almost all the characteristic vices of his race)."[39]

But Kimemeta had, to some degree, played a double game. On the one hand, he had helped Thomson, and on the other, he had seen to it that the expedition did not venture into the ivory-rich territory that lay near Lake Samburu. In so doing, he attempted to limit the direction and scope of Thomson's travels. This proved to be of little inconvenience to Thomson since the trading fields Kimemeta wanted to protect lay to the north of the expedition's areas of interest.

Thomson was given a hero's welcome in Britain, and his book entitled *Through Masai Land*, first published in 1885, was a sensation.[40]

Of note is the fact that Jumbe Kimemeta's name did not even appear in the index, although Thomson did give him credit for his invaluable assistance to the mission. Over the years, scholars have come to realize that although Thomson accomplished a remarkable feat that had enormous implications for Britain's later colonial ambitions, he was hasty and careless in his observations, did things on the run, and lacked the ability to analyze and approach systematically the objects of his observations. In part, this may have been due to his youth and to his fear that the German explorer, Fischer, would beat him to the prize. But these characteristics were evident in the accounts of his other journeys as well.[41] To his credit, Thomson finally gave a precise idea of the size of Lake Baringo, which had been greatly exaggerated in reports from traders and which Speke had erroneously claimed was a part of Lake Victoria.

Thomson also brought back exciting news about the great, mysterious lake to the north, which traders called Samburu. While he was at Lake Baringo, he met some Wakwafi (Samburu or Maasai) visitors who had come south from the area of Lake Samburu. They were quite familiar with the lake:

> This lake they described as from twenty to thirty miles broad; but its length they knew not, as they had never seen the northern end. They further spoke of it as lying between mountains several thousand feet high, though the water does not quite reach their base, and there Wakwafi dwell. They say that the water is salt, and has surprising numbers of enormous *white* fish, with crocodiles and hippopotami. The natives have no canoes.[42]

On the map accompanying his book, Thomson placed Lake Samburu at thirty-seven degrees east longitude, with its southern end at about three degrees north latitude. This represents an accurate placement of the lake today, but the true configuration is different from the one Thomson gave, which was essentially that which had been published by Wakefield and some others. His descriptions of Nile perch and the large number of crocodiles and hippopotamuses were all accurate additions to what was already known about the lake. Thomson's report about Lake Samburu enjoyed enhanced credibility among European geographers because he had gathered his information from people who lived in the region and at a distance of only 150 miles.

Thomson himself never returned to the high plateaus of East Africa, but he did undertake several subsequent expeditions to Nigeria (1885), the Atlas Mountains (1888), and Katanga (1890). He died in London on August 2, 1895, at the age of 37, probably from systemic tuberculosis.

Ten years earlier, his book had been published in German, and in 1886, it appeared in French. In Austria-Hungary, it came to the attention of Crown Prince Rudolf, who had a keen interest in geographic exploration. There on Thomson's map, Rudolf saw a large lake that no European had ever seen—the last of the great African lakes left to be explored. And in that lake, the crown prince saw an opportunity for Austria-Hungary to gain a place in African exploration and perhaps even a stake in the colonial scramble for Africa that was about to begin.

4

Visitors from Vienna

Count Samuel Teleki (courtesy Lajos Erdélyi).

*T*homson's triumphal return in 1884 was one of the few bright spots for Britain with regard to Africa that year. But from the German perspective, the year was characterized by rapid and successful colonial expansion. Germany annexed the Cameroons in July and Southwest Africa in September, and in October, Gerhard Rohlfs, a noted explorer and outspoken advocate for German colonial expansion, was sent to Zanzibar as consul general.[1] Zanzibar's independence had been assured in 1862 by a declaration signed by Britain and France, but the British exercised significant influence over the sultan and his policies. And since Zanzibar claimed sovereignty to much of the East African hinterland, German attempts to claim any territory there brought Britain into direct conflict with Germany through the former's surrogate, Zanzibar.

The British government of the day was indifferent to the acquisition of colonies in Africa in general. However, Germany's successes alarmed several influential private businessmen, including Sir

49

William Mackinnon, who in 1888 obtained a charter for the Imperial British East Africa Company (IBEA). A similar German company, known as the Gesellschaft für Deutsche Kolonisation (Society for German Colonization), had been previously founded by Dr. Carl Peters. In 1884, Peters landed on the East African coast and, eluding agents of the sultan, successfully signed treaties with local chiefs in Usagara, just opposite Zanzibar on the mainland in what is now northeastern Tanzania.[2] Peters was back in Berlin in February 1885, where the Berlin Conference on the Niger and the Congo was coming to an end. This conference had been called in November 1884 to settle issues that were related to those geographic areas and affected the European powers concerned.[3]

The day after the delegates to the conference left Berlin, the kaiser declared a German protectorate over the areas where Peters had signed treaties. This declaration had far-reaching political consequences because it successfully challenged the sultan of Zanzibar's rights and meant that Britain could no longer control German actions by using the sultan as a surrogate for its own interests.

In April 1885, Clemens Denhardt, who with his brother Gustav had been trading along the Tana River since the 1870s, signed a treaty with the chief of Witu, an area located midway up the present-day Kenya coast. This action, coupled with the recently declared German protectorate over Usagara, effectively placed the British sphere of influence between two German ones, with Witu in the north and Usagara in the south. The Germans were thus in an ideal position to lay claim to the interior, circle the British sphere, and render it nothing more than a coastal enclave.

By August 1885, the Germans had forced the sultan to recognize their claims, threatening him with the use of force if he did not do so. Two months previously, realizing the precariousness of their hold in East Africa, the British had requested that a commission with representatives from Britain, France, and Germany be set up to define the limits of the sultan's territories on the mainland. The members of this commission laid out the general issues but were unable to come to an agreement. However, Bismarck was soon willing to settle the Zanzibar issue in the interest of improving relations with Britain. He promised the British that if they made concessions on the East African question, he would support them in their dispute with the French over Egypt.[4]

The East African partition treaty that resulted in late 1886 recognized Witu as German territory and defined the German sphere of influence as extending inland to Lake Victoria between the Rovuma River and a line drawn to the lake from the coast at Umba.[5] The British sphere was north of this line, extending to the Tana River.[6] The line, which essentially constitutes the modern boundary between Kenya and Tanzania, effectively divided the two spheres of influence but did not define their western limits. And of great significance, the treaty set the following northern limits to the British sphere of influence: "On the north by a line which, starting from the mouth of the Tana River, follows the course of that River or its affluents to the point of intersection of the Equator and the 38th degree of east longitude, thence strikes direct to the point of intersection of the 1st degree of north latitude with the 37th degree of east longitude where the line terminates."[7]

What this meant was that the vast area of what is now northern Kenya and where Lake Rudolf is located was as yet unclaimed. With a German protectorate directly across from this area at Witu, on the coast, there was little doubt among many Britons familiar with the issues that the Germans would sooner or later make a grab for it. Thus, as the Austro-Hungarian Count Samuel Teleki made preparations for his journey to Lake Samburu in 1886, the area around the lake still lay outside anyone's sphere of influence. This may have provided Austria-Hungary's Crown Prince Rudolf with some of the impetus for urging Teleki to undertake his journey.[8]

In East Africa and Europe, however, a rapid series of complex events involving the European powers and their agents and surrogates in Africa unfolded, which effectively dimmed whatever vague colonial dreams Rudolf may have had.

In 1887, while Teleki was en route to the lake, the sultan of Zanzibar granted a land concession to his coastal areas to the British East Africa Association, later known as the IBEA (the 1886 agreement granted the sultan full rights to the coastal strip, even that area along German territory).[9] The association's founder, the Scottish businessman Sir William Mackinnon, had had extensive business dealings with Zanzibar since the 1870s. He and the IBEA were destined to play a very significant role in the development of what eventually became modern Kenya and Uganda.

German and British agents in East Africa and the swirl of European big-power politics led the British and the Germans to the bargaining table to settle the East African question in 1890. Their discussions resulted in the Heligoland Treaty of 1890, in which Germany ceded all interest in Witu and in the lands north of the British sphere of influence and accepted a British protectorate over Zanzibar. The British in turn promised to persuade the sultan to sell the Germans his coastal territories adjacent to their sphere of influence and to cede the island of Heligoland, which Germany viewed as crucial to the development of its naval power.[10]

The Heligoland Treaty was signed on July 1, 1890, and shortly thereafter, Carl Peters returned from a marathon trip through what was
now the British sphere, having started out from Witu in 1889. As pre-
dicted by some in Britain, he had not lost any time trying to claim for
Germany those areas not covered by the 1886 treaty. His clear intent
had been to transform the British sphere into a coastal enclave. In the
process, he effectively placed most of what is now Kenya and Uganda
under German control. However, when he arrived on the coast at Bagamoyo, he learned that Bismarck had signed away what he thought
he had just acquired for Germany.[11] In reality, Bismarck's willingness
to sign the Heligoland Treaty had little to do with East Africa. Fearful
for Germany's position in a Europe in which France and Russia had
grown uncomfortably close, he sought better relations with Britain as
part of a strategy to offset any possible Franco-Russian attack.[12]

In 1886, as Crown Prince Rudolf contemplated Teleki's trip, the
Heligoland Treaty was four years off. The lands around Lake Rudolf
were wide open for acquisition, a status that would be confirmed by
the 1886 agreement between Britain and Germany.[13] Rudolf knew the
value of a geographic bargaining chip in the game of big-power European politics, even one in far-off Africa. For Lake Samburu was a possible source of the Nile and thus could become extremely valuable to
the British, French, and Germans in their contest for the heart of
Africa.

Samuel Teleki von Szek, a count of the Holy Roman Empire, was
born at Saromberke in Transylvania (now in Romania) on November
1, 1845, into a noble family that traced its roots to the early fifteenth
century.[14] In 1685, one of his ancestors, Mihaly Teleki, chancellor of
Mihaly Apafi, prince of Transylvania, was made a count for his diplomatic efforts on behalf of the latter with King Leopold of Hungary.
The Teleki family produced a number of renowned scientists, scholars, statesmen, soldiers, and politicians, beginning in the seventeenth
century.

Teleki, who came from the Calvinist branch of the family, studied
at Göttingen and Berlin universities and later became a Freemason.[15]
He entered the armed forces and eventually rose to the rank of lieutenant colonel in the Hussars.[16] Through the efforts of one of his
brothers-in-law, he met Crown Prince Rudolf, with whom he became
close friends. Their mutual love of hunting led Rudolf to spend long
periods at Teleki's country estate at Saromberke. However, shooting
was not the only interest that drew these two men together. Teleki
was also an experienced politician and in 1881 was elected to the Hungarian parliament from the area of Gernyezegi. In 1883, he and other
Hungarian aristocrats induced Crown Prince Rudolf to sign a docu-

ment promising to work for Hungarian independence (Rudolf is said to
have made this commitment while inebriated at Teleki's country
house at Saromberke). Some of Teleki's aristocratic Hungarian friends
then put into motion a plan to make Rudolf king of Hungary and thus
in effect dethrone Emperor Francis Joseph. Although Teleki was away
in Africa while this plot was being discussed, his involvement in efforts to obtain greater autonomy for Hungary and his support of
Rudolf's liberal political views gave the emperor and his government
much cause for concern.[17]

Most contemporaries assessed Teleki as a bon vivant who enjoyed
good food (he weighed close to 250 pounds at the outset of his African
expedition), hunting, hiking, and the company of beautiful women. A
confirmed bachelor, he was also rumored to have a crush on Archduchess Stephanie, Rudolf's wife. This perception and his political influence over Rudolf led the conservative court at Vienna to see the
value of his taking a prolonged overseas journey.[18] Thus, in 1886, he
announced plans to go on a hunting expedition to Lake Tanganyika in
East Africa, in the company of his friend Baron Arz.

What contemporary observers failed to appreciate was that Teleki
was a complex man. Bon vivant that he was, he also possessed remarkable leadership abilities and great political skills that served him well
in both Hungary and Africa. He was equally at ease in navigating
through the tangled web of Austro-Hungarian politics and in negotiating with hostile African chiefs. He knew how and when to persuade,
humor, and cajole, and he was prepared to threaten and use force when
diplomacy failed. He knew the art of taking the measure of people,
could insightfully assess others' motives, strengths, and weaknesses,
and was quick and flexible in his strategies for dealing with them.
Teleki was also a powerfully built man with an iron constitution. He
had a brilliant mind, was courageous in the face of danger, and possessed excellent military skills. Those who saw only his portly frame
shrouded in cigar smoke greatly underestimated him. Indeed, of all the
men who ventured into Africa at this time, few possessed his unique
combination of skills that were sure to result in success.

Crown Prince Rudolf had been the patron of both the Austrian and
the Hungarian geographical societies since 1874, and he took a keen
interest in exploration. After reading the German translation of
Thomson's book in 1886, he decided to promote an Austro-Hungarian
expedition to East Africa to visit Lake Samburu and climb both Mount
Kilimanjaro and Mount Kenya, two peaks that had been visited by
others but had not yet been successfully scaled to their summits.[19]
Rudolf was able to persuade Teleki to lead an expedition of geographic
discovery into what is now northern Kenya. In essence, Teleki still

planned to travel to Lake Tanganyika but agreed to the crown prince's request that he then strike north for the two snow-covered mountains and Lake Samburu.

Teleki's companion on this journey was Lieutenant Ludwig von Höhnel, a 1876 graduate of the Marine Academy at Fiume. In March 1886, von Höhnel was assigned to serve as navigator aboard the emperor's yacht *Greif*, which had been put at the disposal of Crown Prince Rudolf.[20] The prince and his wife, Stephanie, boarded the *Greif* at the port of Pola on March 5, and four days later, they arrived at the island of Lacroma on the Dalmatian Coast, opposite present-day Dubrovnik. At this time, Rudolf, who had first contracted gonorrhea in 1876, was suffering either from a reinfection or from a bout of syphilis, and his physicians had suggested that he recuperate in Lacroma.

Rudolf and Stephanie were lodged at the Monastery of San Giacomo, which Archduke Maximillian (later emperor of Mexico) had converted into a residence in 1859. At first, only Rudolf was confined to bed, but he was soon joined by his wife after she suffered an episode of acute pelvic inflammatory disease as a result of being infected with gonorrhea by her husband. Despite their ill health, both Rudolf and Stephanie got to know of von Höhnel during the trip.[21]

On April 1, Teleki arrived at Lacroma with an entourage of six retainers.[22] That evening, the captain of the *Greif*, whom von Höhnel described as "the daily guest at the princely table," returned from Lacroma and, as was his habit, told the watch officer what had happened that day. By a fortunate turn of events, von Höhnel happened to be the officer on watch: "He [the captain] incidentally mentioned that a Hungarian count had arrived in order to take leave of the Crown Prince before starting on an African expedition. The captain had no idea that with his remark he had touched the most sensitive striving of my inner life [and] was therefore much surprised when I . . . said: 'In this I must have a share.'"[23]

Von Höhnel persuaded the captain to speak with Count Teleki on his behalf. However, Teleki's initial response was a negative one. He had no desire to associate himself with anyone, much less with someone he did not know. But as von Höhnel later wrote, Teleki soon changed his mind: "I had to thank the Crown Prince and the Archduchess who spoke strongly in favor of me."[24] Although Rudolf knew that Teleki was skilled in the use of geographic instruments, he clearly saw the value to the expedition of someone like von Höhnel, whose proficiency was even greater and who was also an excellent cartographer. Thus, his decision to promote von Höhnel's participation was primarily motivated out of a desire to ensure the scientific capability of an expedition that was now placed under his patronage.

Teleki came on board the *Greif* the next day at 3:00 P.M., a copy of Georg Schweinfurth's *Heart of Africa* under his arm. "In the deck saloon he silently spread out the map of the book, pointed to a pencilled line on it and said, 'It is there where I want to go.'"[25] The line ran from Zanzibar to Lake Tanganyika and then north toward Abyssinia. By any calculus, this was an extremely ambitious itinerary. However, Teleki was a flexible pragmatist, and he would change the expedition's route several times as circumstances required.

Von Höhnel's desire to go on this trip was not dampened by Teleki's rotund appearance or vague travel plans. As he said, "To me it was absolutely indifferent where the expedition was to go and how the Count looked if he only allowed me to have a share in it."[26]

Teleki finally agreed to take von Höhnel along, thanks to the intervention of "powerful influence," namely, the imperial couple and the captain of the *Greif*. Although fate had placed von Höhnel in favorable circumstances, he was highly qualified to assume responsibility for the expedition's geographic activities. Born in Pressburg, in what is now Slovakia, on August 6, 1857, he was also fluent in Hungarian, which was an added asset as far as Teleki was concerned.

Von Höhnel was the youngest of four brothers and came from a middle-class family of modest means. His father, a remote man with an exaggerated sense of duty, eventually became provincial director of customs at Trieste in 1864.[27] His premature death in 1868 left the family in precarious financial circumstances. In order to better cope with her reduced means, von Höhnel's mother moved the family back to Vienna, where she had relatives who could assist her. As the youngest son, von Höhnel was given considerable freedom by his mother. He attended a variety of schools, often as an indifferent student. Eventually, he decided on a naval career, influenced in part by his maritime exposure as a young boy in Trieste. With the help of his older brother, he intensely studied for the entrance examination to the Marine Academy at Fiume in 1873. He obtained the highest grade and was granted immediate admission.[28]

After graduating from the naval academy in 1876, von Höhnel served as a midshipman. During this time, he was assigned for three months to the imperial yacht *Minaman*, which in 1879 carried Crown Prince Rudolf on a bird-collecting trip to Spain and Portugal. Von Höhnel could not have imagined that, several years later, the young prince would enable him to achieve his lifelong dream of traveling into the heart of Africa, for aboard the *Minaman*, Rudolf was aloof and distant. Von Höhnel later wrote that "the Crown Prince had, excepting the captain, little intercourse with the ship's staff. Of us midshipmen, who were exactly his age, he took hardly any notice."[29]

Teleki meticulously planned his expedition, spending several months in Vienna, Trieste, Paris, Cherbourg, and London, where he purchased clothing, tents, medicines, and an impressive arsenal of weapons and ammunition. He arrived in Paris on July 11, 1886, and had his boats, tents, and camp furniture custom made. A week later, he left for London, where an equipment supplier from Charles Lori and Company introduced him to Sir Richard Burton. Teleki received valuable advice from Burton and later wrote that "he made my preparations much easier and perhaps even made the success of my enterprise possible."[30]

Perhaps Burton's most valuable advice was that Teleki's plan for a caravan of only a hundred men would result in the expedition's failure. He advised taking a much larger force into the interior and also recommended that Teleki recruit a strong personal armed escort of Somalis. Being far from home, the Somalis were not likely to rebel or defect, and as strangers to the Zanzibari porters, they would be better able to keep the latter in line.

Not all of Burton's advice proved to be helpful. A dissatisfied Teleki wrote the following in his diary: "In London, advised by Burton, I bought my travel equipment from Silver, but I cannot recommend him to anybody. He is only set up to equip tourists buying ready-made products. . . . Besides that I could never speak to him personally during the three weeks I was in London."[31]

Teleki purchased 124 Werndl and Colt rifles and 6 Colt revolvers with which to arm the members of his expedition. He also took along a personal arsenal of 13 Holland, Winchester, and Colt rifles, as well as 4,000 rounds of ammunition and 120 pounds of gunpowder and buckshot. Although his primary interest in hunting was for sport, he also knew that he would have to regularly kill animals in order to supply the caravan with meat. Leaving nothing to chance, he also purchased a 50-day supply of tinned food for a large number of people in the event of famine.

Teleki's untiring efforts in preparing for his expedition were evidenced by the six pages of his diary devoted to detailed descriptions of procuring equipment and supplies. He sought out the best suppliers, but despite his care, the ether in his apothecary kits evaporated by the time he reached Zanzibar and his photo-developing chemicals quickly spoiled.[32]

There were enormous costs associated with equipping an expedition of this size and projected duration. In addition, the combined salaries for the porters, guides, and escort troops were also great. Like most aristocrats of his time, Teleki had the bulk of his wealth tied up in landholdings and therefore did not possess sizable liquid assets that he could quickly draw on to finance the expedition. Thus, in early 1886, he sold off a large parcel of land and a seventeenth-century family heirloom diamond to finance what would be the trip of his lifetime.[33]

Von Höhnel left Trieste on October 5, 1886, aboard the *Titania* and bound for Aden. After transferring to a ship of the Imperial British India Line, he sailed for Zanzibar, where he arrived on October 31. On board was William Oswald, the Austro-Hungarian consular agent in Zanzibar. He urged von Höhnel to use the long days aboard the slow-moving ship to study Swahili. As a result, von Höhnel had a reasonable command of the language by the time the expedition left Zanzibar.[34]

Von Höhnel traveled with the expedition's 140 cases of supplies, whose packing he had supervised in Vienna and Trieste. As soon as he arrived in Zanzibar, he made the acquaintance of the island's leading European personalities, including General Lloyd William Mathews, head of the sultan's army.[35] Mathews was immediately suspicious of the potential political aims of the Teleki expedition and, as a result, was initially cold and distant toward von Höhnel. One day, he candidly asked von Höhnel to give him his word of honor that the expedition would not pursue any political aims. Von Höhnel was happy to oblige since, as far as he knew, Teleki was only intent on geographic discovery and hunting, not in laying claim to territory in the name of Austria-Hungary.[36]

Following Teleki's instructions, von Höhnel tried to hire James Martin, the man who had helped to make Thomson's trip such a success. However, Martin was already committed to taking a group of sportsmen into the interior and could not join the expedition. Von Höhnel then sought out Jumbe Kimemeta, the ivory trader who had accompanied Thomson and Martin across Maasai land. Von Höhnel successfully persuaded Kimemeta to remain in Zanzibar until Teleki arrived, in return for a fixed daily allowance. Kimemeta expressed interest in joining the expedition, provided it traveled north toward Lake Baringo. This meant that in order to obtain Kimemeta's services, Teleki would have to abandon his plan of first going to Lake Tanganyika.

While von Höhnel was in Zanzibar hiring personnel, Teleki was en route via Aden and the Somali coast, securing the services of experienced caravan headmen. He was able to hire Karsa, a trusted Somali gunbearer who would later serve in the expeditions of two American explorers, William Astor Chanler and Arthur Donaldson Smith. He also hired Qualla Idris, a twenty-six-year-old Somali headman who had spent six years with Henry Morton Stanley. Teleki had been advised by Burton that the success of a European expedition in the interior hinged on the quality of its personnel. Thus, he and von Höhnel spared no effort in recruiting the tried and tested.

Teleki arrived in Zanzibar on November 29 and immediately sought a final agreement with Jumbe Kimemeta. This proved more difficult than either he or von Höhnel had anticipated. For one thing, Kimemeta absolutely refused to go to Lake Tanganyika, as there was little ivory to be had there. Ever flexible in his plans, Teleki quickly abandoned this leg of his proposed journey, both to accommodate Kimemeta and because he had learned that hunting was even better in areas to the north. Although Kimemeta then agreed to join Teleki and von Höhnel for a total salary of $2,000, the sultan, fearful of the expedition's possible political aims, refused to give his approval. Unable to change the sultan's mind, Teleki sent Crown Prince Rudolf a telegram asking him to intervene, which he did. The sultan finally agreed after receiving assurances that Teleki had no other objectives but hunting and geographic discovery.[37]

Mathews was eventually satisfied that the expedition posed no political threat to Great Britain's interests, and thereafter, he became extraordinarily helpful to Teleki and von Höhnel. Teleki spoke in glowing terms of him in his diary: "The willing friendship and helpfulness which General Mathews offers every stranger, in his indescribable way, is extremely useful. The general takes care of everything—the crew, the guides; tells you what goods should be taken along, finds out where to get those things. One could claim he fits the expedition out."[38]

It took Teleki and von Höhnel almost two months to hire all of the expedition personnel and repack their goods and supplies for portage in the interior. Kimemeta was put in charge of packing the trade goods, which comprised 100 loads of glass beads, 70 of iron wire, and 80 of cloth. In all, Teleki had 495 loads of 70 pounds each, including 22 that contained the parts for a boat he hoped to launch on Lake Samburu. All these loads added up to 18 tons, according to von Höhnel's reckoning. Each porter had to carry 70 pounds plus a rifle, powder horn, and water bottle, which together often came to 100 pounds. The expedition's 495 loads and 295 guns were carried not only by porters recruited in Zanzibar but also by others hired in Pangani and by 25 donkeys purchased by Kimemeta. By the time it headed into the interior, the expedition numbered close to 400 men.[39]

On January 18, 1887, Teleki advanced three months' salary to the 200 people who had joined the expedition in Zanzibar, including Kimemeta. Three days later, a flotilla of dhows and ships transported the expedition's men and supplies to Pangani, Kimemeta's home base on the coast from where Teleki planned to march into the interior.[40]

Teleki quickly learned that proximity to the coast and a salary advance were powerful inducements for porters to desert. Within a week of arriving in Pangani, several took off. They were soon caught and flogged, as was the accepted custom. Thomson had regularly resorted to flogging, as did other explorers, in order to prevent desertion and theft,[41] for the success of an expedition greatly depended on the imposition of an almost military discipline on the porters. Flogging and chaining were routine, and on occasion, porters were shot for repeated desertion.

On February 6, Teleki led his expedition out of Pangani in the direction of Mount Kilimanjaro.[42] By the standards of the day, it was an enormous caravan, carrying a local fortune in trade goods. Maintaining discipline was uppermost in Teleki's mind, and, not surprisingly, he repeatedly discussed it in the early entries of his diary. Despite his precautions, thirty-seven men soon deserted and left their loads scattered about on the ground. One, however, made off with the metal case containing all of the expedition's maps, astronomical tables, and drawing paper. Because this was one of the most important loads in the caravan, Teleki conducted a week-long search for it but to no avail. Eventually, he sent von Höhnel back to Zanzibar via Bagamoyo to catch up with the deserters and obtain more cartographic supplies.

Unlike most late-nineteenth-century travelers in East Africa, von Höhnel expressed unusually sensitive insights into the plight of caravan porters. Writing in 1924, he said:

> I cannot imagine a harder and more pitiable lot than that which the caravan men had to endure on travels of discovery in Africa. This life they bore for starvation wages, amounting to five Maria Theresa dollars a month. Science is hardly aware of how much is owed to these so-called Zanzibari men—for the most part slaves—and surely does not think that the discoveries in which it rejoices were paid for with the lives of thousands of these poor devils, who have never obtained their due reward.[43]

But as he trekked back to the coast in search of the deserters and his map-making materials, his thoughts about them were no doubt less kind. Meanwhile, Teleki, who had impressed people in Zanzibar as a plump and pleasant sportsman who would probably make it to Mount Kilimanjaro and no further, was already showing his mettle. He disciplined the porters, established tighter control over them and their movements, and rewarded those who proved cooperative and loyal.

For the next six weeks, Teleki marched his men northwest toward Taveta, the caravan staging center near Mount Kilimanjaro. They followed what by then had become a well-trodden trail used by both coastal traders and an increasing number of European hunters. This road led through the Usambara and Pare Mountains, where the plentiful game provided Teleki with marvelous sport. But he was also continuously preoccupied with desertions and the theft of goods by porters who then fled to the coast.

Even though some of the deserters were kept in chains in camp, they managed to escape again. Teleki blamed von Höhnel for this, saying, "I have the feeling that Höhnel does not know how to deal with the men."[44] Yet the fault was not von Höhnel's: Rather, the defections were prompted by Teleki's proximity to the coast and the fact that his prepaid staff carried loads that were worth a small fortune on the Zanzibar market. Despite his acidic comment, Teleki thought very highly of von Höhnel, noting elsewhere in his diary that he was "a very useful, ambitious man and works well—much better than I do."[45]

By late March, Teleki began encountering roving bands of young Maasai *moran* (warriors), who, as was their custom, engaged in continuous efforts to shake down the caravan. Having read of Thomson's great success with the Maasai by passing himself off as a *laibon* (ritual priest), Teleki did the same. He doled out medicines and read fabricated incantations from a French novel, *Page d'Amour*, whose pages he was otherwise using for toilet tissue. Although these efforts placated the Maasai, it also drew them in greater numbers to his tent. One morning, for example, a group of them came to greet him at 6:00 A.M., "covered . . . with thousands of flies" and proudly showed him their nocturnally induced penile tumescence. They were chagrined when Teleki chased them off, thereby showing no interest in the powerful results of his own medicines.[46]

Teleki arrived at Taveta on March 30, some sixty pounds lighter than when he had left Pangani two months before. There, he found James Martin, Thomson's former companion, who was guiding a group of four British hunters; the group included Frederick Jackson, who later fostered British colonial interests in East Africa and became governor of Uganda (1911–1917).[47] Martin and his party were in Taveta not merely to hunt but also to lay claim to the area for Zanzibar on the instructions of General Mathews, who was attempting to forestall German incursions.[48]

It is of more than passing interest to note what Jackson and Teleki had to say about one another. Writing years later, Jackson recalled his meeting Teleki:

> It was also at Taveta that I met Count Teleki when he was on his way to Lake Samburu, at that time represented on the latest maps by an oval of dots, about as big as an average thumb-nail. At the time he had lost much weight on the march up, something between four and five stone, and had shrunk visibly. . . . From what I saw of him, and subsequently heard of him, he was always calm and collected.

He was certainly very amusing and outspoken, and good company generally. Some of his ideas were quaint, if not actually jarring, others were quite brutal; two examples of the former occur to me. During his stay at Taveta, he rarely went out shooting, as he knew that most of the game near by was fairly wild, and a long crawl was not at all to his liking; furthermore, he was assured of as much as he wanted later on.

His name was easy for a Swahili to pronounce, and nearly all the headmen and boys referred to him as Count Teleki, but he was more generally known as *Bwana Tumbo* (stomach).

With the exception of Baker's discovery of Lake Albert, Count Teleki's discovery of Lakes Rudolf and Stephanie was the only one of first importance undertaken by individual enterprise, and entirely at private expense, and it has always appeared to me that the point of difference is not generally recognized or appreciated.[49]

What Jackson did not say was that the reason Teleki had not bothered to go shooting was that there was little game left. Teleki recorded this in his diary: "Met Harvey, Willoughby, Hunter, Jackson, Martin. They have hunted out the whole area; more than 60 rhinos and a few hundred other animals, and what was not killed has fled."[50]

The magnitude of the British party's slaughter was enormous. Thus, Teleki's decision not to hunt was based on the scarcity of game, not any aversion to a "long crawl," as Jackson related. For his part, Jackson gave a very revisionist account of the carnage caused by him and his companions. Writing four decades later for a public deeply sensitized to conservation issues, he said the following of his hunting with Robert Harvey: "That little shoot has always remained one of my most pleasant memories and the commencement of a long friendship."[51]

Teleki was brutally candid in his opinions about the Zanzibari porters. Yet these views were not his alone; they reflected prevailing European racial attitudes at the time:

> Living a long time with these natives I learn to detest and despise them. At first I was astonished that people living among those natives experienced these feelings. The blacks are repulsive but most repulsive are those that have been brought up by the missionaries and have taken in all of the poison of the European civilization. They are born for serfdom without any honest feelings like love, gratitude and courage. . . . I have them beaten a lot but not nearly enough to waken in them a slight feeling of responsibility. The moment I turn my back they fall asleep and let themselves be stirred up by the apprentices of the missionaries. Those that do so I have beatings administered to until they shit in their pants. I was very good to them but never received the slightest show of gratitude.

The other solution is better. If his behind burns he is decent for at least a week.[52]

These opinions stand in sharp contrast to those expressed by von Höhnel four decades later, in which he characterized the porters as "a pitiable lot" who worked "for starvation wages" and as "poor devils, who never obtained their due reward."[53]

After almost two weeks in Taveta, which Teleki described as "a beautiful and peaceful place," the expedition headed for Mount Kilimanjaro. Jumbe Kimemeta had to be carried during part of this trek "because of inflammation of his scrotum."[54] Moving into the more densely populated slopes of the great mountain, Teleki came into contact with increasing numbers of Africans, about whom he recorded earthy and candid comments in his diary. These observations are important because they documented not only existing local practices and behaviors but also Teleki's value judgments about them. These types of observations were largely absent from von Höhnel's otherwise meticulous book about the expedition, entitled *Discovery of Lakes Rudolf and Stefanie*.

On April 28, Teleki received a delegation of *moran* from Arusha and later recorded his impressions of the encounter:

> In the evening a few Moranes arrived from Arusa. Very friendly. They spat in their hands. I had to spit too but I spat at them which was a great honor for them. This way of spitting is a sign of friendship and peace. They rubbed the spit into the palm of my hand, scratched and patted me, all signs of friendship. They pulled their penises out to full length and showed me the marks of their Masai circumcision by which they prove their origin from Arusa. After that they showed me that beneath my chin the same sort of hair grows as around their testicles. Friendly natives. In the end I retreated into my tent to evade further signs of their good will.[55]

Teleki's frequent diary comments about African physical characteristics and bodily functions indicate that these were a significant cause of culture shock for him:

> The sultan is sitting in front of me playing with his penis. These good natives piss wherever they are if they have the urge to do so, even in my tent! But there I throw them out. They are more careful about shitting and I was asked to send my men all to one side for that. . . . They marvel at my writing and think I can exterminate natives, kill the cattle, and inseminate women. If they want to be friendly towards somebody, they rub their chin and run their fingers through their pelvic hair.[56]

Even if Teleki's personal attitudes toward local peoples were patronizing, he was extremely skilled at diplomatically negotiating with them. He never underestimated their abilities and was always patient and calm in resolving potentially dangerous disputes. He was often kind to them, treated their illnesses with his own medications, and preferred peaceful contact and mutual respect to the firepower of his mini-army.

What is also clear from all of the surviving accounts of this expedition is that Teleki really enjoyed himself in Africa. He took pleasure in trekking and shooting, avidly collected geologic, natural history, and ethnographic materials, and was moved by the spectacular beauty of the East African landscape. Except for an occasional mild bout of malaria, he was in good health throughout the trip. At the end of a grueling day that may have included a near miss with a charging rhinoceros or an armed attack by local people, he would contentedly sit in front of his tent, smoking his long-stemmed pipe with Hamis, his pet monkey, on his lap. As the cool of the evening approached, he often sang, as von Höhnel later recounted: "The count had a beautiful singing voice, and in the quiet evenings in the wilderness he often made himself heard, always beginning with some French songs. These soon gave way, however, to melancholic Hungarian tunes."[57]

It is a tribute to the characters of both Teleki and von Höhnel that they forged a lifelong friendship under the adversities of African travel that had made other men bitter rivals. This was due not only to their complementary personalities but also to the fact that Teleki was primarily engaged in this trip for his own personal pleasure. He did not look to the results of this expedition for honors and recognition, and he did not need them to satisfy the expectations of any government or scientific body. The fact that he never published an account of the trip but had his companion von Höhnel do so indicates that, for him, the rewards of the expedition were in Africa, not in the saloons and lecture halls of Europe.

Von Höhnel's career lay at sea and not in Africa. Though this trip fulfilled a long-held dream of adventure in Africa, he did not see it as the prelude to future employment by either a colonial government or private commercial interests. From a certain perspective, his absence from the navy for almost three years while accompanying Teleki put him at a distinct disadvantage as far as his career was concerned. His work and accomplishments in Africa were not transferable as credits toward promotion but instead were viewed as departures from the norm for a young naval officer.

Thus, Teleki and von Höhnel markedly differed from most of their explorer contemporaries in terms of what they hoped to gain from their travels. For Livingstone, the goal was more souls for Christ; for Speke and Thomson, it was fame and patron sponsorship of future trips; and for Stanley, it was a lucrative career in the commercial exploitation of Africa.

In later years, after Teleki's death, von Höhnel expressed fond memories of his former patron:

> His most winning characteristics were simplicity, kind-heartedness, and carefulness. . . . The longer one knew him, the more one appreciated him. . . . My companion disposed of very good nerves, had a great knowledge of all shooting matters, and was a capital marksman. . . . The years we spent in the interior of Africa, during which we were entirely dependent on each other, were the foundation of a friendship that united us for the rest of our lives.[58]

On June 19, 1887, Teleki and von Höhnel began their final attempt to reach the top of Mount Kilimanjaro.[59] Taking seventy-seven men, a light load of equipment, and a few bottles of the 1842 vintage of a Hungarian wine, they began their ascent at daybreak. Teleki took his own barometric, temperature, and altitude measurements, which he meticulously recorded in his diary. Von Höhnel soon became so fatigued that he had to rest every ten minutes. Not wishing to jeopardize the expedition's objective of scaling the peak, he offered to remain behind in his tent. The following morning, Teleki began moving alone up the slopes of Kibo peak. Unfortunately, he did so while smoking his pipe and some expensive cigars Oswald had given him in Zanzibar. This did not help matters when he began to develop signs of altitude sickness, which eventually forced him to stop at 17,387 feet. Teleki was wise enough not to push his luck. Bleeding from his nose and mouth and experiencing difficulty in breathing, he turned around and began to descend. He was comforted to some extent by the fact that he was the first European to ascend the mountain to such a height. Had he been better prepared and ascended more slowly, he might have succeeded in scaling Kibo's 19,340 feet.[60]

After descending the mountain, Teleki and von Höhnel returned to Taveta, where they had left most of their men. There, they met the German explorer and scientist Dr. Hans Meyer, who was preparing an assault on Mount Kilimanjaro. Meyer, an investor in the German East Africa Company, had more than exploration on his mind. An advocate for German colonial ambitions, he was clearly intent on placing Mount Kilimanjaro under the company's control and was eventually successful at this.[61]

Teleki spent two weeks in Taveta, resting and regrouping his caravan for the march across the Maasai grasslands. He sent a large collection of ethnographic objects, natural history specimens, and trophies down to the coast, along with a letter to Oswald instructing him to ship everything to Crown Prince Rudolf. Teleki also used his time in Taveta to take stock of his arsenal, which had been depleted by the theft of twenty-one rifles.[62]

On July 15, 1887, Teleki, von Höhnel, Kimemeta, and their caravan set out for Ngongo Bagas near present-day Nairobi, where they arrived on August 27. During this period, four of the expedition's porters died from causes that Teleki did not record in his diary. However, these and most of the subsequent thirty-two deaths among the expedition's personnel were probably due to either malaria or dysentery, which also troubled von Höhnel for much of the trip. In fact, he became severely ill with dysentery on August 24 and remained incapacitated from it for the next two weeks.[63] This disease had killed other explorers, including New in 1875 and Johnston in 1879, and had invalided Thomson in 1884. Thus, its appearance gave both von Höhnel and Teleki great cause for concern.

Ngongo Bagas was a stopping point for coastal caravans, where food was usually obtained through barter with the Kikuyu people who lived in the nearby fertile highlands and around the base of Mount Kenya. By the time Teleki and von Höhnel reached this area in 1887, the Kikuyu had been subjected to repeated raids and abuses from coastal Arab and Swahili caravans. Their crops and livestock had been stolen, and worse still, many of them had been captured and sold into slavery. Even after slavery had been stamped out by the European powers, the lush gardens of the Kikuyu remained a tempting target for food-starved caravans that had to travel for weeks through arid stretches often devoid of even game. For their part, the Kikuyu attempted to take advantage of caravans through pillaging, demands for tribute, or chicanery, which in turn often led to armed conflicts.

In crossing into Kikuyu country, Teleki and von Höhnel were the first Europeans to enter a region that was extremely unsettled and charged with numerous opportunities for confrontation and open conflict. The political division of the Kikuyu into small and often rival and warring groups complicated contacts with them even further. For Teleki, matters were made worse when von Höhnel became severely ill with dysentery on September 11.[64]

Teleki made enormous efforts to pass peacefully through the country of the Kikuyu in order to achieve the second objective of his expedition—the ascent of Mount Kenya. He patiently underwent blood-brotherhood ceremonies with local chiefs, gave them gifts, paid tribute, and restrained his men, who were frequently provoked. Some Kikuyu groups, however, proved treacherous. They simultaneously showed signs of friendship while plotting to ambush the caravan at the first opportune moment.[65]

Teleki had been warned by Europeans on the coast not to explore Kikuyu country because of the risk of unpredictable and violent ambushes. Even Jumbe Kimemeta "showed much faintheartedness on this matter," as von Höhnel recorded in his memoirs.[66] However, Teleki had promised the crown prince that he would attempt to climb Mount Kenya. In crossing Kikuyu country, he showed great courage and tact, always marching at the head of the caravan and diplomatically dealing with incessant demands for tribute.

His real troubles began on September 14, 1887, when the caravan was attacked with bows and arrows by the Kikuyu while he was paying their chiefs tribute. Supposedly friendly chiefs and guides had actually led the caravan into an ambush, and Kikuyu warriors quickly surrounded and attacked it on all sides. Teleki had no choice but to counterattack, which he did with deadly consequences for the Kikuyu. Some forty-five Kikuyu were killed in the fight, and many more would have been had Teleki not restrained his men.[67]

As von Höhnel later wrote: "It was most unfortunate that hostilities had broken out, for we still had apparently many days' journey before we could reach the northern frontier of Kikuyuland. We were extremely anxious to make peace with the natives."[68]

Teleki went to great lengths to make peace with the local Kikuyu, and in general, he was successful. For the next several days, the caravan was not molested as it slowly progressed across the lush hills and valleys. It became clear to both Teleki and von Höhnel that the Kikuyu were divided among themselves: Some favored allowing the caravan to pass peacefully, but others wanted to pillage it. War cries from those who wanted to attack the caravan kept Teleki and his men on edge for the next several days. Finally, on September 21, the caravan approached a stream where some 800 to 1,000 Kikuyu warriors were waiting. An equal number rushed in on the caravan's rear. Von Höhnel described what happened next:

> An unnatural silence prevailed, and it seemed as if the Kikuyu were waiting for a signal. That signal came. Silently half a dozen arrows whizzed through the air and fell amongst us. . . . In a moment, every other sound was drowned in the noise of the guns fired simultaneously by all our men.
>
> The firing soon ceased . . . but it was a long time before we were all together again. . . . The porters were compelled to give up all their spoils, as this was the only way to check their plundering propensities.
>
> It was very evident that the onslaught had been planned, for we picked up hundreds of leather bags dropped by the fugitives, which were either empty or contained strips of skin intended to tie up the bales, or perhaps even to bind the captives the natives hoped to take.[69]

On September 27, Teleki and von Höhnel sighted Mount Kenya for the first time. Teleki recorded this momentous event in his diary: "To-day, by the grace of God, I have achieved one of my greatest desires, I saw Mount Kenya. The view was breathtakingly grand."[70] Teleki's pleasure at seeing Mount Kenya was soon shattered by renewed Kikuyu hostilities. As von Höhnel said: "The insolence of the natives was constantly on the increase."[71] Eventually, on October 2, the Kikuyu attacked, but they were quickly routed by Qualla Idris and 120 of Teleki's men, who pursued them up a hillside. Teleki gave Qualla Idris orders to burn the villages, take prisoners, and confiscate livestock in the hope that such severe punishment would force the Kikuyu to sue for peace. Writing on November 4, 1887, to Crown Prince Rudolf, Teleki provided very graphic details of the battle and recounted that he had burned 50 hamlets, taken 49 prisoners, and captured 1,400 sheep.[72]

This massive show of force did not completely convince the Kikuyu that they should make peace with Teleki. The following day, they again attacked but were driven off after 10 of their number were killed. One of Teleki's most trusted men, Abedi Wadi Heri, who was suffering from dysentery, was killed in this attack. Teleki wrote in his diary: "My poor Abedi is also lost. The Kikuyus killed him. Höhnel fired at them, but it is too late to save Abedi."[73] Von Höhnel wrote that one of the Kikuyu warriors "was mockingly holding up a blood-stained shirt towards us. A shot from us avenged his [Abedi's] death."[74]

Teleki pushed on toward the western slopes of Mount Kenya despite sporadic attacks by the Kikuyu. As he did so, he and von Höhnel discovered that they were infested with lice. Von Höhnel, still ill with dysentery, decided not to attempt climbing the mountain. On the morning of October 17, Teleki started up the mountain with 40 porters and several guides. Three days later, he reached an altitude of 15,355 feet, according to his own aneroid reading. Ultimately, the cold, ice, snow, and fog forced him to give up his attempt to scale the tallest peak, M'Batian, which is 17,058 feet high. So, on October 21, he regretfully turned back and began to retrace his steps down the south-western face of the mountain. By any standard, his ascent of the mountain during the rainy season was a remarkable feat and one more example of his physical toughness.[75]

The second objective of his expedition partially accomplished, Teleki was anxious to get out of the country of the Kikuyu. He led his expedition northwest along the eastern flanks of the Aberdare range, toward the arid Laikipia Plateau then inhabited by the Maasai. The Kikuyu living on the northern fringes of their territory were extremely friendly toward Teleki and his men. Word had already reached them of the crushing defeat inflicted on their relatives to the south. Moreover, exposed as they were to continuous raids by their enemies the Maasai, these northern Kikuyu feared terrible consequences should Teleki ally himself with the Maasai. They also saw the potential advantages of inducing him to help them drive off the Maasai. Teleki, however, had no interest in taking sides in the conflictual stalemates that then characterized Kikuyu-Maasai relations.

The northern Maasai whom Teleki now encountered also regularly demanded tribute, and they were expert at feigning peaceful intentions while plotting to pillage a caravan. News of Teleki's stunning defeat of the Kikuyu had already reached them by the time he arrived. He succinctly summed up their response to him with a statement in his November 3, 1887, diary entry: "They recognize me as an extremely powerful Laibon, and they are afraid of me because I have conquered the Kikuyus."[76] In a sense, then, his defeat of the Kikuyu rendered the Maasai peaceful and friendly.

On November 4, 1887, Teleki wrote a thirteen-page letter in Hungarian to Crown Prince Rudolf, recounting his experiences with the Kikuyu and his attempt to climb Mount Kenya. This and subsequent letters that he sent to the coast with passing trading caravans amplified his diary entries. He detailed his hunting experiences for the prince and included a litany of the slaughter that was usual for the time (he had shot twenty-five rhinoceroses, four elephants, and one lion). He also expressed regrets about his battles with the Kikuyu and the hope that he would not have to engage in any others in the future.[77]

Teleki also had some harsh words for Thomson in his November 4, 1887, letter to Crown Prince Rudolf: "Everything Thomson has written about the Maasai are pure lies. The Maasai are a peaceful people, honest, intelligent such that four to five people can travel in security among them." In fairness to Thomson, it should be noted that Teleki's crushing defeat of the Kikuyu had made the Maasai more docile and cooperative.[78]

Teleki and his men were now entering a part of East Africa where the greatest challenges would come in the form of climate and topography, not frightened or hostile peoples. Local informants had confirmed that there was a large lake to the north on the other side of the semidesert and scrub-bush country that now lay before them. They did not refer to this lake as Samburu but as the Basso Narok (Black Lake). Some also vaguely hinted that there was yet another lake to the north of the Basso Narok, called the Basso Ebor (White Lake). To complicate matters, people told them that the Guaso Nyiro River flowed through a third lake to the east, called Lorian. Teleki decided to send von Höhnel down the Guaso Nyiro to Lake Lorian while he headed north for Lake Baringo. Unfortunately, von Höhnel's illness and the rocky and mountainous terrain prevented him from reaching the lake. But on meeting up with Teleki on December 8, he was able to describe the upper reaches of a river that had not been previously explored. Teleki had arrived at the village of Nyemps, just to the south of Lake Baringo, the day before, where he planned to wait out the rainy season before striking north for the Basso Narok.[79]

The arrival of a trading caravan heading for the coast prompted Teleki to write a number of letters home—to his sister Agnes, the manager of his estate, to Oswald in Zanzibar, and to Crown Prince Rudolf. He actually wrote two letters to the prince, one on December 22, describing his hunting experiences, and another six days earlier, which laid out his future travel plans. Both letters were brief because, as Teleki told the prince, "I have exhausted my paper and because of this please excuse the brevity of my report. The most modest servant of your Imperial Highness."[80]

In his letter of December 16, 1887, Teleki told the prince about the lakes:

> From here I will leave for Zamburu which is a country near the white and black lakes. The caravans do not approach them, and as a result they do not know at what distance they are and what people live there. There are the Wakwafi who live there and three other tribes also; one is the Turkana and is situated along the shores of the black lake. The rest are unknown. A local told me that the white lake is 15 days march, and the other he estimated at 30 days.[81]

Teleki and his men were now set to strike north into terra incognita. Some 150 miles lay between their camp at Nyemps and the southern tip of the black lake. They secured the services of Sokoni, a Nyemps guide who knew the country ahead of them, and prepared enough provisions for thirty-five days.

On January 10, 1888, Teleki and von Höhnel set out with Kimemeta, 197 porters, 6 guides, 15 askari, 8 Somali guards, 19 donkeys, and assorted cattle, sheep, and goats. Nine sick men and some supplies were left at the base camp. Von Höhnel wrote: "The men were not in the very best of condition . . . but they were a brave and determined-looking little troop. . . . In capital spirits, though I was still a mere skeleton, I mounted my grey steed to bring up the rear of the extended column."[82]

Teleki led his men into a region never before seen by any European and by few coastal traders. It was a harsh country of volcanic slag, boulders, searing heat, and scarce water supplies. Within the first three weeks, four men died. Teleki mournfully recorded their deaths in his diary. On February 20, 1888, he wrote: "Hamis Yinger died in the afternoon. I was very sorry to lose my dear Zanzibari helper. I looked over him for a long time."[83]

After passing over the rugged Larogi range of mountains, they came upon another range that had never before been charted. As Von Höhnel described it, "We wound up our work by naming the newly discovered mountains the General Mathews chain in honor of our friend General Lloyd Mathews, who had done so much to help us in Zanzibar."[84]

By March 2, they reached Mount Nyiru, where they met a Burkeneji (Samburu) by the name of Lembasso who confirmed the existence of two lakes to the north, the Basso Narok and the Basso Ebor. For three days, he led them through a dry, parched landscape that gave no hint of a nearby lake. Finally, on the afternoon of March 5, they struggled up to the top of a dusty ridge and saw in the distance the shimmering surface of an enormous lake. The porters shouted for joy while Teleki and von Höhnel gazed speechless at the object of their quest.

> An entirely new world was spread out before our astonished eyes. The void down in the depths became filled as if by magic with picturesque mountains and ragged slopes, with a medley of ravines and valleys, which appeared to be closing up from every side to form a fitting frame for the dark blue gleaming surface of the lake stretching beyond as far as the eye could reach. ... We gazed in speechless delight, spell-bound by the beauty of the scene before us ... full of enthusiasm and gratefully remembering the gracious interest taken in our plans from the first by His Royal and Imperial Highness, Prince Rudolf of Austria, Count Teleki named the sheet of water, set like a pearl of great price in the wonderful landscape beneath us, Lake Rudolf.[85]

Teleki's diary account is much more matter-of-fact than von Höhnel's almost euphoric response to sighting the lake:

> I can't imagine a landscape more barren, dried out and grim. ... At 1:22 P.M., the Basso Narok appeared, an enormous lake of blue water dotted with some islands. The northern shores cannot be seen. ... As far as the eye can see are barren and volcanic shores. I give it the name of Lake Rudolf. Daudu Muhiman stayed behind, maybe died? One elephant.[86]

The following day, they actually arrived on the southern shore of the lake, where the waters were the color of jade. They had little time to savor their remarkable accomplishment in being the first Europeans to reach the Jade Sea. The early monsoon clouds heralding the beginning of the rainy season were already gathering on the eastern horizon. This, coupled with the scarcity of food and the weakened state of the men, forced Teleki to advance to the northern end of the lake as quickly as possible. Once there, he immediately set out for the Basso Ebor, the second lake that they had been told about that lay to the northeast; on April 19, they reached its southern shore. Teleki named it Lake Stephanie in honor of Rudolf's wife, a name that has since been changed to Chew Bahir by the Ethiopian government. In an almost laconic diary entry, he described the discovery: "At 8:30, I had my first view through the bush tops of the Basso Nabor and gave it the name Lake Stephanie; the lake cannot be very large as I can see the mountains on all sides surrounding it. A dead water eagle is floating on the surface of a swampy puddle. And here, in the world's most barren spot, I set up camp."[87]

They then returned to the northern end of Lake Rudolf, just as the rainy season was getting into full swing. Teleki and von Höhnel had discovered two lakes, and the next geographic challenge was to determine the source of the larger of the two, Lake Rudolf. Because the rains had transformed the Omo River delta at the northern end of the lake into an impenetrable marsh, von Höhnel's explorations of the area were greatly hindered. But based on his limited observations, he concluded that two rivers flowed into the lake—the Nianamm (Omo), which he saw, and to the west of it, the Bass (whose name means "water"). The meticulous von Höhnel was making an educated guess about the Bass because he did not actually see it. The Omo breaks up into many channels and forms a delta before emptying into the lake, and it is possible that his informants were speaking of one of these channels as being another river, the Bass. In fact, he found obtaining information from the local Reshiat people almost impossible: "It was extremely difficult to get any reliable facts about the surrounding country."[88] The Bass to which von Höhnel's informants were referring may actually have been the Kibish River, a secondary source west of the Omo that only reaches the lake during very heavy rainy seasons. Thus, Teleki and von Höhnel would return without definitively resolving the question of the course of the Nianamm and the Bass, which in turn would entice other explorers to do so.

Teleki had originally planned to return along the lake's western shore, but the heavy rains had flooded the Omo River delta and made a crossing practically impossible. In addition, the Reshiat people who lived at the northern end of the lake refused to give the expedition either guides or food. Not wishing to tempt fate so late in the game, Teleki decided to return quickly the way he had come. He had already lost a dozen men to sickness, and von Höhnel was still chronically ill with malaria. By this point, Teleki was exasperated with von Höhnel, who scoffed at taking quinine to prevent malaria. He expressed his frustration in his diary entry of January 24, 1888: "He does not want to take quinine, medicating himself instead according to my idiotic English medical handbook."[89]

The expedition started south again, and on a side trip along the southern end of the lake, von Höhnel discovered an active volcano, which he named Teleki in honor of the count (the gulf at the southern end of the lake near the volcano is still referred to as von Höhnel Gulf; however, the lake has receded since that time, and the volcano is now quite a distance from the lake's southern shore and is dormant). From the southern end of the lake, they made a detour to the western side into Suk and Turkana country, in search of provisions. The march down the eastern shore of the lake had been grueling. The men were fatigued, there was no game since the animals had been dispersed by the rains, and the expedition had run low on food. Consequently, the trip into Suk country was, in fact, a planned raid on food supplies. Von Höhnel summed up their predicament:

> Our caravan was on the verge of dissolving into pillaging gangs, and to avoid this, a decisive step had to be taken. The cattle which the Suk would not—and admittedly could not—sell, had to be taken by force. Necessity has no law. . . . Acts of violence of course do not go off without bloodshed, and this grieved us more than I can say, for the natives had been friendly, and we were the first Europeans they had ever met.[90]

It greatly troubled both Teleki and von Höhnel that they had to forcibly take food and livestock from the Suk, who themselves were close to starvation. However, as they saw it, they had no other choice.

Teleki returned to Lake Baringo on July 29, 1888, after an absence of seventeen months. Twenty of his men had perished on this journey to find the black and white lakes, most falling victim to malaria and dysentery. Although von Höhnel was still ill with malaria (primarily because of his refusal to take quinine), Teleki was as robust as ever.

The expedition arrived in Taveta on September 29, 1888, where Teleki and von Höhnel learned of the enormous political changes that had taken place on the coast during their absence. An Arab revolt in Tanga and Pangani had been suppressed by General Mathews, and there was ample evidence of East Africa's division into British and German spheres of influence. Teleki and von Höhnel also learned in Taveta that William Oswald had committed suicide and that his place as consular officer had been taken by his cousin.

It took Teleki and his men three weeks to reach the coast. They arrived at Mombasa on October 24, 1888, where they met Mathews, who was anxious to hear about their discoveries.[91] They had been in the interior for almost two years and had charted the last of the great African lakes.[92] After a two-month stay in Zanzibar, in part necessi-

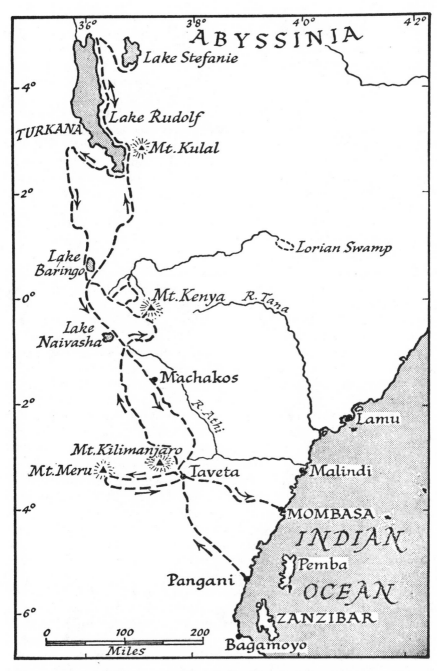

Count Samuel Teleki's route (from Some Historic Journeys in East Africa, 1961).

tated by the fact that they were both very ill with malaria, Teleki and von Höhnel traveled to Harar in Ethiopia, before returning to Europe in the spring of 1889.[93] By this time, Crown Prince Rudolf was dead, having committed suicide on January 30, 1889, at Mayerling. Thus, on his return, Teleki never got to see the man who had been the patron of his successful expedition.[94]

During the time they were in the interior, Teleki often corresponded with Crown Prince Rudolf, sending letters down to the coast with passing caravans (one of which contained none other than Sadi ben Ahedi, the man who had traveled with New and given Thomson so much grief). These letters were passed on to William Oswald, the consul of Austria-Hungary in Zanzibar, who regularly reported on the expedition to Count Kalnocky, minister of the imperial house and foreign affairs. Oswald reported in a letter dated June 6, 1887, that the expedition had visited the Mount Kilimanjaro area.[95] On February 14, 1888, he wrote Count Kalnocky that Teleki had reached Mount Kenya, and on May 8, he informed Kalnocky's ministry that Teleki had arrived at Baringo in February. In this last letter, Oswald dutifully reported on von Höhnel's dysentery as well.[96] William Oswald's successor, Alfred Oswald, wrote to the ministry on October 22, 1888, announcing the good news that the Teleki expedition had reached Taveta a few weeks before.[97] Thus, the expedition was in sporadic contact with the consuls in Zanzibar throughout most of its time in the interior, and, through him, with the Austrian government and Crown Prince Rudolf.

Teleki remained in robust health for most of the trip, and the loss of 97 pounds of weight may actually have been to his benefit. When he reappeared on the coast, he weighed 141 pounds, in contrast to the 238 he weighed when he started out. In fact, in his November 4, 1887, letter to Crown Prince Rudolf, Teleki said: "I will tell you other things when I return home if you still remember the 'fat Teleki' who has had to shrink his trouser strap by three holes. I am in good health."

On reaching Mombasa, Teleki sent a brief report of the expedition's findings to the *Times* in London, which published it on December 25, 1888. The Scottish Geographical Society adapted the report for publication, and it was also subsequently published in Hungarian.

On their return to Vienna via Cairo, Teleki and von Höhnel learned how close they came to being cheated of their prize. Jules Borelli, a French explorer, had left Egypt on September 16, 1885, and headed for Ethiopia in order to explore the Omo River. He was delayed from moving into western and southwestern Ethiopia by Emperor Menelik, who detained him at the capital of Antoto for part of the period from July 1886 to November 1887. Borelli started out in November 1887 for the headwaters of the Omo River and reached a point on the river 300 miles north of Lake Samburu on June 17, 1888, some three months after Teleki and von Höhnel had arrived on the lake's southern shore. Had Menelik not detained him and had he not fallen ill, Borelli might have reached the lake well before Teleki and von Höhnel. He was forced to return north because of illness, which, according to his own report, was probably malaria. Borelli was given a good description of the lake by people in Ethiopia, who called it Lake Schambara.[98]

Borelli arrived in Cairo on November 15, 1888, where he later met Teleki and von Höhnel. He and the two Austro-Hungarians exchanged information, and in the book he subsequently wrote, Borelli thanked von Höhnel for supplying him with the cartographic details that he later included in his maps. It is of interest that von Höhnel made no mention of Borelli in his own book. However, von Höhnel did have a great deal to say about Borelli in his as yet unpublished, English-language autobiography. On seeing the map Jules Borelli had made, he was amused: "According to this map, Mr. Borelli had penetrated south right across the country in which Lake Rudolf is lying without seeing it. . . . I advised him not to show this map to anybody, and promised to make it harmonious with our discoveries and to set it right. This was no easy task."[99]

Clearly, Borelli was not a very good geographer or cartographer. Yet he doubted von Höhnel's assertion that two rivers flowed into Lake Rudolf. Borelli had thoroughly explored the upper and middle reaches of the Omo, and because of the curvature of the river's course, he thought that the Omo would have to join up with the alleged Bass River to the west on its way south, which subsequent explorers found was actually not the case. Borelli deduced that the Omo alone flowed into the lake.[100] In this, he was close to the truth, as another river to the west, the Kibish, rarely reached the lake except during heavy rainy seasons. He also correctly noted that the Omo and Nianamm were really the same river.[101] However, his assertion that the Omo was the only source of the lake was doubted at the time by some because of von Höhnel's claim of a second river to the west.[102]

Teleki and von Höhnel were clearly incorrect in their beliefs about the Omo River. They wrongly believed that Borelli's Omo flowed toward the east, where it joined the Juba (Giuba) River in Somaliland. They were also incorrect in believing that the Nianamm was a distinct river that flowed into the lake to the west of the Omo. And finally, they were wrong in believing that the Bass was another permanent source of the lake.[103] When Teleki and von Höhnel returned to Vienna and Borelli to Paris, the issue of whether the Omo and Nianamm were actually the same river was an open one.

Neither Teleki nor von Höhnel received heroes' welcomes in Vienna when they returned in early June 1889, even though they had given Austria-Hungary an honored place in the annals of African exploration. There were two reasons for this. Jealousy was clearly one, as von Höhnel noted: "On the part of certain other personalities who liked to pretend that they were the only promoters of geographical researches, the expedition had from the outset not been taken seriously; now that they saw that they had been mistaken, they all the more buried it in silence.[104] Even von Höhnel's fellow officers gave him a cool reception. "What did Africa matter to them!" he wrote.[105]

The other reason had to do with Crown Prince Rudolf's suicide on January 30, 1889, when Teleki and von Höhnel were en route to Harar in Abyssinia.

Count Teleki ... did not reap the deserved reward for his enterprise. In consequence of the tragic death of the Crown Prince Rudolf, one was on the look out for scapegoats whom one might hold responsible; the friends of the Crown Prince were of course the cause of the tragic development. My traveling companion had been one of these, and though utterly innocent and though he had been a devoted friend to the Prince, abstentious in every way, he had to suffer for his friendship. His name was unpopular in high circles, and this was a reason not to speak of his travels and achievements.[106]

Despite the importance of Teleki's geographic discoveries, the Royal Geographical Society declined to invite him to lecture on his travels, as suggested by Sir Richard Burton.[107] Colonial competition in East Africa had become so intense by 1889 that the society demurred, citing concerns about possible adverse political consequences for Great Britain. As the society saw it, an invitation to speak would have represented recognition of Teleki's claim of being the first European to visit Lake Rudolf. And in the scramble for Africa then under way, such claims normally gave sponsoring colonial powers the right of territorial annexation.

The society's refusal to hear him and the failure of his own country to take much note of his journey disheartened Teleki to some degree. But he had no desire to force recognition from others for his accomplishments and contented himself with memories of a remarkable journey to Africa. His delegation of the job of compiling an account of the expedition to von Höhnel did not reflect aristocratic indolence on his part, as some have suggested. Rather, it demonstrated that, as an independent man of great wealth who was confident in his view of himself, he had no need for the accolades that such an account might bring. He chose instead to promote his faithful companion von Höhnel by having him write up the account. Von Höhnel's book was published in German three years later and in English in 1894.

Teleki gave his ethnological collections to the Hungarian National Museum in Budapest, and his natural history and geologic specimens went to several museums in Europe. He retained a number of trophies from the expedition as well as some ethnographic objects, which he displayed for many years at his country home at Saromberke.

Teleki returned to East Africa in March 1895, where he hunted for a month around Mount Kilimanjaro. Gout and a deterioration in the general state of his health precluded his climbing the mountain again. Although he claimed that he was not a sentimental man, this return visit likely represented a search for the happiness he had experienced eight years before when he first saw the mountain.[108] His April 8, 1895, diary entry is revealing:

> I could not resist taking another look at Kilimanjaro before I lay my head down to rest forever. To see once more Kilimanjaro in all his glory and the country around in which I had been so serenely happy before. . . . I don't know if I will ever return again, and I took leave from the snow-covered ancient one like from an old friend I would never see again in my life! And if I were sentimental, I would have cried!"[109]

Von Höhnel often visited Teleki at his country estate at Saromberke, a village that had a purely Hungarian population. Von Höhnel wrote that

> Saromberke lies in Transylvania in the upper Maros Valley. Simple as the host himself, were the buildings which he inhabited as well as the people whom I first met there. . . . Simple and modest though Count Teleki had shown himself during the expedition, he now proved he was a gourmet of no mean order. He imported coffee directly from Mokka, his cigars from Havana, and the same thing applied to everything in his household.[110]

Teleki had inherited a remarkable library from his great-grandfather, but his pride was his stud farm. "Saromberke bred half-bloods of special quality, tough horses with gazelle-like eyes and Arab heads," wrote von Höhnel. Looking back on his first meeting with Teleki on the *Greif*, he said, "I then could not see what . . . consequences would result from the first short interview, that many a year of this friendship would bind me together with this man."[111]

After a long illness, Teleki died at his home on Four Reviczky Street in Budapest on March 10, 1916, at the age of 71. Surviving him were his sister Elizabeth, Baroness Banffy Zoltan, and her children, as well as the children of his sister Agnes, Countess Joseph Zeyk, who had predeceased him. A Reformed service was held in his home on March

12, 1916, at 2:00 P.M., and his remains were transported to Saromberke, where, after a service in the local Reformed Church, he was
buried in the family vault.[112]

Teleki's former country home is now an agricultural school occupying much less land than the estate's previous 100,000 acres. The impressive Teleki library, founded by Samuel's great-grandfather in 1802,
is now housed in the nearby small town of Tirgu Mures. In the early
nineteenth century, it had 40,000 volumes for Saromberke's 6,000 inhabitants. There are conflicting accounts of what happened to the contents of Teleki's country house, including his African trophies, ethnographic collections, and photographic plates. During the 1970s and
1980s, the Romanians told visitors that the Soviet army had sacked the
estate during World War II.[113] However, a number of local Hungarians
maintain that Communists actually did so after the war. Some have
graphically described how the Communists threw furnishings out of
the windows into the courtyard, including photographic glass plates
taken on Teleki's Lake Rudolf expedition. Following the looting, a local
Hungarian administrator sent two young men out to salvage documents and photographs from the vandalized estates. Some of Teleki's
photographs, including those from Africa, were collected and deposited
with the Hungarian Cultural Organization in Cluj, whose holdings
were later incorporated into the Romanian National Archives. A number of Teleki's African trophies were placed in the Gongenyszentimrei
Forestry School, a former country estate belonging to Crown Prince
Rudolf, located forty kilometers from Saromberke.[114]

In 1972, Lajos Erdélyi, a photographer from Tirgu Mures, obtained
access to the surviving Teleki photographs. He made copy negatives
and prints of around 100 of these photographs, which he used to illus-
trate his 1977 biography of Teleki.[115]

In 1988, the Hungarian Scientific Africa Expedition, composed of
scientists from several disciplines, commemorated the centennial of
Teleki's journey by retracing its route. They placed a memorial plaque
at Loiyangalani, on the eastern shore of Lake Turkana,[116] marking the
passage of Teleki and his men who, a century before, had sought out
this lake—not in the interests of a colonial power or with a desire to
exploit its resources but simply because it was there.

5

An American Approaches from the South

William Astor Chanler soon after his second East African expedition (courtesy John Winthrop Aldrich).

As Teleki and von Höhnel were leaving the East African coast for home, a young American from Dutchess County, New York, arrived in Zanzibar on March 13, 1889, en route to Mount Kilimanjaro. William Astor Chanler was only twenty-one years old at the time. However, the previous year, he had inherited a fortune on attaining his majority and quickly threw off the shackles imposed by his overly strict guardians. Chanler was born on June 11, 1867, in Newport, Rhode Island. His father, John Winthrop Chanler, was a wealthy lawyer who had served as a member of Congress (1863–1869) and as chairman of the executive committee of Tammany Hall, New York. His mother, Margaret Astor Ward, was a great-granddaughter of John Jacob Astor and the daughter of Emily Astor and Samuel Ward.[1]

Chanler's grandfather Ward began life as a financier and banker. He married the daughter of William B. Astor in 1837 but quickly ran afoul of his Astor in-laws because of his early business failures and love for taking risks. A man of great intellectual interests and social skills, Ward went on to make and lose fortunes at regular intervals. He also became a leader of New York and London high society, was America's leading epicure and gastronome, organized revolutions in South America, and was the most powerful lobbyist in Congress for many years.[2]

The elder brother of Julia Ward Howe, author of the *Battle Hymn of the Republic*, and an uncle to the brilliant writer F. Marion Crawford, Ward was warmhearted, charming, and generous. However, he was also the "prince of good livers," as *Vanity Fair* characterized him in 1889, and was thus viewed as an unreliable father by the Astors. When his wife, Emily, died in childbirth, they quickly removed his daughter, Margaret, from his control and later saw to it that her Chanler children were kept as far away as possible from him.[3] The Astor family circle was eventually in a unique position to do this, as Margaret and John Winthrop Chanler both died prematurely when their children were very young.

William Astor Chanler was only ten years old when his surviving parent (his father) died in 1877. He and his seven remaining siblings were raised under the watchful eye of strict Astor guardians at Rokeby, the Chanler family estate in Dutchess County. He attended St. John's Military Academy in Ossining, New York, and was then sent off to Phillips Academy at Exeter, New Hampshire, in preparation for his entry into Harvard College.[4]

Much to the chagrin of his Astor relatives, Chanler visited his grandfather Ward while still a teenager. Ward greatly impressed him with exciting stories about politics, lobbying, and overseas travel. It was thanks, in part, to Ward that Chanler eventually overcame an early speech impediment to become a brilliant conversationalist.[5] By the time he entered Harvard in 1886, he was bright, daring, assertive, opinionated, and inclined to be impulsive and to spurn advice. His tightfisted Astor guardians kept him on a very short leash at Harvard and on a meager budget as well. In an attempt to extract more money out of them, he set fire to his dormitory room draperies, hoping for a sympathetic response to his appeal of loss by fire. His guardians coldly rejected his plea, leaving him with bare windows for the winter.[6]

On reaching his majority in June 1888, Chanler dropped out of Harvard, where his studies had bored him.[7] In a sense, it was fitting that his first great endeavor in life was in the shadows of Mount Kilimanjaro, Africa's greatest volcano, for he himself was like a piece of molten rock shot out onto the African landscape.

Chanler arrived in Zanzibar with his seventeen-year-old assistant George E. Galvin, who was also from Dutchess County.[8] Fortunately, Galvin's diary, with its detailed record of this first trip of theirs into the East African interior, has survived.[9] They left Rokeby on December 8, 1888, and embarked at New York City the following day for Le Havre, where they arrived eight days later. Chanler spent the next two and a half months in France and England, shooting, playing polo, and riding to hounds. On February 10, he and Galvin arrived in Monte Carlo; after a week at the gambling tables, they left on the final leg of their journey to Zanzibar.[10]

On May 18, 1889, Chanler and 150 porters sailed from Zanzibar for Mombasa, aboard the sultan's small steamer, the *Kilmer*. James Martin, who had traveled with Joseph Thomson six years before, was also on board, with 60 porters. They were part of an Imperial British East Africa Company (IBEA) expedition headed by Frederick J. Jackson, Ernest Gedge, and Dr. Archibald Donald Mackinnon. This expedition was destined for Uganda, which it eventually secured for Great Britain despite the remarkable efforts of Germany's agent Dr. Carl Peters. During the thirteen-hour voyage, Chanler benefited from speaking with Martin, who was then one of the most experienced travelers in East Africa.[11]

Chanler and his expedition started for the interior on May 21. He soon encountered porter desertions, engendered by proximity to the coast and the payment of three months' advance wages. As was customary, he had to locate the deserters and instill discipline among his remaining men. Galvin vividly described the effect of flogging on the porters: "I called on one man to take his load and he refused. I picked up a stick and went at him. After I got through with him and looked around for another, they were quietly lifting their loads on their heads and walking away."[12]

Chanler stopped off at the Rabai Mission Station, where Krapf, Rebmann, New, and Wakefield had all labored years before, and was in regular contact with the 250-strong IBEA expedition, a day's march ahead of him.[13] By this time, Mount Kilimanjaro had become a magnet for European sportsmen. But this was also an area where British and German interests faced off against one another in the tension-filled days before the Heligoland Treaty of July 1, 1890, established the Anglo-German boundary. In May 1889, German-British rivalry in East Africa was fierce, and it was into this setting that young Chanler came marching with his 150 porters and a large, fluttering American flag.

On June 30, 1889, Chanler and his men reached Taveta, where they stayed at Martin's former camp. However, on July 11, they moved to Teleki's old campsite, which Galvin later purchased from the local chiefs. There, Chanler supervised the construction of a six-room, thatched-roof house that stood in one corner of the two-acre compound. Aware of local political sensitivities, Chanler had two flagpoles erected, one for the Stars and Stripes and the other for the sultan of Zanzibar's red standard.[14]

The purpose of Chanler's trip to Mount Kilimanjaro was primarily sport. Still a caravan staging center, it had also become a base for visiting European sportsmen and naturalists. Among the latter was twenty-eight-year-old Dr. William Louis Abbott, an American physician whose inheritance of a fortune a short time before enabled him to abandon medicine in favor of a career as an explorer. Although he was away in Maasai country when Chanler arrived, he left a welcoming letter behind and soon returned, after his porters had attempted mass desertion. Abbott had already spent a year in the Mount Kilimanjaro region and had, in fact, assisted Teleki and von Höhnel when they passed by his camp on their way down to the coast. He was of great help to Chanler, sharing his knowledge of the mountain's fauna and flora and details about the peoples who lived on its slopes.[15]

Chanler's niece, Maddie DeMott, recorded that he had obtained a commission in the German East African Ivory Patrol.[16] Despite this German connection, he maintained cordial relations with Frederick Jackson of the IBEA and flew the sultan's flag over his compound. Thus, as a third-country national in a crucible of local colonial competition, he eminently succeeded in being on good terms with the representatives of the competing powers. This was a remarkable accomplishment for so young a man, and it demonstrates the brilliance of his insights into the political realities he faced in the Kilimanjaro region.

Chanler received high praise from Dr. Hans Meyer, the German scientist and explorer who was the first European to reach the summit of Mount Kilimanjaro. After meeting Chanler on the mountain's slopes, he wrote the following:

> The Kilimanjaro states have been visited by a number of missionaries and sportsmen of whom perhaps the most noteworthy is the young American, Mr. Chanler, who, proceeding to the region merely for the purpose of sport, has nevertheless distinguished himself by a thorough exploration of the lower slopes of the mountain. . . . He stayed with us overnight, and greatly delighted me with his spirited account of his achievements and plans, and with his keen insight into African affairs. Many of our colonial wise-acres might envy the energy and tact which has enabled this youth of 23 with a still more youthful companion, to lead a caravan of 180 men into regions as yet totally unexplored.[17]

Chanler spent four months exploring the Kilimanjaro region and seems to have determined during that time or shortly thereafter to lead an expedition into the vast, unexplored regions between Lake Rudolf and the Juba River to the east. As DeMott noted, he had proved to himself his capacity for leading a large group of men through the African wilderness and wanted to achieve "something more worthwhile than hunting."[18]

After having obtained what sportsmen then considered a respectable bag of trophies, Chanler left Taveta on October 4, 1889, and headed for the coast. He felt satisfied in the knowledge that he had proven himself as a big-game hunter, had successfully negotiated with local chiefs and entered into blood brotherhood with them, and had avoided becoming entangled in the web of Anglo-German political intrigue.[19] Galvin had also proved his mettle, not only at hunting but also in managing the infinite details of a large field expedition. Like Martin, who had traveled with Thomson, he was reliable, resourceful, and patient—characteristics that greatly contributed to the expedition's success.

Chanler and his men walked into Mombasa eight days after leaving Taveta and almost five months since heading into the interior. By now, he had firmly decided to return to East Africa, for he left all of his rifles in the care of his agents, Smith Mackenzie, and put his two headmen, Waziri and Hamidi, on half pay.[20]

Chanler and Galvin sailed from Zanzibar on the *Pei Ho* on November 3, bound for Marseilles, which they reached three weeks later. In no hurry to return home, Chanler spent the next six months in London, Paris, Rome, and Aix-les-Bains, where on April 9, he and Galvin met Queen Victoria taking a ride in a donkey cart. Still subject to recurrent bouts of malarial fevers, they sailed from Liverpool for New York on May 27, 1890, and finally reached Rokeby in early June.[21] During the year and a half they had been away, Africa had transformed them from mere boys into experienced world travelers.

Chanler now knew East Africa well, and he set his sights on exploring the vast patch of unknown territory that lay north of the Tana River between Lake Rudolf and the Juba River. In this, he was no mere dilettante out for sport and adventure. This assertion is supported by the fact that he made meticulous preparations for this expedition in London by purchasing an impressive array of supplies and equipment and contacting respected scientists for guidance. Richard Harding Davis, the turn-of-the-century journalist who, as Lately Thomas said, was the "beau ideal of American youth, the glamorous foreign correspondent and man about town," was very much impressed with Chanler's preparations. As Davis noted: "Part of [Chanler's] day was spent closeted with the officers of the East Africa Company, another part in Whitechapel buying Tommies' discarded redcoats as presents for African kings; and later he was testing smokeless powder and repeating rifles, or choosing canned meats and bottled medicine."[22]

In March 1892, Chanler wrote to von Höhnel out of the blue, asking him to accompany the expedition. As DeMott observed, this also was an indication that his expedition was to be a serious scientific endeavor. The fact that he met with officials of the IBEA clearly shows that he was sensitive to the political realities as well.[23]

Von Höhnel had never heard of Chanler and had already turned down a number of government and corporate offers to return to East Africa, including one from the IBEA. However, during a visit to Vienna in April, Chanler was able to recruit von Höhnel. For his part, von Höhnel may have been attracted by Chanler's proposal because, like Teleki's, it represented an offer from a private patron under whom he could engage in independent scientific inquiry. As a naval officer, he knew only too well that he could never have such independence in the employ of a government. Chanler induced the Austrian admiralty to give von Höhnel a furlough and then left for London, where, as Thomas related, he amused himself by riding in breakneck steeplechases against the best gentlemen jockeys.[24]

Two months later, however, he was ready to start off, and he invited von Höhnel to London to reach a final understanding. They left Europe separately, met in Port Said, and then sailed to Aden, where von Höhnel remained to engage the Somali while Chanler went on to Zanzibar. Von Höhnel also had to go over to Massowa in Eritrea to engage some Sudanese guards. Chanler saw his main task at Zanzibar as the engagement of porters. However, as he noted: "I could not have chosen a more inopportune time for the enlistment of porters at Zanzibar. The British East Africa Company, bent upon the retention of Uganda, had practically exhausted the supply of porters, and a missionary caravan was on the point of starting to the interior."[25]

Chanler, being the enterprising fellow he was, had no intention of sitting in Zanzibar and waiting for tried and tested porters to return from the interior at some vague point in the future. He also did not intend to follow von Höhnel's plan of recruiting porters in nearby German East Africa. As Thomas observed, Chanler was "tough, primitive, and single-minded. His capacity for action was enormous, and he despised dawdling and irresolution, but his inherent pugnacity was disguised by effortless manners and aristocratic ease."[26] True to form, Chanler did what came naturally to him. He went out and hired men from the plantations, sending out word that an expedition was about to leave and that it had the approval of the government. When von

Höhnel arrived in Zanzibar a few weeks later, he was shocked by the news that Chanler had hired 135 porters "by hook and crook."[27] They were largely young and inexperienced men, unaccustomed to the rigors of travel in the interior. Von Höhnel had arranged with the governor of German East Africa to hire Wanyamwezi porters, who then and in later years were renowned as the best porters in East Africa. As von Höhnel said, "We could have chosen the pick out of thousands of stalwart men. The Wanyamwezi, moreover, are cheerful and trustworthy men who never think of deserting."[28] Von Höhnel was distressed and feared the worst consequences of hiring inexperienced youths. He later said of Chanler that "he at that time was not aware that he had made a grave mistake, but he admitted it some months later."[29]

Sir Gerald Portal, who was the British consul general in Zanzibar and a friend of Chanler's, gave every support possible, instructing his subaltern General Lloyd Mathews, the prime minister of Zanzibar, to assist him in every way.[30] It was Chanler's intent to travel up the Tana River from Lamu on the coast to Mount Kenya, climb the mountain, go north to Lake Rudolf, and move east across 600 miles of unexplored territory where the Galla lived and on to the Juba River. He planned to follow the river to the ocean and then move southwest along the seashore to Lamu, covering 3,000 miles in the process. This ambitious plan for the expedition was published by Davis, reflecting Chanler's objectives before departure. But Chanler's own description of his objectives, as related in his book written after the expedition, were more vague.[31] In a letter to his sister Margaret, written on his way to Africa, he said: "If I fail in Africa, I shall not be utterly cast down. Many better men than I have failed in attempting what I am essaying to do. If I die, I die on a decent cause and leave my people nothing to be ashamed of."[32]

The expedition left Lamu for the interior on September 18, 1892. It consisted of three white men, Chanler, von Höhnel, and Galvin, and sixty others, including the Zanzibari porters, seven Somali camel drivers, and twelve Sudanese guards armed with Mannlicher repeating rifles. The expedition also included fifteen camels, ten oxen, goats, sheep, donkeys, horses, and three dogs.[33] Marching along the Tana River, the group reached Hameye, an abandoned IBEA post, two months later. En route, the expedition had encountered the usual perils of travel in that period—illness, hostile groups, desert wastes, and, as von Höhnel feared, more than the usual number of desertions. Chanler tried to mend the situation by sending the most unreliable porters back to the coast and calling for new ones. Since it would take several weeks for new porters to arrive, he and von Höhnel set off to explore the area to the north, leaving Galvin at Hameye. They left on

December 5, 1892, with eighty men.[34] Chanler became ill with fever, probably malaria, but would not consider stopping. Eventually, they came to the Nyambeni Mountains that today fringe Meru National Park, where they encountered the Embu, an eastern extension of the Kikuyu. It was here that they picked up a guide named Motio, who took them to the Guaso Nyiro River and Lake Lorian, which they soon discovered was not a lake but a swamp into which the river emptied.[35]

Chanler had to be carried in a hammock for the first four days of this trek because he was delirious and semiconscious. It was the rainy season, and malaria transmission was at its peak (although this was unknown at the time since the parasite and the vector had yet to be linked).

On December 26, 1892, they came upon a waterfall on the Guaso Nyiro that rose some sixty feet high; they called it Chanler Falls, a name that is still used today.[36] Marching ever eastward through the dry scrub, they reached the Merti Plateau by December 30. On January 12, 1893, they realized that Lake Lorian was really a swamp, swarming with mosquitoes. The members of the caravan were both dejected and angry, for instead of a fresh-water lake where they could rest and recuperate, there was nothing but "an abode of pestilence and death," as Chanler recorded.[37] It took them a month to hobble back to Hameye. Short on rations and sick with malaria, they were attacked by the Wamsara (Meru), and three porters were killed and twelve wounded in the skirmishes that followed. They finally reached Embu country and on February 10, 1893, sighted Hameye, where the Stars and Stripes were proudly waving over the camp. The news that Galvin gave them was not good: The oxen had died, as well as some of the cattle, camels, and donkeys.[38]

While resting at Hameye, Chanler wrote to his sisters Margaret and Alida, telling them what had transpired over the previous months and outlining his future plans:

> I cannot write a long letter because I am not very well. I discovered a most beautiful waterfall which I have called Chanler Falls. So the family will be handed down to history after all. In a day or two and with the whole caravan, I go to Mount Kenya, and then to the unknown north. I hope to be gone eighteen months as there is a great deal of exploring to be done, and should my expedition be the first to do it, I should be famous. Höhnel is a charming fellow, and George is as nice as ever. This letter must go the rounds of the family as I cannot write any more. Love to all.[39]

Tenacious and determined, Chanler set out for the north on March 8, 1893, heading for the Mathews Range, which had never been fully explored. En route to the Nyambeni Mountains, some twenty men deserted. Chanler sent his headman, Hamidi, down to the coast for replacements. This proved to be a serious mistake because the man was not trustworthy, as von Höhnel had suspected all along. Chanler, however, pushed ahead, exploring the southern Mathews Range and Lolokwi Mountain. He then met with the Rendille people, a group of pastoral nomads who had had no previous contact with Europeans. He unwisely communicated these facts in a September 22, 1893, letter to George Mackenzie, the director of the IBEA. His claim of first contact had disquieting political implications. For all the company directors knew, Chanler could have signed a treaty of protection with them on behalf of the United States and handed them some flags, as the British and Germans had been doing all along elsewhere in Africa.

The expedition's fortunes were dealt a serious blow on August 24, 1893, when von Höhnel was seriously gored in the groin and lower abdomen by a charging rhinoceros. Chanler treated the wounds as best he could with permanganate, but he had little in the way of painkillers or other medications. He knew that he had to get von Höhnel back to their base camp at Daitcho, some 280 miles to the southeast, where there was a good store of medicines. On September 1, they started for Daitcho, but their progress was hindered by numerous rhinoceros charges. Von Höhnel later wrote:

> The rhinoceros mating season was apparently at its height, and part of the Guaso Nyiro River that we were following was a favorite trysting place for all the amorous pairs of the entire district, who of course were highly displeased with seeing us disturb their idyll. In the next few days, we had a hundred narrow escapes with these animals, and twenty-five times the caravan was seriously charged and scattered. Many a time the frightened men put my stretcher roughly down on the ground, and the rifle shots of the vanguard led by Chanler, the shots of the guard that surrounded me, the close and distant snorting of the monsters and the constant alarms of the fleeing men created a pandemonium that kept me at a high pitch of excitement the whole time. Under my very eyes, one of our men was thrown high into the air and fell head-first on a hard rock; he was buried twenty-four hours later. To all this must be added my own unbearable pain.[40]

Von Höhnel and Chanler arrived at Daitcho on September 18. Von Höhnel was finally given morphine in regular doses and was able to get some much-needed rest. However, because he had not eaten in almost three weeks, he was in an extremely weakened state.

A passing ivory-trading caravan brought the good news that there was an English physician, Dr. William Charters, at the Kibwezi Mission Station, 380 miles away. As soon as von Höhnel was able to travel again in a stretcher, Chanler sent him to Kibwezi with Galvin and twenty-five men, as well as eighteen unfit porters. The group arrived at Kibwezi fifty-four days later. Charters debrided von Höhnel's wounds under general anesthesia, and after three weeks, von Höhnel left for the coast and home. Meanwhile, Chanler planned his trip to Lake Rudolf and beyond. On October 19, 1893, he wrote to von Höhnel:

> George's letter with the welcome intelligence that you had bought 50 donkeys reached me here a few days ago. You, despite your illness, and the natural desire to hurry on to medical aid, stopped till you had added another good turn to the many I owe you.
>
> Now we are able to go forward with ease and speed you are forced to turn your face to the coast. I cannot tell you the full extent of my feelings at your departure because I do not yet realize all that you were to me, both personally and as one of the leaders of this expedition. From the moment when you lay breathless & bleeding under the tree in the Subugo forest I realized that you could no longer hope to continue your journey; but what your absence would mean to me I had not the energy to conjecture. My whole mind and body were filled & tingling with the desire to get you safely to Daitcho.
>
> We may not see one another in this world so that I can speak my mind freely to you. Your companionship during the past months has been one of the pleasantest incidents in my life. Your influence has been all for the good and I must tell you that I feel to be a better man since I have known you. I fear many & many times I have caused you pain & now I ask your pardon. I have a bad—really bad—temper & on looking back I wonder at the kindliness with which you often met my roughness. If we should be permitted to meet again I hope there will occur some opportunity for me to prove my affection for you.[41]

Chanler wrote von Höhnel several more letters, updating him about his plans for the expedition. He realized that without von Höhnel, the expedition no longer had any real scientific capability. Yet he was tenacious and determined to go on.

On October 7, 1893, Hamidi, the headman, returned to Daitcho from the coast with eighty unfit porters, whom Chanler tried to train for the next two months until Galvin returned. Galvin finally arrived at Daitcho on December 15 with supplies, pack animals, and the news that von Höhnel was making a satisfactory recovery. Chanler wrote von Höhnel a letter the following day: "I am delighted your wound is healed and that there will be no ill after effects—you had a terrible time of it; and deserve good days and many of them to make up for what you have suffered."[42]

On December 17, 1893, the day after Galvin returned with supplies for the trip north, Hamidi and most of the porters suddenly deserted. The next day, the Sudanese guards also left but then returned. This mass desertion effectively caused the collapse of Chanler's expedition. But why had it occurred? Chanler was absolutely dumbfounded at first because it had come as a total surprise to him. Hamidi returned two days later and said that the men felt that their enlistment time had expired and that they had no desire to go farther into unknown country filled with savage people like the Rendille. Chanler was correct when he later said, "I was firmly convinced that he was at the bottom of it."[43] Hamidi confessed that nothing Chanler had done should have caused the mass desertion and that he himself had no complaints to make. Yet on his return to camp, he made every effort to get the Sudanese to desert. "He told them that they should come to him at the river and follow him to the coast as General Mathews of Zanzibar had told him that if he succeeded in inducing the men to desert, he would see that they all received their pay upon reaching the coast."[44]

Chanler went on: "Taking all things into consideration, it looked as if Hamidi had been acting under orders received during his visit to the coast; but what possible reason the authorities at Zanzibar could have for breaking up my expedition could not appear clear to my mind. The ways of diplomacy are devious."[45]

General Mathews, then the custodian of British interests on the mainland, had every reason at this time to see that Chanler was stopped. With seemingly endless personal financial means, Chanler was capable of roaming all over the unexplored British sphere with the American flag in tow, and in so doing, he posed a potential political problem. The easiest way of stopping him was to cause a mass desertion of his men. Speaking of Hamidi's role in this, Chanler cogently made the following observation: "Instead of twenty well-armed men and some donkeys, I had been furnished with a disorderly rabble of eighty unarmed and insubordinate men—that he— [Hamidi] must have received something stronger than a hint that it was the pleasure of the people in power at the coast."[46]

Von Höhnel did not think much of Hamidi, observing that "in Count Teleki's Rudolf Lake Expedition he was a simple porter who after one year had been made an askari."[47] And with von Höhnel, the famous and well-respected explorer, out of the picture, it would have been easier for Mathews to cause the expedition's collapse.

Chanler and Galvin had no choice but to return to Mombasa, which they reached on February 10, 1894. There, Chanler found a letter from Mathews, advising him not to proceed to Zanzibar but rather to leave on the sly at once and have his agents pay off his men.[48] Chanler also found that instead of arresting the deserters, as was the established procedure, the British authorities in Mombasa had sent them on to Zanzibar, lodging them there at his expense. Thus, the deserters had been treated in a unique manner by Mathews, which lends strong credence to Chanler's suspicion that Mathews was behind the plot.

When Chanler met with Mathews, he found that the British official had uncharacteristically concluded that the porters were justified in their desertion, without hearing Chanler's side of the story.[49] When the porters first arrived in Zanzibar, Mathews had taken them to James White Allen, the acting U.S. consul. Together, they listened to the men's statements, which were conflicting. The porters accused Chanler of cruelty, providing poor food, and flogging them, and they claimed that they had been engaged for eighteen months only. As Allen wrote: "One man had been ordered shot by Mr. Chanler for repeated desertions, and this was given as another reason."[50] But even Mathews knew that the porters had not been engaged for only eighteen months. He had also previously heard of the shooting from Hamidi when they met on the coast, where the latter had gone to get more porters. Yet Mathews had made no mention of the shooting to Allen at the time he learned of it, which was several months before the mass desertion.

When Chanler appeared in Zanzibar, Mathews told Allen that he saw no reason to hear the expedition leader's side of the story or the accounts of the men who had remained faithful to him. Regarding this, Allen said: "I asked Gen. Mathews to hear their story. This he said he thought was not necessary, that he had already formed his opinion and quite understood the case. This is but one instance of Gen. Mathews treatment of Mr. Chanler, treatment which has been outrageous in the extreme."[51]

Allen and others in Zanzibar were both shocked and baffled by Mathews's conduct toward Chanler and his lenient treatment of the deserting porters. Up to this time, Mathews had established a well-deserved reputation as a skilled and just administrator. His dramatic departure from established procedures and his blatant prejudice against Chanler raised serious questions early on about his motives and his possible role in the desertion.

A frustrated Allen wrote a lengthy dispatch to the U.S. secretary of state on April 2, 1894, in which he sharply criticized Mathews's conduct:

> Gen. Mathews has placed every difficulty in Mr. Chanler's way, his attitude at all times being decidedly hostile. People familiar with caravan

laws and customs are greatly astonished at the General's actions. The custom is that porters deserting shall be imprisoned, punished, and lose all pay. Yet, in this case, he has refused to take any action against them. Those having to do with caravans are greatly exercised about this.[52]

Although Chanler would claim in his book that the shooting of the porter who repeatedly deserted was an accident, he told Allen that he had ordered him shot:

> Mr. Chanler does not in the slightest attempt to conceal the fact that he found it necessary to order a man shot. The discipline of a caravan has to be like that of an army. The ordinary punishments are flogging and the chain gang, but extreme cases have to be dealt with severely. In the case of this man, he had repeatedly deserted, and the caravan was approaching a dangerous country. He was repeatedly warned but persisted in his attempts to escape, till finally, for the safety of his associates, his caravan and himself, and as a warning to the porters, Mr. Chanler ordered him shot.[53]

At first glance, the shooting of a porter who had repeatedly deserted would appear to be an outrageous act. Yet porters were then held to a standard of armylike discipline. They were armed with rifles and regularly drilled so as to instill in them the organized, defensive combat skills that would be needed if an expedition were attacked. The Sudanese and Somalis who commanded the porters on Chanler's expedition were, in essence, the noncommissioned officers responsible for maintaining discipline. Desertion on just a few occasions was usually dealt with by flogging; porters who repeatedly deserted were often shot. In a March 16, 1894, memorandum to Lord Rosebery, the British prime minister, Mathews laid out the plight of the Zanzibari porters, with whom he clearly sympathized: "For the slightest offense, or alleged offense, they are often flogged, even brutally, the number of lashes ranging in known cases up to as many as 150, and they have on a charge of desertion actually been shot."[54]

Thus, according to Mathews, flogging and execution were routine. This raises questions about why he chose to make issues of them in the case of Chanler's expedition and why he sided with the deserting porters and their leaders. Mathews's persecution of Chanler and his sympathetic treatment of the porters really had little to do with the merits of the allegations. Rather, they reflected a pragmatic approach to local political issues. The British sphere in East Africa was about to collapse, and this was a determining factor in his handling of Chanler and his men.

Sir Gerald Portal became the British agent and consul general in Zanzibar on March 10, 1891. At the same time, the IBEA, which was primarily a trading company, was chartered to administer the British sphere, which included Uganda. By 1892, the IBEA had reached the end of its tether in East Africa and announced its intentions of withdrawing from Uganda by year-end. Undercapitalized and drained by the civil war between the Catholic and Protestant native forces in Buganda (January–March 1892), known as the Fransa-Ingliza War,[55] the company announced its plans to pull out and retreat to Dagoretti, near modern-day Nairobi.[56] Frederick Lugard, the IBEA's man in Uganda who had successfully negotiated a treaty between the French-led Catholics and English-led Protestants, was withdrawn by Sir William Mackinnon, the company's head, and reached London in October 1892.[57]

The British government then in power was indifferent to this event and showed no interest in placing the area under direct protection. In fact, at the time, the British were seriously considering withdrawing from Egypt as well.[58]

Lugard, an archproponent of British imperialism, lost no time in lobbying for the establishment of a British protectorate, delivering speeches, and writing articles and letters in the papers.[59] The specter of Church Missionary Society (CMS) missionaries and their families stranded and unprotected in the interior, coupled with the CMS's own campaign, temporarily swayed public opinion so that immediate abandonment was postponed. In addition, Bishop Alfred Tucker of the CMS, on leave in England, raised £15,000 from the CMS Gleaners Union, and added to the £25,000 raised by Sir William Mackinnon, this enabled the company to limp along until March 1893.[60] The foreign secretary, Lord Rosebery, then succeeded in getting the government to agree to send Gerald Portal on a visit to Uganda to make a report and recommendations. Given Portal's support for imperial expansion, it was almost a foregone conclusion as to what he would recommend.[61] Portal left Zanzibar in January 1893, and Rosebery asked James Rennell Rodd to go to Zanzibar in Portal's absence.[62] Thus, when Chanler arrived in Zanzibar in the summer of 1892 to launch his expedition, the IBEA was on the verge of collapsing, and to the expansionists like Portal and Mathews, the future of the British sphere seemed in peril of foreign takeover. However, Portal clearly did not see Chanler's presence as threatening at the time. If he had, he would not have offered him "every assistance in his power."[63]

Portal pulled down the IBEA flag in Uganda on April 1, 1893, and replaced it with the Union Jack.[64] He declared a provisional British protectorate, which had no legal standing as it had not received the approval of the British Parliament. In both Parliament and the cabinet, many were opposed to establishing a protectorate in Uganda or else-

where on the East African mainland.[65] There was a good possibility
then that the British sphere on the mainland would be abandoned.
And in April 1893, Chanler was moving into the middle of the sphere.
In former times, other lone travelers had succeeded in staking claims
that were subsequently assumed by their governments. To local imperialists like Mathews, bent on retaining the mainland for Britain,
Chanler had now become a serious threat, for if the IBEA pulled out,
the sphere was up for grabs. And there was Chanler right in the middle
of it with his American flag.

In 1893, the year that Chanler was in the interior, things otherwise
went very badly for British interests in East Africa. In February, Todd,
the IBEA's agent in Kismayu, was attacked by Somali, and Rodd had to
rush from Zanzibar to defend the area as best he could. Just then, Cecil Rhodes, the master empire builder, dropped in on Rodd in Zanzibar
and urged the establishment of a protectorate on the mainland.[66] In
Zanzibar itself, matters sharply came to a crisis on March 5, 1893,
when Sultan Seyid Ali died. The succession was contested by Seyid
Khalid, who secured the palace, and Seyid Hamed, whom the British
favored. An armed confrontation between Hamed and the forces of the
challenger Khalid took place at the palace doors, with Mathews
threatening to blow them down with cannons if Khalid did not submit, which he eventually did.[67] While Rodd and Mathews eventually
got the situation in hand and put the more cooperative Hamed on the
throne, Khalid was not without supporters.

Rodd and Mathews did not have much respite because in May 1893,
the IBEA announced its withdrawal from coastal Witu, whose sultan,
Fumo Omari, now defied outside authority.[68] Two months later, Mathews had to take a military expedition against Witu. Fumo Omari and
his bands were routed but not brought under administrative control.
On July 31, Mathews hauled down the IBEA flag at Witu and replaced
it with the sultan's standard. He then placed Witu under Zanzibar,
which itself was a British protectorate.[69] This did not go over well with
the British government, large segments of which were clearly leaning
toward abandoning mainland holdings. Rodd was desperate because
the IBEA was withdrawing its men and not replacing them, and he had
but 150 Zanzibari troops in Uganda and 150 in Witu.

Portal returned to the coast on October 22, 1893, and three days
later, he left for England with Rodd, who was severely ill with malaria.
Mathews was now in charge.[70]

Chanler's headman, Hamidi, had returned to the coast for more
porters after the military confrontation at Witu and the Somali rebellion at Kismayu early in the year. Hamidi would certainly have
known about both events, which would have been threatening to both

him and the porters since Chanler intended to traverse these areas later in his journey.

The fact that both Witu and Kismayu were insecure would not have deterred Chanler. However, it would certainly have frightened some inexperienced porters into cowardly defection. In addition, the IBEA was withdrawing from the areas south of the Tana River while Chanler was moving into the unexplored area to the north. This would have put the porters at even higher risk.

Chanler's men knew of the death of the sultan before von Höhnel left for Kibwezi, the news having been brought up by a trading caravan. Chanler said of their reaction to this:

> I could hear them discussing the probabilities of the successor attempting to free the Sultanate of Zanzibar from British influence. They seemed to think the time had come when the natives of Zanzibar should rise, and, throwing off the European yoke make Arab influence paramount along the coast. Had I been a stranger in Africa, it might have seemed odd to me that these men, for the most part slaves, should feel that their interests were in far greater degree with their masters than on the side of the British, who were ostensibly their friends and anxious to free them from servitude.[71]

Among the porters Hamidi brought from the coast were a group of twenty who, Chanler reported, "had followed the fortunes of Busheri, an Arab patriot, who had endeavored to prevent the Germans from taking that portion of East Africa which they had claimed. Many of them boasted of the numbers of Europeans they had slain. These men, by their boastings, quickly became heroes in my camp."[72]

Hamidi's group also brought distorted tales of Mathews's military campaign against Witu. According to Chanler, "They gave highly colored accounts of victories achieved over the Europeans by the Arabs and outlaws in the neighborhood of Lamoo. They said the time had at last come when the Arabs were about to re-establish themselves in Zanzibar on a firm footing and that messengers had come from Mecca advocating the 'Jihad' (holy war) against the infidel."[73]

Chanler, true to form, called his men together and said that "not for a moment were lies of this sort to be tolerated in my camp; that any one of my men who would take the trouble to think for a moment should know the stories were absolutely untrue; and that I, being a European, would not permit such rumours to circulate while I was there to stop them."[74]

Chanler later learned what had really happened on the coast. However, his disparaging of the news brought by Hamidi and the men from the coast did not and could not prevent his porters from believing it.

Thus, as some of the porters saw it, British rule was collapsing and the Arabs were about to rise again as an independent power on the coast. This was certainly no time to be away in the interior and on the way to a distant lake, particularly if one were a battle-scarred nationalist.

The porters had another reason to desert as well. Most of them had already gone up north to the Rendille country near the Mathews Range on Chanler's first visit there. They knew the road was rough and difficult and that the Rendille were unfriendly and dangerous. They had little stomach for such a difficult undertaking, especially after spending almost nine comfortable months in camp at Daitcho. Galvin's return marked the point in time when an easy camp life would end and the march north would begin. If defection were to occur, it had to take place then, before the men were far from the well-trodden and relatively safe trade routes from the coast.

At the time of the porter defection in December 1893, the British sphere was essentially being abandoned. A protectorate over Uganda would not be confirmed in Parliament until the following August.[75] Thus, the sphere had entered a period of great vulnerability to foreign seizure, as local imperialists saw it. What had been earlier viewed as an innocuous scientific expedition headed by Chanler was now seen as a major threat in the waning days of 1893. Consequently, Mathews had strong motives in promoting the collapse of the expedition, as Chanler himself implied.[76] These motives would have been strengthened by the fact that Chanler indiscreetly gave an American flag to a local chief on the Tana River early in the expedition. Von Höhnel reprimanded Chanler for this in a letter written in 1923, saying: "The dark spot is another one, the flag giving on the Tana River, which a few days later you yourself condemned."[77] Giving a flag to a local chief was a powerful symbolic act of staking a territorial claim for a colonial power. News of this must certainly have reached Mathews through Hamidi, who met with him on the coast in 1893 when he went to secure additional porters for Chanler. Since trading caravans were regularly moving through this area at the time, news of an American flag on the Tana River might even have reached Mathews earlier. In either case, this information would have alarmed him and induced him to cut short Chanler's presence in the interior.

Frightened by the dangers of travel farther into the interior and excited by the turbulent political events on the coast, the porters would have been receptive to Hamidi's inducement to desert. He also promised them immunity from the usual adverse consequences of desertion: "General Mathews of Zanzibar had told him that if he succeeded in inducing the men to desert, he would see that they all received their pay upon reaching the coast."[78]

Hamidi's assurances to the deserting porters that Mathews would see that they were paid and not punished were supported by the general's later actions. Contrary to existing convention, he demanded that the porters be paid, gave immediate credence to their allegations, and tried to force Chanler to make a quick exit. In so doing, he tried to camouflage any role he himself had played in causing the expedition's collapse. However, Mathews overplayed his hand in his effort to victimize and then vilify Chanler. He lost no time in having the acting British agent write to Lord Rosebery, the foreign secretary who later, in 1894, became prime minister.

On January 29, 1894, M. Cracknall, the acting British agent and consul general in Zanzibar, who for many years had been the judge of the British Consular Court, wrote a four-page dispatch to Lord Rosebery about the porter desertion. In this dispatch, he laid out the porters' allegations of ill treatment but added his own caveat that "this story may be a mere tissue of falsehoods." Cracknall also claimed that the incidents occurred in an area "within the British sphere of influence."[79]

Rosebery had been an intimate friend of Chanler's grandfather, Sam Ward, and knew that the United States had no territorial interests in East Africa. He also knew of the Chanler family and was familiar with William Chanler's expedition. Thus, a matter of this nature was of interest to him not only because of his official position but also because of the person against whom the allegations were being made.[80]

On March 15, 1894, Cracknall again wrote to Lord Rosebery, who had just become prime minister. He outlined the complexities of the desertion, which he now characterized as having taken place outside the British sphere. He said that he did not believe he had jurisdiction over the case on these grounds, even though Mathews had been advocating that he bring Chanler to justice. However, he agreed with Mathews that Chanler should not be tried by the U.S. Consular Court, claiming that Allen would be a biased judge.[81] What is transparent in this letter is that Cracknall was having second thoughts about getting deeply involved in Chanler's case and was trying to distance himself from it.

While waiting for a reply from Lord Rosebery, Mathews and Cracknall agreed to have Chanler submit the matter to arbitration. Chanler proposed to appoint one arbitrator himself, have the government of Zanzibar appoint another, and have that individual and Mathews choose a third. Chanler chose Seth A. Pratt, the former U.S. consul at Zanzibar, and the government of Zanzibar selected a Mr. Wilson, then its legal adviser. Pratt proposed eight candidates, German, Italian, and French, all of whom were fluent in Swahili (a necessity since much native testimony had to be heard in that language). Wilson rejected all of these and instead proposed three men, one of whom had just been decorated by the government of Zanzibar for services rendered, and two others whom Pratt knew were hostile to Chanler's interests. Pratt quickly realized that Mathews was intent on stacking the court against Chanler, and he finally gave up, finding Wilson unreasonable and discourteous.[82]

A stalemate now ensued, with Chanler refusing to pay the £1,000 in porter wages demanded by Mathews. Hostile, unreasonable, and unyielding, Mathews refused to negotiate and even threatened Chanler with public exposure through negative publicity. Then suddenly and unexpectedly, he blinked. He agreed to accept half the amount he had originally demanded.[83] This abrupt turnaround was actually in response to an April 16, 1894, dispatch sent by the Foreign Office to Cracknall. Approved by Lord Rosebery, it was devastating to Mathews's position because it told him and Cracknall that they had no jurisdiction over the case: "Where the person implicated is an American citizen, you have no power to interfere judicially. As regards natives of Zanzibar, stringent regulations against their employment already exist, but these regulations do not apply to the Protectorate north of the Tana."[84]

In effect, the Foreign Office told Cracknall and Mathews not only to remove themselves from the case but also that the existing regulations governing porter treatment did not apply to the area where the alleged shooting and floggings had taken place. This decision from London effectively neutralized Mathews's crusade against Chanler and forced him to negotiate.

In order to enable Mathews to save face in a conflict now charged with much personal acrimony, the Foreign Office suggested that he lay the matter before the sultan of Zanzibar, who they knew would opt to settle the case according to local Arab law.[85] The sultan proved very amenable to settling the claims of the porters in return for a partial payment of wages and a blood-money payment of £1,000 to the owner of the porter who was shot.

With the payment issue settled, there now remained the problem of Mathews's original public support for the porters' allegations and his condemnation of Chanler. For the sake of his own career and position, he had to mend fences with Chanler. In a gesture of forced reconciliation, he pronounced a revisionist account of what caused the collapse of the expedition:

I thoroughly believe that the whole trouble was caused by Somali intrigue. The headmen of the porters weakly giving in to other porters who were afraid to proceed inland not knowing where they were going and frightened by Somali tales. I believe the Somalis intrigued to gain their

own ends viz: the return of the expedition to the coast. I propose that Somali headmen should be imprisoned for not remaining with Mr. Chanler,
and that porters be paid only half of pay due. Headmen no pay.[86]

This significant retreat on Mathews's part effectively brought the
matter to a satisfactory closure. Chanler agreed to pay the blood
money and a portion of the wages claimed by the porters. For his part,
Mathews was able to save face and placate Lord Rosebery by blaming
foreign scapegoats, namely, the Somalis. However, Rosebery was still
left with the potentially thorny political problems associated with
Mathews's unwelcome assertions that there was widespread porter
abuse in most European-led expeditions. He expressed this concern in
a file memo: "Were the state of facts disclosed in Sir L. Mathews' principal minute to be disclosed the anti-slavery feeling in this country
would be very justly exasperated."[87]

On April 10, commenting on Mathews's March 16 memorandum,
he wrote to Cracknall, saying: "Sir L. Mathews, I think, generalizes
rather overmuch being moved by the alleged cruelty shown by Mr.
Chanler. The new transport arrangements when in working order will
remedy much of this."[88] This was a further rebuke to Mathews and a
dismissal of some of his exaggerated claims about the general plight of
safari porters.

In saying that "the treatment of my affairs was made subservient to
purely local and, I may say, private ends," Chanler came close to the
truth of the matter.[89] The late William Chamberlain Chanler, the explorer's nephew, succinctly summarized matters in this regard when
he noted that "the British didn't like the idea of an American marching around their unexplored territory carrying the American flag, and
decided to put a stop to it."[90] Yet, it was really Mathews's policy, not
London-directed policy, that was at work here, as evidenced by both
British and American official documents of the time.

The collapse of Chanler's expedition raises two broad and related issues regarding Mathews's possible instigation of the porter defection
through Hamidi, the headman. There is no documentary evidence to
support this scenario, other than Chanler's own claim.[91] He was being
discreet when he asserted that he was at a loss to explain why Mathews would want his expedition to collapse. He had, of course, handed
out an American flag on the Tana River, which he never mentioned in
his account of the expedition. This highly provocative act would have
been reason enough for Mathews to sabotage the expedition. If Chanler had handed out one flag, he was capable of handing out others as
well, thus placing the British sphere at risk of foreign seizure at a time
of great vulnerability.

The second issue has to do with Mathews's treatment of the porters after they had deserted. The established conventions for desertion were imprisonment and forfeiture of wages.[92] These punishments were equally applied to porters deserting from either European or Arab/Swahili-led caravans. Mathews's failure to apply these sanctions represented a very pragmatic, albeit unjust and inconsistent, approach to dealing with a potentially volatile political problem. Instead of imprisoning the porters as was customary, Mathews gave them their freedom, housed and fed them at Chanler's expense, and demanded they be paid their full wages. He justified these highly unusual actions by claiming that Chanler had been the cause of the mass desertion through excessively cruel treatment of his men. Mathews could hardly have done otherwise if he himself had induced them to desert. Even if he had not caused the desertion, he would have run serious political risks imprisoning so many men.

In the end, Mathews was forced to abandon his campaign against Chanler after being rebuked by Lord Rosebery. He withdrew his acceptance of the porters' allegations of unusual cruelty, blamed the desertion on the Somalis who came from outside the protectorate, and dropped his demands for full wages. Taken together, these actions represented a significant retreat for a man who was then the most powerful and influential British colonial agent in East Africa. However, his only other choice was to confront the prime minister, a course of action that would have led to his dismissal or forced resignation. Such an option was untenable for him, not only for reasons of self-preservation but also because the Foreign Office's position was so well reasoned and based on existing laws and regulations. It must have embarrassed Mathews to be reminded that Britain had no jurisdiction over Chanler and that the alleged cruelties had occurred outside the region to which existing regulations could be applied. Having invoked these legal issues, the Foreign Office did not bother to raise the obvious question as to why Mathews was treating Chanler's deserting porters contrary to the very conventions he had helped establish. They clearly knew the answer. Cracknall's realization of these facts early on in the crisis effectively left Mathews isolated in his prosecution of Chanler.

It is obvious that Mathews initially acted in a very high-handed, unjust, and prosecutorial manner toward Chanler. However, he had unwisely chosen a tenacious, combative, and well-connected target, who quickly forced him into retreat. It was certainly no comfort to Mathews that Rosebery expressed the view that the matter of porter treatment in general would be addressed by Arthur Hardinge, who had just been appointed agent and consul general. Hardinge's arrival in Zan-

zibar in May 1894, after Chanler had left, placed Mathews in a chastened, secondary role.

Chanler finally left Zanzibar for home after spending two months
resolving his difficulties. His antagonist, Mathews, continued to serve
in Zanzibar until his death at the age of fifty-one from cerebral
malaria, on October 11, 1901.[93] Rodd thought highly of Mathews, saying that he led "a straight and beneficent life," and he characterized
him as "the most generous of men."[94] Yet Mathews was emblematic of
the colonial proconsuls of his time, and this above all explains his
dealings with Chanler.

Chanler had much to be proud of. He had explored 2,500 square
miles of unknown territory. He and von Höhnel had fixed the exact
geographical position of Mount Kenya's peak, discovered the Nyambeni Mountains, charted the course of the Guaso Nyiro, discovered
the Chanler Falls, and found the Lorian Swamp. Chanler had made the
first European contact with the Rendille and discovered a new species
of antelope—Chanler's reed buck, *Cervicapra chanlerii*.[95] He had collected thousands of specimens of reptiles, beetles, butterflies, plants,
and other flora and fauna, which he donated to the Smithsonian Institution. A number of these were new to science, including two species
of reptiles, *Mabuya chanleri* and *Simocephalus chanleri*, and two
species of butterflies, *Iphthima chanleri* and *Charaxes chanleri*.[96]

Although Chanler's geographic explorations fell short of his original
expectations, it seems he had kept his options open in this regard. In a
letter written from Daitcho on November 16, 1893, to von Höhnel, he
said: "If I get through Borana, I shall make for Ime and Berbera."[97] Even
the day before his men deserted, he wrote to von Höhnel again, saying
that he would wait a year for von Höhnel to return if necessary. He
then said that if he could not get through the Boran country, he would
return to Zanzibar.[98]

Chanler never returned to East Africa. He was elected to the New
York State Assembly as a Democrat in 1896, campaigned in Cuba during the Spanish-American War, and served in Congress for a term
(1899–1901). After 1912, he lived in Paris, breeding racehorses and
running a private intelligence operation. He married Beatrice Ashley,
an accomplished actress and author, and they had two sons, William
Astor Jr. and Sidney Ashley.[99] Chanler wrote two short novels in addition to his book on African exploration—*A Man's Game* (1921), under
the pseudonym John Brent, and *The Sacrifice* (1925), under the pseudonym Robert Hart.[100] For many years, he maintained an apartment in
Paris at 19 Rue de la Tremoille, from where he ran his intelligence operation. He suffered a leg amputation following an accident in 1914
and died at the age of sixty-six on March 4, 1934, in Mentone, France.
His remains were returned to the United States and buried in the

Chanler family vault in Trinity Cemetery in upper Manhattan. Some of his African artifacts and trophies still adorn the Chanler estate house at Rokeby, in Dutchess County, New York.

In August and December 1996, Galvin's son, George E. Galvin Jr., sent to Rokeby a collection of trophies, ethnographic objects, von Höhnel field maps, photographs, camping equipment, and a Mannlicher rifle that had been associated with Chanler's expedition. Included in this collection was the expedition's thirty-eight-star American flag.[101]

Ludwig von Höhnel maintained a lifelong friendship with Chanler. He was at sea between 1894 and 1899, being promoted to captain of corvette in the latter year. Between 1899 and 1903, he served as an aide-de-camp to Emperor Francis Joseph of Austria, and in 1903, he was promoted to frigate captain. Two years later, he was sent by Austria on a diplomatic mission to Emperor Menelik of Ethiopia, and in 1912, he was promoted to rear admiral.

Von Höhnel's last assignment was as commander of the naval arsenal at Pola. There, he encountered frequent difficulties with Vice Admiral Julius von Ripper, who constantly meddled in his activities. In his memoirs, von Höhnel claims that it was because of this meddling and the excessive demands of his post that he retired from the navy on August 1, 1909. However, as Erwin F. Sieche related, there was another reason for his resignation.

In 1909, von Höhnel became engaged to Valeska van Oestéren (1870–1947), who came from a prominent German family in Hamburg. As an Austro-Hungarian officer, he had to obtain official permission to marry. Archduke Franz Ferdinand and his aides objected to the match because her brother, Friedrich Werner van Oestéren, had published a novel in 1906 entitled *Christus nicht Jesus*, which was viewed as being highly anti-Jesuit and supportive of freemasonry. Ferdinand disliked the Freemasons because those based in France had singled him out for especially caustic criticism. Von Höhnel was bluntly told that he could not marry Valeska and remain in the navy. Exasperated with his then current superior and angered by this decision, he eventually chose to retire with the rank of commander at the age of fifty-two. When he and Valeska were married on July 17, 1909, Chanler served as one of the witnesses. Three years later, von Höhnel was given the retirement naval rank of rear admiral.[102]

Following World War I, von Höhnel and his wife, who were childless, fell on hard financial times. At Chanler's urging, he wrote his memoirs, which were published in Germany in 1926.[103] He also wrote an English-language memoir, completed in August 1924. He sent this to Chanler, who in turn gave it to his niece's husband, Edward Motley Pickman, a gentleman-scholar in Boston with connections to publishers. However, Pickman's efforts to place it with a publisher were unsuccessful because of the Great Depression. In 1965, Pickman's widow, Hester, found the manuscript in her husband's library and sent it to Chanler's great-nephew, John Winthrop Aldrich, for inclusion in the family archives at Rokeby.[104] In the late 1920s, von Höhnel completed a book in German about his travels with Chanler in Africa. He was unsuccessful in finding a publisher for it because it lacked a sufficient number of photographs, which by then had become vital to the success of travel books.[105] However, von Höhnel did publish the survey results of the expedition, which were supplemented with astronomical analyses by Dr. J. Palisa. This article contained a map drawn on a scale of 1:750,000, showing the features of the area as well as profiles of mountain ranges.[106]

Beginning in 1931, Chanler arranged to have a remittance of 1,000 French francs (then worth US$40.00) sent to von Höhnel each month from his bank, Bankers Trust Company, in Paris. Chanler stipulated that his name not appear on any of the correspondence and that the exchange costs be charged to his account.[107] Two years previously, he had sent von Höhnel $400 to pay his rent and to get his wife's jewels out of pawn.[108] Without Chanler's monthly remittance, the von Höhnels would have been close to destitution, judging from the Chanler–von Höhnel correspondence in the Rokeby Papers. Chanler also arranged for the stipend to continue after his death, which it did.

Von Höhnel was deeply grieved by Chanler's death, writing about it to Chanler's sister, Margaret Aldrich: "It is with a heavy and sorrowful heart that I console you, he was the truest and staunchest friend, he altogether was a hero, my hero, whom I always admired and dearly loved."[109] Von Höhnel died in Vienna on March 23, 1942, his ashes being buried in an urn in Vienna's Central Cemetery. The Chanler family did not learn of his death until 1946. Valeska von Höhnel died in 1947, leaving his remaining papers and memorabilia to his nephew, Dr. Heinrich Zündel. Zündel's widow, Rosa, gave a small collection of von Höhnel's ethnographic materials to the Ostafrika Museum, which was then located in the schloss (castle) at Bad Deutsch-Altenberg. She also donated a bust of von Höhnel to the museum.[110]

Mathews and other British colonial authorities in Zanzibar may have taken some comfort in the fact that a perceived threat to their interests in East Africa had been removed. Yet, unknown to them, another determined American explorer was about to descend on them from the north. As Chanler was arriving in Trieste in May 1894 from Zanzibar, Arthur Donaldson Smith, a physician from Philadelphia, was preparing to leave London for Somaliland and Lake Rudolf. The authorities in Zanzibar would know about him before long.

6

An American Arrives
from the North

Arthur Donaldson Smith, at the time of his first trip to Lake Rudolf (from Through Unknown African Countries, *1897).*

F ollowing William Astor Chanler's departure from the East African coast in the spring of 1894, the British had no respite from American attempts to reach Lake Rudolf. On July 29, 1894, Arthur Donaldson Smith, M.D., of Philadelphia, set out for the lake from Berbera on the Somali coast, leading a caravan of eighty-two Somalis. He traversed 2,000 miles of unexplored wilderness during the next year and finally, on July 10, 1895, saw the blue-green waters of the lake off in the distant haze. He later wrote about his feelings on seeing Lake Rudolf for the first time: "As I looked upon the bright sheet of water, it seemed to me like a roll of parchment awaiting me—a roll such as I have received on completion of a course of study."[1]

Smith had good reason to feel satisfied about his accomplishment. He was the first white man to reach the lake from the north and the first to see it since it had been visited seven years before by Count Samuel Teleki and Lieutenant Ludwig von Höhnel. Why a man of independent wealth such as Smith chose to risk his life and subject himself to enormous hardships is partially explained by an entry he made in his diary the day he first saw the lake: "One thinks of the great world far away—how circumscribed it seems. Nature appears so immense out here that the greatness of civilized mankind dwindles by degrees in one's estimation the longer the separation from the artificial continues."[2]

Smith's yearnings for sport and adventure were leavened by his training as a physician and his skills as a naturalist. Thus, his self-financed trip was one of the best-organized scientific expeditions into this part of Africa, and it yielded major contributions to the fields of geography, ethnology, geology, paleontology, and natural history. Smith not only filled in the blank spaces of East Africa with the names of lakes, rivers, mountains, and villages but also brought out of this area a wealth of scientific materials that he eventually gave to the British Museum, the University of Pennsylvania Museum, and the Academy of Natural Sciences of Philadelphia.

Arthur Donaldson Smith was born on April 27, 1866, in Andalusia, Pennsylvania, a small community on the Delaware River in Bucks County, close to the city of Philadelphia. The youngest of three children, he was born into a patrician Philadelphia family of considerable wealth. His father, Jesse Evans Smith, and his mother, Martha James Knight, were prominent members of Philadelphia society.[3] Smith's paternal great-grandfather, Joest (Yost) Smith Jr., was a member of the Revolutionary Army who had served in the Richland Company of Bucks County. Joest Smith Sr. "died of the fever taken from soldiers living in his house for whom he was caring" during the encampment of the army at Valley Forge.[4]

Smith's family name was originally Schmidt, his ancestors having come to the United States from Germany. However, at the time of the Revolutionary War, the family Anglicized the name to avoid any hint of association with the Hessian mercenaries who were then fighting with the British. As an adult, Smith dropped Arthur from his name and referred to himself as either A. Donaldson Smith or Donaldson Smith.

Smith grew up in his family's Philadelphia home and at "Wyndlawn," a summer retreat not far from Andalusia. He and his sister developed a keen interest in natural history early in life. He also learned to hunt, fish, and ride, sports for which he maintained a liking all his life. However, his interests in the outdoors went beyond those of a mere sportsman because he studiously acquired an impressive knowledge of plants and animal life that served him well during his trips to Africa and elsewhere.

In 1881, Smith entered the University of Pennsylvania at the very young age of fifteen. On graduating four years later, he applied to the graduate chemistry program at Johns Hopkins University, advancing his age by one year. Although he wrote on his application that he desired "to take a year's course in chemistry with a view either to continue that study . . . or to make medicine my profession," he may also have known that he was too young to be considered by most medical schools. This is borne out by the fact that when he applied to Harvard Medical School in 1886, he advanced his age by two years on the application form. He entered Harvard in the fall of that year and remained there until 1888, when he transferred to the medical school of the University of Pennsylvania. There, he completed a third and final year of study before receiving his M.D. degree on May 1, 1889, along with 123 classmates. Soon after graduation, Smith went to the University of Heidelberg for several months of postgraduate study. He returned to his parents' home at 226 South 21st Street in Philadelphia in early 1890, where his mother died on March 15 of that year.[5]

Smith was twenty-four when he returned from Germany. He was a handsome young man of modest height (about 5'7") with blue eyes, brown hair, a distinctive mustache that he would later regularly wax, and strikingly white teeth that impressed people even in his later years. Although assertive and patrician in his manner, he was never pompous or patronizing. Rather, even as a young man, he was admired for being thoughtful and sensitive about other people's feelings, virtues that helped make him highly successful with patients and in diplomatic negotiations overseas.[6]

For the next two years, Smith practiced medicine in Philadelphia, where he was associated with a number of hospitals. He especially enjoyed performing surgery and was extremely accomplished at it. This skill proved of great value in 1895 when he had to amputate the arm of one of his most trusted Somali gunbearers, Yusef, who had been attacked by a crocodile. Smith was then on the banks of the Guaso Nyiro River in what is now Kenya. This area is still remote, and an upper extremity amputation of the kind Smith undertook would be a terrifying prospect for qualified surgeons even today if they had to do it under the same circumstances. Yet Smith was very modest about this lifesaving operation when he later recounted it in his book: "The poor fellow's arm was nearly torn from him. I was obliged to amputate the arm close to the shoulder. While I was engaged in operating on Yusef's arm, a herd of elephants passed near the camp, but I did not go after them."[7]

On November 24, 1892, Smith's father died of a stroke at the age of sixty-eight. His estate of $208,000 was left to his three children in equal shares. Arthur Donaldson Smith's inheritance of close to $69,000 was a sizable fortune (a century later it would be the equivalent of $2,600,000).[8] It was this inheritance that enabled him to temporarily give up the practice of medicine and devote himself on a full-time basis to some of the pursuits of a vanishing gentry. In his case, these included hunting, fishing, traveling, and enjoying the rugged outdoors. This was the free-spirited life he preferred, compared to the rigid one he had known growing up in a formal, patrician environment. However, he had a highly inquisitive and disciplined mind, which, augmented by his medical and scientific training, was destined to set him apart as a scientific explorer of note.

In early 1893, Smith went on a hunting and fishing trip to Norway with a friend from Massachusetts named William Lord Smith, M.D. (no relation). While they were in Norway, this friend told him that he was planning a sporting trip to Somaliland. This type of trip appealed to Smith: "An exploring expedition offered me an opportunity for gratifying all my desires and ambitions. So, I joined him with the idea that this preliminary journey would give me the requisite knowledge of the natives and beasts of burden that I intended taking with me when I made my exploring expedition."[9]

Hunting trips for wealthy Europeans and Americans were extremely common in northern Somaliland in the 1890s because the area was teeming with big game. Later, as the wildlife was decimated through overhunting, hunters moved on to what is now Kenya, which, in the early part of the twentieth century, replaced Somaliland as the principal magnet in Africa for big-game hunters.[10] Visiting sportsmen placed a heavy burden on local British officials in Somaliland, among them Percy Cox (1864–1937), who was appointed assistant political resident at Zeila, a major port, in 1893. Complaining about the never-ending stream of sportsmen, the resident of Berbera, Lieutenant Colonel William Butler Ferris (Cox's immediate superior), said the following in his 1895–1896 annual report: "The number of sportsmen visiting Somaliland does not abate. They add much to the work and personal expenses of the Assistant Resident [Cox], and the want of a traveler's bungalow is more than ever felt. Some so-called sportsmen have amused themselves by killing everything they came across, large and small, male and female."[11] Cox thought very highly of Smith, with whom he later formed a lifelong friendship.

The British Somaliland Protectorate may have been a sportsman's paradise. However, it was also located on the politically turbulent Horn of Africa, where Britain, France, and Italy were engaged in fierce competition for the arid and semiarid lands surrounding Ethiopia. These three European colonial powers found themselves competing not only with one another but also with Ethiopia, which under Emperor Menelik II, had become a powerful and independent state with a determined policy of imperial annexation of adjacent territories. Thus, in effect, there were four colonial powers vying for supremacy on the Horn of Africa, one of which was indigenous in character.

Britain was initially drawn to Somaliland not by a desire to acquire colonial territory but by a need to protect a vital maritime link with the Suez Canal. Three ports on the Somali coast—Berbera, Zeila, and Bulhar—were crucial to Britain's interests, and until 1884, they were occupied by Egypt, which was a friendly power. That year, however, Egypt withdrew its troops from the three ports in order to deploy them against the Mahdi in the Sudan. Britain quickly recognized that a hostile European power in possession of this coast could control the Bab el Mandab, the strait between the Gulf of Aden and the Red Sea, and could thus wreak havoc on the Suez Canal traffic so vital to Britain's Indian empire. At first, Britain tried to induce Turkey, Egypt's suzerain power, to take over the ports. When Turkey declined to do so, Britain was forced to occupy them in 1885. This inevitably led to the conclusion of treaties with local tribal groups and expansion into the interior. On July 20, 1887, Britain proclaimed the establishment of the Somaliland Protectorate and thereby made a firm commitment to a permanent colonial presence on the Horn of Africa.[12]

As in the British East Africa Protectorate to the south, coast-based officials in Somaliland constantly worried about indigenous challenges to their authority and the covert activities of their colonial rivals. They were even suspicious of the possible political motives of visitors such as Smith. Thus, when he arrived in Somaliland in 1893 with high hopes of launching a subsequent expedition to Lake Rudolf, he knew from the outset that he could not succeed unless he enjoyed the full confidence of the local British authorities.

Even with this support, a journey far into the interior was still a very dangerous undertaking. Somali clans, like the Maasai to the south, were capable of quickly mustering well-organized and powerful armies. This was dramatically demonstrated in 1895, when Smith was well on his way to Lake Rudolf. The Rer Hared clan of Somalis rebelled against the British, closed all the trade routes linking the coast with the interior, and attacked clans loyal to the colonial administration. Smith's friend Percy Cox, who was now a captain, was put in charge of a military expedition against the clan by his superior, Lieutenant Colonel Ferris. At the head of 52 trained Indian and Somali camelry troops and 1,500 irregulars, Cox defeated the Rer Hared in six weeks, detached their allies from them, and forced them to surrender. This quick victory not only established Cox's reputation for ability and decisiveness, it also gave the protectorate an uneasy peace for several years. Had Smith not been so far inland at the time of the rebellion, his expedition could easily have fallen victim to the Rer Hared.[13]

On their hunting trip, the two Smiths traveled as far south as Milmil, about 125 miles from Berbera. Well within the British Somaliland Protectorate the area was frequently visited by European sportsmen. Smith noted that "we had splendid sport, killing six lions, besides many elephants, rhinoceroses, and other big game. But what I valued most was that I was enabled to form my plans for my future expedition through the Galla countries to great advantage."[14]

He went on to say that he perceived that a trip from Berbera to Lake Rudolf would be a difficult and dangerous undertaking: "The preliminary details would require the most careful study, and no expense should be spared in preparing for every possible contingency." He received a great deal of encouragement from Captain H.G.S. Swayne, who had made many trips through Somaliland and had written much about its fauna. On his last trip, Swayne had gotten as far as the Webi Shebeli River (River of Leopards), some 125 miles beyond Milmil. But he was unable to go farther because of the threats of the Galla and the small size of his armed escort (only forty men). Swayne attributed Galla hostility to the clashes they had recently had with Captain Vittorio Bottego and Prince Eugenio Ruspoli, two Italian explorers who had probed what are now the borderlands between Ethiopia and Kenya. Bottego and Ruspoli had gone through some of the same country that Smith proposed to explore, but they had not reached Lake Rudolf. Ruspoli had gone up the Juba River and its tributaries to four degrees north latitude and then turned to the northwest; he was within 150 miles of Lake Rudolf when he was killed by an elephant on December 4, 1893, at Burgi. Bottego had gone as far north as seven degrees north latitude during his expedition of 1893. As Smith well knew, it was just a matter of time before the Italian made another attempt to reach Lake Rudolf.[15]

When the two Smiths returned to the coast from their hunt on February 1, 1894, Arthur Donaldson Smith was determined to start for Lake Rudolf the following July. He left orders with a local merchant, Mohammed Hindi, to buy the best camels he could find. He also engaged many of the Somalis who had been with him on the hunting trip, a wise move since he had already observed them under adverse field conditions. His hunting trip had rightly taught him that a well-equipped expedition could pass through the Galla country, provided it was appropriately armed, and "especially if patience were exercised, and everything done to conciliate the natives." Smith realized the need to protect against what he called "little acts of treachery" by taking an armed escort of seventy men. He made preliminary arrangements with Malcome Jones, the British resident at Bulhar, and with Charles McConkey, the agent of Brown, Shipley and Company at Aden, outfitters and freight forwarders.[16]

Smith did not want his expedition to Lake Rudolf to be just one more hunting trip. Rather, he was intent on making significant contributions to the scientific exploration of Africa in terms of geography and natural history. This, he realized, required the acquisition of skills in measuring latitude and longitude and in collecting and preserving natural history specimens. Like Teleki and Chanler, he could have opted to take an experienced surveyor with him. However, his previous scientific training convinced him that he could acquire these skills himself with little difficulty. He therefore approached the Royal Geographical Society, whose map curator, John Coles, taught him the various methods for precisely determining latitude and longitude. He then asked for the help of the British Museum in learning the best methods for collecting and preserving natural history specimens. In addition, he hired a young British taxidermist, Edward Dodson, to help gather specimens in the field.

Although the Royal Geographical Society did not provide Smith with any financial support, it did lend him several instruments, including a six-inch theodolite, an artificial horizon, boiling point thermometers, aneroids, and prismatic compasses. In addition, the society placed the expedition under its auspices so as to facilitate the cooperation of local British officials in Somaliland. That the society extended so much assistance to Smith is a strong indication that the British government at this time had no objections to someone like him traveling to Lake Rudolf. This lends additional support to the inescapable conclusion that the collapse of Chanler's Lake Rudolf expedition a year earlier was uniquely the work of General Lloyd William Mathews in Zanzibar.

One of Smith's Philadelphia friends, Fred Gillett, asked to join the expedition, primarily to shoot big game. Smith agreed to this because he was anxious to have the company of someone he knew. Gillett did not pay any of the expedition's expenses, but he did hire twelve men of his own and purchase twenty pack camels.

Smith, Gillett, and Dodson set sail for Africa from London on June 1, 1894. Before leaving, they were told by many that it would be impossible to enter the Galla country, let alone reach Lake Rudolf, with less than 200 or 300 well-drilled followers. Smith later noted in his diary that "the expression of such opinion served only to increase the zeal I felt in the enterprise." He had no intention of taking so large a force into the interior. Rather, he planned to rely on the same sort of tact and patience that had enabled Thomson to successfully cross Maasai land.[17]

Smith first stopped in Aden, where Lieutenant Colonel Sealy, political agent for the Somali coast at Aden, and other British officials had overseen preliminary preparations for the expedition. Smith engaged fifty-five Somali in Aden, who signed contracts that had been carefully drawn up by Sealy. Smith and Sealy were extremely cautious in their choice of men, selecting only those with extensive experience and no history of prior desertion. On Sealy's recommendation, Smith hired Qualla (Dualla) Idris as his headman. Idris was a well-known figure in African exploration. He had accompanied Henry Morton Stanley and had later traveled with Samuel Teleki and Ludwig von Höhnel. Although the latter spoke in glowing terms of Idris, Smith was to have serious problems with him. He threatened to desert when they were detained by the Ethiopians, demonstrating that even seasoned and reliable men behaved unpredictably when placed in adverse circumstances.

On June 29, 1894, Smith, Gillett, and Dodson sailed for Berbera with their 55 Somali men. Berbera was their final launching point, and they spent ten days there getting together 27 more men; 150 days' supply of rice, dates, and ghee (rancid butter); an enormous stock of trading goods; a total of 84 camels, and 100 boxes with copper vessels containing spirits for preserving reptiles, fishes, and batrachia. In addition, they took boxes for collecting birds and insects, a collapsible Berthon boat, cartridges, and numerous other supplies.[18]

Captain Percy Cox, the acting resident at Berbera, did all he could to help send the expedition off in the best possible condition. Finally, on July 10, 1894, Smith marched out in the late afternoon and headed southwest for Hargeisa, 95 miles away. The country there is hot and dry, marked by a broad plain that eventually rises up into a high plateau. At the time of Smith's trip, this area of Somalia and that to the southwest (called the Haud and the Ogaden) were renowned for their splendid lion populations and great herds of wildlife. After spending four days at Hargeisa, Smith moved across the Haud, marching nine hours a day and covering about 24 miles per day.

Two days before leaving Hargeisa, Smith wrote to John Coles, the map curator of the Royal Geographical Society. He described his trip from Aden to Berbera and from there to Hargeisa and expressed his concerns about his camels: "There was no food within three or four days of Berbera; I had to push on to Hargeisa as fast as I could to save what few camels I had from starvation. I came with only eighty camels, all loaded very heavily. I should have had 110 camels for the loads. However, I lost only five camels on the way." Smith was understandably preoccupied with his transport animals, for if they died or were too weak to go on, his expedition could collapse.[19]

On July 27, the expedition arrived at Milmil. Thus far, they had traversed secure areas frequented by many sportsmen. In fact, they were unable to hunt between Berbera and Hargeisa as the area was reserved for the garrison at Aden. At Milmil, the local Somalis complained to Smith about a man-eating lion. Hoping to kill the animal, he had a zareba (a thorn bush enclosure) built, in which he and his gunbearer hid themselves at dusk. He then had a donkey tethered as bait ten feet away. Not long after sunset, a group of hyenas appeared and began closing in on the donkey. However, they suddenly fled in all directions as a huge male lion jumped on the donkey. Smith took careful aim and fired at close range. On being hit, the lion made for the zareba and collapsed its walls on top of Smith and his gunbearer. Wounded and roaring, the lion came to rest a foot away from Smith's face, with only a tangle of thorn bush separating them. The lion finally got up and walked off into some nearby bushes, much to Smith's relief. Smith and his gunbearer lay absolutely still, fearful that the animal might charge again. However, they soon heard the barking of a fox nearby that told them the lion was dead. Smith and his gunbearer then spent the night keeping the hyenas away from what turned out to be a magnificent, black-maned lion.[20]

Taking on new camels at Milmil, Smith headed due west, not realizing that the Ethiopians had already penetrated this far south. He could have given himself a safer margin from the Ethiopians by going southwest. However, this area all the way to the Webi Shebeli River had already been traversed by Swayne, by Counts Hojes and Cudenhove, and by the Italians Ruspoli and Bottego. The lure of the country to the west of Milmil was that no European had ever seen it. Like many travelers in Africa of his time, Smith wanted to traverse as much unknown country as possible. But to do so, he had to skirt around patches already explored by others. In mid-August, he arrived at Bodele, on a dry riverbed called the Terfa, 150 miles from Milmil. There, he unexpectedly met Captain C.J. Perceval, who was traveling north. Although pleased to meet someone so far off the beaten track, the encounter was a serious disappointment for Smith, for it significantly reduced the amount of territory he could later claim he was the first to explore.

Ten more days of marching brought Smith to the Webi Shebeli, which he could not cross because it was in flood. So, he moved downstream where the river was narrower and had rafts built to ferry his men, animals, and supplies across. However, the crossing was difficult because of the swift current and the large numbers of hippos and crocodiles. Once across the river, he would have done better had he proceeded southwest as planned. But his usual good judgment left him as he impulsively decided to visit the town of Sheikh Hussein, 160 miles to the northwest. What caused this sudden change in plans was the report of two Galla informants that the town was built of stone. "Stone houses in this part of Africa!" Smith exclaimed in his diary. "This was most interesting news."[21] And so, he led his caravan toward Sheikh Hussein, unaware that it was solidly in the hands of the Ethiopians.

Smith and his caravan gradually marched up into the highlands, passing through herds of elephants and gazelles. Every Galla they met told the same story: They had been reduced to poverty by the raiding Ethiopians. Common sense should have induced him to head south, but the town built of stone was too much of a magnet. On September 17, 1894, after he had named a nearby chain of mountains the Gillett Mountains, in honor of his friend, he met up with the first Ethiopians. Their cordiality was in large measure due to the fact that his caravan represented an armed force superior to their own.

Sheikh Hussein was all that Smith expected, a town of stone houses set high up in the mist-covered mountains. There were only a few Ethiopians in the town, but they were clearly in control of its Galla population. Their presence also represented Ethiopia's progressive imperial aims among the peoples south of its borders. Although the Ethiopians were friendly toward Smith, they made it very clear to him that they were not keen on his going west toward Lake Rudolf. He did not at first attach much significance to their disapproval of his plans since his armed Somalis greatly outnumbered them. He busied himself exploring the surrounding country, in the process determining the source of the Webi Shebeli River.

After two weeks in the fog and rain of Sheikh Hussein, two Ethiopians appeared on October 1, 1894, and told Smith that Menelik's governor of the region wanted him to come to Ginea (Ginir). What was of more concern to Smith was the size of the governor's army, which had just returned from an expedition in the south. Smith, Dodson, and Gillett put their heads together and decided that only one of them should go to Ginea. Gillett agreed to go with eight men, confident the Ethiopians would not attack with the main Somali force and Dodson and Smith at Sheikh Hussein. During the week Gillett was gone, Dodson and Smith collected natural history specimens, and Smith drilled his Somali in preparation for a possible Ethiopian attack.

A week later, a message came from Gillett saying it was safe for the entire caravan to proceed to Ginea. When Smith arrived there three days later, he was warmly greeted by the Ethiopian governor, Wal-da-

Gubbra (Wolda Gabriel), who firmly told him that he could not travel west unless Emperor Menelik approved of it. On October 17, Smith wrote a letter to the emperor, explaining that the purpose of his journey was purely scientific. Unknown to Smith, such a declaration was unlikely to persuade Menelik, who was keenly aware that his imperial aims in the Lake Rudolf region could easily be jeopardized by agents of European powers masquerading as scientific travelers.

While awaiting a reply from the emperor, Smith and his companions made short exploratory trips around Ginea. It was during one of these trips that he came upon the spectacular underground caves of the Web River at Sof Omar, which he called Wyndlawn after his summer home near Philadelphia. This name, like many he gave to various topographic features, did not survive far into the future.

It soon became obvious to Smith's men that they were being detained by the Ethiopians. It was at this point that Qualla Idris came to him and said that he was disgusted with the expedition and wished to return home. Smith was shocked by Idris's demand: "This was a splendid thing for a headman to do, just at the critical point to desert his master, when everything seemed to be going against him."[22] Smith convinced Idris to stay but never trusted him again.

Realizing that his continued house arrest in Ginea might provoke desertions among his men, Smith tried to leave. However, he was stopped by the Ethiopians, who were prepared to use force if necessary. Finally, on November 16, he received a letter from Menelik saying that he must return the way he had come. So he shrewdly headed back east toward Somaliland to fool the Ethiopians and then went south along the Webi Shebeli River, intent on turning west through country beyond Menelik's control.

Eventually, the expedition came to a trading center called Bari that was outside Ethiopian control. It was here that Fred Gillett learned that his father had died three months before:

> But now Fred received a shock that would have been hard enough to bear at any time, but which was still all the more severe as it came when he was far away in the wilderness. Coupled with the sad news were announcements that made it imperative that my friend, who had assisted me so often in my geographical and natural history work, should return home at once. On the third day (January 25), Fred started for the coast, with nine men and ten camels. I sent out the same time to Berbera eight boxes of natural history specimens, and my poor sick headman, Ahmed Aden.[23]

However, Gillett's father's death may have been only part of the reason why he left. Smith and Gillett obviously had some kind of falling out, as borne out in a letter of February 27, 1896, from Smith to J. Scott Keltie, secretary and editor of publications of the Royal Geographical Society:

> In the article for the journal, please change the sentence 'Mr. Fred Gillett agreed to accompany me with a sporting outfit' to 'Mr. Fred Gillett asked me to permit him to accompany me with twelve men, to which I agreed, on account of companionship.' I regret that you ever asked for Gillett's photographs for the journal, but as you spoke to him first I did not like to refuse. I beg you to insert the three Gillett photographs in the center of the article and not in the beginning.
>
> I have spent much money, to say nothing of the risks I ran on the expedition, and I think I should not have an article published by the R.G.S. that will disgust me to look back upon.
>
> Whatever happened between myself and Gillett has been patched up, and I do not think you would want to bring about rows. My friends have got the idea that Gillett shared in the expenses of the whole expedition, whereas I should have saved money in not having him.
>
> You must confess that I have put Gillett forward in the paper, and have given him credit for things I do not believe. I trust that will not be repeated by you. I only give you this information as a hint that there is a very sore point with me in regard to the trip that I wish to forget entirely.[24]

It is unclear from this letter, written after Smith had returned to the United States, whether he and Gillett had a row in Africa or if their misunderstanding arose later over the latter getting undeserved credit for the expedition's successes. They had clearly mended their differences to some degree by early 1896, as Gillett was present at the meeting of the Royal Geographical Society in London on January 6 when Smith presented the results of the expedition. He even praised Smith when he rose to speak at the end of the presentation: "I wish to express my admiration for the persevering way in which Dr. Donaldson Smith mapped out the country, in spite of the broiling and enervating climate, tiring marches, and inaccurate reports given by natives, unaccustomed to precision."[25] This terse but significant public comment by Gillett essentially gave Smith full credit for the expedition's geographic accomplishments and put to rest speculation to the contrary.

On January 31, 1895, Smith and Dodson, with seventy-five men and sixty-five rifles, made a fresh start for Lake Rudolf by heading southwest toward the Juba River. The 200-mile march to the Juba was through monotonous brush, where at the time there were sizable herds of giraffe, waterbuck, oryx, and zebra. On February 17, they crossed the south-to-north lines of march of Prince Ruspoli and Captain Bottego and moved south along the Web to where the Daua River flows into the Ganana. Most of Smith's undeveloped photographic plates were damaged during his crossing of the Ganana, which accounts for the fact that he made few photographs in what is now northern Kenya. He and Dodson moved along the southern banks of the Daua and were soon in what is now the northeastern corner of Kenya, near Mandera. From there, they followed the line of wells that run east to west from El Dere to Egder in what today is southern Ethiopia.

In late March 1895, the caravan approached the country of the Boran people, who, like the Maasai, were expert soldiers and pastoral nomads. At the time of Smith's arrival, the Boran were on a heightened war footing because of recent Ethiopian raids. The Ethiopians had not only killed and wounded Boran soldiers, they had also abducted women and children and stolen large numbers of livestock. As a result, they were extremely hostile toward any group of armed strangers entering their territory. As Smith approached this area, he almost lost his life—not to a Boran spear but to a bolt of lightning that struck him and his gunbearer, Karsa (Karsha), while they were out hunting. It was a perfectly clear day when the bolt hit, knocking both men unconscious.

In hopes of avoiding armed conflicts with the Boran, Smith fired off several rockets at night, which lit up the sky with dazzling fireworks. Although the Boran were impressed, they launched an attack the following day. The trouble began when two of Smith's men were attacked by the Boran, with one of them, Elmi, being fatally wounded. "Poor Elmi lay dead behind a bush," Smith wrote, "horribly mutilated, his intestines scattered about, and a part of him carried away as a trophy by his murderers."[26] Smith was euphemistically referring to the Boran custom of removing the testicles of their victims.

Between April 6 and 10, Smith and his caravan were constantly harassed by Boran war parties consisting of men on foot and on horseback. Employing standard military tactics, Smith used his well-drilled Somali men to drive off the attackers. On April 8, he wrote about the attacks in his diary:

> The punishment the natives received was terrible; but still they came on regardless of those who were falling about them and the din of musketry. Frantic to get away, the poor savages, who had now for the first time realized that a bullet will pierce a shield and kill a horse hundreds of yards away, were taking themselves off as fast as their legs could carry them.[27]

Smith was greatly troubled by having to inflict so much harm on the Boran. He was truly surprised by the ferocity of their attacks since he had done nothing to provoke them. Clearly, the effect of his guns on them and their horses was serious because they quickly sued for peace, returned the pack animals they had stolen, and let Smith proceed unhindered.

After a brief visit to Lake Abaya and the wildlife-rich bush that surrounded it, Smith headed for Lake Stephanie, which lay 100 miles to the southwest. As he did so, he came upon the skulls of thousands of buffalo that had succumbed to a rinderpest epidemic five years before. On reaching Lake Stephanie, he traveled around its eastern, southern, and northern shores and determined that the Galana Amara River flowed into it from Lake Abaya. Unlike Teleki and von Höhnel, who only saw the southern part of Lake Stephanie, Smith virtually walked around it. He found that there was also a small lake 10 miles long and 2 miles wide extending from the northeastern corner of the lake, which he named Lake Donaldson. Since Smith's day, both lakes have virtually dried up, and most of the wildlife that then lived there has vanished.

Moving to the northwest of Lake Stephanie into a region never before visited by Europeans, Smith encountered numerous small ethnic groups. Among these, the Arbore gave him a great deal of difficulty by ambushing his caravan on several occasions. Once he was attacked by 450 Arbore armed with bows and poisoned arrows.[28] He also met the Dume people, whom he mistakenly believed to be pygmies because of their short stature. In fact, on his return to England, his descriptions of the Dume initially provoked more excitement than any of his other discoveries.[29]

Smith had now been in the interior of Africa for a year, and Lake Rudolf was only 100 miles to the southwest. Finally, after wading down a stream for several days, he came into open country, and on July 10, 1895, he saw the lake:

> We saw a long white strip of water gleaming far off in the distance. This was a sight that appealed to the heart of every man in the caravan. It was Lake Rudolf. With one accord, the boys rushed up, and, crowding around me, burst into a loud "hip-hip, hurrah!" led by Dodson. As I looked upon the bright sheet of water . . . I felt that I had attained in a measure the greatest ambition of my life—that of being able to add a little drop to the sea of knowledge possessed by civilized mankind.[30]

On July 14, 1895, Smith and Dodson camped on the same spot where Teleki and von Höhnel had stayed for a month in 1888. Since these two explorers had left the area, no Europeans had ever visited it. However, a Swahili caravan, the first ever to go that far north, had come from Mombasa and reached this area a few years before Smith's arrival. Unknown to Smith was the fact that Arthur Henry Neumann, an ivory hunter, was heading north up to the lake, having come from Lamu on the coast. He finally reached the southern shore of the lake on December 6, 1895.[31]

Smith's next objective was to settle the issue of the lake's source. Von Höhnel had been unsuccessful in his attempts to do so. He had found a river, the Nianamm, flowing into the northern end of the lake. What no one knew was whether this was the same river as the Omo, whose upper course had already been explored by Jules Borelli and others. To resolve the issue, Smith set out to explore a strip of land 100 miles long. His initial attempt failed because he and most of his men were stricken with severe attacks of malaria. However, on July 24, although still sick, he made a second start. His route took him through the fertile country of the Murle and Kere people, who made his transit difficult. Finally, some 80 miles north of the lake, Smith, who had previously thought that the Nianamm and Omo were one, erroneously concluded they were not. The Omo, he said, probably flowed into the Juba or the Ganana, and the Nianamm was a different river and the source of Lake Rudolf.

Today, on modern maps, a mountain chain called Mount Smith, situated in southern Ethiopia, is the only permanent geographic reminder of Smith's gallant but failed effort to solve the mystery of the Omo River. In reality, Smith had gone up the Omo and then up one of its tributaries, the Mago River, which he mistook for the Nianamm and the source of the lake.[32]

Beset by repeated and disabling attacks of malaria, Smith arrived back at his Lake Rudolf camp on August 5, confident that he had settled the question of the Omo River. Having achieved the primary objectives of his expedition, he was anxious to get home and tell the world of his discoveries. So, on August 8, 1895, he, Dodson, and the caravan started down the eastern shore of Lake Rudolf and later veered toward the southeast.

Smith and his men soon entered lands that had never before been seen by Europeans. Ahead of them lay Marsabit, a high volcanic range some 30 miles long, whose summits were and still are covered by dense forest. Léon des Avanchers had referred to this range on his 1859 map under its Boran name, Sakou, and von Höhnel had accurately recorded what the Rendille and Samburu said about it and placed it on Chanler's maps.

Marsabit rises to a height of 5,000 feet. The forest begins at an altitude of 4,300 feet, and below that are dense bush and open glades. The southwestern slopes, consisting of conical hills and extinct volcanoes, rise gradually until three distinct summits are formed. This enormous, verdant range is full of springs, pools, and spectacular ravines, and there is a crater lake at its highest summit. But around it, stretching for almost 100 miles in every direction, is a dry and waterless desert.

Smith and Dodson headed across the desert to the west of the mountain. It took them five days to get to the base of Marsabit, traveling, as Smith said, over a path worn smooth by countless animals: "On the second day, we commenced to ascend the mountain, but we did not reach the top until after three marches. I was attacked by fever on these marches, and twice had to be carried; but the cool bracing air at the top of Mt. Marsabit quickly cured me."[33]

It was not so much the air that cured Smith as the heavy doses of quinine he took. In spite of being very ill, he was most impressed with Marsabit: "According to European ideas, nothing could be more charming than this Marsabit. Surrounded by a large forest and lying at the top of the mountain, is a lake a mile square, clear, and deep. The jagged walls of a crater form a semi-circle about it, while from another side, a broad road leads out from the forest to the open meadow beyond."[34]

Smith left Marsabit on September 13, 1895, after spending only four days on the mountain. Before leaving, he was almost killed by an elephant, after which he wrote the following understatement: "By this time I had begun to look forward to getting home safely."[35] Heading south through 140 miles of uncharted country, the caravan reached the Guaso Nyiro River on September 22, where Smith suffered a severe relapse of malaria. He camped on the northern bank at Melka Koja, a point reached by Chanler and von Höhnel in 1893 on their way to the Lorian Swamp.

On October 1, Smith felt well enough to head south across an unexplored stretch of country between the Guaso Nyiro and Tana Rivers, reaching the latter six days later. Suffering more from the effects of quinine than from malaria, he looked down from the banks of the Tana and thought he was hallucinating:

> Imagine our astonishment when a canoe hove in sight just around a bend in the river—and in that canoe sat a man holding a pink umbrella! Yes, true enough, a pink umbrella, and underneath a man in a white suit! I fired two shots from my Winchester, and the next instant the salute was answered from the canoe. With all the Somalis drawn up in a line behind us, presenting arms, Dodson and I awaited the landing of the white man. As the Rev. Robert Omerod stepped on the sandy beach, he grasped our hands heartily.[36]

Omerod was a member of the Methodist Reformed Mission who was on his way downstream after an exploratory trip for the purpose of setting up a new mission. He helped Smith obtain a half dozen canoes from the Pokomo people he knew along that stretch of the river. This greatly facilitated the expedition's return to Lamu on the coast:

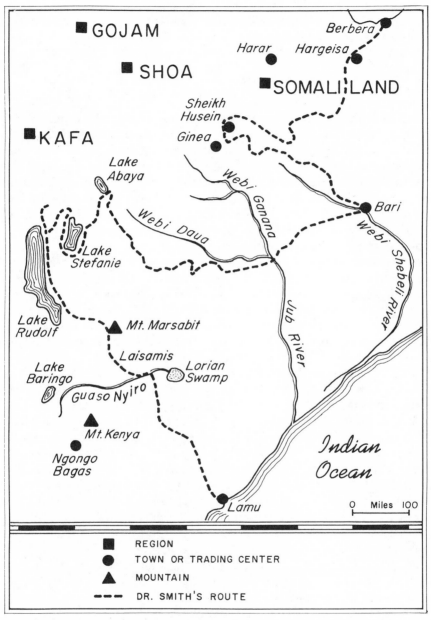

Arthur Donaldson Smith's route during his 1894–1895 journey to Lake Rudolf (drawn by Saturnino B. Villapez).

The camel loads were lightened by our placing many of them in the canoes, while Dodson and I made ourselves comfortable, each in the middle
of a dug-out, reclining on blankets and bags. What luxury it was for us to
be paddled quietly along, after having had such wearying marches! A
more pleasurable trip than this canoe ride I never made in my life. Mr.
Omerod, among his other kindnesses, provided Dodson and myself with
various periodicals, three or four months old, but very recent to us.[37]

On October 29, 1895, Smith, Dodson, and their Somali men sailed
to Aden. They had covered 4,000 miles in sixteen months and had
filled in a number of blank spaces on the map of Africa. A one-word
cablegram sent by Smith from Aden to Philadelphia summed up the
results of his expedition. It simply read: "Successful." A similar message was received at the Royal Geographical Society in London on November 4. Two days later, the *New York Times* declared the success of
Smith's expedition with a bold headline: "A Successful Explorer—Dr.
Donaldson Smith Accomplishes His Mission in Africa."[38]

Smith and Dodson arrived back in England on November 30, 1895.
On the evening of January 6, 1896, Smith presented his findings to the
Royal Geographical Society. He had collected 700 specimens of birds,
24 of which were new to science; 300 reptiles and batrachians, of
which 11 were new; 300 specimens of plants; 1,000 butterflies; 200
mammals; and close to 6,000 insects. The staff of the British Museum
examined all of these specimens, and Smith donated all of the new
species to the museum. The remainder he donated to the Academy of
Natural Sciences of Philadelphia. Of the new species, some were
named after Smith, including the rare crested rat, *Lophiomys smithii*, a
fish, *Synodontis smithii*, and a bird, *Turacus donaldsoni*. His geological collection was examined by J.W. Gregory, noted for his own expedition to Kenya's Rift Valley. Smith donated his ethnographic collection
to the University of Pennsylvania Museum and, in 1914, gave them a
second such collection from his subsequent African expedition.[39]

Smith's verbal presentation about his trip before the Royal Geographical Society was extremely well received. The session was
chaired by Sir George D. Taubman Goldie, one of the society's vice
presidents. The American ambassador cogently observed in remarks
made after Smith's speech that the trip was "an honest, brave, modest
endeavor to let all the world know something of distant regions of
which nothing seems to have been known before." Ambassador
Thomas Francis Bayard (1828–1898) also noted that Smith's trip had
not been undertaken for profit or utility, remarks no doubt intended
for those whose expeditions were motivated by politics or profit.[40]
John Coles, the map curator, praised Smith for the excellence of his

geographic measurements and for the dedication he had shown in preparing for the trip.

Finally, the eminent cartographer Ernst Georg Ravenstein rose to speak. A prominent figure in the Nile source debate of earlier decades, he had helped draw the maps of several eminent explorers, including J. Ludwig Krapf (he also wrote an introduction to Krapf's book). He raised the issue of the Omo River, disagreeing with Smith's conclusions that it flowed into either the Ganana or the Jub and that the Nianamm was the source of the lake:

> I am inclined to think that the Omo, after all, takes its course to Lake Rudolf. I may observe that neither Dr. Smith nor Count Teleki saw the Nianamm at its best. This question of the course of the Omo is perhaps the most interesting problem to be solved in connection with African hydrography, and it would redound to the honor of America if Dr. Donaldson Smith went out again and settled it.[41]

There was both criticism and challenge in Ravenstein's brief comments. It rankled Smith that he had failed to definitively resolve the issue of these rivers through on-site geographic observation. Like von Höhnel before him, he had made an educated guess that Ravenstein correctly suspected was wrong. Despite all of the other successes of his expedition, Smith was keenly aware of this failure and was determined to set it right. For this reason, he immediately began plans for a return expedition to settle the issue of the lake's source.

Smith left Great Britain from Southampton and arrived in New York aboard the *St. Louis* on February 15, 1896. He was met by members of his family, who had not seen him in two years, and reached Philadelphia that afternoon. By any measure, his expedition had been an enormous success, and he could well have rested on his laurels as an explorer for a lifetime. Unlike many other expeditions of the day, his had not been financially supported by any government, scientific society, or private commercial interests. He had spent $6,000 of his own money on it (close to 10 percent of his inheritance), which in today's currency would be equal to $222,000.

Smith was honored and feted. "It has been an agreeable surprise to me that Americans in general have taken great interest in my expedition," he wrote on February 27, 1896, to J. Scott Keltie, the secretary and editor of publications of the Royal Geographical Society in London. "Many dinners and receptions have been given for me. I lecture before the Geographical Club in Philadelphia and New York soon."[42]

Henry Pleasants Jr., M.D., Smith's sister's nephew by marriage, recalled his impressions as a young boy:

It was quite something for us small boys to be even distantly related to a real live African explorer. Personally, I was a bit disappointed when I saw him for the first time after his return. He had not grown two feet taller, and he was thinner than ever. His complexion was yellow, too. Father said it was because of malaria and quinine and bad food. Otherwise, he was just the same Uncle Donnie, as quiet and insignificant as ever.[43]

Smith's major concern during the early months of 1896 was with the delay in the *Geographical Journal*'s publication of his maps and the oral presentation he had made before the society on January 6, 1896. This is reflected in his February 27 letter to J. Scott Keltie: "No proofs yet received. I do not give my permission to have maps published before I see and comment proofs."[44] Smith was clearly upset by the delays and was not in the best of health either. Keltie was surprised to learn of Smith's differences with Gillett during the trip and tried to mollify him about the delay in the proofs of his article.[45]

Smith received the proofs for his paper in late March but not the proofs for the maps. On April 2, 1896, he wrote to Keltie, saying, "I did not write immediately as the map proofs have not come. I hope to get the maps soon—it is getting late for them. There is plenty of work for me now getting my book ready but I feel in good condition, no more malaria or eye trouble. . . . Please forget what I said about Gillett and the photographs, and insert the three pictures where they belong—in the beginning."[46]

The proofs of the maps had still not arrived by June 17, when Smith sent his longest (eight pages) and strongest letter to Keltie: "Mr. Ravenstein's last letter to me stated that the proofs of my maps would be sent at once. No maps have since appeared. The R.G.S. Journal for June has reached me. Not a word has been inserted regarding my expedition. I feel most discouraged."[47] Smith had good reason to be discouraged with the slow pace of producing his article.

Although the Royal Geographical Society seemed to Smith to be dragging its feet in publishing the results of his expedition, he himself was active in disseminating word of it in the United States. The *New York Times* carried an extensive article on his accomplishments, entitled "Exploring Eastern Africa—Dr. Donaldson Smith, an American Traveler, Encounters Queer People to the Northward of Abyssinia," and numerous stories appeared in the Philadelphia newspapers.[48] Smith also lectured to a capacity audience in the American Geographical Society's Chickering Hall and before the Philadelphia Geographical Society.

Unfortunately, he was not a very effective speaker. Henry Pleasants recalled his father's impression of Smith's address before the Academy of Natural Sciences of Philadelphia: "Father said that he acted as if he would rather have faced a wounded bull elephant than the audience.

His knees shook so hard that anyone could see them; and his voice could not be heard farther back than the third row."[49]

The *Geographical Journal*, which made its appearance in 1893 under Keltie's editorship, published both written articles and articles derived from presentations made before the society by explorers, travelers, and others. J. Scott Keltie (1840–1927), whose association with the society began in 1884, was a distinguished and respected editor and writer. Yet despite Keltie's efforts, was the Royal Geographical Society, an often co-operative partner with British imperial aims, purposely suppressing Smith's findings? Smith seemed to have thought so during the period before publication. He was especially suspicious of Ernst George Ravenstein, the society's cartographer. Writing to Keltie, Smith said:

> Mr. Ravenstein's last letter to me stated that the proofs of my maps would be sent to me at once. The letter was received over a fortnight ago, but no maps have since appeared. . . . Now I venture to say after he has gotten from me all the information I could give, he is against my getting any credit. Or else why would he have not published my maps at once?
>
> Mr. Ravenstein made another little remark to me to the effect that most of the tribes I discovered had already been heard of, but this I can prove to you to be absolutely incorrect.[50]

Smith's letter of June 17 crossed with the proofs of his maps, which arrived from London on June 20, 1896. He hastened to write to Keltie four days after his letter of June 17: "Proofs of my maps have arrived (yesterday), and I am greatly pleased. Very sorry I wrote you a few days ago when I had a fit of depression. Mr. Ravenstein has worked well to oblige me as well as to attain accuracy in the five maps he sent me. I have not seen the index map, but I cabled Mr. Ravenstein to publish all, on faith."[51] Smith was clearly very happy with the maps and cheered by the fact that his work would soon be published. He quickly passed from the issue of the maps to future travel.

However, Keltie could not let Smith's highly accusatory letter of June 17 go unanswered:

> Dear Donaldson Smith: I cannot tell you how grieved I am that you should take so erroneous a view as to the attitude of the Society towards your work in Africa. The delay in the preparation of the maps is most annoying. . . . Mr. Ravenstein is undoubtedly the best cartographer we have, and no one knows Africa so well as he does. We felt it was only justice to your admirable work to give the maps to the best man even at the risk of delay. Be assured this delay will do your reputation no injury. No one can take away any of the credit which belongs to you. I am glad the maps are out of hand at last. Too late, unfortunately, for the July *Journal*, but they shall go into the August number.[52]

Keltie acknowledged that there had been undue delay in bringing Smith's work out. However, he firmly countered Smith's allegation that Ravenstein was trying to deny him the recognition he deserved: "You are laboring under a serious misconception; and that the delay in the publication of your maps and paper is purely accidental. Rest assured that we place a high value on your work in Africa." Keltie ended his long letter by encouraging Smith to apply to the society for financial support for his next trip to Africa.[53]

Smith's article finally appeared in two parts in the August and September issues of the journal, the maps being published with the first installment.[54] The three Gillett photographs appeared at the beginning of the first installment. The latter was the second article in the issue, appearing after part two of George N. Curzon's article on the Pamirs region and the Oxus River. Smith's second installment was again the second article, appearing after one on "The Hausa Territories" by Charles H. Robinson and followed by the third installment of Curzon's article. Taken on merit alone, Smith's work should have been treated as a lead article. However, Curzon was a powerful political figure, a member of Parliament and the cabinet, a renowned traveler, and a vice president of the society. One can understand why Smith's first installment followed Curzon's article. But it is less explicable why the second one came after a rather unremarkable article on what is now northern Nigeria. Smith, who was obviously relieved at just getting published, voiced no complaints about the position of his article. On August 20, 1896, he wrote to Keltie thanking him for the journal copies and telling him that he was very pleased with the first part of the article and the maps.

Although Smith was now committed to launching a second expedition to resolve the Omo question, he expressed serious concerns about its costs, which he put at £3,000. He told Keltie that the society would have to pay two-thirds of the expenses. Aware that the Omo question might get resolved by other explorers before he got back to the region, he put forth a back-up proposal of exploring the unknown area between the lake and the Nile.[55] Such a plan was then of little vital interest to the society. In addition, the society had received word, as had Smith, that a wealthy young British aristocrat, Henry Sheppard Hart Cavendish, the nephew of Lord Hartington (Duke of Devonshire), had set out to explore the western shore of Lake Rudolf. What neither the society nor Smith knew as yet was the extent of the area explored by Cavendish. The society had also learned that the Italian explorer Vittorio Bottego had arrived on the northern shore of Lake Rudolf on September 1, 1896, intent on resolving whether or not the Omo River was the principal source of the lake.

Keltie wrote to Smith on February 2, 1897, saying that the society's council members were well disposed to his plans but that they could not at that point approve the funds. What he did not say was that the likelihood of their ever doing so was growing dimmer by the month. Not only were there other explorers in the area—Bottego, Cavendish, and Neumann—but the Upper Nile region and the borders between Ethiopia and the British sphere of influence also were rapidly becoming political flash points in the rivalry between Britain and France for control of the Nile. Keltie was extremely euphemistic when he told Smith that "the regions between Somaliland and the Nile will be in a disturbed state."[56]

Despite the growing political instability in the region and the presence of other explorers around the lake, Smith persisted in his attempts to obtain society financing for a return trip. Referring to Bottego, Cavendish, and Neumann, he told Keltie, "You would do me a great favor if you would send me any accounts of their journeys if you think they bear on the question that is nearest my heart."[57] That question, of course, was the Omo River.

What Smith could not have foreseen was the arrival in the Lake Rudolf region of several European and Ethiopian expeditions, primarily launched to achieve colonial ends. The question nearest his heart was now complicated, not so much by geographic challenges as by political intrigue.

7

Sportsmen and Ivory Hunters

Arthur Henry Neumann, the ivory hunter (from Elephant Hunting in East Equatorial Africa, *1898).*

The three years following Arthur Donaldson Smith's return from East Africa, 1896–1898, were to prove decisive for Britain's plan to control the Nile from its headwaters to the Mediterranean. This period also witnessed the emergence of Ethiopia as an indigenous colonial power that was destined to play an important role in the complex competition for the Nile. Ethiopia not only inflicted a humiliating military defeat on the Italians in 1896 but also allied itself with the French in the interests of pushing its borders to the south and west. This territorial expansion eventually brought Ethiopia into confrontation with British interests around Lake Rudolf and the Nile. A clever and prudent man, Ethiopia's emperor, Menelik II, knew the value of shifting his alliances in the interests of self-preservation. Thus, he eventually moved from a policy of confrontation with the British to one of accommodation when it became clear that Britain had emerged as the most powerful colonial power in the region.

Four British expeditions arrived at Lake Rudolf during these turbulent years. Yet only one of them was politically motivated and sponsored by the British government. The others were essentially led by sportsmen with little interest in scientific exploration and no inclination to become involved in their country's attempts to expand its East African possessions. Still, the arrival of these men at the lake later proved advantageous to Britain in its territorial disputes with Ethiopia, for the claim of earliest presence was a very persuasive one in the discourse of colonial powers.

Arthur Henry Neumann was the first to arrive, reaching the southern tip of the lake on December 6, 1895, shortly after Smith returned to London. The contrasts between these two men could not have been more dramatic. Whereas Smith was a meticulous geographer and skilled naturalist, drawn to the lake by a desire to advance science and human knowledge, Neumann was primarily an elephant hunter intent on amassing a hoard of ivory.

Born in Bedfordshire on June 12, 1850, where his father was the rector of the Hockliffe village church, Neumann was a solitary and retiring child. By his own admission, he was stigmatized by his family as a "cruel boy" because of his harsh treatment of domestic animals. In later years, he wrote, "I am prepared to be denounced as cruel. I admit at once that I am." He was also a shy man who craved solitude and who had an "unquenchable thirst for prying further and further into remote wastes."[1]

Neumann was to slaughter elephants for close to two decades, first in southern Africa and later in what is now Kenya. It was not only the ivory that appealed to him but also the pleasure and excitement he derived from stalking and killing elephants. This is abundantly clear in many of the passages from his book *Elephant Hunting in East Equatorial Africa*. Toward the end of his life, he became disheartened when game regulations were put in place and hunters such as himself were subject to public censure. He tried to justify his years of killing by claiming that the elephant's continued existence was "incompatible with the advance of civilization."[2] To his credit, though, he advocated the creation of game reserves where elephants and other wild animals could be preserved.

In 1868, Neumann left England for South Africa, where he unsuccessfully tried his hand at farming in Natal and gold mining in the Transvaal. He then took up hunting in Swaziland, where he also set up a trading post and learned to speak the local language. When the Zulu War erupted in 1879, he became an interpreter for Norman Magnus

Macleod of Macleod who was the British government's political agent for Swaziland. Neumann and Macleod formed a lifelong friendship that was galvanized by their compatible personalities and a mutual interest in hunting.[3]

When the Zulu War ended in 1880, Neumann joined his brother Charles, who had established a small farm. Since farming was scarcely to his liking, he soon set off for the then remote Limpopo River valley, where he hunted for several years. The proceeds from hides and ivory provided him with a reasonable income for a time. However, the inexorable destruction of wildlife in this region by Europeans eventually forced him to find other remote areas where he could hunt in solitude. One such place was East Africa, which he briefly visited in 1888 in order to inquire about hunting elephants. Although elephants were abundant, the costs of outfitting a caravan were well beyond his means. The other obstacle was his total ignorance of the character of the country. He shrewdly concluded that the solution to both of these problems was an employment opportunity that would enable him to travel into the interior and thereby acquire the experience necessary to launch an elephant hunt.

In May 1890, George S. Mackenzie, the administrator of the Imperial British East Africa Company (IBEA), hired Neumann to help with the construction of a 300-mile road from Malindi on the coast to the company's station at Machakos. Mackenzie was under intense pressures to get this road built and had only a small budget to cover wages for Europeans. Not surprisingly, he took Neumann on without references and gave little thought to either his abilities or his character.

Neumann's immediate superior was Captain Frederick Lugard, who was a high-powered, ambitious, and efficient ex-soldier who would later become a leading figure in Britain's African empire. He immediately put Neumann in charge of a work gang of fifty men, with orders to hack as straight a path as possible through the bush along the Sabaki River. Neumann found the work monotonous, but it at least gave him an opportunity to familiarize himself with the country and to shoot wildlife.

From the outset, Lugard was greatly dissatisfied with Neumann and the quality of his work. He wrote in his diary that Neumann was excessively deliberate, reclusive, obdurate, potentially insubordinate, and often lacking in common sense. For instance, instead of cutting a straight road, as the flat land easily permitted, he created a meandering one unsuitable for telegraph lines.[4] Although Lugard's judgment of Neumann might be attributed in part to his own driving personality, it is also likely that it represented a fair assessment of a peculiar man who had spent most of the previous two decades as a rover in the wilds of Africa.

When Lugard moved on to Uganda, he effectively packed Neumann off to the coast by saying that his orders contained no provisions for him. Mackenzie quickly overlooked Lugard's candid evaluation because he was hard pressed to find Europeans of even modest abilities. Thus, instead of dismissing Neumann, he promptly assigned him to work with a survey party that was to identify possible routes for a railway from Mombasa to Lake Victoria. Led by Captain Eric Smith, the group also included James Martin, who had traveled with the explorer Joseph Thomson in 1883–1884. In December 1890, the survey party left Mombasa and headed for the lake and Uganda, which they reached after an uneventful trek of a few months. Once the work was completed, Neumann returned to the coast. En route, his camp at Loita was attacked by the Maasai, who killed thirty-eight of his ninety-two men. He and the remaining survivors managed to escape under the cover of darkness but not before he was speared through the forearm.[5]

When Neumann arrived in Mombasa, he found a letter from South Africa offering him the position of magistrate among the Zulu. He decided to accept it because he knew it would quickly provide him with the additional funds he needed to finance an elephant hunt in East Africa. His year with the IBEA had not made him a rich man, but it had given him the opportunity to become familiar with the country and to discover where elephants could be found in great numbers.

One of the consequences of Teleki's sale of ivory in Zanzibar in 1889 was that it drew attention to the elephant herds in the Lake Rudolf region. This was an area not previously hunted by Europeans or frequently visited by coastal traders. However, some of the latter soon began to travel up toward the lake in search of ivory gathered by the Wanderobo, who were expert elephant hunters.

In December 1893, Neumann was back in East Africa at the head of a caravan of fifty men armed with Snider rifles. In Mombasa, by a stroke of good luck, he met von Höhnel, who was on his way home to Austria-Hungary after having been wounded by a rhinoceros. Von Höhnel recorded the meeting:

> A Mr. Neumann was just equipping a caravan with his modest means in order to visit the Rudolf lake district. He wanted to undertake the shooting of elephants on a business basis. He was about 40, fair, of slight build, and did not look very enterprising. . . . He was said to be a crack shot. I was able to give him good information about the districts which he intended visiting, and he consulted me on many points.[6]

In late January 1894, Neumann met William Astor Chanler, who was returning to the coast following the desertion of his men. They spent a pleasant night talking and smoking Neumann's Havana cigars.

Chanler gave Neumann much useful information about the districts to the west and on parting gave him his little terrier, "Frolic."[7] Neumann essentially headed for areas recently visited by Chanler and von Höhnel, and in February 1894, he killed his first elephants. He then headed for the Guaso Nyiro River, where he was so successful at shooting elephants that he was able to send his first shipment of ivory back to Mombasa by July.

With the help of Wanderobo trackers, Neumann continued hunting until early 1895, when he decided to return to the coast. He had amassed a large hoard of ivory, had become intimately familiar with the dry bush country of what is now northern Kenya, and had made friends with expert Wanderobo hunters, who greatly facilitated his success.

Using some of the ivory sale proceeds from this first trip, he then outfitted a second but smaller caravan of thirty-five men, which left Mombasa on May 16, 1895. Neumann headed for Lake Rudolf, whose large elephant populations had only been hunted by the Wanderobo and Count Samuel Teleki. The scale of his elephant killing in the area north of the Guaso Nyiro River earned for him the Swahili language sobriquet *Nyama Yangu* (My Meat).

Killing as many elephants as he could, Neumann finally got a glimpse of Lake Rudolf's southern shore on December 4, 1895. Von Höhnel and Smith had recorded their first views of this body with poetic descriptions and philosophical reflections; Neumann, by contrast, dispatched his with a terse comment: "A fine sight it was, looking blue like the sea."[8] More important to him, he soon found many old bull elephants carrying large tusks, three of which he killed in one day.

There was hardly an elephant along the eastern shore of the lake that escaped the sights of his rifles. By late December, he had reached the northern end of the lake, from where he moved into the forests along the banks of the Omo River. It was here that the first serious tragedy of the expedition occurred. On January 1, 1896, Neumann's servant, Shebane, was washing in the shallow waters of the riverbank when suddenly an enormous crocodile seized him. Neumann described what happened next:

> I was still looking down when I heard a cry of alarm, and, raising my head, got a glimpse of the most ghastly sight I ever witnessed. There was the head of a huge crocodile out of the water, just swinging over towards the deep with my poor Swahili boy in its awful jaws, held across the middle of the body like a fish in the beak of a heron. He had ceased to cry out, and with one horrible wiggle, a swirl and a splash, all disappeared. One could do nothing. It was over; Shebane was gone.[9]

Once he had shot the area clean of elephants, Neumann marched south toward the lake, where he went on a massive killing spree. He was so busy shooting elephants that wounded animals were left to die, for as Neumann said, "we had other things to think about."[10] However, his zeal for killing almost resulted in his own death when a cow elephant broke his ribs and pierced his arm with a tusk. When he raised his rifle to shoot her as she charged, he found that the cartridge had not entered the barrel. He turned and ran, but the elephant easily overtook him. Neumann escaped with his life but remained an invalid in camp for three weeks. In one of his rare philosophical reflections, he said of his near brush with death, "Just retribution, perhaps you will say; and for my part I harbored no ill-will against the elephant for avenging its kith and kin. It was the fortune of war."[11]

Still greedy for ivory and scarcely chastened by his injuries, he continued to hunt his way south even though his men and donkeys could scarcely carry all the ivory he had already accumulated. Eventually, he had to resort to a relay system in order to get all his ivory to the coast. When he arrived in Mombasa on October 1, 1896, he was a far richer man than when he had left a year and a half before. But the elephant populations of Lake Rudolf were now doomed to extinction. Hoping to imitate Neumann's success, other hunters soon came and eventually wiped them out.

On returning to Britain, Neumann wrote his book *Elephant Hunting in East Equatorial Africa*, which was published in 1897. Except for an important butterfly collection of 170 species, his contributions to advancing either geographic knowledge or science were modest. Yet John G. Millais, the famous naturalist-artist, who met Neumann at this time, thought highly of him and became a close friend.[12]

After a brief period of service in the Boer War, Neumann returned to East Africa in 1902. He again hunted elephants near the Guaso Nyiro River, on Mount Marsabit, and near Lake Rudolf. Using Mount Kenya as a base, he relentlessly pursued these animals as much for their ivory as for the thrill of killing them. In 1902, he wrote Millais the following telling words: "I take but damned little interest nowadays in shooting any other beast but the elephant. . . . Nothing else thrills me."[13] The magnitude of his slaughter can be judged from the fact that in March 1903, he traveled down to Mombasa with a ton of ivory.

Time, however, was running out for both Neumann and his relentless killing of elephants. In 1905, much-needed game regulations were put into place, which he wrongly interpreted as being directed at him personally and out of spite. The authorities gave him a grace period in which to wind down his affairs, and he left Mombasa in October 1906 a very angry and unhappy man. Writing to Millais, he poured out venomous criticism of the Game Preservation Society that had pushed for the new regulations: "It seems that your intrepid, sanctimonious, giraffe-slaying, bastard-missionary, self-appointed protector of beasts . . . and almighty law-giver for Africa in general, psalm-smiter-in-chief, this stroll through the country . . . coadjutator . . . in the Game Preserving Society has been trying to put a spoke in the wheel of your humble servant."[14]

When Neumann arrived in London, he sold his ivory for £4,500, realizing a profit of £1,500 after covering his expenses. This sale marked the end of his adventurous life as an elephant hunter.[15] The vast and lonely wilderness of northern Kenya that had been his home for so long was slowly coming under administrative control, and elephants were being protected through hunting regulations.

As the world Neumann had known in East Africa was changing, he himself was slipping into a severe depression. Writing to Millais from Mombasa on July 28, 1906, before his final departure, he said: "The prospect of leaving my country and giving up the life I love makes me sad. . . . Here in my 'nowhere' I have been happy, and never suffered from those terrible fits of depression that weigh me down there."[16]

Following his arrival in London, Neumann pursued his plans for obtaining government permission to administer a tract of land north of the Guaso Nyiro as a reserve for the Wanderobo and Samburu, in which controlled elephant hunting could take place. Although the bureaucracies in London and Nairobi moved slowly, they did favor his scheme. However, Neumann had slipped into a deep depression, exacerbated when his proposal of marriage was rejected by a woman with whom he had fallen in love. On May 29, 1907, he wrapped himself in his hyrax-skin rug and shot himself through the head with one of his old hunting rifles.[17]

Neumann made no pretenses to being either a naturalist or a geographer. He was an elephant hunter to such a degree that it overwhelmingly defined his adult life, almost to the exclusion of all else.[18] He was also a troubled and unhappy man who managed to deal with his emotional problems by choosing an unusual life of solitude, seclusion, and slaughter. His killing of elephants not only satisfied the demands of the ivory market but also enabled him to contain his own inner turmoil.[19] Of all the men who went to Lake Rudolf in these early years, he revealed the least about the land and its peoples but the most about the traveler himself.

The next British visitor to the lake was Henry Sheppard Hart Cavendish, who, unlike Neumann, was a member of the British aristocracy. Born in 1876 at Thornton Hall in Buckinghamshire, he was the son of William Thomas Cavendish and the grandson of Henry

Manners Cavendish, the third Baron Waterpark. After completing his studies at Eton, he traveled to South Africa in 1895 to spend a year sight-seeing and shooting.[20] It was while there that he read in the newspapers of Arthur Donaldson Smith's successful expedition to the lake from Somaliland. Seeing an opportunity to combine both sport and exploration, he decided to organize a trip to Lake Rudolf: "It occurred to me that somebody ought, as soon as possible, to explore the west coast of Lake Rudolf, and that as no Englishman had yet attempted exploration in that part of Africa, it was high time for British travelers to bestir themselves in the matter."[21]

Cavendish, of course, had no idea that his fellow countryman Arthur Neumann had already arrived at the lake. Even if he had been aware of this, it is doubtful that it would have altered his plans since he was intent on exploring the western shore of the lake.

Cavendish returned to London from South Africa in June 1896 and by the end of August was en route to Aden. There, he met Lieutenant H. Andrew, a young military officer on leave, and persuaded him to join the expedition. The two left Berbera on September 5, closely following the route that Smith had taken inland. With them was a headman who had served in Count Samuel Teleki's expedition, as well as a number of men who had traveled with Smith. During the early part of the march, they met Professor Daniel Giraud Elliot, Carl Akeley, and Smith's former companion and taxidermist, Edward Dodson, who were collecting natural history specimens for Chicago's Field Museum. Knowing of Smith's interest in returning to Lake Rudolf, Dodson wrote him about meeting Cavendish and hearing his plans to travel down its western shore. Smith was somewhat disconcerted by this news because he had high hopes of settling the question of the Omo River himself.[22]

After crossing the Webi Shebeli River, Cavendish and Andrew came into a region that had recently been raided by Ethiopian military parties:

> We were in the rear of an Abyssinian war-party, which had left only the day before, after looting the surrounding villages and driving off all the unfortunate natives' livestock. . . . For the next four days, we marched through desolate country that had been devastated immediately before by the Abyssinian hordes. . . . They brought us numbers of people who had been horribly mutilated by the Abyssinians, and again begged us to stay with and protect them.[23]

This graphic description of Ethiopian atrocities confirmed the observations made by Smith two years before. Although Ethiopia was engaged in a courageous battle to preserve its independence against

European colonialism, it was also an expending imperial state. Emperor Menelik II's brutal campaigns to annex the areas south of the Ethiopian highlands are often overshadowed in both European and Ethiopian accounts by his valiant efforts to remain free of foreign domination. At the time, Menelik presented this annexation under the guise of an irredentist movement whose purpose was to unify lands that had allegedly been part of Ethiopia hundreds of years before. To some extent, this doubtful claim obscured Ethiopia's prominent role as a contemporary but indigenous colonial power competing with European rivals for parcels of Africa to which none of them held any legitimate rights. Ethiopian imperial expansion took a very high toll by any objective measure in the form of theft, tribute, slaves, and destruction. The imperial center, which was feudal in character, provided nothing to conquered peoples, whose best hope was to be left alone.[24]

In December, Cavendish and Andrew arrived at the Daua River, where elephants were abundant. From this point on, their expedition focused more on amassing ivory than contributing to science. They killed ten elephants in as many days and continued in this manner for the remainder of the trip. The insatiable demand for ivory in the United States and Europe had created a lucrative market for tusks, which, when sold in large numbers, could easily offset the costs of an expedition.

Cavendish later claimed that he encountered no hostility from the Boran, who he said had attacked Smith because they thought he wanted to rob them of their salt. He painted an idyllic picture of his relations with them: "They treated us in the most friendly manner, pressing every kind of present that they considered valuable upon us, and we had the greatest difficulty in making them accept a return present."[25] Lord Delamere followed Cavendish through the country of the Boran a few months later. On his return to London, he complained to the Foreign Office that Cavendish had treated the Boran very harshly. Such an accusation, based on reports gathered in the field, might at first glance be suspect. However, further documentation of Cavendish's looting and plundering of local peoples was later provided by Herbert Henry Austin.[26]

Cavendish moved on to Lake Stephanie, where he continued shooting elephants. It was while in this area that he was attacked by a wounded elephant and almost lost his life. After recovering from his narrow escape, he headed south for Lake Rudolf, which he reached on March 12, 1897. Sparing in his comments on seeing the lake for the first time, Cavendish merely said, "In our satisfaction at the sight of Lake Rudolf, we immediately determined to take a few days' rest."[27]

Cavendish split his expedition at this point, sending the main body of men down the eastern shore of the lake with Andrew while he himself marched along the western shore. Andrew spent most of his time shooting elephants and amassing more ivory, while Cavendish claimed that he was constantly attacked by the Turkana, with whom he tried to establish friendly relations. Finally, on May 3, he captured a woman and, using her as an interpreter, established contact with the Turkana. Writing of this, he said: "After much palaver and a few presents, we satisfied them that we only wished to pass through the country and had no intention of stealing anything, nor was fighting a pleasure to us."[28]

This account was eventually disputed by a later traveler, Herbert Henry Austin, who noted in his diary that Cavendish had disgracefully looted and plundered the Turkana.[29] Thus, based on the testimony of two eminent British travelers, it appears that Cavendish's behavior toward some local peoples was abusive and exploitative in the extreme.

Cavendish and Andrew finally met on the eastern shore of the lake and proceeded south toward Baringo. En route, they came upon a small soda lake in the Suguta Valley, known today as Lake Logipi.

On July 6, 1897, they arrived at Lake Baringo, where Andrew was charged and seriously injured by a rhinoceros. He required several weeks of convalescence, after which they marched south toward Fort Smith in the newly established Uganda Protectorate. There, they met Frederick Jackson, the deputy commissioner, who was keenly interested in hearing about their journey. He was very impressed by the size of their ivory hoard but somewhat disconcerted by their boasting of the huge profits they would realize when it was sold in Zanzibar. After resting at Fort Smith for a brief time, they marched southeast toward Kibwezi, where von Höhnel had been treated for his wounds in 1893. From there, they moved on to the railhead of the Uganda Railway, then under construction. The entire caravan was placed aboard a special train and carried over the newly laid tracks to Mombasa.[30]

Cavendish spoke before the Royal Geographical Society on January 31, 1898. As Turton has observed, the scientific results of his expedition were negligible, and his account of local populations was "confusing and not very informative."[31] Yet he and Andrew were the first to carry the Union Jack around the lake, and in so doing, they made an important statement on behalf of British colonial interests. This was not lost on Frederick Lugard, for whom Neumann had worked and who was in the audience:

> He is the first Englishman who has traversed that country—his predecessors, one of whom we welcomed here, were Dr. Donaldson Smith and

Signor Bottego, the Italian explorer. They have done excellent work, but they are not of our own nationality. . . . The more British explorers that go into that country, the better, provided they work in the way Mr. Cavendish worked.[32]

Lugard was blinded by his own jingoism and a dedication to promoting Britain's colonial empire. As Turton has succinctly noted, Cavendish's geographic accomplishments were "clearly negligible."[33] True, he had been the first European to completely travel down the western shore of Lake Rudolf. But as Karl W. Butzer found, his map of the Omo delta was by and large adapted from Smith's.[34] Many were receptive to Lugard's comments because they needed to attach more importance to Cavendish's accomplishments than they deserved for the sake of facilitating Britain's claim to the area.

Not everyone at the meeting heaped praise on Cavendish. Dr. R. Bowdler-Sharpe of the British Museum was obviously irritated by the poor quality of the expedition's natural history collection and Cavendish's neglect of it. In polite and diplomatic language, he expressed strong regrets that the British government had left the collecting of natural history specimens to people like Cavendish, whom he regarded as an "incompetent amateur." Bowdler-Sharpe's stinging comments surely must have embarrassed Cavendish:

> Since his return, he has been so busy that he has not been able to give us the time necessary to help in getting his collection in order . . . and only Mr. Cavendish himself can sort out this enormous mass of skulls and skins, and bones and limbs. . . . It is a national disgrace to England that all our great natural history expeditions depend upon private enterprise, and that our Government does absolutely nothing in the matter.[35]

In February 1898, soon after Cavendish's presentation before the Royal Geographical Society, Lugard tried to persuade him to lead another expedition in East Africa. Instead, Cavendish traveled to Patagonia; then, from 1899 to 1902, he served as a captain in the South African Light Horse during the Boer War. He served in the army again in World War I, and in 1932, he became the sixth Baron Waterpark. Four of his five marriages ended in divorce, and none produced a male heir. Thus, when he died on November 26, 1948, the title passed to his nephew.[36]

Only a few months after Cavendish had left Berbera, another British aristocrat set out from the same port for Lake Rudolf. Hugh Cholmondeley, the third Baron Delamere, was born on April 28, 1870, and grew up on his parents' estate, Vale Royal. An indifferent student at Eton, he inherited the title when his father died in 1887.[37] High-strung, slight of build, and endowed with fiery red hair and a temper to match, he quickly abandoned his parents' plans for a university education and began fulfilling his passion for hunting.

On reaching his majority in 1891, Delamere set off on what was to be the first of five hunting trips to Somaliland. Though not physically robust, he possessed remarkable stamina and determination, which enabled him to overcome enormous hardships, injuries, and illness. During his third trip in 1894, he contracted typhoid fever in Aden. After recovering, he crossed over to Zeila on the Somali coast and proceeded into the interior, where he spent three months shooting lions and sticking wart hogs. While there, he was charged by a lion; his ankle was so badly mauled that he was left with a permanent limp.[38]

Delamere arrived back in England in 1894, not only with a limp and peritonitis but also in financial distress. But neither debts nor illness and injury could keep him from his passion for hunting, and thus, within a few months, he was back in Somaliland for the fourth time. On this trip, he hunted lions by using dogs.

On learning that Arthur Donaldson Smith had successfully returned from a trip to Lake Rudolf, Delamere resolved to do the same. In 1895, he began making serious preparations for this journey to the lake. His mother, who had reasons to be concerned for his health and safety, insisted that he take a physician along as a companion. She left the selection to the Rowland Ward Company, the taxidermists and travel book publishers, who eventually chose twenty-six-year-old Dr. A. Eustace Atkinson, just out of medical school. Atkinson was a charming and powerfully built man who got on extremely well with Delamere.

The Lake Rudolf trip was delayed because Delamere first went on a tiger hunt in India and then to Norway to shoot elk. While in Norway with Atkinson, he was thrown from a horse and suffered spinal injuries. Back at Vale Royal, his mother had good reason to dissuade him from yet another hunting expedition to Somaliland. However, stubborn and determined to reach Lake Rudolf, he left with Atkinson for Aden in the summer of 1896.[39]

Delamere was an experienced traveler and quickly able to organize his caravan. It consisted of himself, Atkinson, a taxidermist, a photographer, and an army of porters. In December, they marched out of Berbera with 200 camels loaded with 100 rifles, a Maxim gun, instruments, ammunition, food, provisions, and bales of beads and cloth. They headed southwest, more intent on hunting than on geographic discovery. In March, they arrived at the Italian post of Lugh on the Juba River, where Captain Ugo Ferrandi welcomed them, as he had Cavendish and Andrew four months earlier. Since he was running low on trade goods, Delamere sent Atkinson to Zanzibar aboard an Italian gunboat, with a £1,000 credit to replenish his stock. It was while in

Zanzibar that Atkinson realized the huge profits to be made in ivory. He rejoined Delamere with a determination to kill as many elephants as he could.[40]

In May 1897, Delamere and Atkinson met as planned at the water-holes of El Madow (now Muddo Erri). They then passed along the line of wells that fringe the Mega escarpment, basically following Smith's original route. Then departing from this line of march, they headed south toward Marsabit Mountain, where they arrived in August. The mountain was home to large herds of elephants that had not been extensively hunted before. Delamere prolonged his stay in the Marsabit forest to enable Atkinson to accumulate ivory. He shot twenty-one elephants in as many days.[41]

Thus far, Delamere had avoided Ethiopian raiding parties because the rains had failed and the wells along the raiding routes were dry. Also, the Ethiopians were preoccupied with military defenses elsewhere. Yet Delamere found ample evidence of the destruction caused by Menelik's armies in their attempts to extend his imperial frontiers.

Delamere finally left Marsabit for Laisamis to the south and from there went northwest to Lake Rudolf, which he reached in September 1897. He led his caravan around the southern shore and then a third of the way up the western shore before moving on to Lake Baringo. Atkinson, who had shot his first elephant at Marsabit, continued shooting the animals just as Delamere did. At the end of the expedition, Atkinson's ivory brought in £1,000; Delamere's totaled £14,000, most of it obtained in the Baringo District.

Eventually, they arrived at Ravine, where James Martin, who had traveled with Joseph Thomson, was serving as the collector of the Baringo District for the Uganda Protectorate. Martin had also set up an elaborate, illegal ivory-collecting scheme, through which he eventually pocketed between £12,000 and £15,000. Because of his illicit trafficking in ivory, he was later removed from Baringo and sent to the remote Sese Islands in Lake Victoria.[42]

Delamere was captivated by the cool, lush highlands of East Africa, with their forests and well-watered meadows. They were a dramatic contrast to the hot, dry scrub of Somaliland. He decided to explore them further with a smaller expedition. He sent half his men back toward the coast with Atkinson, while he traveled through the Laikipia Plateau. It was probably during this trip that he first thought of settling in this fertile land. Leaving the plateau, he trekked toward Marsabit, where he camped near a spring that was later known as Delamere's Njoro (Delamere's Water). Atkinson joined him there to shoot more elephants, and eventually, they headed south toward the Guaso Nyiro River. While at this river, they met Dr. Johann Georg

Kolb, the German naturalist who was a good friend of Arthur Neumann. The two caravans had barely parted company when Kolb was charged by a rhinoceros and killed.[43]

Delamere continued his sinuous wanderings to the Mount Kenya region and then headed for Mombasa and the coast. He arrived in England in 1898 after a two-year absence and with so thick a beard that his mother did not at first recognize him.

Neither Delamere nor Atkinson kept a diary of their unusual trip, nor did either of them ever publish an account of it. It was not until some thirty years later that the full story of this expedition was finally recorded by the late Elspeth Huxley, who interviewed Atkinson in Kenya after Delamere had died.[44] The natural history and geographic accomplishments of this expedition were negligible and added little to what was already known about the region.[45]

Delamere married Lady Florence Cole, the daughter of the earl of Enniskillen, in July 1899. That same year, he returned to East Africa with his bride, where he eventually became the leader of the white settlers. As such, he played an important role in the early political life of Kenya Colony. He died of coronary artery disease on November 13, 1931, and was buried on his estate, Soysambu, on a knoll overlooking Lake Elementita.[46]

Atkinson also settled in Kenya, where he at first hunted for ivory. In fact, he not only hunted for ivory himself but also hired both white hunters and Africans to do it for him.[47] In 1902, his relentless pursuit of ivory led to a terrible tragedy and a criminal trial in Nairobi. He and two accomplices, Smith and Vincent, had been hunting elephants in northern Kenya near Mount Kulal. In addition to hunting, they regularly purchased ivory from the Rendille people, whom they supplied with guns and ammunition. On July 30, 1902, word reached Sir Charles Eliot, the governor of the British East Africa Protectorate, that Atkinson and his partners had killed some Rendille in order to obtain their store of ivory.[48] Eliot promptly dispatched H.R. Tate, the district officer at Fort Hall, into the area south of Lake Rudolf to verify this story, which had been brought to light by disgruntled porters.[49]

Tate discovered that Atkinson, Smith, and Vincent had haggled for several days with a Rendille chief over the price of a load of ivory he had accumulated. Exasperated, Atkinson invited the Rendille hunters to congregate around a keg that he said contained their payment in Maria Theresa dollars. The keg was actually filled with gunpowder, but because Atkinson had been sitting on it, the Rendille did not doubt his claim that it contained the silver coins. Pretending he had to relieve himself in the bush, he surreptitiously lit the fuse and walked away. Most of those near the keg were either killed instantly or seriously wounded when it exploded. Atkinson and his accomplices then quickly gathered up the Rendille ivory, which their 200 porters carried down to Nairobi.

When Tate submitted his report in October 1902, it contained sufficient evidence to hang all three men. However, the Africans who had witnessed the killing were fearful of retaliation if they gave testimony in court. Consequently, the prosecution was only able to call three witnesses, one of whom was Arthur Neumann, who was not present when the incident occurred. Much to Eliot's dismay, the all-European jury promptly acquitted Atkinson and recommended that Smith and Vincent be deported.[50] After the trial, Atkinson returned to his farm at Karura, where he gave up both medicine and ivory hunting for farming, sawmilling, and the manufacturing of roof shingles.[51]

With the conclusion of Delamere's trip, travel to Lake Rudolf by sportsmen and ivory hunters temporarily came to an end for several years. Important political interests involving the Upper Nile, the Mahdist state in the Sudan, Ethiopian expansionism, and colonial rivalries forced the British to prevent any but officially sponsored expeditions from reaching the lake. Scientific exploration and sport had dominated European interest in the lake over the previous decade, but such pursuits were now supplanted by the political goals of competing colonial powers.

8

Italians at the Source

Captain Vittorio Bottego (courtesy Manlio Bonati).

A few months before Henry Sheppard Hart Cavendish arrived at Lake Rudolf in March 1897, an Italian expedition had come down from the north, following the course of the Omo River. Headed by Captain Vittorio Bottego and sponsored by the Società Geografica Italiana and the Italian government, the purpose of this expedition was to resolve the riddle of the Omo River and its relationship to Lake Rudolf. However, launched as it was at a time when Italy was attempting to impose a protectorate over an independent Ethiopia, this expedition had political objectives as well.

Eleven years before Bottego arrived at Lake Rudolf, Italy had landed 1,000 troops at Massawa on the Eritrean coast, with the knowledge and consent of Great Britain. Massawa had been occupied since 1865 by the Egyptians. But in 1884, Egypt withdrew its garrison for use in the war with the Mahdi in the Sudan. The vacating of Massawa left it vulnerable to possible seizure by a European power hostile to Great Britain's interests, especially its Indian empire lifeline via the

Suez Canal. Britain supported Italy's action in order to allow an ally to realize its colonial ambitions and to prevent a hostile power such as Germany from occupying this key port.

This occupation was immediately protested by Ethiopian (Abyssinian) Emperor Yohannes IV and by Menelik, the *negus* (king) of Shoa, a vassal state of Ethiopia (Abyssinia). It was not long before the Italians began moving up into the adjacent highlands, on the pretext of protecting the trade route from the coast.[1] However, Yohannes and Menelik were eventually mollified by Count Pietro Antonelli, who had been Italy's diplomat in Ethiopia since 1877. He had also been supplying both Menelik and Yohannes with guns, the former for his efforts to strengthen his bid to succeed Yohannes and the latter for his war with the Mahdists and his efforts to keep vassals like Menelik in line. Among these vassals was Tekle Haymanot, the *negus* of Gojam, who, in 1888, joined with Menelik in a conspiracy to depose Yohannes. As part of this plot, Menelik enlisted Antonelli's help, asking the Italians to create a military diversion for Yohannes on the borders of Eritrea. The succession to the position of emperor was finally settled in Menelik's favor when Yohannes was killed by the Mahdists at the Battle of Metemma on March 11, 1889.[2]

Strengthened by Italian military help, Menelik was able to declare himself *negus negast* (emperor) soon after Yohannes's death. He demanded and received declarations of loyalty from most provincial rulers, except from the *ras* (prince) Mengasha of Tigray, who was the son and aspiring heir of Yohannes IV. In an effort to discourage Mengasha from making good his legitimate claim, Menelik, now Menelik II of Ethiopia, encouraged the Italians to occupy the highlands around Asmara, adjacent to Tigray. He then sent an army into Tigray in order to obtain what proved to be only a temporary submission from Mengasha.[3]

To strengthen his position as self-proclaimed emperor, Menelik signed a treaty with the Italians on May 2, 1889, at Wuchale. Not yet crowned or fully recognized as emperor, he was extremely anxious to make an accommodation with Italy in order to consolidate his power. Also, he needed Italy to control Mengasha of Tigray, who was a continuous and legitimate threat to his claim as emperor.[4]

The Treaty of Wuchale established the colony of Eritrea, and according to Article Seventeen of the Italian version, it also gave Italy authority over Ethiopia's foreign affairs. On October 11, 1889, Italy gave formal notice to Britain, France, Germany, Russia, the United States, and other countries that this article of the treaty placed Ethiopian foreign affairs under its control.[5] This interpretation was soon denounced by Menelik, who claimed that his Amharic version stated that

Ethiopia could use Italy's good offices in the conduct of its foreign affairs but was under no obligation to do so.[6]

Menelik had good reason to be concerned about Italy's interpretation of Article Seventeen because it formed the basis for later Italian attempts to establish a protectorate over Ethiopia. Between 1890 and 1896, Italy progressively attempted to foster its colonial ambitions in the country, with the overt support of Britain. At the same time, Italy provided Menelik with a continuous flow of modern weapons and financial support. These were intended to increase his dependency on Italy for remaining in power, thus clearing the way for the establishment of a protectorate. Unfortunately for their colonial ambitions, Menelik was shrewd in playing the Italians off against France and Russia, which had sizable legations in the country. As a result, political intrigue became intense and complex at Menelik's court during these years. Yet in 1890, he was forced to yield to Italian demands for a new boundary with Eritrea.[7] This gesture of appeasement on his part, however, was to no avail, as Italy continued to make advances into Ethiopian territory.

An inevitable military collision between Italy and Ethiopia was virtually assured when Francesco Crispi became Italy's prime minister on December 15, 1893. Confrontational, megalomaniacal, and determined to absorb Ethiopia into an Italian East African empire, he ordered the occupation of territory beyond the 1890 boundary.[8] As Bottego began preparations for his expedition to Lake Rudolf, Crispi was busy rallying diplomatic support from France and Britain for his military conquest of Ethiopia.

Vittorio Bottego was born in Parma on July 29, 1860. His mother, Maria Acinelli, who was from Parma, and his father, Dr. Agostino Bottego, who was born in Albareto near Parma, provided him with a comfortable childhood. As a teenager, he was expelled from a local school for fighting and sent to the military training center at Modena. Following a year there, he entered the Military Academy at Turin for three years and then went on to the cavalry school at Pinerolo in 1886.[9]

In 1887, Bottego volunteered for the Special Africa Corps that was sent to Massawa in response to the massacre by Ethiopians of a column of Italian troops under Colonel De Cristoforis. Arriving in November, he was placed in charge of a battery of indigenous troops. But he was also a keen naturalist who spent much time and effort collecting birds, reptiles, fish, arthropods, and minerals, which he shipped back to the Parma Museum. His scientific interests in natural history and geographic exploration brought him to the attention of the governor of Eritrea, Major General Antonio Gandolfi, who suggested that he explore the unknown areas of the interior. What appealed to Bottego most was an expedition to the unexplored headwaters of the Juba River. This river was of significant political and economic interest since it flowed out of the Ethiopian highlands and south toward the Somali coast, where Italy was engaged in establishing another colony, Italian Somaliland.[10]

Bottego's expedition to the Juba was temporarily delayed when Crispi's government fell on January 31, 1891, after three and a half years in power. Recalled to Italy, Bottego continued to advocate for his expedition. During this time, he met the Marquis Giacomo Doria, president of the Società Geografica Italiana di Roma. Doria suggested that Bottego first undertake a brief exploratory trip to the country of the Danakil, which he did in May 1891. On his return, he was assigned to the Nineteenth Artillery Regiment in Florence. There, he spent a year studying astronomy, zoology, and photography in preparation for his projected trip to the Juba. Bottego was driven by a genuine desire to advance scientific knowledge, but the Italian government had a very different agenda.

The new prime minister, Antonio Di Rudini, was not a colonialist and indeed was an opponent of Crispi's designs in eastern Africa. However, he was also a pragmatist and realized he could not walk away from Crispi's colonial commitments. On March 24, 1891, he and Lord Dufferin signed a protocol outlining the Italian and British spheres of influence in East Africa. The boundary ran up the midchannel of the Juba River to six degrees north latitude and then turned west along that parallel to thirty-five degrees east longitude, where it turned north along that meridian to the Blue Nile.[11] This protocol, in effect, placed Ethiopia in the Italian sphere of influence without anyone bothering to inform Menelik, who soon found out about it. The most that he could do was to notify the great powers of the boundaries of ancient Ethiopia and declare that he was prepared to defend them.[12]

In order to take possession of the Somali coast, Italy had to form an Italian East Africa Company, notify the sultan of Zanzibar (who had long claimed this area as his own), and establish a presence along the coast and in the interior. Exploration of the source of the Juba was essential to the success of Italy's claim to this part of the Somali coast and to preventing Ethiopian incursions into it. Not surprisingly, Doria, who had been lobbying on Bottego's behalf, was able to tell him in March 1892 that the government would provide financing for the expedition.

In August 1892, Bottego and a wealthy companion, Captain Matteo Grixoni, arrived in Massawa. From there, they went on to Berbera in British Somaliland and then began their trek toward the source of the Juba, with a caravan of 124 men. Grixoni was not up to the rigors of such a difficult trip, and on February 15, 1893, he defected after threatening Bottego with a pistol. Grixoni headed back to the coast with 33 men, while Bottego and the remainder of the expedition moved toward the river's source. Although traveling with greatly reduced resources, Bottego was able to reach the upper Juba and accurately determine its origins. He then headed south for the coast, moving along the river's valley. On July 17, 1893, he arrived at the settlement of Lugh, where two European members of Prince Ruspoli's expedition, Walter Borchardt and Emilio Dal Seno, were being held prisoner. He was able to obtain their release before moving south toward Brava on the coast, where he arrived on September 8 with 46 of his original 124 men. After stopping at Zanzibar, Aden, and Massawa, he reached Naples in November, to be greeted by a hero's welcome. The geographic society awarded him its Grand Gold Medal, and he was invited to give lectures in Rome, Parma, Florence, and Naples.[13]

Although the Italian government took note of Bottego's natural history collection and the 600 photographic plates he had exposed, it attached greater significance to the political outcomes of his expedition. His thirteen-month trek to the headwaters of the Juba had clearly strengthened Italy's hold on the Somali coast and given tangible evidence of an Italian presence along some of the boundaries put forth in the 1891 protocol. However, the declared Italian sphere of influence also extended far to the west to the sources of the Omo River, where Italy had not yet shown its flag.

In December 1893, Crispi once again became prime minister. During 1895, he relentlessly tried to impose protectorate status over Ethiopia. This was an extremely thoughtless decision, given that Ethiopia was a highly hierarchical society with a powerful central government. Its army was also formidable and modern, having been armed by Italy and France with the latest weapons and trained by French and Russian officers. Despite Menelik's best efforts, Crispi not only refused to negotiate but also recklessly pushed matters toward armed conflict by ordering the invasion of Tigray, Ethiopia's northernmost province. Alfred Ilg, Menelik's Swiss counselor, tried to get the French to dissuade Italy from this course of action. However, he was unsuccessful largely because France needed Italy's support for its occupation of Tunisia.[14]

Realizing that he could not count on European diplomatic support in his efforts to get Italy to pull back its troops behind the 1890 border and renounce protectorate claims over Ethiopia, Menelik prepared for war. As he did so, Bottego was in Rome organizing what would prove to be his most important expedition to Africa. Given Italy's political and economic aims in Africa at this time, it would be unreasonable to assume that the purpose of Bottego's expedition was purely scientific and geographic. Though he himself attached far more importance to these objectives, he was not unaware that his efforts would be of great political and economic importance to Italy.

On May 3, 1895, Italy's foreign minister, Baron Alberto Blanc, signed an agreement with the Società Geografica Italiana, in which the parties mutually agreed to support Bottego on an extensive expedition to eastern Africa. The government committed 60,000 lire to the endeavor, King Humbert I provided 40,000 lire, and the society assumed responsibility for organizing the expedition. This agreement was, in effect, a marriage of convenience between the government, which wanted to promote its political and economic interests, and the society, whose objectives were purely scientific.[15] Yet, as was so often the case with European travelers in Africa at this time, sponsorship by a scientific organization conveniently provided cover for political and military activities. As G.N. Sanderson cogently noted, "European military explorers at the head of very small detachments were able . . . to penetrate Africa and to impose their authority with unprecedented ease and rapidity."[16] Thus, Bottego's modest caravan was capable of reaping a rich political and economic harvest for Italy.

The government-society agreement was quite specific about the political and economic objectives of the expedition. Bottego was "to see to the establishment of a commercial station at Lugh" on the Juba River and identify the surrounding areas where Italy could conclude "political and commercial agreements in order to tie the trade of these areas to the Lugh station and to the ports of the Benadir."[17] In effect then, Bottego's principal goal in the Somali hinterland was to extend Italian control over it. But this was not all. He was also instructed to explore the lands along six degrees north latitude and west toward thirty-five degrees east longitude, the lines that constituted the boundaries in the 1891 protocol defining the Italian and British spheres of influence.[18] This westward march would take Bottego to the Omo River and Lake Rudolf and into the eastern watershed of the Nile.

This was not the first time that Italy had attempted to assert its political control along the southern and western boundaries of its self-proclaimed sphere of influence. In 1893, the experienced Italian explorer Prince Eugenio Ruspoli had traveled up the Juba and concluded protectorate treaties at Lugh and Dolo. He then trekked west toward the country of the Boran and the Omo River, with the intent of placing these areas under Italian control. However, these objectives were never achieved, as he was killed by an elephant while hunting near Burgi on December, 4, 1893.[19]

Bottego took three other Italians with him on this expedition: Carlo Citerni, his brother-in-law's nephew, was an infantry lieutenant responsible for photography and the daily diary; Dr. Maurizio Sacchi was placed in charge of the meteorological observations and the natural history collections; and naval lieutenant Lamberto Vannutelli was to record all the geographic data.[20]

Bottego left Naples on July 3, 1895, some three months before Italian troops invaded Tigray. At Massawa, he took on 250 men and a large quantity of ammunition and then headed for Brava on the Somali coast. There, he was joined by Captain Ugo Ferrandi, and together they moved north to Lugh, which they reached on November 18. Although Bottego was trekking through familiar territory that he had covered on his previous trip, it was in an extremely volatile state. The Ethiopians, equipped with modern weapons by the Italians and other Europeans, had been raiding the area with devastating consequences for the local populations. This in turn placed the local Somali clans on an almost constant war footing. Not surprisingly, they launched an offensive attack against Bottego's caravan on November 5, during which Sacchi was speared through the shoulder and a bugler, Adum Jusuf, was wounded through the left hand.[21]

When Bottego reached Lugh, he found it a smoldering and deserted ruin full of decaying corpses. The Ethiopians had raided it a few days before, and the Somalis who had not been killed had fled into the surrounding countryside. Eventually, the population of the settlement returned, and on November 21, Bottego concluded a treaty of protection with the local sultan. He also built a fort and trading post, which now represented a permanent Italian presence in the interior.[22]

Leaving Ferrandi and 45 soldiers in charge, Bottego and 180 men left Lugh on December 27 and marched up the Juba, eventually reaching its junction with the Daua River. From there, he headed west along the route taken by Arthur Donaldson Smith the year before. Toward the end of February, two months out of Lugh, they entered the country of the Boran, where the expedition was warmly received. En route, they had not encountered any of the Ethiopian raiding parties that had previously hindered Smith. They thought themselves lucky in this regard but were unaware that Menelik and his empress, Taytu, had marched out of their capital, Addis Ababa, on October 11, 1895, heading for a confrontation with the Italians in Tigray. By late February 1896, Menelik had assembled a well-equipped and well-trained army of 100,000 men at Adowa and was prepared to do battle with Italy's 17,700 men who had invaded Tigray. Until the very end, Menelik tried to resolve his differences with Italy through diplomatic means. However, Crispi ordered his military commanders not to negotiate until the Ethiopians had been defeated. In taking this unwise course, he in effect threw his flimsy field force, half of which comprised African recruits, against Menelik's superior force, which was well equipped with modern rifles and cannons.

The inevitable battle began at Adowa early on the morning of March 1, and by noon, the Ethiopians had prevailed. Close to 11,000 men from both sides lay dead on the battlefield. The Ethiopians severed the genitals of their dead foes and carried them aloft as trophies. The surviving Italian prisoners were brutally treated, but their Eritrean troops suffered a worse fate at the hands of the Ethiopians, who cut off their right hands and left feet as punishment for their alleged treason.[23]

The Italian defeat at Adowa came as no surprise to those intimately familiar with the size, discipline, training, and equipment of Menelik's army. However, it shocked many Europeans, who had inherently assumed that African soldiers were so inferior to white men that they could easily be defeated, even when present in overwhelming numbers. This view, which was an expression of European racial attitudes of the time, was regularly reinforced by accounts of the white man's easy military victories over hoards of undisciplined and poorly equipped African soldiers. In part, Italy's defeat at Adowa was a shock to Europeans because it sharply challenged their entrenched beliefs in African racial inferiority.

Crispi's government could not survive so crushing a military defeat. On March 7, he submitted his resignation to King Humbert and went into permanent retirement. He was replaced by Antonio Di Rudini, whose principal tasks were to secure the release of some 1,900 prisoners of war and to conclude a permanent peace with Ethiopia.[24] Both proved to be complex undertakings involving third countries, including Russia, the Vatican, and France. Eventually, Italy and Ethiopia signed a peace treaty in Addis Ababa, on October 26, 1896. Under the terms of this treaty, Italy paid Ethiopia an indemnity of ten million lire, which was publicly camouflaged as reimbursement for expenses incurred in housing and feeding prisoners of war. Ethiopia recognized the 1890 Eritrean border, and Italy dropped its protectorate and sphere of influence claims.[25] In renouncing the latter, Italy no longer had any vital interests in the region of the Omo River or in the lands along the eastern Nile watershed. Yet this was precisely the area that Bottego and his caravan were about to explore in the interests of now defunct Italian political ambitions.

When Bottego and his men reached the top of the Amar Mountains on March 23, 1896, they were completely ignorant of Italy's crushing defeat at Adowa. They visited Ruspoli's grave and then moved on to the largest of the Ethiopian Rift Valley lakes, Abaya, which they named after Queen Margherita.[26] After charting this lake, they trekked up higher into the damp and mist-covered highlands in search of the Omo. Like Smith, they soon encountered armed groups of Ethiopians, who harassed them as they struggled over the mountains. Bottego hoped to go as far north as six degrees, forty-four minutes north latitude, the farthest point on the Omo that the French traveler Jules Borelli claimed to have reached several years before. In so doing and in locating the river, he hoped to definitively chart its southward course and relationship to Lake Rudolf. In a certain sense, this effort was misguided since Borelli's geographic data and maps were grossly inaccurate. As it was, the Ethiopians barred his way, and he was forced to retreat south.[27]

On June 29, 1896, the expedition arrived on the banks of the Omo River, nine months after having set out from Brava. Despite continuous harassment from bands of Ethiopian soldiers, they were overjoyed when they finally saw the river. "The 29 of June, a day that will remain memorable for us; we give much thought to solemnizing it on the banks of the majestic river finally conquered. The joy of finding it makes us even forget the nearness of our enemy. . . . Here across from Cullo, residence of *Ras* Wolda Giorgis, our flag now flies on the banks of the mysterious river."[28]

Bottego had not only found the Omo but had also discovered that this stretch of it was in Ethiopian hands. This was of little concern to him, however, since as he saw it, the entire region would soon be part of a vast Italian protectorate stretching from the Red Sea to the Nile watershed. *Ras* Wolda Giorgis was the powerful and trusted prince to whom Menelik had entrusted the conquest and annexation of the lands to the south of Ethiopia. In flying the tricolor in Giorgis's face, Bottego was, in effect, proclaiming Italian supremacy in the region. This challenge did not go without a response from Giorgis, who must have thought Bottego mad, given the defeat at Adowa. His troops pursued the Italians, eventually driving them away from the river and across the highlands until they escaped into the plains near Lake Rudolf.

Bottego was sorely disappointed in being unable to scientifically establish that the Omo before him was the same one seen by Borelli. In point of fact, it was, but that would be proven by another traveler. However, the Italians were soon rewarded by the discovery that the Omo flowed into Lake Rudolf. On August 30, they saw the river coursing into a "silvery expanse of water," as they described the lake.[29] They summed up their feelings when they wrote that "finally, after so much effort and suffering, we had finally achieved the principal objective of our journey."[30]

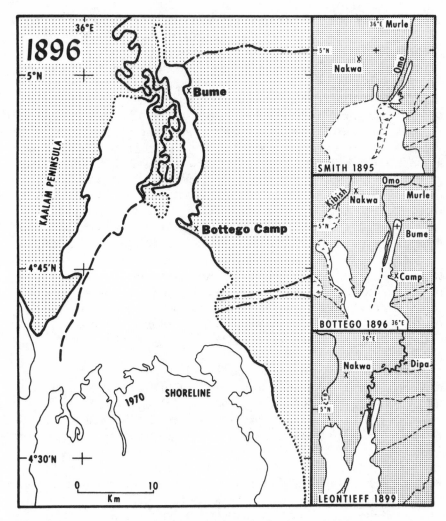

The changing contours of the northern end of Lake Rudolf (courtesy Professor Karl W. Butzer, University of Texas).

But the meticulous Bottego, instead of heading south and for the coast, proceeded to explore areas to the north of the lake. He did this both out of geographic curiosity and in the interest of what he and his companions believed was the dawn of a new era of progress and civilization for the peoples of the region, under the Italian flag. While most of the expedition remained at one of Arthur Donaldson Smith's former campsites, Bottego and Vannutelli explored Lake Stephanie.[31] On their return, Sacchi and Citerni went up the Omo to purchase ivory from the Murle people. They soon returned with fifty-seven tusks, thus bringing their ivory haul up to 4,410 pounds.

It was impossible for them to carry all this ivory, and so Bottego entrusted Sacchi to take it to Lugh with the expedition's reports and natural history specimens. Accompanied by an escort of twenty-three soldiers, Sacchi met up with a Somali caravan at Lake Stephanie and then proceeded to Lake Abaya, where they had left ivory and supplies in the care of local people. However, on February 5, 1897, Sacchi was killed in an attack launched by the Ethiopians, who then stole the ivory. Some of his men and the Somalis carried his papers and scientific specimens on to Lugh.[32] Unaware of Sacchi's death, Bottego crossed the Omo on November 5, 1896, and spent a few weeks exploring the northern two-thirds of Lake Rudolf's western shore. Once this was completed, he trekked north again for the Nile watershed.

Unaware of Italy's defeat at Adowa and its renunciation of any claims to lands along thirty-five degrees east longitude, Bottego was ever faithful to his original charge. He headed north into this area, believing that in so doing, he would place Italian protectorate claims on a firm footing. By the time he arrived in the Ethiopian highlands, Menelik was aware of his presence. The emperor gave orders that no harm should come to the Italians, but he ordered that they be brought to Addis Ababa.[33] Yet Menelik could not fully control the actions of his provincial leaders. In addition, local princes knew from experience that Menelik's public pronouncements were sometimes meant to be disobeyed. Thus, an order to bring the Italians to Addis Ababa alive could, in fact, have meant that Menelik wanted them killed. There is no certain proof of this, and it seems unlikely since Menelik had just concluded a peace treaty with Italy and would not have profited from a gratuitous provocation.

Bottego and his men were initially well received by the Ethiopians, and they requested permission to pass through their territory to Addis Ababa. However, these local officials had to defer to Giote, the *dejaz-mach* (commander) of Lega. Not wishing to wait for a response from him, Bottego set out for Ghidami, where the governor resided. Giote received them warmly, and there was the usual exchange of gifts and letters.[34] However, Bottego was uneasy about these expressions of friendship, especially when some of Giote's soldiers tried to induce expedition members to desert. On March 16, twelve men deserted with two cases of ammunition.

Taking the best possible precautions against a surprise attack, Bottego camped on a small hill, Daga Roba. On the morning of March 17, he awoke to find the camp surrounded by a thousand armed Ethiopian soldiers. Bottego tried to negotiate but to no avail.[35] Being a soldier, his instincts were to fight and not to surrender, even though the odds of victory and escape were slim. Despite Bottego's heroic stand, he and his eighty-eight men were overwhelmed in less than an hour. Shot in the chest and left temple, he fell to the ground, urging his men to continue fighting even as he died. Citerni, who was wounded, and Vannutelli, who escaped injury, were quickly captured and brought to Giote, who had them shackled in irons. The caravan's possessions were soon looted, and most of its scientific collections were destroyed.[36]

Ghidami was 300 miles from Addis Ababa, and as travel over the highlands was slow, it took many weeks before word of the destruction of Bottego's expedition reached Menelik. He quickly ordered Giote to bring the prisoners to Addis Ababa, where they arrived on June 22, 1897, after spending ninety-eight days in chains. There, they were warmly received by Dr. Cesare Nerazzini, the Italian envoy, and by Menelik himself, who met with them twice and who invited them to an official dinner.[37]

Menelik was anxious to put this unfortunate episode behind him. He had already repatriated most of the Italian war prisoners taken at Adowa, was negotiating an important trade treaty with Italy, and was greatly concerned by possible British threats to his independence. He had no desire to antagonize Italy, which was still a major military power and a close ally of Britain.

Bottego quickly became the heroic icon of Italian colonial sacrifices in Africa. His tragic death provided Italy with the kind of martyr that Adowa had not produced. For unlike the Italian soldiers at Adowa, he was perceived as neither aggressor nor combatant but rather as a man of peace trekking through Africa in the interests of science. His legacy to science was substantial, for of all the late-nineteenth-century explorers who visited the Omo, he contributed the most to an understanding of its course, thereby resolving one of the last great geographic puzzles of the African continent. He was the only expedition leader to lose his life in this region at the hands of an African people. Yet he was also the only European traveler to secure an honored place in the oral history of other Africans, who still speak of his passage along the Omo a century ago.[38]

After their return to Italy, Citerni and Vannutelli wrote an excellent account of the expedition, which was published in 1899. The city of Parma erected a memorial statue in Bottego's honor and also created a new home for the Museo Zoologico Eritreo Vittorio Bottego to house his collections.[39]

Citerni continued his interest in eastern Africa and returned there several times. In 1903, he traveled to British Somaliland as an adviser to the Italian government on the uprising led by Muhammed Abdullah Hassan, head of the Salihiya religious brotherhood. In 1910–1911, he served as a member of a joint Italian-Ethiopian mission to delineate the border between Ethiopia and Italian Somaliland. Promoted to colonel, he served in the Balkans in World War I; he died of pneumonia in Rome in 1918 at the age of forty-five.[40]

Vannutelli led two expeditions to Turkey, in 1904 and 1906, on behalf of the Italian geographic society and later served in the Italian-Turkish War of 1911 and in World War I. The last surviving member of the Bottego expedition, he participated in a documentary produced by Italian state television in 1960, commemorating the centennial of the explorer's birth. He died in Rome in 1966 at the age of ninety-five.[41]

Bottego's death and the Battle of Adowa effectively brought to closure Italy's involvement in the lands around Lake Rudolf.[42] Although Bottego had correctly documented that the lake was a closed basin with no connection to the Nile, some still doubted this conclusion. As a result, the struggle for control of the lake after 1897 reflected broader colonial interests, involving the Upper Nile and Ethiopian attempts at territorial annexation.

9

Showdown on the Upper Nile

Commandant Jean-Baptiste Marchand (from Vers le Nil français avec la mission Marchand, *1898).*

Vittorio Bottego's death symbolically ended Italy's colonial aspirations in the Lake Rudolf region and the Omo River basin. However, shortly before his death, three European colonial powers—Belgium, France, and Great Britain—intensified their efforts to seize control of the Upper Nile. They were joined by Ethiopia, which under Menelik had adopted a foreign policy of aggressive colonial annexation of territories beyond the Amhara heartland. These competing interests came into sharp conflict during 1897 and 1898 and led Menelik to establish opportunistic but fragile ententes with the Mahdist state and France.

The years 1897 and 1898 also witnessed heightened interest by Menelik in Lake Rudolf and attempts by him to claim it and the Lower Omo River for Ethiopia. This brought him into direct competition with Britain, whose interest in the lake at this time had more to do with ensuring the integrity of its East Africa Protectorate than in gaining control of the Upper Nile. Yet the lake was not completely di-

vorced from Britain's Upper Nile policy. A British expedition specifi-
cally directed at securing the Nile also staked out a claim to the lake
given its proximity and the possibility that it somehow fed the river.
The likelihood of the lake being a source of the Nile seemed remote to
many, based on Bottego's detailed survey showing that it and the Omo
comprised a closed system. Nonetheless, this view was not yet fully
accepted as the showdown for control of the Nile got under way in
1897.

Of all the colonial powers, Britain had the greatest stake in the fate
of the Upper Nile. This stemmed from its occupation of Egypt fifteen
years before and its vital interests in the Suez Canal. The liberal prime
minister William Gladstone had hesitated to invade Egypt in 1882.
However, his uncompromising conservative successor, Lord Salisbury,
a powerful advocate of British imperialism, had no doubts whatsoever
in 1896 about seizing the entire course of the Nile.[1] In a sense, Salisbury's hand was forced by the clear attempts of Belgium and France to
lay claim to parts of the upper course of the river and its watershed.
But between British-controlled Egypt and the Upper Nile lay the powerful Mahdist state, which had recently entered into an entente with
Ethiopia. The challenge for Britain then was to destroy the Mahdist
state by moving on it from the north and to neutralize European en-
croachments on the upper river by sending an expedition in from the
south. This pincer movement did not go unnoticed by Menelik, who
suspiciously viewed it as a potential threat to his independence.

It had been a hesitant Great Britain that occupied Egypt on September 13, 1882, after defeating a mutinous Egyptian army under Ahmed
Arabi at Tel-el-Kebier. Arabi's anti-Christian and antiforeign nationalist movement had a measure of popular support because its causes ran
deep. The legitimate Egyptian resentment against foreign domination
of national life partially originated in the spendthrift habits of the previous khedive, Ismail, who brought the country to the brink of bank-
ruptcy and French-British financial receivership in 1875. On June 26,
1879, Turkey, still the suzerain power, deposed Ismail at the request of
France and Britain and replaced him with Tewfik. Arabi's popularity
rapidly grew after his revolt, as did anti-European sentiment, forcing
the flight of some 14,000 Europeans by June 1882. On June 11, 1882, a
serious riot broke out in Alexandria, in which several hundred people
were killed, including fifty Europeans.[2]

Gladstone was averse to invading Egypt in order to restore order and
Tewfik. Nonetheless, public pressure in favor of an invasion mounted,
and this, coupled with all of the historic circumstances that tied
Britain to the Nile, forced his hand. In an attempt to avoid a permanent British commitment in Egypt, Gladstone tried to get France and

Italy to join in the invasion. However, these two powers refused, a decision the French later regretted when they saw Britain installed as the master of Egypt.

Sanderson cogently observed that

> The basin of the Upper Nile was rapidly becoming an object of serious political concern to Britain, and within the next three years British concern was greatly increased by the growing interest of other European powers. This rapid and surprising transformation had its roots in the British occupation of Egypt in September, 1882, and in the Mahdist insurrection which, combined with heavy British pressure, forced Egypt into withdrawal from the whole of the Sudan.[3]

Nineteenth-century Egyptian efforts to conquer the Sudan had actually begun in 1820, when the Ottoman viceroy Mohammed Ali sent his son, Ismail, with an army to annex the area. Egyptian efforts at consolidating control in the Sudan went into high gear under Ismail, who became the Ottoman pasha of Egypt in 1863. He employed Europeans such as Sir Samuel Baker, the noted British explorer, who remained in the Sudan from 1869 to 1873 and established the Equatoria Province.[4] Baker was followed in Equatoria by Charles George Gordon, who had won fame for his military and administrative successes in China. Gordon's assignment, like Baker's, was to consolidate Egyptian authority in the region of the great central African lakes and to stamp out the slave trade.

In 1877, Gordon was appointed governor general of the Sudan. From the outset, he was saddled with a corrupt Egyptian bureaucracy and tax policies that were harsh and exploitative. Against this unpopular background, he quickly tried to abolish slavery, on which much of the cash economy functioned. Gordon's crusade obviously alienated the powerful slave-trading interests, and ordinary people saw Egyptian tax policies and the concurrent economic depression as uniquely due to the actions of a Christian foreigner. In 1879, Ismail, the khedive, was no longer able to pay the interest on his loans and was forced by the European powers to resign and go into exile. Gordon also resigned, leaving behind in the Sudan a severe economic depression and a rising tide of discontent.[5]

Two years after Gordon's departure, Mohammed Ahmad ibn Abd Allah, the son of a Dunqulah boat builder, declared himself to be the Mahdi (the divinely guided one). The Mahdi was a magnetic personality who was able to galvanize diverse sectors of discontent with Egyptian rule into a broad-based revolt. This included the powerful slave traders, the holy men (fakirs), who despised the "legalistic and unappealing orthodoxy of the Egyptians," and the Baqqarah cattle nomads of Darfur and Kordofan, "who had had enough of taxes and unbearable Egyptian behavior."[6] As Alan Moorehead noted: "Taxes were gathered with extreme harshness, and every Egyptian official was known to be corrupt. There were about 28,000 of them stationed in the various garrisons throughout the country, and their behavior towards the Sudanese had become unbearable."[7] The Mahdi's military successes were startling. By September 1882, he was in control of all of Kordofan, and on November 5, 1883, he annihilated an Egyptian army at El Obeid under the command of Colonel William Hicks.[8] Gordon was then sent back to the Sudan in order to ensure an orderly evacuation of Khartoum, the capital, but others saw in his return a chance for forcing the British government into action against the Mahdi. But Gladstone was strongly opposed to a military invasion of the Sudan. The Mahdists eventually captured Khartoum, on January 26, 1885, and killed Gordon and most of his men. With the fall of Khartoum, the Mahdi's control of the northern Sudan was virtually complete. However, this stunning victory for the Mahdists was clouded six months later when the Mahdi died at Omdurman, across the river from Khartoum. The Mahdi was succeeded by the khalifa Abdallahi, who possessed sufficient charisma and ability to hold the Mahdist state together for close to thirteen years.

As Sanderson noted, "Since the Mahdist state neither sought nor obtained the recognition of other powers, the Sudan could be plausibly and temptingly regarded as *res nullius*."[9] As such, it was vulnerable to seizure by any European country able to defeat the Mahdist army. Yet of all the colonial powers, Britain alone had the most to lose in the conquest of the Sudan by a European competitor, for the occupation of Egypt had given Britain a new and enviable strategic position in the Mediterranean. However, that position was dependent on the Nile, whose annual flood was vital to Egyptian agriculture. The late Victorians firmly believed that European technology could divert the course of the Nile. Thus, an unfriendly European power in control of the Nile headwaters could hold Egypt for ransom and extract concessions from Britain.

These fears on the part of the British were heightened by an address made before the Egyptian Institute by a French hydrologist, Victor Prompt, in 1893.[10] He speculated on the consequences to Egypt if an unfriendly power were to control the Upper Nile. Prompt was able to convince President Sadi Carnot of France of the feasibility of damming the Nile at Fashoda, just below the point where the Sobat joins it.[11] Carnot, an engineer by training, quickly endorsed Prompt's idea, as did French politicians who saw in this possibility a means of forcing Britain to negotiate a withdrawal from Egypt. Thus, Fashoda, an otherwise insignificant Egyptian post first set up in 1855, became the focus of French military expeditions to the Nile.[12] However, this was not the only reason why the French wanted to get to Fashoda. They also felt justified in extending their central African territories to the left bank of the Nile and having a share in the spoils of the Sudan when the Mahdist state fell apart.

Other nations besides France also posed a significant threat to Britain's interests in the Nile. King Leopold of the Belgians, who ruled the Congo Free State as an independent ruler, was anxious to get a foothold on the river, as were the Italians, who had signed the Treaty of Wuchale on May 2, 1889, with Menelik. By this treaty, the Italians thought they had gained a protectorate over Ethiopia and with it, access to the Nile. However, Menelik later repudiated this treaty, saying that his version did not contain a protectorate provision. Francesco Crispi, Italy's pugnacious and at times reckless prime minister, was bent on seizing a stretch of the Nile. Lord Salisbury was resolutely opposed to this but did not immediately raise the issue with Crispi. In the complex game of quid-pro-quo European politics, he first played the role of intermediary on behalf of Germany in successfully dissuading Italy from entering into an alliance with France. Thus in his debt, Germany was willing to renounce any claims to the Nile basin. This left Salisbury with the delicate problem of dealing with Italian aspirations for a portion of the river. He had to oppose their desires without damaging the Anglo-Italian alliance so crucial to the success of Britain's colonial schemes in Africa. He was finally able to get Italy to renounce any claims to the river in 1891, in return for British recognition of an Italian sphere of influence over Ethiopia and elsewhere in East Africa.[13]

Negotiations with King Leopold II proved much more difficult. However, through much diplomatic effort, Britain was able to get him to sign the Anglo-Congolese Agreement of May 12, 1894. This less-than-perfect treaty gave Leopold an enclave at Lado on the Upper Nile, leased to him for life, and claims to the Bahr el Ghazal, which would later prove nettlesome for the British. Nonetheless, the treaty effectively excluded Belgium from the Nile in the long-term future.[14]

Victor Prompt's 1893 proposal to dam the Nile at Fashoda was quickly followed by a French expedition, whose intent was to reach the Upper Nile. In June 1893, Commandant Parfait-Louis Monteil was appointed officer in charge of posts in the upper Ubangi region of France's central African possessions. He arrived at Loango on the coast on August 24, 1894, intent on moving up to Ubangi and then on to the Nile. However, while still on the coast, he was abruptly reassigned to West Africa to deal with an urgent military threat posed by an imam-warrior, Samory Toure.[15]

Aware of this first French attempt to reach the Nile, Sir Edward Grey, the Foreign Office undersecretary, told the House of Commons on March 28, 1895, that a French move on the Upper Nile would be considered an "unfriendly act." The Grey Declaration was, in effect, a veiled threat of war, but it had no immediate deterrent effect on the French.[16] Salisbury returned to office in 1895, and attempted to secure the Nile by pushing the construction of a railway through East Africa, from Mombasa to Lake Victoria. Although £3 million were eventually appropriated for this project, it would not be completed until 1901, long after colonial control of the Nile had been resolved in Britain's favor.[17]

Meanwhile, a second French expedition was dispatched to central Africa, with orders to seize the Upper Nile. Placed under Commandant Jean-Baptist Marchand, a soldier with much African experience, this expedition arrived at Loango on July 24, 1896. Because of civil disorders in the Congo, which Marchand had to put down, he and his column of 128 Senegalese soldiers and staff of Europeans were unable to leave for the interior until January 1897. They traveled up the Ubangi River and then followed the M'Bomu River, which, thanks to heavy rains, was navigable for a distance of almost 300 miles. Taking the *Faidherbe*, the upper Ubangi post-boat, they sailed as far as the M'Bomu cataracts, beyond which lay 125 miles of unnavigable river. They then dismantled the boat and portered it to the Sueh River, an affluent of the Bar el Ghazal. Marchand finally reached Fashoda on July 10, 1898, where he raised the French tricolor. By the standards of the day, he and his men had accomplished a remarkable feat by traversing 2,000 miles of jungles and swamp in a year and a half.[18] This extraordinary journey across the then largely unexplored center of Africa made Marchand an instant hero in France but the detested symbol of colonial interloping in Great Britain.

Unfortunately for Marchand and France, a combined Anglo-Egyptian force of 25,000 men under General Sir Horatio Kitchener was cautiously but steadily moving up the Nile toward Khartoum. Kitchener's expeditionary force represented a sharp reversal of Britain's previous policy of abandoning the Sudan. The decision to invade and destroy the Mahdist state was primarily driven by the growing risk of a French seizure of the Upper Nile and the serious consequences that action would hold for Britain's vital interests in Egypt. The seriousness of the French threat was all too obvious to Salisbury and his government. Like the British, the French had organized a pincer movement on the river, but this one was coming from the east and west. While Marchand was marching toward the river from the west, a separate expedition was sent out from Ethiopia after complex and frustrating negotiations with Menelik. However, the emperor played a crafty double

game with the French by feigning support for their plans while secretly entering into an entente with the khalifa.

Menelik's victory at Adowa and peace treaty with the Italians
strengthened his standing with European states and enabled him to
foster Ethiopia's role as an indigenous colonial power. At the same
time, he made peaceful overtures to the khalifa, drawing on their mutual interest in deterring European colonialism. His major concern between mid-1896 and 1898 was possible British aggression against
Ethiopia. As Sanderson noted, he feared "that the subjugation of
Ethiopia was the ultimate objective of British action in north-east
Africa." He therefore saw a Mahdist victory against Kitchener on the
Nile as his best insurance for preventing British aggression against
Ethiopia. Yet he had no desire to gratuitously antagonize the British,
with whom he would have to deal in the event of their victory over
the khalifa. As a consequence, his entente with the Mahdist state consisted of little more than a declaration of good intentions and some
vague expressions about fostering trade; it was devoid of any commitments that would provoke the British.[19]

For their part, the British were extremely concerned about Menelik's suspicions of them and about French and Russian influence at his
court. They were also greatly troubled over his friendly contacts with
the khalifa and the possibility that he might supply the Mahdists with
arms and ammunition for the upcoming military confrontation on the
Nile. Salisbury recognized the immediacy of the need to neutralize
Menelik as a possible ally or arms supplier to the khalifa. For this reason and to counter French influence at Menelik's court, he sent James
Rennell Rodd to Addis Ababa in April 1897. Rodd negotiated a secret
treaty with Menelik, in which the latter agreed not to ship arms to the
Mahdists. In return, Ethiopia was granted duty-free privileges at the
British Somaliland port of Zeila and recognition of its claim to the
vast Somali-populated Ogaden region, based on the principle of effective occupation. That the British gave Menelik such favorable territorial and economic concessions in this treaty demonstrated the strength
of their desire to keep him out of political and military events along
the Nile. Despite Rodd's strong assurances that the British had no desire to subjugate Ethiopia, Menelik remained suspicious of them, sustained in his view by Russian and French representatives at his court.[20]

When Rodd signed the Anglo-Ethiopian Treaty on May 14, 1897, he
had no idea that Menelik had concluded the Convention pour le Nil
Blanc (the White Nile Treaty) with the French barely two months before. In this treaty, Menelik agreed to provide assistance to any French
expedition approaching the Nile from the East, and France recognized
Ethiopian sovereignty on the right bank of the river. Menelik was

scarcely in a position to deny a French request of this kind because France had provided significant military and diplomatic support during Ethiopia's recent war with Italy. He had no interest in pressing Ethiopian claims along the eastern bank of the Nile, as this would have unnecessarily provoked both Britain and the Mahdist state. Yet Menelik needed to maintain close relations with the French as a foil against possible British aggression.[21]

As part of its effort to secure the Upper Nile, the French government sent the governor of its Somali coast colony, Léonce Lagarde, to Addis Ababa in 1897. He successfully negotiated the Convention pour le Nil Blanc, which he and Menelik signed on March 20. Despite the terms of the treaty, Menelik had absolutely no intentions of fostering French advances on the Nile. He knew that the French could offer him little in the way of military protection in the event that their activities on the Nile resulted in conflict with the Mahdist state. Therefore, to ensure Ethiopia's independence and to promote its own colonial interests, he played a shrewd political game of secretly cooperating with all sides while publicly committing to none. Thus, he almost simultaneously signed secret treaties with France and Britain while entering into an entente with the khalifa.[22]

The French sent out two expeditions from Addis Ababa in 1897 for the purpose of joining up with Marchand on the Nile. The first of these was placed under the command of Captain Clochette, whose death in Ethiopia on August 27 would lead to the expedition's collapse.[23] A second expedition was later organized by Christian de Bonchamps and Gabriel de Bonvalot, under the auspices of the French Ministry of Public Instruction. This sponsorship was intended to disguise the expedition as a scientific one organized for the purpose of ethnographic and natural history research. In order to absolutely ensure the camouflage of this political mission, an entomologist, Charles Michel, a mining engineer, Léon Bartholin, and a landscape painter, Maurice Potter, were assigned to it.[24] Unfortunately for France, the expedition was plagued from the start by less-than-enthusiastic support from Lagarde, who was resentful because he had no direct control over it, and by logistical support problems exacerbated by sabotage on the part of the Ethiopians, who feigned support for the enterprise. Menelik had no wish to see the mission succeed, for if it did, it held the potential for dragging him into an unwanted conflict with the Mahdist state, his bulwark against possible British aggression.

Lagarde was an extremely vain man, who was furious that Paris had given him no authority over the Bonchamps-Bonvalot mission. He expressed his anger over this decision by leaving Addis Ababa before Bonvalot arrived. However, on his way down to the coast, Lagarde met

Bonvalot and quickly got into a heated argument with him. Bonvalot knew that the mission stood little chance of success without Lagarde's diplomatic support. Still, Bonvalot traveled on to Addis Ababa, where he insightfully concluded from his encounters with Menelik that the Ethiopians were less than enthusiastic about supporting the expedition. He therefore returned to France, leaving Bonchamps in charge.[25]

Bonchamps was optimistic that the expedition could succeed. He eventually marched out of Addis Ababa with guides and a letter of introduction to the *dejazmach* (commander) Tessama, governor of the western province of Gore. Menelik's instructions to Tessama were to both cooperate and obstruct. This was expressed through delayed supplies, incompetent guides, indifferent local officials, and porters who disappeared.

After four months in the field, Bonchamps returned to Addis Ababa to solicit Menelik's intervention. He was joined by Lagarde, who was ordered by Paris to speak with the emperor. Menelik was sympathetic and understanding and profusely apologetic for the incompetence and negligence of his provincial officials.[26]

Bonchamps again marched out of Addis Ababa, slightly more hopeful and with instructions from Lagarde to plant the French tricolor on the western bank of the Nile and the Ethiopian flag on the eastern. He was also told to avoid all contact with the Mahdists. While Tessama became more cooperative, the expedition was instructed by Menelik to march along the left (south) bank of the Sobat River, which was farthest removed from Fashoda and covered by swamps and traversed by several tributaries. This decision proved fatal to the small, poorly equipped expedition, as Menelik hoped it would. Bonchamps and his men only managed to get to the confluence of the Baro and Adjouba Rivers, which mark the beginning of the Sobat, in December 1897. They were some 90 miles from Fashoda, but, afflicted by disease, hunger, and the seasonal flooding of the area, they had to turn back on January 1, 1898, again as Menelik had hoped they would.[27]

In March 1898, Tessama was instructed by Menelik to lead a reconnaissance party down the Sobat because he was worried about possible British moves into the area from the south. The region was reputed to hold rich gold deposits, and for this reason, Menelik wanted to lay claim to it. While Bonchamps returned to Addis Ababa seeking instructions, a boat that had never materialized, and supplies, two members of his expedition, M. Faivre and Maurice Potter, went along as Tessama's guests.

Faivre and Potter persistently urged Tessama to move on to the Nile instead of following a more southerly route toward the region of Lake Rudolf.[28] They were finally successful in inducing him to allow a flying column of armed men to go down the Sobat River to the Nile. While Tessama remained behind with the bulk of his army, one of his lieutenants led 800 men down the Sobat. Faivre and Potter accompanied the group, as did Russian Colonel Artamanoff and several Cossacks. They left Tessama on May 18, 1898, and reached the Nile on June 22, seventeen days before Marchand passed the same point on his way to Fashoda. Colonel Artamanoff and two of his Cossacks, in a display of Franco-Russian solidarity, swam to the left bank of the Nile and planted the French tricolor (there were no available boats). Meanwhile, the Ethiopians hoisted their flag on the right bank. France's attempt to lay claim to the Upper Nile now consisted of a makeshift tricolor fluttering above a lonely stretch of the river. Marchand would reinforce this claim a short time later, installing himself at Fashoda, some 60 miles downstream from the Sobat-Nile confluence.[29]

The highland Ethiopians refused to remain in these swampy lowlands. Out of fear of encountering the Mahdists and despite repeated pleas by Faivre and Potter, they left the flags and headed toward Ethiopia. The small expedition of Ethiopians, Frenchmen, and Russians rejoined Tessama on August 5, 1898, almost three months after having left him.[30]

In terms of scientific accomplishments, the Bonchamps expedition was a great success. It mapped a large, unexplored area to the west of Ethiopia, collected many natural history specimens, and produced detailed descriptions of regions largely unknown to outsiders.[31] Yet it had fallen far short of its political aim, which was to establish a meaningful French presence on the river. Menelik was not unhappy about this turn of events since he had demonstrated sufficient goodwill toward the French to reap political benefits if they were successful. At the same time, he had avoided any unpleasant entanglements along the Nile that might have jeopardized Ethiopia in the event of either a British or Mahdist victory in the Sudan.

Of far greater concern to Menelik than French attempts to claim the Upper Nile was the possibility of a British move from the south. This posed an obvious threat to his designs on the lands around Lake Rudolf. In 1897 and early 1898, he was fully prepared to meet the British with force in this area so as to preserve Ethiopia's independence and imperial expansion.[32] His willingness to militarily confront the British was in part the result of his having successfully defeated the Italians; it also stemmed from the mistaken belief that Britain had in effect launched a converging invasion intent on destroying both the Mahdist state and Ethiopia. Menelik eventually changed his foreign policy following Kitchener's dramatic victory over the Mahdist state. Eschewing military confrontation, he then opted for a diplomacy based on the principle of effective occupation, in which he believed he held the upper hand.

Increasingly concerned by reports of Marchand's expedition to the Nile, Lord Salisbury resolved to send an expedition from Uganda to the Upper Nile.[33] The man chosen to lead it was Major James Ronald Macdonald of the Royal Engineers. Macdonald, who was thirty-five years old at the time, had already had a brilliant military career in India and much African experience. He had served as the chief engineer for the preliminary survey for the Uganda Railway in 1891–1892 and as acting commissioner for the Uganda Protectorate in 1893.[34]

Macdonald was asked to submit to Lord Salisbury plans for an expedition to the Upper Nile in April 1897. Salisbury kept both the treasury and most of the cabinet in the dark about the expedition's true purpose. On the surface, the expedition was to explore the sources of the Juba River. In reality, Macdonald was instructed to move up the eastern bank of the Nile to just below the tenth parallel, which would take him into the area of Fashoda. Sanderson summed up the expedition's purpose by quoting Lord Salisbury's note to Macdonald: "Secure the allegiance of the chiefs by presents and the grant of the British flag . . . secure the territories in question against other powers." In other words, Macdonald was to "stake claims by means of treaties."[35]

Macdonald's second in command was Herbert Henry Austin, a thirty-year-old captain who had served with him in India and on the Uganda Railway survey. Austin was born in Burma on June 1, 1868, the second son of Colonel Edmund Austin of the Indian army. He was educated at Clifton College and then at the Royal Military Academy at Woolwich, where he was commissioned as a second lieutenant in the Royal Engineers on February 2, 1887. He then went on to the School of Military Engineering at Chatham, Kent, where he spent two years. He first met Macdonald on the northwest frontier of India in 1889 and worked under him on a number of railway surveys. Austin got on extremely well with Macdonald, who, in 1891, offered him a place on the Uganda Railway survey. Once this work was completed, Austin returned to India to serve as a district engineer. During that time, he participated in the Waziristan Expedition of 1894–1895 and the Tochi Valley Expedition of 1895–1896.[36]

Once assigned to lead a column up the Nile from Uganda, Macdonald immediately asked Austin to join him. The public was told that the Juba Expedition was to explore the sources of the Juba River, which in reality are several hundred miles from the Nile. Yet those in the know were well aware that these sources had already been previously charted by Vittorio Bottego in 1893. The true purpose of the mission was to head off Marchand and his men. Austin later summarized this in his unpublished memoirs: "The Macdonald Expedition, consisting of nine British officers, arrived at Mombasa from England early in July, 1897, with sealed orders to forestall, if possible, the French expedition known to be bound for Fashoda from the west under Marchand."[37] The reason for the secrecy about the true objective of the expedition was to prevent both the French and the Mahdists from learning about it.

Macdonald's party consisted of 9 British officers, 500 porters, 30 Sikh sepoys, 300 pack animals, and 25 two-wheeled Indian bullock carts. The group left the railhead on July 22, which then was but a short distance inland, and moved west toward Uganda with 2,000 loads of supplies.[38] Their arrival in Uganda in September coincided with a revolt by Sudanese soldiers who had been settled there by Frederick Lugard in 1891. The soldiers' principal grievance was poor pay, but the rumor that Macdonald was going to force them to fight their Moslem brothers to the north also incited them to rebel. Before long, other discontented elements in Uganda joined them. As a result, Macdonald had to delay the start of his mission to the Nile by several months. It was not until April 1898, after he had put down the rebellion, that he was able to head for the Upper Nile.[39]

Menelik had reason to be concerned about a British expedition to the Juba headwaters since he considered them to be in Ethiopian territory. With Kitchener moving up the Nile and Macdonald coming from the south, it seemed plausible to him that a pincer movement against Ethiopia was under way. The British, in fact, had no intentions of annexing Ethiopia, but this was scarcely credible to Menelik in 1898. In order to check Macdonald's possible advance into Ethiopian-claimed territory, he had sent out *Dejazmach* Tessama in March 1898, moving toward the Sobat-Nile confluence. This was the journey that enabled the Frenchmen Faivre and Potter, who were part of the Bonchamps mission, to plant the French flag on the Nile. Menelik heightened his rhetoric in Addis Ababa in an attempt to keep the British out of Ethiopian-claimed territory. Regarding Macdonald, he remarked, "I'll send out *Ras* [prince] Wolda Giorgis with 20,000 men—they can check his passport."[40]

Salisbury was extremely concerned about avoiding unnecessary provocations with the Ethiopians at the crucial time when Kitchener was rapidly moving toward the heart of the Mahdist state. Such provocations held the potential for jeopardizing the entire military campaign and Britain's hopes of securing the Upper Nile. Macdonald had received clear instructions to avoid contacts with the Ethiopians that could be misconstrued as hostile. Thus, Salisbury was "dismayed and intensely irritated" when Macdonald decided to split his force in two and send Austin up to Lake Rudolf while he made for Fashoda. A British advance on Lake Rudolf not only belied repeated diplomatic assurances to Menelik but also "might have brought about the dreaded clash with the Ethiopians at the very climax of the Nile campaign."[41]

Macdonald sent Austin and surgeon-captain J.D. Ferguson up to Lake Rudolf with a relatively small force of 180 men. They left their base at Save at Mount Elgon on August 1, 1898, and trekked toward the lake. The lake was only 140 miles away, but Austin wisely decided to move northward up the bed of the Turkwell River until it turned east, and from that point, he marched northeast across the dry scrub. This brought him and his men within sight of the lake on August 31, at a point two-thirds up the western shore.[42] On seeing the lake, Austin wrote: "Early on August 31, through a gap in the hills, we saw the waters of the lake shimmering in the morning sunlight . . . there before us lay this grand expanse of water, with no visible horizon north, south, or east."[43] That night, as he sat outside his tent, Austin reflected on being on the shores of the lake: "It was a full moon that night, and . . . looking across the lake, one felt at peace with all mankind. . . . I had often longed to see Lake Rudolf, and my desire was now fulfilled."[44]

Austin and his men rapidly made for the Omo delta, which they reached on September 12. As they did so, they signed treaties with local chiefs and planted Union Jacks, activities that were purposely deleted from Austin and Macdonald's accounts of the expedition.[45] Austin soon discovered, to his dismay, that the Ethiopians had recently invaded the Omo delta with a large military force. What he could not have known was that the head of this Ethiopian expedition, *Ras* Wolda Giorgis, had also planted Ethiopian flags on the northern shore of Lake Rudolf on April 7. Giorgis and his men had not troubled to sign treaties with local chiefs; rather, according to Ethiopian practice, they had decimated the countryside by foraging for food and booty. Austin vividly described what he found north of the lake:

> The Abyssinians had done their work thoroughly. They had scoured both banks of the river, carried away all the cattle, goats, and sheep, cut down the crops, burnt the granaries . . . and taken away captive men, women, and children. The state of those who had escaped was pitiful in the extreme, as, in addition to their starving condition, they were also visited by an outbreak of smallpox. No food . . . was procurable here, and as Kerre and the more northerly districts had also been laid waste, it was impossible to proceed further.[46]

It was just as well that Austin did not proceed further since Giorgis had left behind a series of forts constructed by Lieutenant Alexander

Xavieryerich Bulatovich, a Russian officer in the Imperial Guard who had accompanied this Ethiopian military invasion.[47] Austin's 180 men were no match for Giorgis's army of some 5,000 that had so recently decimated this region.

On September 17, Austin started down the western shore of the lake to the Turkwell River and from there returned to his base at Save, arriving on November 12, 1898, after an absence of some three and a half months.[48] Macdonald's column only got as far north as Torit, in what is now the southern Sudan, but in November it was forced to turn back because of insufficient provisions.

In terms of scientific accomplishments, Austin's expedition produced a detailed mapping of the western and northern shores of Lake Rudolf as well as a valuable survey of the Turkwell River and the lands it drained. This expedition also imparted two British names to geographic features of the lake. Austin named the large gulf at the lake's northwest corner Sanderson's Gulf, in honor of Sir Thomas Sanderson, the permanent undersecretary at the Foreign Office, who had been largely responsible for helping Salisbury organize the Macdonald Expedition. He also attached Ferguson's name to a small gulf on the western shore, where, on their return, they had to battle the Turkana who were intent on stealing their transport animals and supplies.

Austin signed some thirteen treaties on his trip to Lake Rudolf, although he made no mention of them in either his book or his article describing the expedition. A.T. Matson cogently observed in the introduction to the 1973 reprint of Austin's book, "There seems little doubt that Austin knew the government would not welcome a discussion of them [the treaties] in his book."[49] Any mention of the treaties arranged by either Macdonald or Austin was censored out of their reports and writings. Sanderson, in fact, refused Macdonald permission to publish a true account of the expedition and its purposes, called *Uganda in Revolt*, and Austin's book had to pass through careful government scrutiny and censorship before he was able to sign a contract with his publisher on May 22, 1902.[50]

Although Salisbury was a dedicated imperialist, he was anxious about "increasing Parliamentary and press criticism of his East African policies, which were providing the opponents of further costly and provocative colonial commitments with grounds for attacking the government."[51] Austin's book was finally published in 1903, the delay being due both to his subsequent preoccupation with a second expedition to Lake Rudolf (undertaken in 1899–1900, when he reached the lake coming down from Omdurman in the Sudan) and to his having to deal with British government censorship efforts. Ironically, his book describing the second successful expedition to Lake Rudolf appeared in 1902, a year before the one describing the first.[52]

In addition to his article in the *Geographical Journal*, Macdonald wrote four official reports on the Juba Expedition, which contained no material that would have led to either parliamentary or press criticism of Salisbury's policies in Africa. These policies had already come under attack as excessively costly and unnecessarily provocative at a time when the government was already overstretched in its commitments in South Africa and elsewhere.[53] Salisbury and Sanderson were concerned not only about criticism of their colonial policies but also about Macdonald's negative comments regarding inept British officials in Uganda. As a result, they effectively banned Macdonald's manuscript and heavily censored his other writings. Aware of the fate of Macdonald's manuscript, Austin probably crafted his so as to avoid mention of facts that would cause the government to respond in a similar fashion. As a result, his book, *With Macdonald in Uganda*, is very much a personal narrative.[54]

Austin's trip to Lake Rudolf was one of the most important accomplishments of the Macdonald Expedition. Salisbury and Sanderson were clearly angry about Austin's thirteen treaties because, in 1898, they seemed to them irrelevant to their primary objective, which was to secure the Upper Nile. Yet in later years, these treaties gave Britain the upper hand in its negotiations with Ethiopia over the lake, for it was largely on the basis of Austin's expedition that Britain was able to lay claim to Lake Rudolf.

Macdonald was unsuccessful in heading off Marchand at Fashoda. By the time Marchand arrived there on July 10, 1898, Macdonald had barely started for the southern Sudan. Yet Macdonald played a vital role in making Uganda more secure for Britain and thereby strengthening its control over the great central African lakes.

On September 2, 1898, Kitchener made a triumphal entry into Omdurman, where the Mahdist army under the khalifa had made a last desperate stand. Although preoccupied with defending Omdurman, the khalifa had nonetheless dispatched two steamers up the river to route the French from Fashoda. Both had engaged the French but were forced to withdraw after suffering serious damage.[55] The captain of one of these steamers, the *Tawfigia*, arrived back at Omdurman much relieved that Kitchener was now in charge since he would otherwise have been severely punished by the khalifa for his military failure. The captain told Kitchener of his military engagement with unidentified white men at Fashoda. Kitchener had no doubts about who they were and immediately went up the Nile in force on the steamer *Dal*, escorted by four gunboats.[56]

Anchoring 12 miles downstream from Fashoda, Kitchener sent Marchand a letter informing him of the khalifa's defeat. Marchand promptly replied, not only congratulating Kitchener on his victory but also informing him that he had signed a treaty on September 3 with the local chiefs, placing the entire area under French protection. Kitchener then sailed closer to Fashoda and invited Marchand aboard the *Dal*. The two men exchanged gifts and fortunately took an instant liking to one another. Kitchener's fluency in French was clearly an important asset in the delicate negotiations that followed.

After some initial confrontational verbal exchanges, both Marchand and Kitchener realized that this potentially volatile situation could not be resolved on the Nile but only by their respective governments. Marchand left Fashoda for Cairo on October 24, 1898, so that he could directly communicate with Paris. Kitchener traveled to London later that month for consultations, where he received a hero's welcome.[57]

Riding on the wave of popular good feelings over the stunning victory at Omdurman, the British press became hysterical about the French presence on the Upper Nile. The French press was no less restrained, claiming that the British had abandoned the Sudan in 1885 and that now the area around Fashoda and the Upper Nile belonged to France by right of first occupation. The political polemics reached a fever pitch during the first two weeks of October 1898, and for a time, it seemed that war would break out between Britain and France.

Lord Salisbury viewed the French occupation as illegal and ineffective and put forth the right of conquest argument. He reasoned that Britain had conquered the Mahdist state and captured the capital, Omdurman, and thus, by right, the entire country was British.[58] The French did not see matters that way at all. They claimed that Britain had abandoned the area for many years, and according to the rules of colonial acquisition, the French could now stand on the right of first occupation. There were obviously merits to both arguments, and Africans living in the affected areas today would cogently reason that neither the British nor the French had any right being there at all.

British public opinion was unanimous that the French must withdraw. French public opinion, on the other hand, was deeply divided. In addition, the French army was, at the time, seriously split over the Dreyfus Affair, and the navy was in deplorable condition.[59] The French government gradually came to the conclusion that it would be better to put pride aside and come to an honorable compromise.

On December 11, 1898, Marchand, who had returned to Fashoda, lowered the French tricolor according to instructions he had received from Paris.[60] As British and French negotiators worked toward an agreement, Marchand firmly stated that he did not wish to return via the Nile to Cairo through British territory, for in so doing, he would appear to be little more than a British prisoner. Instead, he proposed returning via the Baro and Sobat Rivers and through Ethiopia. Lagarde, who was still in Addis Ababa as French ambassador, asked for and obtained Menelik's permission, and, on December 13, 1898, Marchand and his men started on the long journey to Addis Ababa, where they arrived on March 8, 1899. After a month in the Ethiopian capital, Marchand left for Djibouti on the coast, arriving there on May 16. Two weeks later, he and his men disembarked at Toulon and were received in Paris as heroes.[61] Although Marchand's mission to the Nile represented a French political failure, it nonetheless was one of the most remarkable and courageous journeys ever undertaken across Africa.

The French and British finally worked out a settlement, which became an additional declaration to the West African Convention signed on March 21, 1899. According to the terms of this treaty, France abandoned the Nile Valley but received territorial concessions in regions to the west of the river.[62] The Nile was now British from its source all the way to the Mediterranean.

Thomas Wakefield, a Methodist missionary who published one of the earliest descriptions of Lake Rudolf in 1870 (from Thomas Wakenfield, *1904).*

James Martin (Antonio Martini), a Maltese sail maker who assisted Joseph Thomson on his expedition across Maasai country (from Through Masai Land, *1885).*

Lieutenant Ludwig Ritter von Höhnel, who provided the scientific and cartographic expertise for the expeditions of Count Samuel Teleki and William Astor Chanler (courtesy John Winthrop Aldrich).

Jumbe Kimemeta (center), a leading ivory trader who accompanied both Joseph Thomson and Count Samuel Teleki on their expeditions (courtesy Lajos Erdélyi).

Illustration dramatizing Count Samuel Teleki's armed conflicts with the Kikuyu (from Discovery of Lakes Rudolf and Stefanie, *1894).*

Count Samuel Teleki (center) and Jumbe Kimemeta (seated left) with buffalo head trophy, Lake Baringo, January 1888 (courtesy Lajos Erdélyi).

Maasai moran *(warrior) of the 1880s (from* Discovery of Lakes Rudolf and Stefanie, *1894).*

Count Samuel Teleki with two elephants shot south of Lake Baringo, December 16, 1887 (from Discovery of Lakes Rudolf and Stefanie, *1894).*

Turkana man of the 1880s with a knobkerrie, wrist knife, and mud chignon (from Discovery of Lakes Rudolf and Stefanie, *1894).*

Qualla Idris, who served as the head of the Somali guard in Count Samuel Teleki's expedition and as Arthur Donaldson Smith's headman (from Discovery of Lakes Rudolf and Stefanie, *1894).*

George E. Galvin in 1901
(courtesy George E. Galvin Jr.).

One of William Astor Chanler's camps, 1892. Seated, left to right: Chanler,
Ludwig von Höhnel, and George E. Galvin. Standing behind von Höhnel in a
striped shirt is Sururu, Chanler's tent servant (courtesy John Winthrop
Aldrich).

Romanticized illustration depicting Arthur Donaldson Smith and his men fighting off the Boran, March 1895 (from Through Unknown African Countries, *1897).*

Arthur Donaldson Smith with a lion shot at Milmil in Somaliland, July 1894 (from Through Unknown African Countries, *1897).*

Arthur Donaldson Smith being charged by an elephant at Marsabit,
September 1895 (from Through Unknown African Countries, *1897).*

Carlo Citerni, an infantry lieutenant who kept a daily diary of Vittorio Bottego's expedition to Lake Rudolf (courtesy Manlio Bonati).

Maurizio Sacchi was responsible for the natural history specimens and meteorological observations on Vittorio Bottego's expedition (courtesy Manlio Bonati).

Lamberto Vannutelli served as the geographer for Vittorio Bottego's expedition (courtesy Manlio Bonati).

Major James Ronald Macdonald, who headed the Juba Expedition of 1897–1898 (from With Macdonald in Uganda, *1903).*

*Mabruk Effendi Faki (center) and the survivors of the Tenth
Sudanese Battalion who accompanied Herbert Henry Austin to
Lake Rudolf in 1900–1901 (from* Among Swamps and Giants in
Equatorial Africa, *1902).*

*Count Nicholas Leontiev (far right) standing next to Léonce Lagarde,
Ethiopia, 1897 (from* Une visite à l'Empereur Ménélick, *1898).*

Sir Lloyd William Mathews, the prime minister of Zanzibar, in full colonial dress uniform (from An Apostle of Empire, *1936).*

A portion of the east window in St. Mary's Church, Westham, Sussex, erected in memory of Montagu Sinclair Wellby by his parents (courtesy Nancy Marples).

10

An Orthodox Partnership

Captain Alexander Xavieryevich Bulatovich, circa 1899 (courtesy Prince and Princess André Orbeliani).

European colonial expansion in East Africa coincided with the reemergence of Ethiopia as a powerful indigenous state. State formation in Ethiopia at this time involved the centralization of power by a well-organized and hierarchical military society, territorial expansion into lands beyond the Amhara highlands, and both confrontation and cooperation with European colonial interests.[1] During this process, the Ethiopian Orthodox Church was a powerful cultural and religious force in unifying the nation. It maintained close formal ties with the Coptic Church of Alexandria and, through it, with the rest of Orthodox Christianity.

In April 1891, Menelik served the European powers with notice that Ethiopia's legitimate boundaries extended to Khartoum in the west and well to the south of Lake Rudolf.[2] He framed this claim within the context of an irredentist movement whose aim was to reunite all the lands that allegedly had once been part of previous Ethiopian states. This late-nineteenth-century Ethiopian irredentism eventually assumed the form of military conquest as well as a Christianizing mission no less zealous than that of European missionaries. The territorial claims made by Menelik were exaggerated, as he well knew. However, they gave him a powerful bargaining position from which to negotiate with his European colonial rivals.[3]

Under Menelik, Ethiopia evolved into an imperial state that drew much of its wealth and power from the exploitation of conquered peoples. The agents of this policy were a warrior class of tens of thousands of well-armed men who had been trained in the use of European-made weapons. When these warriors invaded the lands around Lake Rudolf, their objective was nothing less than the appropriation of all portable resources and the destruction of whatever they could not carry away.[4] Their aim was not so much the occupation of land as its immediate exploitation and the future extraction of tribute "to enhance the life of the leisure class."[5]

Late-nineteenth-century European travelers to Lake Rudolf gave numerous accurate accounts of the destructive effects of Menelik's armies on local peoples. As Richard Pankhurst noted, "The fact that the soldiers of former times were unpaid meant that they were obliged to loot whatever they required from the countries through which they passed."[6] The looting and predatory extraction of tribute did not end, however, once areas were brought under Ethiopian colonial control. Many of the administrators placed in charge of these areas were warriors themselves who regularly launched plundering campaigns in order to acquire additional wealth and consumable products.[7] These subsequent campaigns and those launched earlier to seize the lands around Lake Rudolf and elsewhere often resulted in famines and epidemics that further decimated local populations.[8]

The Ethiopians treated locally conquered peoples no better and often much worse than did their European colonial counterparts. As a twentieth-century Ethiopian historian observed: "Paternalistic and arrogant, Abyssinians looked upon and treated the indigenous people as backward, heathen, filthy, deceitful, lazy, and even stupid—stereotypes that European colonialists commonly ascribed to their African subjects. Both literally and symbolically, southerners became the object of scorn and ridicule."[9]

Ethiopian conquest led to the creation of black-upon-black colonialism. Though fully recognizing this, some Ethiopian historians have put forth a well-reasoned case that this colonialism was devoid of racism. They present convincing evidence that conquered peoples could cross the culture-class divide into the Ethiopian mainstream by adopting Amharic customs and Orthodox Christianity. This sharply distinguished Ethiopian colonialism from its European analog, in which the adoption of Western cultural and religious identities did not lead to full and equal acceptance by the white ruling class.[10] However, those who refused to surrender their ethnic and cultural affinities remained the victims of Ethiopian discrimination. Thus, the argument that Ethiopian colonialism was devoid of racism can only be applied in circumstances where conquered peoples opted for full assimilation.

Late-nineteenth-century Ethiopia was characterized not only by its hierarchical warrior class but also by Orthodox Christianity. It was the latter that gave the Russians a point of entry for broad involvement in the country in the last two decades of the century. The Russian agenda in Ethiopia was a complex one, consisting of colonial territorial ambitions, a desire for influence and access to riches and trade, dreams of solidarity between the Russian Orthodox Church and the Ethiopian Church, and the opportunity to use yet another stage on which to maneuver in the interests of big-power European politics.

The Franco-Russian alliance in Europe drew the Russians to the side of the French in Ethiopia and elsewhere in this part of Africa. It also placed them in opposition to British colonial interests when they came into conflict with those of France, as in the Fashoda crisis of 1898. The various elements of the Russian agenda in Ethiopia did not always function in concert or with the official sanction of the czar's government. Religious, Slavophile, and powerful commercial groups promoted unofficial contacts in Ethiopia, thereby eventually drawing their government into sending a semiofficial diplomatic mission to Menelik in 1895.[11]

The Russian mission was headed by Professor Alexander Elisseiv, a prominent explorer who had distinguished himself for his travels in North Africa. His third in command was Nicholas Stephanovic Leontiev, a scheming sociopath who was then a lieutenant in a reserve regiment. Although he was only thirty-four years old, Leontiev had already left behind an impressive trail of gambling debts and confidence schemes and had embezzled his sister's inheritance. Born in 1861 at Kherson in Poltava Province, he was a member of the petty nobility, which gave him some access to those in positions of power. As a young man, he was tall, powerfully built, handsome, extremely intelligent, charming, and friendly, characteristics that enabled him to dupe many. Expelled from his army regiment for gambling debts, he set off for India and Persia, where he falsely passed himself off as an emissary of the Ministry of Finance while engaged in a variety of dubious commercial dealings.

Ever resilient, he returned to St. Petersburg, where, thanks to his friendship with the son of the editor of *Novoe Vermja*, he published a highly flattering account of his Asian travels. This in turn gave him access to the Russian Geographical Society, a sponsor of the Elisseiv mission. He was also able to insinuate himself with the Holy Synod of the Russian Orthodox Church and especially with its procurator general, who was a powerful advocate of church expansion and pan-Slavism. Quickly sensing opportunities for himself, Leontiev embraced the procurator general's views and in so doing, secured Christian forgiveness for past transgressions and a place in the Elisseiv mission.[12]

The initial purpose of the Elisseiv mission was to sound out Menelik about closer contacts between the two Orthodox churches. However, this religious purpose was but a point of departure for more ambitious plans, which included political, commercial, and military objectives. The mission left Odessa on January 3, 1895, and disembarked at Djibouti, where it was warmly greeted by the French governor. En route to Addis Ababa, Elisseiv suffered heat exhaustion while crossing the Danakil Desert and had to return to the coast. It was then that Leontiev assumed leadership of the expedition. He quickly upgraded everyone's title, including his own, prior to their arrival at Menelik's court on March 23, 1895. He became a colonel and a count; Father Ephorem was made a bishop; and the physician, Dr. C. Zviaghin, was promoted to general.

Menelik was impressed with Leontiev's powerful and persuasive manner of speaking, but he was not deceived by his lies and fanciful boasting. Leontiev went too far when, a month after his arrival, he produced a concocted letter from the czar. Although Menelik and his wife, Taytu, immediately saw through this scheme, they continued to tolerate Leontiev for their own political purposes. It was, after all, early in 1895, and Menelik was anxious to cultivate European support for his diplomatic efforts to prevent Italy from making further territorial incursions into Ethiopia. These efforts eventually proved futile, forcing him to militarily confront the Italians at Adowa a year later. But during the first half of 1895, he saw Russia as a potential ally, and thus he allowed himself to be blessed by Leontiev's "bishop" while Abune Matewos, the head of the Ethiopian Church, cringed on the sidelines.

One of the objectives of the sponsors of the Elisseiv mission was to bring about some kind of union between the two Orthodox churches. This became apparent to Menelik soon after Leontiev's arrival and was of concern to both him and Ethiopia's religious leaders. They knew that the czar claimed to be the protector and leader of all Orthodox Christians, including themselves. Since this was a claim they were unwilling to accept, they were vague in their response to the issue of religious unification. However, Menelik was more open to Leontiev's suggestion that he send a diplomatic delegation to St. Petersburg, not because he sought unification of the two churches but out of a need to secure Russia's support in his struggle with Italy. Leontiev pushed Menelik hard for sending this delegation since it would enable him to reach the pinnacle of Russian power, namely, the czar.[13]

Leontiev did not tell Menelik that he had no official authority to request that such a mission be sent, nor did he bother to inform the Russian foreign ministry about it. Ever the skilled confidence artist, he waited until the mission had reached Cairo before sending word to the foreign ministry that it was on its way. The czar and his foreign minister had no choice but to allow the delegation to proceed. The bold and confident schemer was now on his way to meet the czar.

On June 29, 1895, the delegation arrived at Odessa, carrying the Ethiopian Order of Solomon for the czar and gifts that included a crown, a gold cross, an illustrated manuscript of the Bible, and artifacts and jewelry made from gold, ivory, leather, and horn. Menelik also sent a personal letter to the czar, congratulating him on his recent marriage and accession to the throne, and Taytu sent a note to the czarina.

The members of Menelik's delegation occupied modest positions in the imperial Ethiopian hierarchy, and Leontiev was seriously concerned that the czar would take offense at receiving such low-ranking representatives. So, as he had done before, he simply promoted everyone to ranks certain to impress the czar. Fitutari Damtew and Kenyazmach Genemye, who were army commanders, became generals and close relatives of the emperor, Belackew was made a prince, and the priest, Gebre Egziabeher, was elevated to bishop.

On orders from the czar, the government rolled out a glittering reception for the Ethiopians. They met with the leaders of the Orthodox Church and most of the imperial grand dukes and were honored guests at banquets, parades, and religious ceremonies. Finally, on July 13, they and Leontiev were ushered into the presence of Czar Nicholas and Czarina Alexandra. Damtew presented the monarchs with the gifts from Menelik and Taytu and gave a speech in French that greatly impressed the imperial couple. Not to be outdone, Leontiev gave the czarina a colorful basket that he said had been filled with flowers by Taytu and carried on the head of a servant girl from the capital to the sea. This concocted tale came under suspicion even as Leontiev was telling it to the czarina.

Nicholas and Alexandra then presented the members of the delegation with gifts and decorations, including the Order of St. Anna, second class, and the Order of St. Stanislaw, third class. Nicholas also gave Damtew the Grand Cross of the Order of St. Anna for Menelik. Leontiev was a major beneficiary of this imperial audience since it gave him the credibility, authority, and respect he previously lacked.

During the forty-three days they stayed in Russia, the Ethiopians received excellent press, largely due to Leontiev's shrewd public relations campaign. But the cracks in his grand scheme began showing when one newspaper, *Grazdanin*, questioned the ranks of the delegates and told readers that the emeralds they had strewn left and right as gifts were really colored glass made in St. Petersburg. Quick on his feet, Leontiev said that he would respond to the allegations only after the Ethiopians had left Russia.

However, other Russian newspapers, anxious to get scoops of their own about this highly publicized diplomatic mission, began to uncover additional unpleasant details. They found that Leontiev had tried to get the mayor of St. Petersburg to pay for the costs of some of the gifts the Ethiopians presented to the czar and czarina. They also charged that he had made a commitment of Russian military assistance to Ethiopia in the czar's name but without any official authorization. They disclosed Leontiev's unsavory past, accused him of falsely assuming the title of count, and claimed that he had tried to get various Russian cities to fete the Ethiopians in the interests of his own personal profit. Although the Ethiopians' public comportment was beyond reproach, it was revealed that they drank 160 rubles worth of champagne every day, the biggest drinker being "Bishop" Gebre Egziabeher, who consumed two bottles for breakfast alone.

As soon as these revelations began to pour out in the press, the foreign ministry moved to send the delegation back to Ethiopia. The entourage left not only with the gifts the czar had given them but also with a consignment of rifles and ammunition and a cash credit for Menelik. Leontiev was allowed to accompany them as far as Djibouti but was ordered to return immediately to St. Petersburg to answer the charges made against him. These charges were given additional credence by Leontiev's Ethiopian interpreter, Redda, who remained behind in Russia out of fear of retribution from Menelik. He told Grand Duke Vladimir that Leontiev had promised Menelik that Russia would give him 100,000 rifles.[14]

Meanwhile, Leontiev took his time returning to Russia in the hope that the scandal he had created would fade from view. He stopped in Paris, where he met Léon Chefneux, a French arms merchant who had previously represented French interests in Ethiopia and supplied Menelik with modern weapons and ammunition. The purpose of Leontiev's visit with Chefneux was to explore possibilities in the private arms trade in Ethiopia. There was a fortune to be made selling guns and ammunition to Menelik since he had enormous ivory-based wealth with which to pay for them.[15]

Leontiev finally returned to Russia and to a temporary disgrace, from which he rapidly recovered. Through boldness and deception, he successfully gained audiences with the Italian ambassadors in Paris and St. Petersburg, where he offered his services as mediator between Ethiopia and Italy before the Battle of Adowa. Rebuffed by them, he set sail for Massawa in February 1896, just before the Battle of Adowa, claiming he was the head of a Russian Red Cross mission. He then asked the Italians for permission to cross their lines in order to give humanitarian aid to the Ethiopians. The Italians, on making inquiry of the Russian government, found that the two doctors Leontiev claimed were in his party were actually Cossacks with no medical training whatsoever and that the group had no connection to the Russian Red Cross. Denied transit, Leontiev took the long way around and arrived in Addis Ababa after the Ethiopian victory at Adowa.

Menelik knew full well that Leontiev was a scoundrel. However, since he had found him so useful in the past, he now sought to use him to draw Russia closer to Ethiopia's side in peace negotiations with Italy. The sticking point in the negotiations was Italy's insistence that Ethiopia never seek the protection of another power. Menelik refused to agree to this because it would have meant foreclosing possible future alliances with other European powers. Because of Italian intransigence on this point, he decided to reach out to Czar Nicholas as a possible mediator. He wrote a letter to the czar and sent it to St. Petersburg with Ato Yosef, one of Leontiev's Ethiopian companions. He then allowed Leontiev to escort fifty Italian prisoners of war to the coast to commemorate the czar's coronation. Leontiev and his Cossack companions, no longer masquerading as representatives of the Russian Red Cross, arrived at Djibouti, where they handed the prisoners over to Dr. Cesare Nerazzini, Italy's chief negotiator.

Anxious to exploit this humanitarian mission to the fullest, Leontiev presumptuously communicated news of it directly to King Humbert I of Italy, from whom he received no reply. However, Prime Minister Antonio Di Rudini directed Nerazzini to go to Djibouti to meet Leontiev and receive the prisoners. Their reports of Leontiev's many kindnesses to them on the trip to the coast only served to increase Italy's indebtedness to him. Although he had not been officially designated as such, Leontiev went to Rome and declared himself Menelik's ambassador to Italy. The prime minister had no choice but to meet with him, and during the discussions that followed, Leontiev pressed Menelik's demand for the payment of an indemnity.

Leontiev's star soon rose to new heights. He went on to Vienna, where Czar Nicholas arrived on August 27 with his foreign minister,

Prince Lobanov. Now self-designated as Menelik's special envoy to Russia, Leontiev was immediately received by the czar and Lobanov. He was invited by the czar to ride on the imperial train to Kiev and to join in meeting Ato Yosef, who was carrying Menelik's request for Russian mediation.

Unfortunately for Leontiev, Italy soon dropped its demand and signed a treaty with Menelik on October 20, 1896, thus negating any need for the czar's mediation. However, Leontiev's latest foray into international diplomacy had significantly bolstered his reputation. He had clearly demonstrated his great personal influence with Menelik and enjoyed the czar's favor since he had placed him in the respected position of international mediator between two warring parties. The competing colonial powers also knew that Menelik was now in Leontiev's debt since the czar's willingness to serve as mediator represented tacit Russian recognition of Ethiopian independence.[16]

When Leontiev returned to Ethiopia in late 1896, Menelik was fully prepared to reward him for his excellent services. He offered him the governorship of the newly established Equatoria Province adjacent to Lake Rudolf. In so doing, Menelik was also serving his own ends. He was aware of how well General Horatio Herbert Kitchener was serving the khedive of Egypt in the Sudan, and he saw the obvious advantages of having a European administer a frontier area that would soon be challenged by Britain.[17]

However, Leontiev was no Kitchener, and Menelik did not foresee the serious consequences of propelling someone like him into the swirl of colonial competition around Lake Rudolf. Although he knew that Leontiev was a brilliant schemer, he wrongly assumed that he would be content to take up his post in a remote area and simply enjoy the material rewards associated with it. As Menelik would soon discover, Leontiev was far too manipulative and devious to assume so straightforward a role. He had no sooner been appointed than he began to inveigle venture capitalists in Belgium, Britain, France, and Russia in a phony gold-mining scheme in his new province. He also stoked the faint hopes of some in France for gaining a foothold in the lands near the lake.[18]

Before Leontiev ever got to Lake Rudolf, another Russian officer, Alexander Xavieryevich Bulatovich, traveled there with an Ethiopian army under the command of *Ras* Wolda Giorgis. Bulatovich had first arrived in Ethiopia in April 1896, with a Russian Red Cross detachment of sixty-one men sent to provide medical care for Menelik's soldiers following the Battle of Adowa.[19] Like Leontiev, he was from a noble Russian family, but there all similarity ended.[20] Bulatovich was born on October 8, 1870, in Orel, to Major General Xavier Vikentyevich Bulatovich and Eugeniya Andreyevna. He was raised on the family's estate, "Lutskovka," in Markovskaya Volost, where he enjoyed all of the privileges of Russia's noble class.

In 1884, Bulatovich entered the exclusive Alexandrovskiy Lyceum in St. Petersburg at the insistence of his very strong-willed mother. He graduated in 1891 and on June 9 of that year entered the Life Guard Hussar Regiment of the Second Cavalry Division, where he received the rank of cornet a short time later. He became an excellent fencer and was highly admired for his skills as a horseman.

Bulatovich was assigned to the Russian Red Cross mission to Ethiopia on April 7, 1896. Although he had received a superb education in the humanities and was well trained in military matters, he knew little about Ethiopia and its peoples. Because he was a serious scholar and a man of broad intellectual interests, he tried to remedy his language deficiencies by studying Amharic and Geez before his departure.[21]

The Russian mission arrived in Djibouti on April 30, and on May 3, the group's leader, Major General N.K. Shvedov, sent Bulatovich to Addis Ababa at the head of an advance team. Bulatovich arrived there in record time and prepared the way for the entire mission, which reached Addis Ababa on July 24. The Russian Red Cross mission rendered valuable medical service to the Ethiopians, a fact grudgingly acknowledged even by their British and Italian rivals. Bulatovich himself made a very positive impression on Menelik and other Ethiopian leaders, not only because of his military and medical skills but also because of his integrity, honesty, and genuine interest in them and their country.

Bulatovich's arrival in Ethiopia following the Italian defeat at Adowa coincided with the rapid implementation of Menelik's foreign policy of colonial annexation of adjacent territories. As part of this policy, Menelik was prepared to militarily confront the British in the south—that is, until he saw the results of the crushing power of Kitchener's war machine in the Sudan. But in 1896, the fall of the Mahdist state was two years off. Flushed with his victory over Italy, Menelik seriously believed that he could militarily challenge the British. He had also come to realize that though effective occupation by his army could provide a strong hand in future border negotiations, possessing his own maps drawn by Europeans would give needed scientific credibility to his territorial claims.

With a view toward consolidating his western frontier, Menelik decided to send an army toward the Baro River. He placed this army under the command of *dejazmach* Tessama, who, in 1898, would accompany the French on their failed attempt to secure the Upper Nile. Menelik also invited Bulatovich to participate in this expedition and

gave him a personal audience on November 9, the day before Bulatovich left to join Tessama. Following his return three months later,
Bulatovich made two other trips to explore the course of the Angar
River and the valley of the Didepa. On all of these trips, he recorded
detailed geographic, anthropologic, and natural history observations
that were among the finest made by Europeans in this part of Africa at
that time.

Menelik personally hosted a reception for Bulatovich on April 8,
1897, after he returned from his travels. This distinct honor reflected
the esteem and affection with which the Ethiopians held him. Of all
the Europeans who had come to Ethiopia, he stood out as a deeply religious man of impeccable integrity and dependability, a man who had
used his scientific skills to help them and not to further any personal
interests. Bulatovich left Africa on May 2 but promised Menelik that
he would soon return.[22]

In St. Petersburg, his work with the Red Cross mission was recognized by a promotion to the rank of lieutenant and receipt of the Order
of St. Anna, third class. While at home, Bulatovich wrote a book describing his year of travels in Ethiopia. Published in September 1897,
this volume not only chronicled his travels but also presented valuable information on Ethiopia's history, government, commerce, military, land tenure, peoples, and religious beliefs. Although he was not
an anthropologist by training, he had the instincts of one and was
driven to record the peoples he observed and their customs out of an
awareness that their world was in a state of rapid transition and would
soon disappear.[23] There were defining characteristics about the
Ethiopians that appealed to Bulatovich. Among these were their military traditions and their Orthodox Christianity. Although he tried to
be objective in his descriptions of them and the peoples they conquered, his perceptions were strongly influenced by Ethiopian values,
many of which he embraced.

On October 17, 1897, Bulatovich returned to Addis Ababa as part of
a Russian diplomatic mission to Ethiopia. He was soon invited to join
the army of *Ras* Wolda Giorgis, the governor of Kaffa, who was ordered to "establish a foothold at Lake Rudolf."[24] Establishing
Ethiopian authority at the lake meant invading large areas outside the
historical boundaries of predecessor highland Christian states.
Though he condemned European colonialism for its disregard of the
rights and interests of indigenous peoples, Bulatovich presented Menelik's identical actions as "carrying out the traditional mission of
Ethiopia as the propagator of culture."[25]

Bulatovich left Addis Ababa for southwestern Ethiopia on January 8,
1898, with a retinue of thirty men. Twelve days later, he entered Kaffa

Province, where Giorgis was mustering an army at his provincial capital of Andaracha. There, he showed Giorgis the map he had brought, marked in Amharic, and instructed him in the concept of degrees of latitude and longitude. Giorgis, who was literate in Amharic, quickly understood the great distances involved, and like most of his men, he was greatly worried about venturing into lands completely unknown to any living Ethiopian. As Bulatovich later wrote:

> He had been ordered to subdue and annex . . . the huge territory which lies among Kaffa, Lake Albert, and Lake Rudolf from two degrees north latitude, and, while doing this, to oppose any other force which might have a similar intention. . . . Provision for the troops could only be supplied by way of requisition. . . . The Emperor Menelik, demanded that the *Ras* complete the task given to him this very year.[26]

Menelik had confided information about this invasion to Giorgis, one of his ablest and most trusted generals, who had originally been the head of his personal guard. After several years of service in that capacity, Giorgis was promoted to *dejazmach* and finally given the rank of *ras*.[27] On February 2, 1898, Giorgis marched out of Andaracha at the head of an army of 16,000 men. During the weeks of preparation, he and Bulatovich developed a close personal relationship that would be sustained throughout the duration of the expedition.[28]

Giorgis's troops felt great trepidation about entering lands none of them knew. They also considered Bulatovich's presence as a bad omen since they believed that they were being led to fight against the English on his behalf.[29] Yet they obediently followed Giorgis into the unknown out of loyalty to him and to their emperor. Despite its size, this army was, for the most part, strictly disciplined under a hierarchy of officers subordinate to Giorgis. Giorgis himself traveled with an escort of retainers, guards, a library, a medicine chest, and a telescope.[30]

On February 15, they came to the Oyma River valley, a rich agricultural area outside the borders of Ethiopia. By now, Giorgis's army had swollen to 30,000 men, who had to provision themselves from the lands through which they passed. Giorgis sent word ahead to the people in this valley that if they submitted, they and their property would not be touched. Such assurances were scarcely credible since this army had to live by confiscating all the grain it could lay its hands on.

The evening before the invasion, Bulatovich climbed a mountain overlooking the valley and described the scene below:

> As far as the eye can see, the valley and hills were densely settled. Smoke arose from the houses. . . . Cattle were returning from the pasture, and the sight of marvelous white cows aroused the appetite of my traveling companions. . . . The quiet hard-working life of a peaceful people was evi-

dent in all, and it was sad to think that tomorrow all this would be destroyed. The picture will change; the inhabitants will flee, driving their livestock and carrying their goods and children. They will, most probably, be killed, wounded, and captured. Their houses will go up in a blaze, and all that will remain of them will be the hearths.[31]

The following day, as Giorgis's hoards rushed into the valley, the "populace was . . . in full flight."[32] Bulatovich graphically recorded what happened next:

The *Ras'* army poured into the valley, where they scattered in various directions, rushing to replenish their supplies. Any prohibition would be unthinkable and fruitless, since the whole provisioning system of the campaign depended on such commandeering. . . . Soon all trails that led to our stopping place were covered with soldiers who were heavily loaded down.[33]

Bulatovich attempted to describe the ethnic groups his Ethiopian hosts were pillaging and to provide some information about their way of life. However, he was obviously limited in this effort by the fact that his encounters with these groups took place while they and their way of life were being destroyed. Assuming an Ethiopian perspective, he grouped most of these peoples under the general rubric *Shuro*, which means black in the language of the Kaffa.[34] By contrast, his descriptions of the army with which he was traveling and its behavior under varied circumstances were extremely reliable and detailed.

Although this army was well organized and generally disciplined, Giorgis and his commanders were often unable to stop the massacres once they began because "a thirst for blood and murder" overtook the troops.[35] And on occasion, foot soldiers misunderstood the peaceful overtures of local peoples and shot them as a result. One such misunderstanding occurred near the Kori River, and Bulatovich later vividly wrote about Giorgis's reaction when he arrived on the scene. "The commander-in-chief was deeply grieved by what had taken place. He practically wept from compassion and rode silently covering his face. . . . The officers who were accompanying him were also upset. It was distressing and disagreeable to all of them."[36]

Bulatovich frequently intervened to prevent the Ethiopian soldiers from killing their prisoners. Yet in the frenzy of an attack, these men often lost control and "seemed drunk with killing and the sight of human blood."[37] They sometimes competed with one another for pride of place in killing villagers and invariably returned with the testicles of their male victims as trophies.[38]

Once Giorgis's army entered the fringes of the Omo River valley, Bulatovich's account became a continuous recitation of butchery and pillaging. He described these events with mixed emotions. In some circumstances, his training as a soldier prevailed, and he framed his assessments within the context of military necessity. Yet in others, he was generally appalled by what he saw and tried to stop it. As a guest of this army, he had little control over its actions, and he was torn by his sense of loyalty to his hosts and pity for their innocent victims. Nonetheless, he did not shrink from providing vivid descriptions of the Ethiopian massacres:

> The winner seized his victim by the hair and slit his throat with the customary dexterous motion of the saber. . . . The sight of the bodies with enormous wounds was horrid. There were practically none of them which did not have the gaping wounds of saber strokes, since natives who were shot almost always also had their throats slit by saber. . . . Most of them [the men] returned with trophies of victory [the genitals of their victims]. . . . They showed no mercy, not only to men, but also to animals. The corpses of animals with slit throats lay all about the road in masses.[39]

Whatever the range of his attitudes, Bulatovich was a meticulous observer who recorded these experiences in detail as to date and place. He was also unique in that he was the only European to document events from the Ethiopian side. Given his integrity and rigorous scholarship, it is no surprise that his accounts corroborated the reports of other European travelers, such as Austin, Bottego, Cavendish, and Smith, who observed the devastation caused by Ethiopian military expeditions. Menelik and other Ethiopian leaders could not have been happy with Bulatovich's book about his trip to Lake Rudolf. Yet he placed recounting the truth above pleasing his hosts.

On March 11, Giorgis decided to form a detachment of only 5,664 men for a quick trip down the Omo River valley to Lake Rudolf. The rainy season was about to begin, and he was anxious to secure the mouth of the river for the emperor. Leaving most of his men at Kolu (called Cullo by Bottego) on the Omo, he, Bulatovich, and the small detachment set out on March 16. En route, they received reports of Europeans in the area, whom the local peoples referred to as *guchumba* (itinerants). They were said to have come from the east and were but a day's march away.[40] Since there were no European expeditions in the area at that time, it is likely that these visitors were coastal traders from Zanzibar on an ivory-collecting trip.[41]

Giorgis now had little time to spare. He therefore decided to head for the Omo delta and the northern shore of Lake Rudolf and leave conquest of the lands beyond to the following year.[42] As they trekked south, he kept asking Bulatovich when they would arrive at Lake

Rudolf and teased him by saying, "God grant that we soon give birth to your lake."[43] Finally, on April 7, 1898, they came in sight of the lake: "About eight o'clock in the morning, the surface of the lake shows in the distance. Here, finally, is the cherished goal of our expedition. Soldiers greet the long-awaited lake with joyous cries."[44] A week later, they ceremoniously raised a silken Ethiopian tricolor atop a 28-foot-tall pole set in a pile of stones. Bulatovich vividly described the pageantry of the evening ceremony:

> The detachment formed up . . . in front of the flag. . . . With his face to the lake, stood the commander-in-chief and his suite, and behind them the drummers, flutists, and pipe players. The *Ras* took a gun in his hands. All became quiet. . . . In front, the lake glistened, that same long-wished lake, to which we for so long and steadfastly had striven . . . and against this background the front of the Abyssinian army stood out brightly. The silk shirts shone, the animal hides, the gold and silver decorations, and Abyssinian flags fluttered. Finally, a shot rang out, and five thousand guns saluted the new domain of Menelik and . . . erected his flag. They beat drums, blew on pipes, and broke out in military songs. Moved, *Ras* Wolda Giorgis embraced me, and I, warmly, and with feeling, congratulated him.[45]

Despite this moment of solemn ceremony, Giorgis's men soon resumed their raiding and pillaging as they made their way north again. While in the Omo delta, Giorgis's Kullo mercenaries raided a village, leaving among the survivors a three-year-old boy whom they brutally castrated. Bulatovich adopted this boy and took him back to Russia:

> They brought me a small boy, abandoned by his parents and terribly mutilated by our blood-thirsty Kulo. . . . A priest found him in the reeds, where he lay in a helpless state near the river itself. . . . The boy stood silently before me, with his legs spread wide. He was terribly covered with blood. . . . I cleaned the wound, washed it with a mixture of mercuric chloride and cocaine, and, having made a bandage, laid the boy in my tent. Vaska, which is what I called him, turned out to be a good, healthy, big-bellied little boy.[46]

On May 26, 1898, Bulatovich returned to Andaracha, where he took his leave of Giorgis. Three weeks later, he was in Addis Ababa, and a pleased Menelik awarded him a gold shield in recognition of his services during the expedition that had added 18,000 square miles to his empire. Bulatovich left Addis Ababa on June 26, with Vaska in tow, and arrived in St. Petersburg on July 31.[47]

Bulatovich was promoted to captain in recognition of his accomplishments in Ethiopia. On January 25, 1899, he presented the results

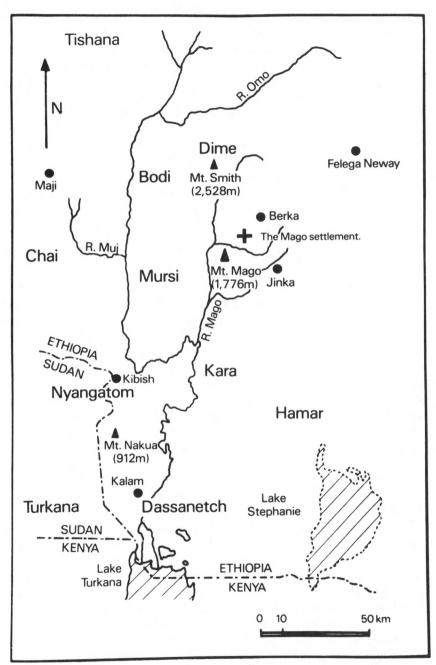

Current map of the lower Omo River, showing the locations of the region's major ethnic groups (courtesy Professor David Turton, University of Oxford).

of his trip at a conference hosted by the Imperial Russian Geographical Society. This brief report was published in French in St. Petersburg and later in Italian in Rome, along with a map similar to Bottego's for the Omo delta and the northern end of Lake Rudolf.[48] Unfortunately, the Italian translation of Bulatovich's conference was "unnecessarily and abusively footnoted by G. Roncagli."[49] This, no doubt, reflected a desire to denigrate Bulatovich's accomplishments since Italy had long viewed Russia as hostile to its colonial designs in Ethiopia.[50]

Bulatovich returned to Ethiopia in July 1899 and spent four months on Menelik's behalf charting several affluents of the Blue Nile. During this stay, he approached Menelik about obtaining a governorship, as Leontiev had done. However, the Russian envoy in Addis Ababa, P.M. Vlassov, vetoed this proposal due to legitimate concerns that it would unnecessarily entangle Russia in internal Ethiopian political affairs, much as the Leontiev scheme recently had done near Lake Rudolf.[51]

In July 1900, Bulatovich was sent to Port Arthur, where he participated in the Russo-Japanese War.[52] Although he had a brilliant military career ahead of him, he requested discharge into the reserves on February 8, 1903, and subsequently entered the small monastery of Nikiforskoye Podvorye, along with a half dozen enlisted men who had been under his command. At the same time, he enrolled Vaska in the Aleksandrovsky Lavra Academy in St. Petersburg. However, as Vaska approached puberty, he was subjected to discrimination from the other students, not because of race but rather because he increasingly displayed the physical characteristics of eunuchoidism. In 1906, Bulatovich took monastic vows, and known as Father Anthony, he later entered a monastery at Mount Athos in Greece, where he lived for several years. Before leaving for Mount Athos, he repatriated Vaska to Ethiopia.[53]

Bulatovich made a final trip to Ethiopia in 1911 to visit Vaska and to seek Menelik's permission to construct a Russian Orthodox monastery. Although he visited the emperor and treated him for his illnesses with icons, holy water, oils, and prayers, his request was denied. Returning to Mount Athos, he soon became embroiled in a theological controversy that resulted in his expulsion from the monastery. He then traveled to Russia, where he lived with his sister, Princess Mary Orbeliani, in St. Petersburg and later at his family's estate, "Lutskovka."

During World War I, Bulatovich served for a while with the Sixteenth Advanced Detachment of the Red Cross. Following the armistice with Germany in 1918, he unsuccessfully tried to reenter monastic life. His persistent adherence to a then heretical belief in the divinity of Christ's name prevented this on terms acceptable to him. While waiting for a final decision on his application to enter the St.

Andrew Monastery in Petrograd, he lived in a modest cabin near "Lut-skovka," where, on the night of December 5–6, 1919, he was murdered by bandits.[54]

Bulatovich's life as a monk stands in dramatic contrast to his earlier career as a soldier and explorer. Yet even as a young man, he exhibited characteristics that foretold his later years. The Italian general Gherardo, who was taken prisoner at Adowa, got to know him well in Ethiopia and described him as "a young man from a noble family, strange, full of energy and vitality, quasi-mystical, and of delicate sentiments."[55] He was also a man devoid of selfish, personal interests, a man whose integrity and intellectual curiosity helped create important travel accounts that are now of great historical value.

Although Bulatovich's remarkable geographic and ethnographic contributions are now better appreciated, Menelik was primarily grateful to him for the string of well-built forts he constructed between Kaffa and the northern end of Lake Rudolf. These and the excellent maps he made served Menelik well in future years when he began negotiations with the British over his southern frontier.

When Bulatovich and Giorgis had left for Lake Rudolf in early 1898, Menelik's foreign policy was driven by a willingness to stand up militarily to the British, especially the Macdonald Expedition. However, following Kitchener's defeat of the Mahdists and the British victory over the Ashanti in West Africa, Menelik reversed this policy. He now realized that unlike Italy, Britain possessed a powerful military machine capable of defeating him and transforming Ethiopia into just another colonial possession. As a result, in late 1898, he adopted a conciliatory posture toward the British, which included negotiating his southern border with them.[56]

As part of his effort to solidify his claims over the lands annexed by Giorgis, Menelik decided to place Leontiev in charge of them. He granted him the title of *dejazmach* of Equatoria, the newly created province in the south.[57] Once appointed, Leontiev found no paucity of bankers, merchants, aristocrats, and others who were willing to invest in what they were told was one of the potentially richest corners of Africa. Leontiev saw this new province as a sort of personal fiefdom, the Russians saw it as a future colony or protectorate, and the French saw it as a foothold for themselves in Ethiopia. They all quickly fell in with Leontiev's scheme, led by Prince Henry of Orléans, who planned to travel with Leontiev into the new province.[58]

Leontiev spent several months in Europe buying up arms for sale to Menelik and obtaining supplies for his trip to Lake Rudolf. His store of weapons was so great that he chartered a steamship in Holland, which set sail on December 3, 1897, for Djibouti via London. The stopover in

London proved to be a fatal mistake because the ship was impounded on the grounds that its dangerous cargo of ammunition and weapons violated regulations that required advance notification. Leontiev and the ship's captain were heavily fined, and the matter was to go to court for a public hearing. Leontiev, however, avoided this by fleeing to Paris, where he recommenced buying arms. The port of London's action was viewed in Paris and St. Petersburg as a calculated attempt to stall Leontiev, whose arms shipment was clearly not in Britain's interests. The British were terribly afraid that these arms might end up with the Mahdists in the Sudan, just as Kitchener was moving on Khartoum.[59]

The impounding of the ship had the net effect of rousing strong patriotic feelings in Russia and anger in Paris, which resulted in the original investment being rapidly replaced. In addition, the French government soon entered the picture in an official manner by promising Leontiev 300 Senegalese riflemen, who were to join him in Djibouti. Leontiev and Prince Henry finally arrived at Djibouti on March 16, 1898, with all of their supplies, weapons, and ammunition. They brought with them a number of French nationals who had been told that they would all eventually become shareholders in the new dominion, Equatoria, that Leontiev was about to establish.

Leontiev was personally invested as *dejazmach* in Addis Ababa by Menelik and given almost absolute authority over all of the lands to the northeast of Lake Rudolf. No Europeans except the Swiss Alfred Ilg, who was Menelik's chief foreign affairs adviser, had risen so high at the emperor's court.[60] Not surprisingly, Leontiev soon became the object of both European and Ethiopian envy. His plans temporarily went awry when, on June 30, 1898, he was accidentally wounded in Harar while demonstrating a machine gun to the governor of the city. The Russian ambassador, P.M. Vlassov, refused to send Russian doctors to help him, in hopes that the injuries might prove fatal and thereby eliminate the freelancer who had caused him so much grief. This did not go over well with Menelik and the Ethiopians, who saw in Vlassov's actions the abandonment of a fellow countryman in distress. Menelik sent his own physician to treat Leontiev, and although Vlassov continued to be a powerful diplomatic and political presence in Addis Ababa for a while, his handling of this incident caused him to fall from the emperor's favor. Fearing that he might be assassinated by Leontiev's supporters, he eventually left Addis Ababa.[61]

Leontiev rapidly recovered in Europe and was back in Ethiopia within a few months. However, Prince Henry had to return to France for family reasons and was unable to accompany him to Equatoria. Leontiev's military expedition to the Lake Rudolf region was, by far, one of the largest and best equipped ever to enter the area up to that time. His second in command was Baron Chedeuvre, an officer of the Russian regiment of Dragoon Guards who had been given the Ethiopian title of *fitaurari* (colonel) by Menelik for the purposes of the expedition. Under him were Ensign Babitchev and a French lieutenant named Sebillou. In addition, there were several Cossacks of the Imperial Personal Bodyguard Squadron, a physician, Dr. Kahn (the expedition's medical officer), and two Croatian brothers, Mirko and Stepan Seljan, who had falsely passed themselves off as physicians when they first arrived in Ethiopia. The French component of the expedition consisted of 130 Senegalese riflemen brought in from Dakar in West Africa, Marius Bouchier, a French colonial administrator who acted as the quartermaster for the expedition, and Captain Leymarie who commanded the Senegalese troops. In addition, Leontiev recruited a troop of Arab scouts in Harar, who were mounted on camels. The Ethiopians sent 2,000 cavalry and infantry with Leontiev under the command of *dejazmach* Tessama, who the year before had traveled with the French in their attempt to reach the Nile from the east.

Leontiev had 1,200 modern repeater rifles and two Maxim guns at his disposal, all of which did not bode well for the peoples of the Omo River valley, who had been recently decimated by Giorgis's army.[62] After passing through Walamo, he headed west toward the Omo River, eventually arriving at the town of Bako, where he established an Ethiopian military and administrative presence. Moving farther south toward the lake, he encountered "forte resistance" from the local populations.[63] This resulted in devastating armed conflicts, which he falsely described as minor and benign. He also provided idyllic descriptions of the country he traversed in his published accounts mainly for the benefit of his investors, who were interested in everything from copper and ivory to cattle breeding. However, as Czeslaw Jesman noted, "news from other sources about Leontiev's activities in this faraway corner of Ethiopia were less rosy."[64] There was a drought in progress at the time of his visit, which forced him to "resort to harsh methods in order to feed his men."[65]

The expedition reached the northern end of Lake Rudolf on August 21, 1899. There, Leontiev found the Union Jacks put up by Austin when he had come up from the south the year before. Indifferent to the political implications of his actions, he quickly replaced the Union Jacks with the Ethiopian colors, on the grounds that the territory had already been claimed by Menelik.[66]

Leontiev's stay at the northern end of the lake was never peaceful because he and his followers were constantly engaged in raiding, pillaging, and wanton killing. The local inhabitants finally joined forces in an attempt to drive them out. Armed with only spears and poisoned arrows, they succeeded in killing 216 of Leontiev's men in one 4-hour-long engagement, but they certainly suffered far greater casualties themselves. Leontiev later described this battle in almost casual terms and expressed regret that the thick brush prevented him from using his machine guns to good effect on these Africans.

Sebillou hoisted several Ethiopian flags near the Omo delta and supervised the construction of a fort on a rise overlooking both the lake and the Omo estuary. The fort was built on the left bank of the Omo while Leontiev returned to Addis Ababa on unexpected orders from the emperor. Before he left, Leontiev unwisely instructed Baron Chedeuvre and Dr. Kahn to take a column down into British-claimed territory to explore the lands near the Nile. Chedeuvre and his men only traveled down the western shore of the lake to just below the Turkwell River, where, on October 1, 1899, they set up Post Menelik II before returning north again.[67]

Despite its record of wanton killing and pillaging, Leontiev's expedition made a modest contribution to an understanding of the geography of the Lake Rudolf region. Dr. Kahn and the Frenchmen in the party drew a map that accurately depicted, for the first time, many of the meanders of the Omo River delta. This rendition of the Omo River remained unique for geographers until the 1930s.[68] However, this singular geographic accomplishment was greatly overshadowed by Leontiev's criminal activities around the lake.

When Menelik recalled Leontiev to Addis Ababa, it was not so much because of his incursions into British-claimed territory or his removal of the Union Jacks. Leontiev had actually served Menelik well by invading territories around Lake Rudolf where Britain had yet to establish an effective permanent presence. In the process, he had strengthened the emperor's hand in negotiating a favorable frontier with Britain. Menelik conveniently achieved several objectives in recalling Leontiev. While still claiming that his frontier extended to the south of Lake Rudolf, he was able to appear conciliatory toward the British by removing the man whose actions had caused them so much concern.[69]

Menelik had anxieties of his own with regard to Leontiev because he knew that he was fiercely anti-British, and the emperor was fearful that these sentiments could get out of hand and drag him into an unnecessary conflict with Britain. More important, Menelik had grown increasingly worried by Leontiev's claims that his self-styled province of Equatoria was his personal domain. The presence of so many Europeans on the expedition and French colonial troops only served to heighten his suspicions that they might be there to help Leontiev take over the region and eventually declare it independent or else offer it to a European power.[70]

Of equal concern to Menelik were the widely circulated reports of how Leontiev had treated the local populations. Percy Horace Gordon Powell-Cotton, who was in Ethiopia in 1899 preparing to travel with the Harrison-Whitehouse expedition to Lake Rudolf, recorded the following about Leontiev:

> M. Gattiker, the brother-in-law of M. Ilg, rode up, and after mutual salutations, gave us some very interesting information about Count Leontieff's expedition to the Omo, in the direction of Lake Rudolf. This Russian officer, had, it appeared, found a great drought, as a result of which the cattle were dying and the crops burnt up. M. Gattiker added that Leontieff and his men boasted of having shot natives down at sight for the sake of the ornaments they wore, that they raided every village they came to for ivory, and that if the natives did not fly at their approach they poured volleys into them until they did. All this augured ill for the success of our expedition.[71]

Menelik was painfully aware of these accounts and of their negative impact on the international image he was attempting to establish for Ethiopia. The eventual desertion of Dr. Kahn and some of the Senegalese riflemen lent strong credence to the widespread charges of Leontiev's irresponsible and criminal behavior. Menelik moved quickly to strip Leontiev of all authority over the frontier regions near Lake Rudolf and to assure John Lane Harrington, the British agent in Addis Ababa, that the Union Jacks would be replaced.[72]

Leontiev's star was beginning to set, although his expulsion from Ethiopia was still two years off. The precipitating cause of his final disgrace was Menelik's outrage on learning from swindled Belgian investors that he had set up several companies in Britain and Belgium for the purpose of mining gold in his Equatoria Province. Since gold mining was the exclusive monopoly of the Ethiopian crown, Leontiev had seriously infringed on a major imperial prerogative.

In a sense, Leontiev's gold-mining scheme was the last straw. He was ordered out of the country, and on May 8, 1902, Menelik sent a circular letter in French to all of the European ambassadors in Addis Ababa, informing them that Leontiev had made a number of false statements in Europe concerning the alleged gold-mining concessions he had obtained. The emperor stated that Leontiev had inaccurately translated the text of an Imperial Letters Patent that had been addressed to him on June 10, 1897, and that all of this had resulted in heavy financial losses for a Belgian company. The emperor asked the diplomats to inform their governments of Leontiev's misdeeds so as to prevent him from repeating them in the future. Expressing his disappointment in a man who had, to some degree, served him well, he said: "Je ne pensais pas que le dédjas Leontieff sortirait ainsi de ma volonté et de ma service" ("I did not think that Governor Leontieff would thus depart from my wishes and service").[73] Leontiev spent the winter of 1902–1903 in Djibouti, and by April 1903, he had liquidated all of his interests in Ethiopia.

Leontiev briefly fought in the Russo-Japanese War in Manchuria and returned to Djibouti in 1906, from where he made a brief but unsuccessful attempt to return to Ethiopia. He set up an agricultural plantation in Djibouti and an arms-importing firm with the help of the Oriental secretary of the Russian embassy in Addis Ababa, but both efforts failed.[74] He eventually returned to Paris, where he died in very reduced circumstances in 1910.[75]

With Leontiev's departure from Ethiopia, Russian involvement in the borderlands near Lake Rudolf came to an end. However, both Bulatovich and Leontiev played extremely important roles in establishing the southern boundaries of the modern Ethiopian state and in giving Menelik control of the Omo River and a foothold on Lake Rudolf. It now remained for other travelers and diplomats to decide how much of the lake would become part of Ethiopia.

11

A Courageous Young Soldier

Captain Montagu Sinclair Wellby (from 'Twixt Sirdar and Menelik, 1901).

*I*n the interests of aiding the conquest of the Mahdist state in the Sudan and securing the Upper Nile, Lord Salisbury sent a special mission to Ethiopia in April 1897. Its multiple purposes were to counter French influence at Menelik's court, prevent the shipment of arms from and through Ethiopia to the Mahdists, delimit the common frontier between Ethiopia and British possessions, foster trade, and establish a permanent diplomatic presence at Menelik's court. The man placed in charge of this mission was James Rennell Rodd, an experienced and skilled diplomat who had previously served in 1893 as the British agent in Zanzibar and commissioner for British East Africa. Since 1894, he had worked as the assistant to Sir Evelyn Baring (Lord Cromer), the British agent and consul general in Cairo. Rodd made special efforts to assure Menelik that the sizable army under Horatio Herbert Kitchener then beginning its campaign against the Mahdists would not be directed against Ethiopia.[1] These assurances, though convincing to some degree, did not prevent the pragmatic Menelik from establishing a diplomatic entente with the Mahdists.

One of the significant outcomes of Rodd's visit was the establishment of diplomatic contacts between Britain and Ethiopia. In order to avoid offending its ally Italy and to leave open possible future Italian protectorate options over Ethiopia, Britain set up an agency in Addis Ababa. This represented a diplomatic presence, but it was one step below the level of an embassy and thus reflected a less than complete recognition of Ethiopia's independence. The man chosen as the first agent was John Lane Harrington, a thirty-three-year-old army captain who had served as vice consul and consul at Zeila in British Somaliland during the previous three years. Although young, Harrington was thoroughly familiar with the complex political currents in Ethiopia and the Horn of Africa. He was to remain in Ethiopia for a decade, eventually becoming minister plenipotentiary and envoy extraordinary in 1908.[2]

As Britain's diplomatic representative at Menelik's court, Harrington was to play a crucial role in negotiating the borders separating Ethiopia from British territories. This was especially true with regard to Ethiopia's southern border and the lands around Lake Rudolf. Although he greatly influenced the course of these negotiations and tried to foster Britain's best interests, he was often hindered by a Foreign Office policy that viewed this stretch of Africa as being of only marginal importance.[3] That policy was primarily dictated between 1895 and 1902 by Lord Salisbury, the prime minister, and his permanent undersecretary in the Foreign Office, Thomas Sanderson. The latter was extremely knowledgeable about African affairs and viewed the Upper Nile and the Sudan as vital to British interests in this part of Africa. Not surprisingly, he and Salisbury sought to keep Ethiopia neutral as they gained control of the course of the Nile. As a consequence, by 1898, they were adamantly opposed to sanctioning any official or unofficial expeditions to Lake Rudolf and beyond. These, they reasoned, might provoke Menelik into retaliatory military initiatives or shipping arms to the Mahdists, which in turn could seriously jeopardize Britain's conquest of the Sudan.

Despite this policy of prohibiting all travelers from going to the lake, there was a steady stream of petitioners. Among them was Captain Montagu Sinclair Wellby, a thirty-two-year-old officer in the Eighteenth Hussars who had been educated at Rugby and Sandhurst.[4] Wellby was no stranger to Africa, having undertaken two expeditions to Somaliland, in 1895 and 1896. However, it was an 1896 journey through western Tibet that established his reputation as an explorer of note. In early May, he and Lieutenant Malcom of the Ninety-Third Highlanders began traveling through the western part of Tibet, which, up to that time, had never been visited by Europeans. They successfully crossed this uninhabited region, some 15,000 feet in elevation, and thereby opened "a way from west to east between the great snowy ranges of the Kuen-lun system."[5] This was an incredible feat since there was little food or water in the area and the high altitude made trekking extremely difficult. At one point, they had to subsist on wild onions, and they later survived the desertion of a number of their men. Wellby and Malcom finally arrived in Peking in late November, seven months after setting out on their remarkable journey.[6]

Despite the difficulties of this trip, Wellby collected eighty species of flowers, which he carefully packed in tins and sent off to J. Scott Keltie at the Royal Geographical Society.[7] Back in India with his regiment, he was soon off to the northwest frontier, where he participated in the Tirah campaign of 1897 as a transport officer. He was no sooner back from this campaign than he tried to obtain permission to march up from Uganda to Khartoum with a handful of men in time to meet Kitchener's troops.[8] Sanderson promptly rejected this proposal, which was obviously made without any knowledge on Wellby's part of Macdonald's secret mission. Still, Wellby was not easily deterred, according to Arthur Donaldson Smith, who was also trying to obtain permission to travel to Lake Rudolf and from there to the Nile. In a letter to his friend Percy Cox, who since 1895 had been assistant to the governor general's agent at Baroda, India, Smith said:

> Sanderson whom I saw at the Foreign Office did not give me much encouragement. The last thing he said was "you know if Lord Salisbury gave you permission he would bring down a hornet's nest around his ears." This means that he has refused permission to many and all applicants. Wellby was refused among others so he hit upon the plan of going with Harrington to Menelik's capital with the idea of crossing to the Nile north of Fashoda. I do not think he will succeed. Harrington told me that Menelik would not give permission to anyone to go through southern districts.[9]

As it turned out, Harrington was wrong. But when he met with Smith in London in the summer of 1898, he could not have foreseen Menelik's shrewd change in policy. For his part, Wellby was an eternal optimist, pushing forward on high hopes. On July 28, he wrote to Keltie that he planned to travel to Lake Rudolf and onward to Khartoum.[10] Wellby's letter to Keltie also contained a not-so-subtle hint about obtaining some form of Royal Geographical Society endorsement. Yet this was scarcely necessary since his lobbying of the military command coincided with Kitchener's final push against the Mahdists in the Sudan. The Intelligence Division of the War Office saw the value of having an officer of Wellby's abilities in Ethiopia as the war in the Sudan approached its climax. Thus, in August, they telegraphed him in Simla, where he had gone for a ten-day rest, telling him that Harrington was returning to Ethiopia and was willing to take him if he cared to go. Wellby jumped at the offer since it was the "only way of getting into Abyssinia."[11]

Wellby had to hurry out of India in order to meet Harrington, who was scheduled to arrive in Zeila on the Somali coast on September 7, 1898. Luckily, Wellby reached Zeila via Aden the day after Harrington's arrival. He immediately told him that he wanted to go to Lake Rudolf and up to the Nile. Harrington's response was hardly encouraging. He told Wellby that he and his party stood very little chance of "being able to travel beyond Menelik's capital."[12] On hearing this, Wellby decided to bypass Ethiopia altogether and head for the lake from Berbera, farther down the Somali coast. This decision could not have pleased either Harrington or the Intelligence Division, which was counting on him for military information about Ethiopia. Leaving Harrington's caravan outside Zeila, Wellby and his small party sailed for Berbera, arriving on September 11. Much had changed in Berbera in the three years since Wellby had last been there. He later wrote, "Every stone of it is under the official thumb, entailing endless rules, regulations, taxes, and certificates."[13] This meant that his plans for making a quick and surreptitious dash out of Berbera for Lugh and the southern shore of Lake Rudolf were quickly uncovered and vetoed by local British officials. They told him that such a journey would violate boundary treaties, and as a result, his plans "speedily vanished into dreamland."[14]

Effectively blocked from reaching Lake Rudolf through Somaliland as Smith had done in 1894–1895, Wellby had no choice but to rejoin Harrington and go on to Addis Ababa. He and Harrington reached the Ethiopian capital on October 25, where they were well received by Menelik. The following day, the emperor set off on military maneuvers with a 50,000-strong army, which he planned to send against *Ras* Mengasha, the prince of Tigray and son of the late Emperor Yohannes IV. Wellby was greatly impressed with the organization and discipline of this army, observations that Menelik hoped would eventually reach London.

It was while this army was on the march that Harrington presented Menelik with a phonograph record on which Queen Victoria sent greetings. This so impressed Menelik and Empress Taytu that a salute was fired in honor of the occasion.[15] Shortly afterward, Harrington asked Menelik if Wellby could travel to Lake Rudolf. He pressed the matter with the emperor but not solely to satisfy Wellby's quest for adventure. Rather, he thought that such a trip would provide him and the Foreign Office with vital intelligence about the extent of effective Ethiopian occupation near the lake and the Nile. One evening, he returned to Wellby's tent and told him that Menelik had consented to let him go. Wellby was ecstatic.[16]

In effect, Menelik was allowing Wellby to tour his domains under Ethiopian escort. He reasoned that this would substantiate his territorial claims all the way to the lake and to the headwaters of the Sobat River. He was also confident that Wellby's maps would help refute British claims to the areas where he had established a visible presence. Clearly, the British would have been hard put to dismiss the maps and reports of one of their own officers, whose expedition they had promoted.

Flushed with excitement, Wellby was hardly concerned about the political underpinnings of what was to be the trip of his lifetime. On December 16, he wrote to Keltie from Addis Ababa, outlining his proposed travel route and telling him that he planned to draw his maps on a scale of four miles to the inch.[17]

Wellby recruited forty-four men, including thirty Ethiopians, nine Somali, and five Sudanese. The Sudanese had been members of the Bottego expedition and had been acting as artillery instructors to the Ethiopians. Also traveling with him was Duffadar Shahzad Mir, an experienced surveyor of the Eleventh Bengal Lancers who had participated in the expedition to Tibet. Wellby chose as his headman a seasoned caravan leader, Mohamed Hassan, and with his help obtained thirty-one mules, nineteen donkeys, and eleven horses. He packed four months' supply of food in skins, most of it consisting of flour, salt, and pepper. In addition, he carried the usual assortment of camping equipment and a plane table, barometers, thermometers, hypsometers, and a theodolite for survey work. His arsenal consisted of 35 Martini-Henry rifles and 6,000 rounds of ammunition, and his fox terrier, "Lady," became the expedition's mascot.[18]

Wellby and his men marched out of Addis Ababa on December 18, 1898, in a southwest direction that took them along the chain of Ethiopian Rift Valley lakes. Menelik had sent letters ahead to his provincial administrators, ordering them to assist the expedition in every possible way. As he trekked over the high hills of southern Ethiopia, Wellby was warmly greeted, feted, and showered with gifts by Menelik's local officials. Spirits were high, the men were happy and well fed, and the expedition made good progress over the mountainous terrain. However, the solicitous attentions of Menelik's administrators created a number of unforeseen problems for Wellby. They were keen about having visitors, and so they insisted that he remain their guest for prolonged periods of time.[19] Wellby could not accept such offers because they would have delayed the progress of his expedition and led to a breakdown of the daily routine and discipline of camp life. These officials also worried about Wellby's safety and the repercussions for themselves if anything happened to him. Consequently, they insisted that he follow secure routes, which were often the long way around. He regularly rejected these suggestions but only after much protracted and tiring discussion. Finally, they often provided him with armed escorts to the limits of their territories. These he found were usually more trouble than they were worth because they tended to loot local villages along the way.[20]

While Wellby was in the Hammar-Koke Mountains, he obtained a Reshiat guide named Kulo and his son, who knew the way to Lake Rudolf. Both had been taken prisoner by the Ethiopians and were pleased to escort the expedition to the lake in return for their freedom.[21] Descending the cool highlands, Wellby trekked across the hot plains toward the lake that the Ethiopians called Gallop. As he did so, he came upon sparse remnant populations that had survived recent devastating Ethiopian raids. The area still had abundant elephant herds, and Wellby began collecting a sizable amount of ivory.

In mid-March, the caravan caught sight of Lake Rudolf and a few days later reached its northeastern shore: "Soon after daybreak, Lake Gallop was in sight, and, though we traveled at a rapid rate along a splendid track for most of the way, yet we did not reach the shores of this beautiful water till after noon. We then pitched our camp fairly close to the edge, that all might enjoy the water, for we were thoroughly hot and thirsty, having had none along the road."[22]

The following day, Wellby moved his camp to the higher, shady ground where Bottego and Smith had previously camped.[23] However, his triumph in reaching the lake and the idyllic location of his camp were marred by an outbreak of anthrax that began killing off his transport animals, including his own horse. This was a potentially disastrous development since the entire caravan was dependent on these animals for transporting food, equipment, and a growing supply of elephant tusks. Fortunately, the Ethiopian chiefs who had hosted Wellby had given him gifts of cattle, which now numbered thirty. Anticipating the loss of all his pack animals, he had his men train the cattle to carry the loads.[24]

As most of his European predecessors had done, Wellby decided to spend several days exploring the Omo River. Unlike them, however, he found the left bank virtually uninhabited, as the people had "shifted across to avoid the raiding parties."[25] He crossed over to the populated right bank of the river, but the villagers fled out of fear of being attacked. As a result, he was unable to make direct contact with them. The forest gallery contained large numbers of elephants, and Wellby shot several. Unfortunately, when he returned to the lake, he found that the anthrax epidemic had further decimated his animals, requiring that he dispose of some of his ivory.

Wellby had hoped to obtain large amounts of grain from the peoples living to the north of the lake for his trek south. However, as he sadly discovered, they had been so decimated by the Ethiopians that there was virtually no grain available. As there was no food to be had in this area, he began his march down the eastern shore of the lake the following day. In order to save time, he walked to the west of the rocky Longodoti Hills that fringed the lake shore. Then, toward the end of March, he met with an unfortunate accident: "While opening a tin, I drove the instrument—the three-sided pointed weapon usually found in any big hunting knife—clean through the first finger of my left hand, causing me to lose half my finger."[26] This was a remarkable understatement on Wellby's part, for as Harrington later wrote, "he marched miles in intense agony, holding a mortifying finger upright during the whole of the long and miserable march, concealing his pain, so that his followers should not lose heart."[27]

Recognizing his desperate need for transport animals, Wellby sent Mir and several men ahead toward the south end of the lake, with instructions to purchase them. Mir soon came upon a herd of several hundred donkeys and many sheep and goats, whose owners fled at his approach. He took sixty donkeys and a large number of sheep and goats and drove them toward the main caravan. When Wellby arrived at the southern end of the lake on April 8, 1899, he was delighted at the sight of Mir's herds. However, he soon learned that Mir had effectively confiscated the animals since the owners had fled "through unreasonable fear and would not stop to barter them."[28]

Like a number of travelers before him, Wellby was faced with the terrible dilemma of either perishing or taking food and property by force from owners who refused to barter. He spoke to the truth of the matter when he said, "Had not Shahzad Mir then helped himself to donkeys and sheep, we should probably be still struggling along the shore of the lake."[29] Yet he was also faced with the additional problem of his Ethiopian escort. These were men "whose chief topic of thought and conversation was killing and raiding." The Sudanese were not any better, according to Wellby, because they "had been accustomed to shoot natives and carry off property in the most regrettable manner."

To some extent, Mir had become influenced by these men and "was perfectly convinced in his own mind that we should never be able to come to a friendly understanding with any tribes at all on our journey, and that we should have to take what we required by force."[30]

Wellby now headed northwest, away from the lake and into the land of the Turkana people, following a route similar to that taken by Teleki a decade before. Despite his extreme caution, there were two unfortunate incidents in which his headman, Mohamed Hassan, was speared in the back and an Ethiopian and Turkana were killed. Once they crossed the Turkwell River, their relations with the Turkana became friendly. Still, Wellby had to constantly lecture the Ethiopians about not pilfering property, but he was only partially successful in this regard. He noted that "the Abyssinians, who in other respects were doing well, could not for the life of them understand why I was so particular to leave alone things that did not belong to me, as their own ideas on this point were totally at variance with my own."[31] Only the death of one of the Ethiopians from touching the poison on some arrows he had stolen made the others heed Wellby's message.

Wellby next trekked into a vast expanse of semiarid country lying between the Turkwell and the Sobat Rivers. This was the unmapped region to the west of the lake that both Cavendish and Smith so much wanted to explore. Their plans were to march east to west from the lake to the Nile. Wellby chose to cross it from south to north, parallel to the lake and the Nile, aiming for the Anglo-Egyptian outpost of Nasser in the southern Sudan. Contrary to then prevailing European preconceptions, Wellby found the land relatively flat. He surveyed the headwaters of the Pibor River, which he mistakenly called the Ruzi (meaning water), and traced it north to where it joined with the Sobat. Trekking for 500 miles from the Turkwell, he arrived at Nasser on the Sobat in late June, where he was greeted by an Egyptian garrison under the command of Lieutenant MacEwen.[32] After resting at Nasser for only a day, he immediately set off for the post of Sobat on the Nile, 180 miles away. There, Wellby and his men were placed on a gunboat, the *Fateh*, and transported the short distance to Fashoda, where only several months before Britain and France had confronted one another over possession of the Upper Nile. From Fashoda, Wellby and half his men were taken by paddle steamer to Omdurman, reaching it in mid-July. The remainder of his men and animals soon followed.

On arriving in Omdurman, Wellby promptly wrote to Keltie at the Royal Geographical Society, telling him of his successful trip:

> I have just arrived here from a very jolly trip. After visiting the southern districts of Abyssinia, and satisfying myself that the Omo flows into

Rudolf, we struck south along the E. shore of Rudolf. . . . Unfortunately, half my animals died from glanders. . . . On arrival at S. Rudolf we passed Teleki's Volcano and struck west. . . . We came across no end of tribes and had no trouble with any of them. I would willingly retrace my steps with ten men only.[33]

Wellby had made a truly extraordinary journey in seven months, during which he had successfully mapped the unknown lands between Lake Rudolf and the Nile. His maps were superb because they were based on meticulous observations of latitude and elevation that he himself recorded, as well as the plane table work done by his skilled and experienced surveyor, Duffadar Shahzad Mir. His ethnographic observations were not extensive because, as David Turton observed, the highland Ethiopians with whom he traveled had a "natural bent for shooting and stealing," which did little to foster peaceful contacts with local peoples.[34] In addition, the Omo River valley and the area to the north of Lake Rudolf had been depopulated in 1897–1898 by the devastating military invasion of *Ras* Wolda Giorgis. Those who survived had fled across the Omo to the right bank to avoid contacts with the Ethiopians.

Von Höhnel summed up Wellby's dilemma in traveling with Ethiopians: "It is natural that the natives who had been repeatedly and cruelly dealt with by the Abyssinian hoards, could have no desire to enter into relations with a caravan composed largely of individuals whom they had every reason to avoid. Wellby therefore came very little into contact with the population living by the lake."[35]

Wellby's largely Ethiopian entourage also influenced the names he attached to geographic features. Von Höhnel said the following of this: "His retinue consisted mostly of Abyssinians, who were also his informants along the route. Therefore the names for lakes, rivers, and places given by Wellby often differ from those used by other travelers."[36] In writing to Keltie on August 9, 1897, Wellby insistently said that "Rudolf is properly speaking Gallop."[37] This Ethiopian name, of course, did not survive, primarily because the lake eventually came under British colonial control.

It is clear that Wellby was a courageous soldier and a skilled diplomat, endowed with superior endurance and a unique ability to get on well with people. Harrington highly praised him: "His unfailing tact, his cheerfulness, resource in dangers and hardships, and the winning qualities which endeared him to all who ever knew him, won him the confidence and affection of the natives with whom he came in contact."[38]

Wellby very much admired the Ethiopians and planned to return to Addis Ababa as an assistant to Harrington. He fully acknowledged the evils created by their armed raids but also challenged his countrymen to look into their causes and to find ways of bringing them to an end. His challenge showed great insightfulness and no doubt made European arms traders uncomfortable:

> In previous pages I have made repeated references to the raids carried out by the Abyssinians, and have, like everyone else, condemned these raids. . . . Yet to straight away throw blame on the Abyssinians without entering into the causes of these raids . . . would be unfair. . . . We have furnished them with the means of carrying on successful and destructive raids; we have supplied them with rifles, and it cannot be expected that they would do otherwise than try their level best to wipe out old scores with their less fortunately armed neighbors.[39]

Wellby's journey strengthened Menelik's negotiating position with the British because it provided confirmation of effective Ethiopian occupation of the lands north of Lake Rudolf. Yet Wellby had also documented a vast buffer zone where neither British nor Ethiopian control was evident, and he "wondered what would eventually be the fate of the country and tribes situated 'twixt Sirdar and Menelik.'"[40] Lake Rudolf lay in this unclaimed stretch of Africa and represented a prize that both the British and the Ethiopians were anxious to seize.

Wellby returned to England in late 1899 and delivered a paper on his trip before the Geographical Section of the British Association at Dover. However, he was unable to accept Keltie's invitation to open the Royal Geographical Society's 1899–1900 session on November 13 with a similar presentation. Writing to Keltie, he said, "Much as I regret saying no to November 13, I don't see how it can be managed as war seems more probable than ever. I must join my regiment as I would not miss the war for anything."[41] The war he was referring to was the Boer War in South Africa.

Less than a year later, on July 31, 1900, Wellby and his small patrol came under heavy Boer fire at Mertzicht in the southern Transvaal. As the Boers advanced, he ordered his men to safety, while he provided covering fire. Fighting alone and surrounded, he was called on to surrender but refused. Eventually, he was shot in the abdomen and lay wounded on the field until the next morning, when he was carried to a nearby military hospital at Paardekop. He died there on August 5.[42] His death caused profound grief for his family and all who knew him. As Harrington noted, the regret was "that a brilliant career should have been thus cut short with its bright promise but partly fulfilled."[43]

Six weeks before, on June 18, John Wellby read his son's paper before the Royal Geographical Society, where it was enthusiastically received.[44] His book, entitled 'Twixt Sirdar and Menelik, was published in 1901, the same year that his parents erected a stained glass east window in his memory in St. Mary's Church, Westham, Sussex.[45] Wellby was buried in Paardekop, where his family had a large white stone cross erected above his grave. However, his grave and monument were later moved to Volksrust, which his grand-niece's husband, Simon Horn, visited in the fall of 1996.[46]

Wellby stood in sharp contrast to Nicholas Leontiev, who arrived at Lake Rudolf five months after him, on August 21, 1899. His incursions into British-claimed territory around Lake Rudolf represented a threat that even a somewhat indifferent Foreign Office could not entirely ignore. Harrington was anxious to quickly replace the Union Jacks originally put up at the northern end of the lake in 1898. Though primarily symbolic, such a gesture served to reinforce Britain's claim to the lake at a time when Menelik was prepared to negotiate his southern border. Concerned that the Foreign Office would take its time sending an official expedition to the lake to do the job, Harrington entrusted it to a joint Anglo-American sporting expedition headed by James Jonathan Harrison and William Fitzhugh Whitehouse. However, before they reached the lake in March 1900, Arthur Donaldson Smith surreptitiously made a run from Berbera, intent on exploring the land between Lake Rudolf and the Nile. His presence in this politically contested area greatly upset Harrington and other British officials. But once Smith had gotten into the interior, there was nothing they could do to stop him.

12

Doctor Smith Returns

Arthur Donaldson Smith as he appeared following his second trip to Lake Rudolf (from The Nile Quest, *1903).*

Since his return from Lake Rudolf in late 1895, Arthur Donaldson Smith had been preoccupied with the idea of exploring the Omo River and the lands to the west. Throughout 1896, he extensively corresponded with J. Scott Keltie of the Royal Geographical Society about obtaining financial support for such an expedition. In early 1897, the society's council finally agreed to give him £2,000 toward the trip.[1] However, Smith was unable to start for the lake, as he was already committed to a natural history collecting trip in the Khingan Mountains of Manchuria and Inner Mongolia with two other Philadelphians, George L. Farnum and J. Edward Farnum.

Smith and the Farnums left Peking on March 19, 1897, and after spending several months in the mountains collecting and hunting, they headed for Vladivostok in Russia. Although in eastern Asia, Smith was in regular correspondence with Keltie, asking for information about the Bottego expedition and James Rennell Rodd's mission to Ethiopia. At the same time, he told Keltie that he estimated that the Lake Rudolf–Nile expedition would cost £4,500 and asked that the council increase its contribution to £3,000.[2] It was now October 1897, and political and military events in that part of Africa had dramatically changed since the council had made its tentative commitment several months before. General Horatio Herbert Kitchener was slowly moving up the Nile, Commandant Jean-Baptiste Marchand was racing toward Fashoda, the French were trying to launch an expedition from Ethiopia to the Upper Nile, and Major James Ronald Macdonald was on a secret mission to secure the Nile headwaters from the south. The prime minister, Lord Salisbury, refused to allow any unofficial expeditions access to Lake Rudolf out of fear of provoking Emperor Menelik II of Ethiopia.

Smith arrived in Shanghai in October 1897 and from there went on to India, where he remained until June 1898. While in India, he spent most of his time with Percy Z. Cox, who at the time was assistant to the governor general's agent at Baroda, a position he had assumed three years earlier. Cox and Smith knew each other well from the period when Cox was the assistant resident at Berbera in Somaliland. Smith spent the 1897 Christmas holidays with Cox and his wife at Baroda and then put his medical training to good use by serving as a physician to the military, for which he was given a stipend. It was at this time that Afridi tribesmen from Afghanistan launched a religious war against the British, captured all the posts in the Khyber Pass, attacked British forts near Peshawar, and overran Tirah, a mountainous tract southwest of the Khyber Pass in what is now northwestern Pakistan. British and Indian troops were sent into Tirah, and in a series of military encounters in 1897–1898 known as the Tirah Campaign, they drove the invaders out and retook the Khyber Pass.[3]

Smith participated in the Tirah Campaign as both a physician and a foreign news correspondent for the *New York Sun*. He continued to provide medical care to the military until the spring of 1898, when he went on a hunting trip with Cox to the east-central state of Bastr.

By this time, Smith had gotten Cox extremely enthusiastic about joining him on the expedition to Lake Rudolf and the Nile. Cox, who had spent several years in Somaliland, planned to take a two-year furlough for the purpose of making the trip.[4] All of Smith's letters to Cox during 1898 dealt with the expedition and the various options and schemes he had worked out for financing it. In fact, by late 1897, Smith, sensing a lack of support for the idea by the Royal Geographical Society, came up with the idea of inducing the gaekwar, the ruler of Baroda, to support the expedition financially. On December 29, 1897, Cox laid this proposal before his superior, Colonel Martelli, in a detailed letter. After describing Smith's reputation and qualifications, Cox related that the expedition would last two years and cost £6,000, of which Smith was prepared to put up £1,000. He proposed that the gaekwar, who had set up the Baroda State Museum in 1894, be asked to contribute £5,000. In return, the expedition would be formally under his auspices and all specimens collected would go to the Baroda Museum. Allowing for the possibility that the gaekwar might find the expedition too ambitious, Cox proposed a more modest alternative in the form of an expedition to Somaliland for the purpose of collecting natural history specimens.[5]

Martelli was favorably disposed to the proposal, and the gaekwar expressed interest. However, Cox, because of his official position, could not discuss financial arrangements with the gaekwar; this was something Smith had to do.

On May 29, 1898, a letter was sent from the office of the gaekwar of Baroda to Cox, informing him that £1,200 had been granted "for a Scientific Expedition to Somaliland for the purpose of collecting Natural History specimens for the Baroda State Museum." The gaekwar had opted for a modest specimen-collecting expedition more in keeping with the interests of the museum. He understandably had no interest in becoming entangled in the political risks of a far-off corner of Africa, nor was he interested in sponsoring geographic exploration of Africa. No doubt, the British authorities in India would not have allowed him to finance the Lake Rudolf–Nile expedition, and there was a hint of this in the letter Cox received: "I beg it to be clearly understood that no further amount will be paid by His Highness' Government over and above that now sanctioned in connection with the Expedition, nor will His Highness' Government undertake any other responsibility in regard thereto."[6] Cox wired the good news about the gaekwar's £1,200 grant to Smith, who was then in Bombay.[7]

Smith arrived back in Baroda in early June, where he spent two days with Cox prior to leaving India for Aden. From the Smith-Cox correspondence over the next several months, it is clear that they elaborated a fairly sophisticated plan of action for obtaining British and Ethiopian government approval for the Lake Rudolf–Nile expedition, financial backing from the Royal Geographical Society, and additional funding from the gaekwar of Baroda. Cox was unwilling to trust the Somalis as guards for the larger expedition and was instead inclined to recruit ex-soldiers of the Indian army. This move was fraught with complications because it required bringing the Indian government into the picture as well.

Smith left for Aden on June 8 on the SS *Oriental*. He wrote to Cox from Aden on July 3, 1898, saying that he was doubtful that the

Ethiopians would let them proceed. Because the Somaliland Protectorate officials reported to Aden, Smith was able to get a good idea of
what was going on in Somaliland, and he provided Cox with a detailed
update on the price of camels, the monthly wage for Somali men, and
a description of conditions in the interior.[8] While in Aden, Smith also
learned of Lord Delamere's trip from Somaliland to Lake Rudolf. Back
in Baroda, Cox wrote to George Curzon, who was then a member of
Parliament but would be named viceroy of India just six weeks later.
Cox wrote him in his capacity as a vice president of the Royal Geographical Society, asking him to help Smith.[9]

Moving on to London in late July 1898, Smith engaged in an intense
effort to get the Royal Geographical Society to provide him with funding and the Foreign Office to intercede with Menelik to let him pass
unhindered. Both efforts were to fail.

On August 6, 1898, Smith wrote to Cox, briefing him on what had
transpired so far. He said: "The Government has refused permission to
half a dozen Englishmen who had strong backing and who wanted to
go into the country west of Rudolf. The fact that I am an American
gives me an advantage, as Curzon hinted." However, Curzon was non-
committal, as was Keltie, whom Smith characterized as "humble as
pie on account of the Cavendish affair."[10]

On September 1, 1898, Smith received a polite but flat refusal from
the British government.[11] This decision not to allow Smith to proceed
was made at the highest echelon, reflecting the level and degree of influence he must have brought to bear in pursuing his request.

Smith was fully aware of the political and military turmoil in this
part of Africa, including the Fashoda crisis that had largely determined
Salisbury's decision.[12] Persistent as ever, he was back in London in October, still trying to get the Foreign Office to approve his trip to the
lake and the Nile.[13] Writing to Cox, he said, "I expect answer any day
from Foreign Office. I will wire you if *not* successful Cox Baroda, this
will mean short trip. If successful, I will wire Cox Baroda, good—and
in this latter case pick up fifteen Gurkhas." Toward the end of his letter to Cox, he said: "If we only go on a short trip, which is most probable, bring your own tent and personal kit, but plenty of boots and
clothes for yourself just in case we make a run for it."[14] In other words,
Smith did not rule out defying the British authorities and making a
run for the lake and the Nile.

Smith and Cox arrived in Berbera on December 20, 1898, and on
Christmas Eve, they set off with thirty camels, three ponies, and two
riding camels for their collecting trip. The Gaekwar's Expedition to
Somaliland was under way. Cox kept a daily diary of the trip, written
in a very legible hand. It recounted in detail their stalks, hunting expe-

riences, and natural history observations and thus is a valuable historical document for conservationists. Cox also took along a camera and made numerous photographs during the trip. Both men were in contact with the outside world while in Somaliland, receiving and sending letters and reading slightly dated newspapers.[15]

On Thursday, December 29, Cox received a letter from John Lane Harrington (1865–1927), the British agent in Addis Ababa. In it, Harrington told him that they might be able to obtain Menelik's permission to visit the lake and the Nile but that this would require their coming up to Addis Ababa.[16] Cox replied to Harrington the same day, saying that it would be too expensive for them to go to Addis Ababa and requesting that he obtain Menelik's permission to go on from where they were.[17]

On January 22, the mail from Berbera and Bombay arrived in camp, and Cox noted in his diary, "I see in the paper . . . that Macdonald is pushing on N. from Uganda to Rudolf etc." He also noted that Lieutenant Colonel James Hayes Sadler (1851–1922), the resident in Berbera, "writes he hopes we have got what specimens we want now!!"[18]

March 26, 1899, was a "red letter day" for Cox. He received "an enormous mail . . . six letters . . . best of all a letter from Harrington saying Menelik's permission to travel in Abyssinia granted. Hurrah! Now we only have Sadler i.e. Br. authorities' scruples to overcome. Cracked a bottle . . . in honor of the occasion."[19]

Although Menelik had given his approval, two other obstacles remained—the local British authorities in Somaliland and the recruitment of good men. It was clear to Cox and Smith that many of the men who had gone on their hunting trip were not suitable for the trip to Lake Rudolf and the Nile. Therefore, they decided to recruit Gurkhas in India. However, Sadler proved uncooperative, saying that he had to refer the matter to the Foreign Office since he had clear instructions not to allow any armed parties to travel beyond the Webi Shebeli River.[20]

Cox tried to find out from the assistant resident in Berbera, Cordiaux, what Sadler's real objection was and learned that it was the idea of their recruiting Gurkhas, the best fighting men in India, that troubled him.[21] Cox saw Sadler again the next day:

> I went over to see Sadler and again urged that he should throw the matter on to Harrington's shoulders, but he insisted that he must write and refused to wire. And also refused to show me what he wrote, but he swore he had no objection to offer. . . . Cannot see why, if he has no objection to offer, he won't show us what he writes. . . . He said that he had said all he could in our favor but he mentioned having said that we were accompa-

nied by 50 men 30 Esc sepoys and 20 natives of India. The Esc sepoys is just the thing to scare them. Begged him to change it.[22]

The following day, April 8, Cox saw Sadler again:

Repeated request to change Esc sepoys, and he agreed to put partly ex-sepoys and partly porters! He also showed me the letter he had written and I found he had put "Rudolfland" as our objective! This is quite enough to put them off, and quite inaccurate. In my official notice for the Harrar authorities, I said "Lake Abaya and the Omo"—quite a different pair of shoes. He however agreed to change it and put as in my official.[23]

Sadler, of course, had the destination correct, but Cox and Smith had misstated it to Harrington so as to disarm any official opposition to the trip. Sadler was an experienced soldier and diplomat, having served in India and as consul at Muscat (1892–1896) before taking up his post at Berbera, and he could not be fooled. Lake Abaya and the Omo were viewed as Ethiopian. The Lake Rudolf area was still an open question, and Salisbury was concerned about possible armed clashes with the Ethiopians in the region. Menelik had, in effect, approved a trip through Ethiopian territory, not one to Lake Rudolf and the Nile.[24]

Smith and Cox left for Aden on April 9, 1899.[25] Cox was in India for the next two months, helping Smith to recruit ex-sepoys for the Lake Rudolf–Nile expedition. However, Cox was never to go on the trip. On May 2, 1899, Lord Curzon, the new viceroy of India, appointed Cox resident at Muscat, where the French were challenging British supremacy at the entrance to the Persian Gulf. The news reached Cox in Bombay, where he was helping Donaldson Smith. Curzon made the offer very appealing by promising to raise the allowance at Muscat and by arranging a permanent appointment for Cox under the Foreign Department.[26] Smith was now on his own as far as the trip to the Nile was concerned.

The Gaekwar's Scientific Expedition to Somaliland was a success, and descriptions of the birds and batrachians collected were published in the *Proceedings of the Zoological Society of London*. Some of the 103 bird specimens collected were presented by the gaekwar to the British Museum. Sixteen specimens of batrachians were also collected, and these were added to those that Smith had given to the British Museum following his 1894–1895 trip. Also included was an excellent butterfly collection.[27]

Smith continued his preparations in India, spending most of May and June 1899 recruiting Sikhs and Gurkhas in the Punjab. By July, he was back in Berbera, ready to leave for Lake Rudolf and the Nile. Accompanying him were Carlysle Frazer, a Scottish taxidermist who had recently been with him and Cox on the Gaekwar's Expedition, and Gaetano, a Goanese cook. From the outset, Sadler tried to sabotage the expedition by inducing desertions and making it difficult for Smith to hire a Somali headman. However, while he succeeded in these efforts to some degree, he was unable to prevent Smith from marching out of Berbera with seventeen Somalis and as many Gurkhas.

Smith's route eventually crisscrossed his 1895 one, as he tried to move through as much parallel unexplored country as he could. He continuously surveyed as he went, using instruments borrowed from the Indian Survey Department. By October, he was in the country of the Boran, whom he found friendly this time. He also had some good words to say about the Ethiopians: "In 1895, I saw the worst side of their treatment; but on my recent journey, I found that their treatment of the tribes, once thoroughly brought to submission, was commendable." When he arrived at El Dere, he had reached the midpoint of his journey, 750 miles from Berbera and an equal distance from the Nile. Thus far, he had had a number of serious problems with both the Somalis and the Indians in his party, and he had some rather harsh words to say about them.[28]

In early November, Smith passed Egder, which he had visited on his first expedition. In 1895, it had taken him nine months to reach this place from Berbera, but now he had done so in just three. Smith found Arab and Somali traders from Kismayu in the region, trading in ivory and cattle. He and his men then moved on toward Mega and headed for the southeast end of Lake Stephanie. Before reaching the lake, Smith obtained a specimen of a tiny gazelle, which he later presented to the British Museum; it was found to be new to science and was named *Madoqua guntheri smithii*.[29]

Smith reached Lake Rudolf on December 10, 1899, some four months after leaving Berbera (during his 1894–1895 trip, it had taken him a year to reach the lake from Berbera). He found that the Murle of the Omo delta had been reduced to poverty, and he concluded that it was the result of Ethiopian raids. However, this was only part of the story since the region had also been affected by a severe drought. Concerning the source of Lake Rudolf, Smith admitted that he had, in fact, traveled up the Mago, not the Omo, on his first trip.[30] He then put forth the opinion that the Mago and the Omo contributed equal volumes of water to a third and final stream, the Nianamm, which then flowed into the lake. He could not have accurately assessed the two rivers from a hydrological point of view and was thus making something of an educated guess at best. The Omo River is, in fact, the principal source of Lake Rudolf, and the Mago, which Smith explored, is a major tributary.

On January 3, 1900, Smith left the Omo and started west across the 300 miles of unexplored land that lay between him and the Nile. Late in the month, he crossed Wellby's line of march at right angles and entered the country of the Margois people, whom he described as cow worshipers. He continued to collect natural history specimens as he had done all along, and in this area, he secured a Ruppel's reed-buck and a pair of spotted bush buck, which the British Museum did not possess at the time.

In late February, Smith entered the country around Tarangole, the northernmost point reached by Macdonald in November 1898. It was there that a local chief named Amara told him the British had set up a post on the east bank of the Nile considerably south of Lado. Previously unaware of this, Smith had planned to exit via the Congo.[31] Quickly changing his plans, he headed for this post, which he reached on March 14, 1900, seven and a half months after he had left Berbera in Somaliland. At Fort Berkeley, he was welcomed by Captain William K. Dugmore of the Uganda Rifles, with whom he remained for seven weeks.

Although Smith had filled in a number of gaps on the map of Africa and had achieved his goal of being the first to cross from Lake Rudolf west to the Nile, he was now faced with the logistical problem of getting his men, equipment, and specimens out through the best possible route. The river route did not at first seem a likely option, even though the British had begun cutting a navigable channel through the *sudd*, the vast area of floating vegetable matter that covered a large area of the Upper Nile. However, he was eventually able to travel down the Nile by boat, while Frazer trekked to Mombasa with the men and the expedition's collections.

Smith reached Cairo in early June, from where he traveled to London. By any measure, his expedition had been a great success. He had mapped over 500 miles of unexplored territory and had brought back several hundred different species of birds, mammalia, plants, reptilia, batrachia, fishes, and butterflies.

A week after arriving at Fort Berkeley on the Nile, Smith had written to J. Scott Keltie at the Royal Geographical Society, not only outlining the accomplishments of his expedition but also detailing the problems he had with Colonel Sadler in Somaliland. He also told Keltie that he planned to exit via the Congo under Belgian auspices.[32]

This statement about traveling under Belgian auspices was sure to irritate the British, who in 1900 were moving toward a showdown with

Belgium in the Bahr el Ghazel area that borders on the Upper Nile. Smith's subsequent comments were also intended to nettle the Royal Geographical Society: "I am sorry that President Sir Clements Markham [of the Royal Geographical Society] expressed the wish that it [the trip from Lake Rudolf to the Nile] should be done by an Englishman. I do not know whether the President will forgive me or not, but I shall probably find this out before I leave Antwerp for America."[33]

This was a loaded statement that contained a not-so-veiled threat. Smith was now the conquering hero, scornful of whatever Markham and the British had to say. Moreover, he was not planning to visit England, candidly saying he would sail from Antwerp to America. He intended this as more than a snub to the Royal Geographical Society. There were clearly serious political and military dimensions to his projected plans. He now possessed unique maps of British-claimed territories and detailed information about them that could be placed in the wrong hands, as the Foreign Office saw it. And Smith gave a not-so-subtle hint that he was considering doing just that:

> I am undecided to whom I shall give my maps. The Germans so far have treated me with the most honor in doing justice to my maps. They like just what I can hand over to them, viz everything triangulated and checked and re-checked. You must acknowledge that the Germans have treated my maps far better than the R.G.S., and also that subsequent to an ephemeral puff after reading a paper, I found no one to stand up for me when I was snubbed on the occasion of Cavendish's paper. If the latter were only the affair of a night, so must the former have been.[34]

Smith had apparently been deeply hurt by Cavendish's allegations that he had treated the Boran badly. Moreover, he was angry that no one at the society had stood up for him. This is not surprising, given that they only had his side of the story and Cavendish's. In addition, the latter was the first British explorer to reach the lake, and his fellow countrymen were not about to publicly denounce him and side with Smith, an American.

In his letter of March 21, 1900, from Fort Berkeley, Smith asked Keltie for a quid pro quo. In essence, if the society wanted his maps and the other fruits of his expedition, they would have to give him the previously promised £2,000 that he now said he would use for future scientific trips.[35]

Given the contents of the letter, it is clear that Smith was not averse to Keltie's sharing all of it with the leadership of the society. He had, after all, achieved his goal of exploring the lands between Lake Rudolf and the Nile in the highly professional manner respected by all of the European geographical societies. He had done this despite incredible obstacles placed in his path by the British government and local British officials such as Sadler in Somaliland. He had what the British now wanted and was clearly in a position to dictate terms. They had no desire to see his maps fall into either German, Belgian, French, or Italian hands for a number of reasons, among which was the obvious embarrassment that would have ensued if British-claimed territory were laid out in map form for the first time in the publication of a rival European colonial power.

The Royal Geographical Society moved rapidly to both mollify Smith and imply that Britain had assisted him on his expedition. In a notice published in the *Geographical Journal*, the society announced that part of the mapping was done by Smith's taxidermist-assistant, a British subject, that most of Smith's men and collections had exited through British territory, and that Smith himself had traveled down the Nile on a British gunboat.[36] To appease Smith, the society promptly invited him to read his paper at a November 12, 1900, session chaired by Sir Clements Markham, the president. Smith received lavish praise from Markham and others present at the meeting, including Oldfield Thomas of the British Museum, who named two antelopes in his honor.[37] This was not all. The society promptly published his paper, and leading members of the council privately apologized to him for past misunderstandings. On May 20, 1901, Markham personally presented Smith with the society's Patron's Medal, which was one of the most coveted prizes in the field of geographic exploration.[38]

After so many accolades, Smith could not refuse to give his maps to the society. Yet for the rest of his life, he frequently complained that the society's council had reneged on its promise to give him £2,000 to offset the costs of his expedition.

None of those who were present at the medal-awarding ceremony could have surmised that Smith's career as an explorer had, in effect, come to an end. He never returned to the regions of Africa he knew so well, nor did he lead scientific expeditions into other parts of the world. Many would follow in his footsteps to Lake Rudolf and the Omo River, enlarging on the geographic discoveries he had made. But his own life would take a different turn.

One of Smith's friends in the first decade of the twentieth century was Theodore Roosevelt, who admired him as a sportsman and naturalist.[39] In 1909, Roosevelt appointed him as U.S. consul in Mersine, Turkey, at an annual stipend of $2,500.[40] By this time, Smith was financially strapped because of some poor investments and had also become dependent on alcohol. Unfortunately, he often became violent when inebriated, which in turn led to his being transferred from Mersine to Patras, Greece, after a few months. However, his stay there was also brief, and in April 1910, he was transferred to Aguascalientes, Mexico, where he remained for a year.[41]

Returning to Philadelphia, Smith became active in the Boy Scout movement, hoping to help boys appreciate the wonders of the natural world. In 1917, he joined the United States Army as a captain and was assigned to Fort Oglethorpe in Georgia.[42] Shortly thereafter, he moved to Roulette, a small town in northern Pennsylvania, where he practiced medicine until 1934. Smith's income was supplemented by a small military pension and a remittance from his niece's husband, Charles A. Potter Jr., a successful Philadelphia businessman. Around 1934, Smith retired from Roulette, in part because of failing eyesight. He then lived for most of the year with his niece, Margaret Spencer Potter, and her husband in Philadelphia and spent the winters in St. Petersburg, Florida. His health began to fail in 1938, and on February 19, 1939, he died of coronary artery disease at the United States Naval Hospital in Philadelphia at the age of seventy-two years.[43]

Smith's second journey to Lake Rudolf essentially brought to an end the era of exploratory travel around Lake Rudolf that had begun with Count Samuel Teleki and Lieutenant Ludwig von Höhnel. Smith had filled in the last large remaining blank space on a map that was now accurately charted with rivers, mountains, lakes, and swamps. Triangulation, however, had not resolved the question of where British East Africa ended and Ethiopia began. Most of the travelers who next visited the lake carried chronometers and theodolites and had a knowledge of the stars. They also carried a mandate to draw political lines across the map.

13

Replacing the Union Jacks

The members of the Harrison-Whitehouse Expedition of 1899–1900 on their return at Nairobi. Left to right: William Fitzhugh Whitehouse, R. Perks, Archibald Edward Butter, Donald Clarke, and James Jonathan Harrison (courtesy Scarborough Borough Council, Department of Tourism and Amenities, Wood End Museum).

*I*n November 1899, three months after Arthur Donaldson Smith had left Berbera on his epic journey from Lake Rudolf to the Nile, an Anglo-American expedition under James Jonathan Harrison arrived at Zeila, on the Somali coast. Its purpose was to "carry a complete survey through the Hawash Valley to Lake Rudolf, and if possible across to the Nile, at the same time combining a sporting trip in which attention was to be directed to the beasts and the birds of the countries visited."[1] Fortuitously, the group met Colonel John Lane Harrington, the British agent in Ethiopia, who was himself traveling from Zeila to Addis Ababa. He had already secured permission for the expedition to travel to the Ethiopian capital and was intensely interested in their plans to go to Lake Rudolf. Yet only a few months before, the Foreign Office had done its best to prevent Smith and Percy Cox from undertaking just such a journey.

There were two principal reasons for this difference of attitude. The first and foremost was that Menelik, the Ethiopian emperor, had agreed to again place the Union Jack at the northern end of the lake. This standard had first been placed there in 1898 by Herbert Henry Austin but was removed by the Russian buccaneer Nicholas Leontiev in 1899. In the complex negotiations over the Anglo-Ethiopian border, Harrington was anxious to return the flag to this location since it essentially proclaimed Britain's ownership of most of the lake. He did not have the resources to send an expedition to the lake for this purpose, nor was the Foreign Office willing to fund one. Thus, Harrington seized upon the idea of having Harrison do the job and then march over to the Nile in order to secure British claims to this stretch of territory. As the Foreign Office saw it, Smith's expedition would only have complicated matters since as a third-country national, Smith could not have achieved these objectives. In addition, his presence in this geographically contested area might have further complicated matters between Britain and Ethiopia.

Harrison was not a newcomer to Africa, where he had previously hunted. A keen sportsman, he was born in 1858 at his family's estate, Brandesburton Hall, in Yorkshire and educated at Elstree, Harrow, and Christ Church, Oxford. In 1884, he joined the Prince of Wales Yorkshire Hussars and eventually rose to the rank of lieutenant colonel.[2] Although a man of great wealth, like Smith he sought ways to defray the enormous costs of an expedition of this kind. He first approached the Royal Geographical Society by writing to J. Scott Keltie on July 24, 1899:

> In case our trip from Berbera to Lake Rudolf and then attempt to explore the country down to the Sobat River comes off this autumn, could we not interest the Geographical Society to aid us with a grant towards taking out a fully qualified man to map and take observations. I have all but £1,000 required for such a trip. . . . Hoping your Society may be endowed to give us some financial assistant in the matter.[3]

Wary of possible Foreign Office opposition to the trip at a time prior to Harrington's need for restoring the flag, he warned Keltie to "kindly keep the matter as private as possible."[4] Keltie did but flatly refused to allocate any funds to support the expedition. However, the society did provide Harrison with a set of surveying instruments and later helped draw the final versions of his maps.

Harrison was successful in recruiting several other prominent sportsmen to participate in the expedition. The first of these was an American, William Fitzhugh Whitehouse, whose significant financial contribution made him a cosponsor of what became known as the Harrison-Whitehouse Expedition. Whitehouse was born in Elmhurst, Illinois, on September 6, 1877. The son of Fitzhugh Whitehouse, an international lawyer, and Frances Sheldon, he spent most of his youth in England, attending Cheam School in Surrey and Winchester College. In 1895, he entered Yale, where he graduated four years later with honors in history and economics. At twenty-two, Whitehouse was the youngest member of the party. However, he was endowed with remarkable leadership skills, a pleasant and engaging personality, and a love of the outdoors. Over six feet in height, he was a superb athlete and a superior marksman. Whitehouse was also insightful and observant, qualities that helped him produce two of the four firsthand accounts of this expedition.[5]

Harrison also invited a well-known sportsman, Percy Horace Gordon Powell-Cotton, to join the group. Powell-Cotton was the scion of wealthy London merchants, and in 1894, he inherited his family's estate, Quex Park, in Kent. In contrast to the forceful and at times brash Harrison, Powell-Cotton was extremely courteous, thoughtful, and observant. Although he was eight years Harrison's junior, he was equally experienced as a hunter and had already led several collecting expeditions of his own to Asia and Africa. The sharp differences in the personalities of these two men were bound to emerge under the unpredictable circumstances of field travel. However, neither foresaw the inevitable breakup of their partnership or the litigation that followed.[6]

Harrison recruited a second Britisher, Archibald Edward Butter, the twenty-five-year-old laird of Faskally, a 33,000-acre Scottish estate in Perthshire. Educated at Eton, Butter was a keen sportsman who also bred Labrador retrievers. Although he had never been to Africa before, his trip with Harrison set the stage for several subsequent journeys in which he played a prominent role in delineating Ethiopia's borders with Britain's possessions.[7]

Harrison also engaged Donald Clarke, an experienced surveyor with the Royal Engineers, and R. Perks, a skilled taxidermist. After arriving at Zeila, Harrison was able to hire as his headman Mohamed Hassan, the man who had served Captain Montagu Sinclair Wellby in the same capacity just a short time before. He also recruited sixty-one Somalis who had previously traveled with Smith, Lord Delamere, Henry Hart Cavendish, and Wellby. Among them was Karsa (Karsha), a gunbearer who had accompanied William Astor Chanler on his 1892–1894 trip and Smith on his 1894–1895 expedition to Lake Rudolf. Having men who had already passed through an expedition's proposed route was a great advantage. They knew the country well, and based on their prior experiences, they were able to provide valuable advice that was vital to an expedition's success. Yet these heroes of late-nineteenth-century travel in Africa are only occasionally identified or merely mentioned in passing in most European accounts.

On November 12, 1899, Harrison led the expedition out of Zeila toward Addis Ababa. In his train were sixty camels carrying supplies, camping equipment, and ammunition. The route from Zeila to Addis Ababa passed through what was then rich game country less frequently visited by Europeans than the area just beyond Berbera. After a month of successful hunting, they approached the Awash River, at which point relations between Harrison and Powell-Cotton began to sour. The essential problem was that Powell-Cotton selectively hunted in order to collect natural history specimens that he thought would be useful to science. Harrison, on the other hand, tended to hunt more indiscriminately for trophies, a trait that resulted in the regrettable killing of immature elephants in the Awash River valley. Powell-Cotton had some sharp words with Harrison over this and later wrote the following rebuke in his book: "The net result of our hunt was, that H. killed five elephants, and W. and B. one each, while I had also seen two drop. As none of the natives here eat the flesh, it seemed a pity to have killed so many for the sake of such small ivory, and I was sorry I had taken part in the hunt."[8]

The inexperienced Butter and Whitehouse were pleased with the hunt, primarily because they felt satisfied in bagging their first elephants. However, Harrison should have known better than to have pursued elephants whose tusks only averaged some seventeen pounds each. In part, he was motivated by a need to present Menelik with a gift of ivory on arriving in Addis Ababa. As it turned out, Menelik, who had no great inclinations toward wildlife conservation, was surprised that Harrison would have killed such young elephants. Harrington had to apologize to Menelik for this and later reprimanded Harrison and the others.

The expedition arrived in Addis Ababa on January 1, 1900, and four days later, the leaders were invited by Menelik to a formal reception and dinner. Menelik was especially keen on seeing Whitehouse since he had never before met a high-ranking American. While in the capital, Whitehouse met up with another sportsman, Frederic Ernest Allsopp (Baron Hindlip), with whom he would undertake a hunting trip in Ethiopia in 1902. More relevant to Harrison, however, was the news that there was a drought in the south and in the lands around Lake Rudolf. He wrongly concluded that it would be impossible to travel from the lake to the Nile because of a presumed lack of water. What he did not know was that despite the drought, there were adequate water sources between the lake and the Nile, a stretch of country that Smith began traversing on January 3, 1900. In view of the information about the drought, Harrison decided to change the expedition's itinerary. Instead of crossing over to the Nile from Lake Rudolf, he decided to head south from the lake into the British East Africa Protectorate. He also informed his companions that until they left Lake Rudolf, surveying would take precedence over hunting, which would largely be postponed until they reached the game fields to the south. This was a wise decision, given the information at hand. Nonetheless, Powell-Cotton disagreed with it and saw an opportunity to disassociate himself from Harrison, with whom he was increasingly in conflict. On January 3, Powell-Cotton wrote a terse entry in his diary summarizing his break with Harrison: "I drop out of trip as J.J. and I can't hit it off."[9]

The expedition members used their time in Addis Ababa to rest, regroup, and ship out the trophies they had obtained thus far.[10] They met on January 17 to sort out their financial arrangements and the following day parted company. Powell-Cotton headed north for the Simien Mountains, where he planned to hunt ibex, while Harrison and the others set out for Lake Rudolf.[11] Menelik provided them with letters to his local officials, requesting that they provide every possible assistance.

Harrington gave Harrison several Union Jacks and instructed him to place one at the north end of the lake. Menelik had agreed to the replacement of the flag initially hoisted by Herbert Henry Austin in 1898 but removed by the Russian Nicholas Leontiev the following year. However, he was unaware of Harrington's instructions to Harrison to set up other flags as well.

Harrison eventually followed Wellby's southward route of the previous year. But he was disappointed to find that the vast herds of elephants were "a thing of the past, cleared out by the constant shooting of Abyssinian soldiers who are now following the ivory right through the Boran country."[12] In the two months prior to Harrison's arrival, some 1,500 Ethiopian soldiers had killed 750 elephants, whose tusks had been sent to Addis Ababa and then shipped to Europe and Asia. Ivory had now become a principal export for Ethiopia and a major source of hard currency earnings that Menelik primarily used to purchase arms and ammunition.

As Harrison and his companions got closer to the great lakes, their worst fears were realized. The severe drought had dried up rivers and streams, caused crops to fail, and created a severe famine. As a result, the entire countryside had been depopulated of those who had survived the Ethiopian raids of the previous several years.[13]

Once they climbed down from the hills, Harrison and his companions found themselves on parched plains devoid of people and game. Yet the rainy season had just begun, and "during heavy thunderstorms the whole country was a running sheet of water six to twelve inches deep."[14] But the water soon evaporated or was absorbed into the dry earth.

On approaching Lake Stephanie, they found "nothing but a vast extent of ground strewn with shells and heaps of fish-bones."[15] The entire lake had dried up, and all the life in and around it had died off. They were able to obtain water by digging deeply into the floor of the lake bed, and they put their rain barrels to good use by collecting the pure water that fell from the sky.

The expedition now headed southwest toward its principal goal, Lake Rudolf. Whitehouse later wrote that "the trek to the lake was terrible, and indeed but for finding a large rock pool of water, the journey would have been impossible."[16] On March 25, they sighted the lake across a sea of hot mirages: "At last the trying days were over and we sighted Lake Rudolf. The water was extremely brackish and alkaline, but even the camels enjoyed it. Here was plenty of game, oryx, topi, and many other species." Harrison set up a camp on the lake shore, where both camels and men were able to recover from the ordeal of the previous weeks. While there, they sighted the albino topi that Wellby had seen the year before, and "Butter obtained this great trophy by a lucky shot with his Mauser."[17] Wellby's description of this unusual animal had caused great excitement in natural history circles in Britain. As a result, the expedition had been asked to bring a specimen back to London in the interest of science. Butter not only brought back the skin and horns but also the entire skeleton, which he donated to the British Museum.

On the last day of March, the party headed for Murle on the Omo River in order to run up the Union Jack. However, to their dismay, they found the area devoid of people and the riverbed completely dry. The absence of people had political significance, as Harrison later implied:

> Having scouted round the whole country-side in the hopes of finding some natives, we returned, and with difficulty selected a single tall thorn tree near Murle. Sending our shikarees up with axe and saw, we dressed all away, leaving only a centre arm, on which we hoisted the English flag; doing so at the request of Colonel Harrington and with the acquiescence of the emperor, to denote the Abyssinian and English boundary-line. Had we been able to discover any inhabitants, we should have hoisted a second flag further north. Needless to say, as the flag went up, the whole party sang "God save the Queen," a bottle of champagne having been brought along in which to drink her Majesty's health.[18]

As part of his efforts to prevent the Ethiopians from further encroaching on British-claimed territory, Harrington had asked Harrison to run up several flags well to the north of the lake, in addition to the replacement flag closer to the lake. In so doing, he tried to purposely push Britain's territorial claims well north of the area originally staked out by Austin. He did this not so much to seize more territory but rather to better position himself for future border negotiations, which he knew would be difficult.

Unfortunately for Harrington, Harrison was unable to locate any local peoples to whom he could give flags and place under British protection. Therefore, he had to be satisfied with merely replacing Austin's flag, which in itself was a significant political accomplishment. Once this was done, he and the others headed down the previously explored eastern shore of the lake, where they were able to hunt. On April 19, they passed the Teleki Volcano at the lake's southern end and moved on toward Lake Baringo. A month later, they arrived at the railhead of the Uganda Railway, just east of Lake Naivasha. There, they sold off their pack animals, including the thirty camels that had survived the trip (of the original sixty), and took the train to Mombasa. From Mombasa, they returned to Britain via India since an outbreak of plague had placed Aden under quarantine.

Harrison was extremely proud of the maps the expedition's surveyor Clarke had made and promptly submitted them to the Royal Geographical Society. But the society's leaders were less than enthusiastic about them on two accounts. Although Clarke had used a plane table and theodolite to chart his positions, he had failed to use a sextant, which would have produced greater accuracy. However, this minor technical deficiency was overshadowed by the fact that Harrison had attached a host of alien names to major landmarks, most of which had already been documented by other explorers, such as Smith and Wellby. Unlike Harrison, these earlier explorers had given most landmarks their local names, though Smith and others had strayed from this principle on a few occasions. Since Smith's first trip, the society had adopted and published a policy strongly urging travelers to give local names to landmarks. Harrison was obviously unaware of this and pled innocence when Keltie and other society figures criticized his maps because the landmarks bore such names as the Brandesburton Range, Whitehouse Range, James Peak, Mount Clarke, Mount Faskally, and Edith Lake. Writing to Keltie, a chastised Harrison said:

I regret the enclosed notes on "naming places" has never been given me before. But you can rely on Clarke having retained every name known or used by natives. He always tried both Abyssinian and Galla for every place—and kept a careful list of anything without a local name. He was just as careful about that as he was not inserting what he had not seen—for he never could put in a yard on chance.[19]

Although the Harrison-Whitehouse Expedition was primarily a sporting trip, it served a vital political role in reasserting British claims to Lake Rudolf. Its various members collected a number of personal trophies, but they also obtained natural history specimens for several museums. Whitehouse, for example, gave a large collection to the American Museum of Natural History in New York City.[20] The expedition also documented the dramatic effect of weather on the level of Lake Rudolf, which had dropped by a dozen feet during the previous year. Prior to this time, it had been assumed that the lake's size only underwent modest seasonal changes.

Harrison continued to hunt in various parts of the world, filling Brandesburton Hall with a huge collection of trophies. In 1905, he undertook a second trip to the Congo, where he recruited several Mbuti pygmies in the Ituri Forest and brought them to London and to Brandesburton Hall.[21] In November 1910, when he was fifty-two years old, he married an American widow, Mary Stetson Clark of Illinois, and began to lead a more settled life. He died at Brandesburton Hall on March 12, 1923, in his sixty-fifth year. Shortly after his death, his family donated 300 animal heads and skins and 1,000 mounted birds to the Scarborough Borough Council. The remnants of this collection are now housed in the council's Wood End Museum of Natural History, along with his papers, diaries, photographs, and photographic plates. Included in this collection are 390 glass negatives taken on his trip to Lake Rudolf.[22]

Harrison wrote an article about the expedition that was published in the *Geographical Journal* in 1901, and Powell-Cotton produced a book, *A Sporting Trip Through Abyssinia*, describing the first phase of the trip and the subsequent months he spent hunting in Ethiopia. He continued to travel in Asia and Africa until the year before his death in 1940 at the age of seventy-four. Over a half century, he made a total of twenty-eight collecting trips, many of them to Africa. In order to house his enormous natural history and ethnographic collections, he established the Powell-Cotton Museum at his ancestral estate, Quex Park. The museum currently contains eight galleries with some striking dioramas of animals in their natural habitats.[23]

On his return from Africa, Whitehouse wrote an article about his trip to Lake Rudolf. Written from a personal perspective, it described his adventures and experiences in detail, documented the expedition's progress, and provided important information about the lands and peoples he observed.[24] Twenty-five years later, he wrote an even more extensive account for the Boone and Crockett Club.[25]

Less than two years after returning to New York City, Whitehouse set out again for Africa with Lord Hindlip, whom he had met in Addis

Ababa. He and Hindlip spent ten months hunting around the Ethiopian Rift Valley lakes, but they did not visit Lake Rudolf.[26] President Theodore Roosevelt later sought his advice about organizing a hunting trip to Africa, but Whitehouse himself had no immediate interest in returning there. In 1904, he became a member of the New York Stock Exchange and began a lifelong career as an investment banker. During World War I, he served as a captain in the army with the Seventy-Seventh New York Division and was exposed to poison gas while in combat.

In 1926, Whitehouse moved to Newport, Rhode Island, following a bout of pneumonia. He served for two terms in the Rhode Island State Senate and was active in the Boy Scout movement and other philanthropic causes.[27] A pioneer balloonist in his younger years, he later enjoyed quail shooting at his brother Sheldon's estate near Tallahassee, Florida. In 1952, he returned to Africa after a lapse of almost half a century. However, he did not visit either Ethiopia or Kenya but rather accompanied his brother to the Belgian Congo, where his nephew, Charles Whitehouse, was serving at the American consulate.[28]

At his wife's gentle prodding, Whitehouse eventually parted with most of the African trophies that had hung for many years in the hall and dining room of their Newport home. He gave them to a local restaurant, where they remained for a dozen years. He often spoke to his wife and children of his adventures and hunting experiences in Africa. On May 25, 1955, he died of a heart attack in his Newport home at the age of seventy-six.[29]

Butter returned to his estate, Faskally, for a while but was soon back in Africa, helping to secure Britain's claim to Lake Rudolf. As he well knew, the era of exploration had ended and was being supplanted by colonial rule. This was much in evidence in the British East Africa Protectorate, which was being organized into provinces and districts sewn together by telegraph wires and roads. Butter realized that there was significant urgency in settling the ownership of the lake in Britain's favor, especially as the Ethiopians had not abandoned hopes of claiming it as their own. What he could not have foreseen was Britain's unstated policy that wavered between determination and indifference.

14

A Lakeside Tragedy

Major Herbert Henry Austin, following his second expedition to Lake Rudolf (from Among Swamps and Giants in Equatorial Africa, *1902).*

Following the fall of the Mahdist state, British concerns in the Sudan shifted to establishing an official border with Ethiopia. This was viewed as crucial to protecting Britain's control of the Nile. Emperor Menelik II of Ethiopia was amenable to concluding a treaty over his western frontier, primarily because he saw no value to the mosquito-infested swamps that lay below the highlands he had already occupied. Though geography strongly discouraged Ethiopian expansion to the west and the Nile, it encouraged it to the south around Lake Rudolf. There, flat plains with vast elephant herds and large numbers of domestic stock made for profitable raiding.

Sir John Lane Harrington, the British agent and consul general in Ethiopia, and Sir Evelyn Baring (Lord Cromer), who held the same rank in Egypt, were the two officials on the spot who were most concerned about Ethiopian expansion into territories claimed by Britain. Both of them realized that the only effective deterrent to this expansion was British occupation of all claimed territories. However, this was impractical because Lord Salisbury was unwilling to finance such an effort due to competing commitments elsewhere in Africa. This left Cromer and Harrington, who worked closely together on this issue, with little more than diplomatic maneuvering as a means of containing Menelik.

In 1899, Menelik agreed to Harrington and Cromer's proposal that they mutually delimit Ethiopia's western border with the Sudan.[1] That summer, Harrington returned to London with a map of the area on which he and Menelik had mutually traced a blue line marking the border. Harrington and Cromer pushed hard for Salisbury to authorize a formal survey so as to give the tentative border clear meaning in terms of topographic features and ethnic boundaries. Salisbury finally agreed to the proposal, and in October 1899, two separate survey parties were sent to the Sudan. One was headed by Major Charles William Gwynn of the Royal Engineers, the other by Major Herbert Henry Austin, who, as a member of Major James Ronald Macdonald's Juba Expedition of 1897–1898, had laid claim to most of Lake Rudolf for Britain.

The two survey parties were collectively called the Abyssinian Frontier Expeditions. Gwynn took the northern portion, and Austin traveled to the south. Both parties were instructed to pose as semiscientific and shooting expeditions and to avoid discussing the true purpose of their activities with local chiefs, many of whom were eager for British protection from incessant Ethiopian raids.[2] However, Gwynn and Austin were free to discuss their work with high-ranking Ethiopian officials, who, in any case, were fully aware of the true purpose of their travels.

Between October 1899 and July 1900, Austin surveyed the Sobat River basin, while Gwynn worked along the course of the Blue Nile. Among other things, their surveys determined points of effective Ethiopian occupation, which helped Harrington in negotiating with Menelik. However, Austin's survey was not carried all the way down to Lake Rudolf or through the lands to the northwest of it where the proposed borders of Ethiopia, the Sudan, and the British East Africa Protectorate came together. This area to the west of the lake had been traversed by Montagu Sinclair Wellby in early 1899 and later in that year by Arthur Donaldson Smith. Despite the valuable surveys produced by these unofficial visitors, Harrington viewed this entire region as vulnerable to Ethiopian seizure since no official British expedition had ever visited it. Therefore, after Austin and his associate, Major Richard George Tyndall Bright, returned to London and completed their maps, Harrington requested that the government send them back to the Sudan to complete the survey down to the lake. Of course, Harrington had more than surveying in mind. He wanted to reinforce British claims to Lake Rudolf, block possible Ethiopian seizure of lands to its west, and link up the Sudan survey with that of the British East Africa Protectorate.

With these objectives in mind, Austin and Bright arrived back in Khartoum on December 10, 1900. With them was Dr. John Garner, who had been serving as a military physician to British troops in Cairo. Austin recruited 32 Jehadia transport drivers, 23 African soldiers from the Tenth Sudanese Battalion under Sergeant Mabruk Effendi Faki, and 4 servants, including an Arabic-English interpreter, Bakhir Ahmed. In place of porters, Austin took along 124 donkeys, 10 mules, and 23 camels to carry the food and equipment necessary to support his expedition of 62 men.

Austin and his entire expedition left Khartoum in late December and arrived at Fort Nasser on the Sobat River on January 11, 1901. After resting for a week, they started out on foot in a southerly direction through the grasslands surrounding the Pibor River. Because Austin, Bright, and some of the Africans had traversed this country in 1899–1900, they did not need guides, and they made good time in getting to the junction of the Akobo and Pibor Rivers. Although the swamps along the Akobo were relatively dry, the cracked and hardened mud made the going extremely difficult. Worse still, swarms of mosquitoes descended on their camp with a fury at sundown.

On February 5, Austin led his expedition in a southeasterly direction along the Akobo River, toward the base of the Ethiopian highlands. They spent most of February trekking through the swamps and open grasslands near the river, where they met friendly groups of Anuak people, who provided them with guides. On February 24, they arrived at Mount Ungwala, which rises to 3,550 feet, and three days later began their ascent of the hilly Boma Plateau.

Still following the Akobo River, Austin and his men eventually turned south along the Kibish River and entered country previously visited by Vittorio Bottego, Smith, and Wellby. As they did, Austin continued to survey the line that would ultimately become the Sudan-Ethiopia border.[3]

On April 4, Austin and his men sighted Mount Nakua, which rises 3,295 feet, near Lake Rudolf. Four more days of marching brought them to Austin's camp of September 15, 1898, where he linked together his current survey with those he had previously conducted. In so doing, he provided the British government with an accurate survey of all the land that lay astride a 2,300-mile-long line from Omdurman in the Sudan to Mombasa. In addition, he accurately documented the true extent of effective Ethiopian occupation and strengthened Britain's claim to the no-man's-land that Wellby had described as "'twixt Sirdar and Menelik." All of this information later proved to be extremely valuable to Harrington in his border negotiations with Menelik.

Austin's arrival at the base of Mount Nakua effectively brought his survey activities to an end.[4] All that remained was to reinforce British claims to the lake and get the expedition safely out of the interior. Thus far, the members of the expedition had enjoyed good health and had not encountered any hostile actions from local peoples. Austin's most pressing problem was that their food supplies were running low. However, Harrington had arranged for the Ethiopians to send a relief column down to the lake, and Austin hoped to buy food from the local agriculturists around the Omo River.[5]

In the hopes of accomplishing both objectives, Austin and his men set off on April 9 on what they assumed would be a rewarding trek along the river. The Ethiopian relief column was nowhere to be found, and, in fact, it never materialized. Worse still, local Africans fled from their approach or else refused to barter food. This behavior was hardly surprising since these peoples had been subjected to the brutal military invasions of *Ras* Wolda Giorgis and Nicholas Leontiev a short time before. Still hopeful, Austin and his men headed farther north into the country of the Mursi, but the reception there was much the same. Although large patches of the riverbank were cultivated, the crops were at least two months from maturity. This meant that grain could not be confiscated from the fields, as some travelers had done when starvation threatened. The only available grain was stored in granaries, but Austin was unwilling to raid villages to take it by force. To make matters worse, the rainy season then under way was especially heavy and had turned the riverbank into a bog.[6]

Austin, Bright, and Garner weighed their options. They and their men now had only ten to twelve days of food available on full rations. They quickly decided against going north into the Ethiopian highlands where food was available since the cold and rain en route would have killed most of the transport animals on which their own lives depended. Therefore, they chose to return south and make for the British post of Ribo, which lay some 300 miles away in the Uganda Protectorate. This decision to exit the Omo River delta along the lake's western shore was really their only viable option. Yet it meant trekking over harsh terrain devoid of much in the way of wildlife and inhabited by the Turkana. The Turkana had every reason to be intensely hostile toward strangers after the recent punishing visit of Leontiev's men.

Austin, Bright, and Garner believed that the expedition could survive on its transport animals, now consisting of 11 camels, 10 mules, and 114 donkeys. But Austin frankly projected "a loss of 25 percent of our men and about 50 percent of the animals."[7] With that grim prospect in mind, he led the expedition south around the enormous swamps that had formed at the northwestern corner of the lake. Things got off to a bad start when one of the transport drivers was killed by local Africans, his body thrown into the crocodile-infested river. For the next two weeks, the expedition slowly made its way around and through the swamps, barely sustained by reduced rations and continuously harassed by local villagers.

On May 5, two of Austin's Sudanese soldiers and his cook, Mahomed, were killed in an ambush.[8] That night, the local Murle people launched two armed attacks against the camp but were quickly driven off by bursts of gunfire. Austin sadly noted that "the whole tribe was bitterly hostile."[9] The reason for the hostility was the recent brutality to which they had been subjected at the hands of the Ethiopians. Three years earlier, these very people had sold Austin food, provided guides, and warned of imminent attacks by the Turkana.

To complicate matters, Austin himself became so ill with gastritis that Garner insisted they take a two-day rest.[10] On May 11, Austin led his men south again, carried on a camel at the head of the column. They had now entered into the land of the Turkana people, whom they expected would be hostile and unwilling to barter food. With their own rations running ever lower, Austin reduced the men's daily allotment to a quarter of a pound of meat and grain on May 17. The Sudanese camels, unwilling to eat the local scrub, soon wasted to skin and bones and were killed for their meat.

It was at this time, approximately a month after they had started on reduced rations, that some of the men began to show signs of severe illness. Those primarily affected were the Jehadia transport drivers, who occupied the lowest rung in the hierarchy of the expedition. Austin gave his own interpretation of why they suffered more than the whites and the Sudanese soldiers: "All the men were most visibly suffering greatly from the want of carbo-hydrate food . . . and on meat alone they appeared quite incapable of maintaining their strength. The askaris [soldiers] all messed together, and derived considerable benefit from clubbing their rations, and obtained, moreover, a sustaining soup from the meat, which was always boiled by them."[11]

Garner, the medical officer, later threw additional light on the matter in his official report:

Our transport drivers now showed signs of the insufficient flour ration. Their meat ration as served out to them was adequate. Owing to inability to trust each other, they would not run a combined mess, as our soldiers did. The consequence was their meat was improperly cooked; on the other hand, our escort clubbed their rations together, the result being their meat was always well boiled.[12]

Austin also reported that the rations available to the Jehadia and the Sudanese soldiers were identical.[13] He, Bright, and Garner, however, had tinned foods to supplement their diet and obviously benefited to some degree from this advantage. Austin made a very cogent observation concerning the preexpedition nutritional status of the Jehadia. He said that they had led "a hand-to-mouth existence," meaning that their nutritional status was marginal at the outset. This would have placed them at the highest risk in a situation of reduced caloric intake. He added that the soldiers had received a far more liberal scale of rations than the Jehadia prior to leaving on the trip.[14] Thus, they, like the Europeans, had significant fat stores on which to draw when faced with starvation.

By mid-May, the Jehadia were in terrible condition. A dozen of them were so weak that they had to be carried on donkeys. On May 19, three of them died, and a fourth was speared by the Turkana. This was the beginning of a massive mortality that was to ensue over the next six weeks.

Desperate for food, the Jehadia naturally broke into the stores when they could and foraged the countryside for anything edible. Austin attributed this behavior to their lack of discipline and contrasted it with that of the Sudanese soldiers, whom he described as "sterling good fellows . . . made of the right stuff."[15] Yet the Jehadia were clearly suffering more severely than the soldiers, and it was this above all else that drove them to acts of desperation. The killing of donkeys for food in late May did little to alleviate either their sufferings or those of the soldiers.

The Jehadia started dying at an unbelievable rate in late May and early June. By June 2, 1901, half of the original thirty-two were dead, mostly from starvation. By contrast, only three soldiers had died. Of these, only one had died from starvation; another died from eating poisonous berries, and a third was speared to death.

As the situation grew more desperate, some of the Jehadia surreptitiously killed the expedition's domestic stock and ate the raw meat on the sly. They also pilfered the grain stores, for which Austin had them flogged. One young Jehadia, Abdul, was flogged on two occasions for stealing donkey meat and for pilfering a sack of grain. In the latter instance, one of the soldiers was an accomplice. Several days later, Abdul killed a donkey and cut up the meat using only a small pocketknife. He was eventually caught, and Austin had him shot by a firing squad at 4:00 A.M. the following day as an object lesson for the remaining men.[16]

As he had done on his previous trip, Austin left Lake Rudolf by following the Turkwell River bed. Before doing so, he burned many loads, including tents, trophies, saddles, and other items that were not indispensable. The Turkana continuously harassed the starving column from the thickly wooded riverbanks and refused all attempts at friendly contact. On June 14, Austin led his men across the Weiwei River, which marked the limit of the Turkana's territory. They were finally freed from daily ambushes, but their food supply included only five pounds of flour and four pounds of rice.

Austin had now lost thirty men, most of them Jehadia. Over the next two weeks, twelve more would die, so that by June 30, only seventeen Africans out of the original fifty-nine were left. Although some had been killed, most had died of starvation.[17] Garner later wrote a detailed account concerning the symptoms of those who died: "The patients' faces became puffy, so much so indeed as to cause almost complete obliteration of the features; the oedema of the eye-lids and ankles being especially pronounced. They complained of severe pains in the head as well as in the muscles of the neck. . . . Referring to my notes, I find that thirty-five men died from this cause."[18]

Although these symptoms are compatible with severe starvation, they can also be seen in people suffering from trichinosis.[19] This is a parasitic disease caused by a worm, the *Trichinella spiralis*, and transmitted when humans consume raw or inadequately cooked contaminated meat. Although the disease is most often associated with the ingestion of poorly cooked pork, a number of animal species can serve as intermediate hosts for the parasite.[20] The suggestion that Austin's men succumbed to an epidemic of trichinosis is strengthened by the fact that most of the dead were those who ate raw or poorly cooked meat. It is also probable that they caught and ate rodents, which are frequently infected with the disease. However, based on the evidence provided by Austin and Garner, it is difficult to come to any other conclusion than that the cause of death among most of their men was starvation.[21]

On June 19, as the column entered the country of the Suk, Austin noticed purple spots on his legs, and a few days later, he developed hemorrhages in his mouth. Garner immediately recognized that he was suffering from scurvy. By this time, British physicians were extremely familiar with this disease and knew that it could be prevented by the ingestion of lime juice, which Garner periodically issued. He was at a loss to explain why only Austin developed the disease and in spite of the fact that he had regularly eaten compressed tinned vegetables, grains, and meats. From the perspective of modern medical science, there are a few possible reasons to explain Austin's development of scurvy. The foods he ate may have been cooked to such a degree that the vitamin C in them was rendered inactive. Alternatively, if he had an adequate intake of vitamin C, he may have been unable to sufficiently absorb it because of the gastroenteritis from which he periodically suffered during the trip.

Whatever the reasons for Austin's scurvy, it progressively grew worse over the ensuing weeks despite Garner's administration of lime extract. Austin's failure to respond to this therapy may have been due to the inadequacy of the dose, or perhaps the lime extract itself had become inactivated in the brutally hot climate. Austin soon developed severe nasal hemorrhages, which left him extremely weak and unable to walk. Garner confined him to bed between July 21 and 28 when he began hemorrhaging into his face, shoulder, joints, and other parts of his body. He temporarily lost his vision due to retinal hemorrhages, suffered from excruciating pain, and ran a fever of from 101 to 104 degrees Fahrenheit.[22]

Despite his desperate physical condition, Austin, driven by sheer willpower, set out again on July 29, leading his greatly diminished column south toward Lake Baringo. Of the original thirty-two Jehadia, only two were left. Eleven of the twenty Sudanese soldiers had survived, one of the four servants, and the three Europeans. In all, Austin had lost 73 percent of his men.

As they neared Lake Baringo, a local guide told them that there was a European stationed nearby. Bright sent a note off to him with the guide, and two days later, Henry Hyde-Barker, the collector of the Baringo District, arrived with eighteen porters carrying provisions and a litter. As Garner noted, the relief was timely, for without it, Austin would have certainly died. He was carried to the Baringo post, where, over the next two weeks, he quickly recovered on a diet of fresh vegetables, milk, and eggs.

Austin and his greatly reduced force left Baringo on August 14 and reached the railway at Nakuru a week later. They sailed form Mombasa on September 8 and arrived at Suez nineteen days later. Austin then traveled by train to Cairo and accompanied the survivors of the Tenth Sudanese Battalion to Assuan, where they rejoined their ranks.[23]

By any measure, Austin's second expedition to Lake Rudolf had resulted in an unprecedented human catastrophe, for the loss of life was far in excess of that experienced by any other expedition to the lake.

Yet the Royal Geographical Society blandly described the tragedy: "Majors Austin, Bright, and Garner . . . arrived at Mombasa early in September, after suffering great hardships during the journey. . . . During the last two months, the party subsisted almost entirely on the donkeys, and out of fifty-nine Sudanese only fourteen survived. Some good survey work was, however, done between the Sobat and the lake."[24]

This terse account, in which the staggering loss of human life is mentioned only in passing, reflected prevailing British values and attitudes of the time, as well as an attempt to avoid fixing official responsibility for an overwhelming disaster. Within the social construct of the time, "natives" were generally viewed as part of an anonymous mass whose lives were frequently dispensable. Yet the loss of so much life was bound to raise uncomfortable questions for a government that had clearly failed Austin and his men in terms of adequately supporting and relieving the expedition. The Royal Geographical Society had no desire to point an accusing finger at Lord Salisbury's conservative government, especially as the three British members of the expedition had survived. Rather, the society chose to brush over the human tragedy and emphasize the expedition's scientific and geographic accomplishments. Foremost among these was the linking of the Sudan survey with those of the British East Africa Protectorate. The political consequences of this were that it placed Britain in a strong position in its frontier negotiations with Ethiopia and prevented further Ethiopian expansion into British-claimed territory. The latter was especially important with regard to Lake Rudolf, which, thanks to Austin's two trips, was now largely in the British sphere. Still, these accomplishments had come at a very high human price and had almost cost Austin his life.

In recognition of Austin's exceptional services, he was made a companion of the Order of St. Michael and St. George in 1901 and promoted to brevet major. Although the government invited him to return to Africa to work on the boundaries he had surveyed, he had to decline because of the lingering effects of scurvy. These included partial blindness in his right eye due to the retinal hemorrhage that occurred when he was near Lake Baringo.

Austin spent the following twenty years of his military career in a variety of posts in India and the Near East and retired in 1920 with the rank of brigadier general.[25] Following his retirement, he authored a number of books based on his experiences, including *Some Rambles of a Sapper*, which was published in 1928.[26] He died on April 27, 1937, at the age of sixty-eight.

Austin's 1900–1901 trip to Lake Rudolf effectively brought to an end the era of mapping the unknown in this part of Africa. His surveys, based as they were on astronomical observations and positions precisely calculated by triangulation, were viewed as definitive. What remained now was the task of drawing a border between Ethiopia and the British East Africa Protectorate and determining where the lake would be divided.

15

Dividing the Spoils

Menelik II, emperor of Ethiopia (from Une visite à l'Empereur Ménélick, 1898).

The tragedy that struck Herbert Henry Austin's 1900–1901 expedition to Lake Rudolf did little to deter others from traveling there. Even as Austin and his surviving men were struggling down the lake's western shore, an Austrian nobleman, Count Eduard Ernst Karl Maria Wickenburg, was approaching the lake from the northeast.

Wickenburg first visited Somaliland and Ethiopia in 1897, hoping to travel to the Omo River valley, down the western shore of the lake, and then on to Uganda. However, 1897 was a politically unsettled year, for Menelik was pushing his frontier southward toward the lake. Not surprisingly, Wickenburg's request to visit the lake was denied. He contented himself with traveling extensively through Ethiopia and Somaliland, where he carried out geographic surveys, collected natural history specimens, and promoted Austro-Hungarian commercial interests. Returning to Vienna for a brief time, he soon set off again for Africa, this time heading for the British East Africa Protectorate. He trekked inland to

Taveta and visited Mount Kilimanjaro, where he put together a large collection of ethnographic objects and natural history specimens.[1]

In 1901, with the political climate greatly charged, Wickenburg requested Menelik's permission to travel into the lands near Lake Rudolf. By now, the emperor was extremely willing to have European travelers document the extent of effective Ethiopian occupation so as to strengthen his border negotiations with the British. Wickenburg actually was no longer interested in Lake Rudolf but rather wanted to explore the lands between it and the Lorian Swamp. This region had been previously traversed by Arthur Donaldson Smith in 1895 and Lord Delamere in 1897.

Wickenburg arrived in Djibouti in January 1901, and by April, he was in Addis Ababa. From there, he set out for the southwest, with forty-five Somalis and Ethiopians and forty camels, donkeys, mules, and horses. He carried with him an impressive array of surveying instruments, supplies, equipment, arms, and a Kodak camera. He meticulously surveyed the country he passed through and combined hunting with specimen collecting. Although he spent three weeks camped at Lake Stephanie, he only paid a brief visit to Lake Rudolf in July 1901. He then trekked southeast toward Mount Marsabit, moving on to the Guaso Nyiro River and basically following Smith's previous route. After a visit to the Lorian Swamp, he marched to the Tana River and reached the coast at Lamu in late October.[2]

Unfortunately, Wickenburg did not publish a book-length account of this trip, and his diaries of it were destroyed at the end of World War II. His brief article about it provides few details and is not chronological in character. Among the travelers who reached Lake Rudolf in these years, he and Lord Delamere stood out as the only two for whom the lake was not their primary goal. In fact, in his article, Wickenburg was candidly dismissive of his brief visit to the lake: "As this trip was not in my original itinerary plan, I do not make any mention of it."[3]

Although Wickenburg never returned to Africa, he began a three-year trip in 1911 through South America, during which he covered 5,000 miles on horseback. He died while mountain climbing at Hollengebirge, Austria, in June 1936, in his seventieth year.[4]

Wickenburg had scarcely left Djibouti when the French Vicomte Robert du Bourg de Bozas arrived there, intent on leading a scientific expedition to Lake Rudolf, the Nile, and the Congo. Only thirty years of age, de Bozas put together a multidisciplinary team of Frenchmen, who spent close to a year traveling through Ethiopia and Somaliland before arriving in Addis Ababa on December 28, 1901. From there, de Bozas and his caravan set out for Lake Rudolf on March 4, 1902, with 20 mules and 110 donkeys. They followed the chain of Ethiopian Rift

Valley lakes, crossed over the mountains, and finally reached the Omo River on June 2. While exploring the lower Omo River valley, they found a large number of fossils and noted for the first time the highly fossiliferous nature of the entire region.[5] Approaching the swampy terrain just to the north of Lake Rudolf, they were attacked by the Murle people who had given Herbert Henry Austin and his men so much difficulty a short time before. This response was a direct result of previous Ethiopian raids that had made the Murle intensely hostile to all outsiders. They killed two of de Bozas's men and a number of his transport animals, prompting him to organize a punitive raid against them the day before he reached the lake.[6]

De Bozas did not linger at the northern end of the lake for long. He set out for the Nile in early July and reached it two months later at Nimule, which was now a British military post. In the process, he crossed Montagu Sinclair Wellby's 1899 south-to-north route and marched west along a line somewhat to the south of that taken by Arthur Donaldson Smith in 1900. This phase of the expedition completed, de Bozas repatriated his Ethiopian, Somali, and Swahili men via the British East Africa Protectorate. He then prepared for his trip through the Congo, which he never completed.

On October 16, 1902, de Bozas and his new caravan marched out of Nimule and headed west for the Congo River. By December, they were at the headwaters of the Uele River, where de Bozas contracted tetanus. This was an invariably fatal disease in those times and circumstances, and thus, despite the best efforts of the expedition's physician, he died on December 24 at Amadi.[7] His death effectively brought the expedition to an end, and the remaining members then traveled down the Congo River to Leopoldville, which they reached on February 7.

The Wickenburg and de Bozas expeditions represent the almost silent closure of a frenetic period of exploratory activity around Lake Rudolf that had begun with Count Samuel Teleki fifteen years before. There was little justification now for further scientific missions to the lake. It had been geographically situated, measured, and described, and its fauna and flora had been collected, analyzed, and classified. Given the then general state of science, there was really little that could be added to what was already known about the lake. It would require several more decades before advances in science would make further geologic and paleontologic studies possible.

Although Lake Rudolf ceased to be a magnet for adventurers, geographers, and scientists, it and the adjacent border area now became the focus of intense diplomatic discussions between Menelik and John Lane Harrington, the British agent and consul general in Addis Ababa.

Despite Harrington's repeated expressions of concern to Lord Salisbury about progressive Ethiopian expansion, little was done to protect British-claimed territories. In part, this was due to Salisbury's preoccupation with problems elsewhere in Africa, as well as the perception that this region of arid wastes was of little strategic or economic importance. For his part, Menelik played a shrewd diplomatic and political game between 1899 and 1902 by making outrageous territorial claims to test British reaction while steadily advancing southward, thereby measuring the British resolve. Harrington was well aware of the nature of this game, but he was unable to rouse up much support in London for an effective border force, which he viewed as the only means of stopping the slow but steady Ethiopian advance.[8]

It was not until 1902 that Salisbury's government decided to do something about Ethiopian advances into British-claimed territories. Unfortunately, it did so in a miserly fashion by asking Archibald Butter, the laird of Faskally, to finance and conduct a border survey. Butter was extremely familiar with this area of Africa, having participated in the Harrison-Whitehouse Expedition of 1899–1900. He had also made a few return hunting trips to Ethiopia and Somaliland, so he welcomed the opportunity of combining official business with sport. Yet he did not foresee the enormity and complexity of this undertaking or its true cost, which eventually reached £10,000.

The border issue was equally complex in diplomatic terms because Britain continued to honor its 1891 protocol with Italy, which recognized Ethiopia as being in the Italian sphere. This exasperated Harrington to no end since the 1896 Italian defeat at Adowa had rendered this agreement meaningless. But the Foreign Office continued to insist on Italian concurrence with any proposed Anglo-Ethiopian border.[9]

Harrington's original instructions to Butter still survive in the Public Record office at Richmond: "The object of your expedition is to place in my hands sufficient information to enable me to arrange with the Emperor Menelik a frontier between Abyssinia and British East Africa." Harrington also told Butter to set up a line that followed natural features, did not cut through the territory of various tribal groups, and was to some degree in conformity with an 1899 understanding reached by him and Menelik. Furthermore, Harrington instructed Butter to distinguish between areas under permanent Ethiopian occupation and those simply subject to raids since the latter could still be claimed as British.[10]

Menelik had little to fear from Butter's survey since he was confident it would substantiate his claims of effective occupation. He readily gave his assent and assigned three Ethiopians and an entourage to the expedition. They were led by Ato Mama, an educated Ethiopian who had lived for six years in France and who served as the official recorder for the Ethiopian side.

Butter recruited Captain Philip Maud of the Royal Engineers, a man who had previously done extensive survey work on India's northwest frontier. At thirty-two, he was four years older than Butter but a world apart in terms of temperament and personality. Whereas Butter was a leisurely and good-natured country squire little interested in details, Maud was a fastidious and meticulous surveyor whose thoroughness and great sense of duty were often perceived as rigidity. Although these diverse character traits led to irritations between the two men under the stresses of field travel, they never disrupted their overall relationship or the work of the expedition.

Harrington added two other men to this caravan, his assistant John Lawrence Baird, who was an old Etonian school chum of Butter's, and Dr. Wakeman, the British residency physician. Butter himself hired Wellby's caravan leader, Mohamed Hassan, and his surveyor, Duffadar Shazad Mir of the Eleventh Bengal Lancers. Against his will, Harrington also asked him to take along Count Giuseppe Colli di Felizzano, the secretary at the Italian legation in Addis Ababa. This was in response to the Foreign Office's wish to include Italy in any border arrangements worked out with Ethiopia.[11]

Butter led his expedition of five Europeans, two Indians, seventy Somalis, and twelve Ethiopians out of Addis Ababa on November 6, 1902. With them was a train of 160 transport animals, including camels, mules, donkeys, and horses. They headed for the intersection of six degrees north latitude and the Ganale River, which represented the demarcation between the Italian and British spheres as set out in the 1891 protocol. However, Menelik's steady southward advances had long made a farce of this geographic claim. Butter and his European colleagues were chagrined by the extent of Ethiopian occupation below this line, and they communicated their findings by letter to Harrington in Addis Ababa.[12]

Over the next six months, Butter's expedition broke up into smaller parties, regrouped, and crisscrossed from east to west the region where effective Ethiopian occupation ended. Maud meticulously triangulated his positions with a theodolite, thus improving on the surveys of previous travelers who had used prismatic compasses. Fortunately, they discovered the impressive Megado Escarpment, which rises 300 feet and forms a natural divider between the higher northern areas and the dusty plains below. Smith had been the first European to note this unusual landmark, running for some 170 miles from east to west, and Lord Delamere had also come upon it in his travels.

Although Maud spent most of his time surveying, he also engaged in shooting game on a grand scale. But Butter outdid all the Europeans on this score, killing nineteen of the thirty-nine lions shot and his share of the twenty rhinos that fell to their guns. Maud kept a meticulous daily diary recording his activities, opinions, and observations, albeit in a very illegible hand.[13]

One of the expedition's tasks was to determine the distribution of the Boran people who lived along the Anglo-Ethiopian borderlands in three distinct regions—Liban, Dirre, and Tertala. This proved exceedingly difficult, as the Ethiopians in the party threatened potential informants with retribution if they spoke to the Europeans. On January 13, 1903, Baird wrote to Maud about this problem:

> I have had a perfectly damnable time, and felt about ready to chuck the whole show. I will not weary you with the details of my experiences, but they have been identical with yours. The two Abyssinians gave orders to the Borans that they weren't to come into my camp or to talk to us or to our boys . . . and any men who did would have a hand cut off. They beat one Boran, whom they suspected of having spoken to us and told him he would be killed if they suspected him a second time. They gave orders to the Borans that they were to tell us nothing about the country except misleading information.[14]

Baird and the others were eventually able to overcome these obstacles and speak directly with the Boran. Nonetheless, it was at times difficult to determine whether a given stretch of country was under effective Ethiopian occupation or simply periodically raided.

In mid-May, Maud reached the north end of Lake Rudolf, where the boundary was least in dispute thanks to Austin's 1898 treaties and flag placements. Climbing to the top of Rocky Hill, which rises 3,574 feet to the east of the lake, he made his final triangulations of the frontier. With his survey work finally completed, he hurried down the east shore of the lake and joined up with the main expedition on May 24. There, he found that Baird had been mauled by a lion a few days before. Luckily for Baird, his two African companions had come to his rescue, one pulling the lion by the tail while the other shot it.[15]

Butter and his companions had now been in the field for seven months and had essentially achieved all of the expedition's goals. They had trekked over 1,000 miles of difficult terrain, and Maud had produced a detailed survey that would become the basis for future Anglo-Ethiopian border negotiations. In June, the Ethiopians left for Addis Ababa, while Butter led his expedition south toward the Uganda Railway and home.[16]

Butter's report was presented to both houses of Parliament in November 1904. In it, he made a strong case for establishing a boundary that followed major topographic landmarks and separated the Galla from the non-Galla peoples. Maud, on the other hand, advocated for a line to the north of this, demarcating the southern limit of Ethiopian occupation. Although Maud's line was in Britain's favor, Lord Lansdowne, the foreign secretary, opted to negotiate on the basis of Butter's line. This line, which became known as the Red Line, ceded to the Ethiopians not only effectively occupied regions but also those regions regularly raided by them. It also had the advantage of following major topographic features.[17]

In December 1903, Lansdowne instructed Harrington to consult with the Italians in Rome about the proposed border. Holding Britain to the obviously defunct 1891 protocol, the Italians were concerned that an agreement might be struck that was prejudicial to their interests. Harrington and the British ambassador, James Rennell Rodd, who had earlier served in East Africa, met with the Italians and, in return for some concessions, obtained their support. There now remained the all-important matter of negotiating with Menelik. His strategy was to delay while secretly promoting further Ethiopian penetration into British territory.[18]

Harrington was convinced that only a British presence along the proposed border could halt Ethiopian advances. However, the Foreign Office was unwilling to fund the force proposed by Butter and Maud in their report. Harrington was persistent, and finally in 1905, the newly established Colonial Office allocated £1,200 annually to patrol the border. The man chosen for this task was Fotios (Philip) Zaphiro, a Greek subject who had lived in Ethiopia for many years. He was fluent in Amharic, enterprising, and politically shrewd, and above all, he knew how to beat the Ethiopians at their own game. In November 1905, Harrington appointed Zaphiro to the post of boundary inspector, at an annual salary of £200.[19]

Zaphiro and his two dozen policemen patrolled the border from the Ganale River to Lake Rudolf, a distance of about 600 miles, and in so doing, brought the Ethiopian advance to a halt. He remained on the border for four years, during which he constructed posts (including Moyale, which lay equidistant on the Red Line from Lake Rudolf and the Ganale River). Seeing little hope of advancing southward, Menelik agreed in 1907 to a frontier that basically was the Red Line.[20] This agreement called for the establishment of a delimitation commission, which was finally appointed in May 1908. The man chosen to head this Abyssinian-East African Boundary Commission was Major

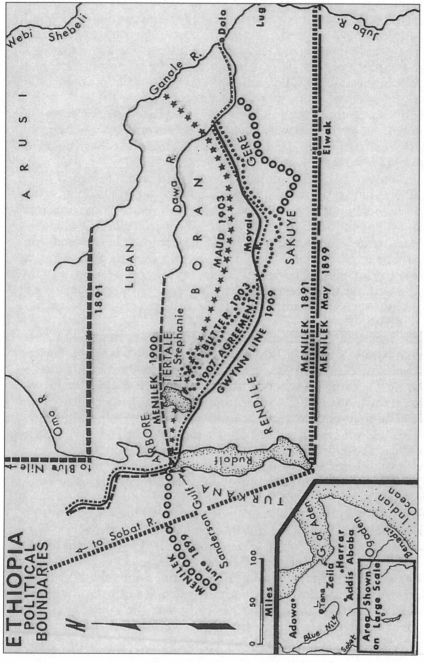

Various boundaries proposed between Ethiopia and British East Africa, 1891–1909 (courtesy Professor Harold G. Marcus, Michigan State University).

Charles William Gwynn of the Royal Engineers. A man of considerable experience in Africa, he had previously served in Sierra Leone and had demarcated the northern part of the border between Ethiopia and the Sudan. During this latter effort, he had worked with Austin as coleader of the Abyssinian Frontiers Expeditions.[21]

Gwynn arrived in Addis Ababa in late August 1908 with two noncommissioned engineers, Corporal Carter and Sapper Favier, a physician, Dr. R.E. Drake-Brockman, who had previously spent five years in Somaliland, Captain R. Waller, who served as second in command, and Captain G. Condon, a transport officer.[22] Matters got off to a bad start because Menelik was ill, and no one in the Ethiopian government would nominate commissioners to accompany Gwynn. After waiting in vain for two months, Gwynn was told by the Foreign Office to proceed without the Ethiopians. There was precedent for this since Menelik had authorized Gwynn to act alone when delimiting Ethiopia's western border with the Sudan.

Gwynn finally joined his caravan in October at Ginir, where it had proceeded while he was in the Ethiopian capital. From there, he headed southeast to Dolo, at the confluence of the Ganale and Daua rivers. At Dolo, he met Zaphiro, who then accompanied him. Over the next two months, he retraced Maud's survey, making minor adjustments in the Red Line that gave Britain access to vital wells necessary for patrolling the border. He arrived at the northern end of Lake Rudolf on February 22, 1909, where he found an Ethiopian post just opposite the mouth of the Omo River. It had taken him only two months to cover the entire border from the time he set out from Dolo. Despite the brevity of his time in the field, Gwynn produced meticulous maps and provided detailed descriptions of the areas he visited.

After reaching Lake Rudolf, Gwynn returned to Addis Ababa, arriving on April 20, 1909.[23] His demarcation line, though conforming for the most part to the British Red Line, departed from it in critical areas. Gwynn had made most of these adjustments at Zaphiro's suggestion since they gave Britain access to wells necessary for patrol activities. Gwynn's line became known as the Blue Line, and it was immediately contested by the Ethiopians, who soon sent a German, Lieutenant Schubert, to survey the Red Line. However, his greatly delayed results did not alter Britain's now firm resolve to hold to the Blue Line. That line actually gave Ethiopia several more miles of the northern end of Lake Rudolf than were demarcated by the Red Line in 1903. Yet the Ethiopians considered that poor compensation for their loss of strategic ground and wells.[24]

Gwynn's demarcation of the border effectively marked the end of the era of colonial competition for the Jade Sea. That competition had begun with large scientific expeditions and military invasions, treaties with local chiefs, and the unfurling of national colors. It ended less dramatically with meticulous surveyors who drew lines across the map separating the colonial spoils. Over the ensuing decades, nature had a final word in this saga, for Lake Rudolf progressively receded 35 miles from its late-nineteenth-century northern shore, thus pulling itself out of Ethiopia.

Epilogue

A late-twentieth-century traveler, Stephen Pern, at the southern end of Lake Rudolf, 1978 (courtesy Stephen Pern).

Britain and Ethiopia continued to disagree over the details of their common border for many years. It was not until 1947 that a new boundary was proposed and a bilateral demarcation commission established. The commission held its first meeting on March 17, 1951, and continued working for the next five years. However, Ethiopia declined to ratify the commission's recommendations, thus nullifying the 1947 proposal. This meant that the 1907 Anglo-Ethiopian agreement was still operative. Only in 1963 did the independent government of Kenya and Ethiopia initiate border negotiations, resulting in a border treaty that was signed in 1970. Throughout

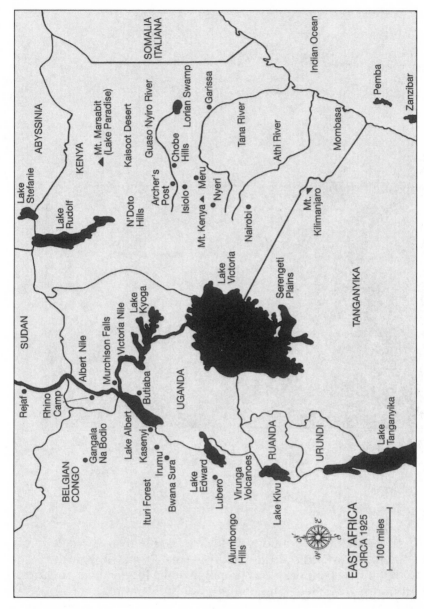

East Africa following the establishment of colonial borders, 1925 (drawn by Douglas Dunn/Joan Simpson).

all these decades, the original 1907 boundary across Lake Rudolf was never in dispute.[1]

During the first decade of the twentieth century, most of Lake Rudolf became part of Kenya's Northern Frontier District, which was infrequently visited and then primarily by administrators, hunters, and occasional scientists. In 1907, George Escherich made important observations about the Omo River delta while on a hunting trip.[2] The following year, Captain Chauncey H. Stigand, a British military officer, traveled up to the lake from Gilgil and on to Addis Ababa. A man of superior observational skills, he was also an excellent naturalist and historian. He moved up the eastern shore of the lake and then entered the Omo River valley, where he was the first to document the recent arrival of tsetse flies, the vectors of trypanosomiasis (African sleeping sickness).[3] After their visits, the British severely restricted travel to the lake because of Ethiopian raids across the border and their own efforts to pacify the Turkana.[4] The Turkana pacification program lasted for a dozen years, between 1914 and 1926.[5] Yet the border with Ethiopia remained closed until World War II, in an effort to control cattle raids and elephant poaching, which continued throughout the 1920s and 1930s.

Although Lake Rudolf was situated in an officially closed district, entry permits were occasionally given to travelers and scientists, including L.F.I. Athill in 1919 and Camille Arambourg in 1932–1933.[6] Arambourg's geological and anthropological mission on behalf of the Natural History Museum of Paris gathered important scientific information about the lake's rich fossil deposits.[7] In 1930–1932, Vivian E. Fuchs led a Cambridge University expedition to Lake Rudolf and returned in 1934 with a multidisciplinary team of scientists. Two of these scientists mysteriously disappeared while on a visit to the lake's South Island.[8]

In 1934, Martin and Osa Johnson, famous American wildlife photographers and filmmakers, flew with their pilot, Vern Carstens, to Lake Rudolf. Using a twin-engine Sikorsky S-38BS amphibian named *Osa's Ark*, they landed at Ferguson's Gulf on the western shore. From there, they flew across to Center Island, which they extensively filmed and photographed. The Johnsons were the first to fly over the lake and gain access to its islands by plane. Their aerial film footage of Lake Rudolf appeared in their 1935 feature film *Baboona*, which was shown in theaters throughout the United States and Europe.[9]

Robert Du Bourg de Bozas was the first to note the rich fossil deposits along the shores of the lake, an observation confirmed three decades later by Arambourg. However, it was not until the early 1970s that Richard and Meave Leakey began uncovering important hominid fossils at Koobi Fora on the lake's eastern shore. The long-forgotten desert lake now became famous for its fossil yields, which quickly rewrote the record of humankind.[10] Since then, additional important fossils have been found, not only along the eastern shore but also on the western side of the lake.

In 1965, Alistair Graham, a wildlife conservationist, and Peter Beard, an internationally acclaimed photographer, undertook a year-long study of the lake's crocodiles, then noted for both their numbers and their enormous size.[11] By this time, however, the lake's long period of solitude was slowly being eroded by lakeside settlements and tourist fishing camps served by airstrips and planes. Still, overland travel remained difficult and often dangerous because of armed cattle raiders who increasingly turned to robbing travelers.

During the 1960s, the security situation in this region sharply deteriorated as armed Somali units roamed the desert wilderness at will and attacked even well-protected convoys. In the ensuing years, wars in Ethiopia, Somalia, and Sudan caused an influx of refugees, some of whom obtained arms and engaged in banditry. Yet the more serious security problem has been caused by the procurement of modern arms by various ethnic groups, including the Karamajong, Turkana, Boran, and Somali. Equipped with these weapons, they now engage in cattle theft with deadlier consequences and have also turned to robbing and killing innocent civilians. In 1997, for example, sixty Kenyans were killed near Ileret, on the eastern lake shore, by armed bandits who had come from Sudan.[12]

Despite the newer dangers, some late-twentieth-century travelers have been drawn to the lake in search of challenge and adventure. In the early 1970s, the late John Hillaby, a naturalist and long-distance walker, trekked through the Northern Frontier District and two-thirds of the way up the eastern shore of the lake.[13] Later in that decade, a young Englishman named Stephen Pern walked around the lake, starting in the southeast, as Teleki, Neumann, and Stigand had, and moving north into Ethiopia, where he was detained for a while by the local police. He then traveled down the western shore, retracing in part the routes taken almost a century before by Henry Hart Cavendish, Vittorio Bottego, and Herbert Henry Austin. He accomplished this remarkable trip in fifty days and traveled with only African companions, including a child and a pregnant woman who accompanied him part of the way.[14] Two years later, Mohamed Amin, a highly acclaimed Kenyan photographer, drove around the lake. His expedition carried 800 liters of gasoline, 20 spare tires, 275 liters of drinking water, a quarter ton of photographic equipment and film, and a radio-telephone with a range of 900 miles.[15]

Roads, schools, clinics, and small towns now dot the countryside through which Count Samuel Teleki and Lieutenant Ludwig von Höhnel once passed. A paved road leads to the western shore of the lake, and modern explorers white-water raft down the Omo River. Although this corner of Africa has dramatically changed since Teleki's time, there is much that remains the same. He would still find northern Kenya and southern Ethiopia familiar places, with their great landscapes and splendid views. And the lake is still there, a shimmering jade sea, remote and lonely, set like a jewel in a vast expanse of thornbush and desert.

Chronology

Date	Event
1843	Antoine Thomson d'Abbadie and Arnaud Michel d'Abbadie explore the upper reaches of the Omo River.
May 11, 1848	Johann Rebmann sees Mount Kilimanjaro.
Dec. 3, 1849	Johann Ludwig Krapf sees Mount Kenya.
1852	Armchair geographer William Desborough Cooley publishes his book *Inner Africa Laid Open*, in which he criticizes the discoveries of Johann Ludwig Krapf and Johann Rebmann.
1855	Jacob J. Erhardt publishes the "slug map," showing a large inland sea in East Africa called Lake Uniamesi.
1856	The Royal Geographical Society sends Captain Richard Francis Burton and Lieutenant John Hanning Speke into East Africa to investigate the reports of Lake Uniamesi.
1858	Johann Ludwig Krapf publishes a map on which Lake Zamburu is depicted south of the Ethiopian highlands.
1858	John Hanning Speke arrives on the southern shore of Lake Victoria and claims to have discovered the source of the Nile.
1859	Léon des Avanchers publishes a map on which Lake El Boo is depicted south of the Ethiopian highlands.
1860	Armchair geographer Charles Tilstone Beke publishes his opinions about the source of the Nile in his book *The Sources of the Nile*.
1860–1863	John Hanning Speke returns to Africa with James Augustus Grant to trace the Nile from Lake Victoria through the Sudan.
1861	Baron Carl Claus von der Decken and Richard Thornton attempt to climb Mount Kilimanjaro.
Dec. 1863	John Hanning Speke's *Journal of the Discovery of the Source of the Nile* is published.
Mar. 14, 1864	Samuel and Florence Baker reach the Luta Nzigé, which they name Lake Albert, and determine its relationships to Lake Victoria and the Nile.

Sept. 16, 1864   Scheduled debate over the source of the Nile between Richard Francis Burton and John Hanning Speke canceled because of the latter's sudden death.

1870   Thomas Wakefield publishes a detailed map depicting Lake Samburu, based on information gathered from coastal traders.

1871   Charles New attempts to climb Mount Kilimanjaro.

1871   Henry Morton Stanley "finds" Dr. David Livingstone at Ujiji on Lake Tanganyika.

1874–1877   Henry Morton Stanley leads extensive expedition into Africa, during which he circumnavigates both Lake Tanganyika and Lake Victoria, and sails down the Congo River.

Sept. 13, 1882   Great Britain occupies Egypt.

1883–1884   Joseph Thomson crosses Maasai land and brings back news of a great salt lake to the north called Samburu.

Jan. 26, 1885   The Mahdi's forces capture Khartoum. General Charles George Gordon dies defending the city.

1885   Joseph Thomson's book *Through Masai Land* is published.

1886   Crown Prince Rudolf of Austria-Hungary reads the German translation of Joseph Thomson's book and decides to send an expedition to East Africa to find Lake Samburu.

1888   Sir William Mackinnon establishes the Imperial British East Africa Company (IBEA), which is chartered to administer Britain's sphere of influence in East Africa.

Mar. 5, 1888   Count Samuel Teleki and Lieutenant Ludwig von Höhnel arrive at the Basso Narok, which they rename Lake Rudolf.

Mar. 10, 1889   Emperor Yohannes IV of Ethiopia mortally wounded by Mahdist forces at the Battle of Metemma.

May 2, 1889   Italy and Ethiopia sign the Treaty of Wuchale, by which the former believes it has gained protectorate powers.

May–Nov. 1889   William Astor Chanler and George E. Galvin visit Mount Kilimanjaro and set up a compound at Taveta.

Nov. 3, 1889   Menelik II, king of Shoa, crowned emperor of Ethiopia.

July 1, 1890   Anglo-German agreement signed governing respective colonial spheres in East Africa.

Mar. 24, 1891   Italy and Britain sign a protocol delimiting their spheres of influence in East Africa, effectively placing Ethiopia under Italian control.

Apr. 1891   Menelik II of Ethiopia declares that his legitimate southern boundary extends beyond Lake Rudolf.

1892   The Imperial British East Africa Company (IBEA) withdraws from Uganda because of financial difficulties and its inability to deal with serious local political problems.

1892–1893   William Astor Chanler, George E. Galvin, and Ludwig von Höhnel explore much of what is now northern Kenya.

1893	Victor Prompt, a French hydrologist, proposes damming the Nile at Fashoda and speculates on the adverse consequences for Egypt if an unfriendly power controlled the Upper Nile.
Apr. 1, 1893	Sir Gerald Portal, the British consul general in Zanzibar, leads an expedition to Uganda, where he replaces the Imperial British East Africa Company (IBEA) flag with the Union Jack, thus making Uganda a provisional British protectorate.
Aug. 1894	British Parliament confirms protectorate status for Uganda.
1895	Robert Arthur Talbort Gascoyne-Cecil, marquess of Salisbury, becomes Britain's conservative prime minister for seven years and chief architect of British imperialism in Africa.
Mar. 23, 1895	Russian mission, headed by Nicholas Stephanovic Leontiev, arrives at the court of Ethiopia's Emperor Menelik II.
May 28, 1895	Sir Edward Grey tells the House of Commons that a French move on the Upper Nile would be an "unfriendly act."
July 10, 1895	Arthur Donaldson Smith arrives at the northern end of Lake Rudolf, having traveled from Berbera on the Somali coast.
July 13, 1895	Czar Nicholas II receives an official Ethiopian delegation in St. Petersburg.
Dec. 6, 1895	Arthur Neumann arrives at the southern end of Lake Rudolf, having trekked up from Mombasa in search of ivory.
Mar. 1, 1896	An Ethiopian army of 100,000 well-armed soldiers defeats Italy's colonial force of 17,000 at the Battle of Adowa.
Aug. 30, 1896	Vittorio Bottego and his expedition arrive at the northern end of Lake Rudolf, having traveled from Brava on the Somali coast.
Mar. 12, 1897	Henry Sheppard Hart Cavendish and H. Andrew reach the northern end of Lake Rudolf, six months after leaving Berbera on the Somali coast. Cavendish explores the lake's western shore.
Mar. 17, 1897	Vittorio Bottego dies battling an overwhelming Ethiopian force at Ghidami.
Mar. 20, 1897	Menelik II of Ethiopia and French leaders sign the Convention pour le Nil Blanc, by which Ethiopia agrees to help French expeditions approaching the Nile from the east.
May 14, 1897	Anglo-Ethiopian Treaty signed in Addis Ababa, in which Ethiopia agrees not to assist the Mahdists in return for territorial concessions.
July 9, 1897	James Ronald Macdonald and his Juba Expedition arrive in Mombasa.
Sept. 1897	Hugh Cholmondeley, Lord Delamere, and Dr. A. Eustace Atkinson arrive at the southern end of Lake Rudolf nine months after leaving Berbera on the Somali coast.

Apr. 7, 1898   Alexander Xavieryevich Bulatovich and *Ras* Wolda Giorgis arrive at the northern end of Lake Rudolf with a large military force.

June 22, 1898   A joint Franco-Ethiopian expedition reaches the Nile in hopes of meeting up with Commandant Jean-Baptist Marchand, coming from the west.

July 10, 1898   Commandant Jean-Baptist Marchand and his party reach Fashoda on the Nile, which they claim for France.

Aug. 31, 1898   Captain Herbert Henry Austin and his party arrive at the western shore of Lake Rudolf a month after leaving their base camp at Save on Mount Elgon.

Sept. 2, 1898   General Sir Horatio Kitchener defeats the Mahdists and occupies Omdurman.

Sept. 12, 1898   Captain Herbert Henry Austin plants Union Jacks and signs treaties with local chiefs at the northern end of Lake Rudolf.

Sept.–Dec. 1898   The Fashoda crisis erupts over France's occupation of a stretch of the Upper Nile.

Dec. 11, 1898   The French back down from their claims to the Upper Nile and withdraw from Fashoda.

Mar. 1899   Captain Montagu Sinclair Wellby and an Ethiopian escort arrive at the northern end of Lake Rudolf three months after leaving Addis Ababa.

Mar. 21, 1899   France and Britain sign the West African Convention, by which the Fashoda crisis is formally brought to closure. France abandons all claims to the Nile River in return for territorial concessions to the west of the river.

May 1899   Menelik II of Ethiopia offers to settle his southern frontier with Britain.

Aug. 21, 1899   Nicholas Stephanovic Leontiev and his military expedition arrive at the northern end of Lake Rudolf and remove the Union Jacks put up by Herbert Henry Austin in September 1898.

Dec. 10, 1899   Arthur Donaldson Smith returns to Lake Rudolf, following his previous route from Berbera on the Somali coast.

Mar. 25, 1900   James Jonathan Harrison, William Fitzhugh Whitehouse, and their party arrive at the northern end of Lake Rudolf and replace Union Jacks removed in August 1899 by Nicholas Leontiev.

May 8, 1901   Major Herbert Henry Austin arrives at the northern end of Lake Rudolf after traveling down from Omdurman in the Sudan.

July 1901   Count Eduard Wickenburg pays a brief visit to the northern end of Lake Rudolf, having set out from Addis Ababa on April 20.

June 1902	Vicomte Robert du Bourg de Bozas and his expedition arrive at the northern end of Lake Rudolf three and a half months after leaving Addis Ababa.
May 1903	Archibald Butter and Captain Philip Maud arrive at the northern end of Lake Rudolf while delimiting the Anglo-Ethiopian border. Their line between Ethiopia and British East Africa becomes known as the Red Line.
Aug. 1903–Feb. 1904	J.W. Brooke leads the East Africa Syndicate Expedition from Mount Elgon to the northwestern end of Lake Rudolf.
Nov. 1905	Philip Zaphiro appointed by John Lane Harrington, British agent and consul general in Addis Ababa, as boundary inspector charged with patrolling the Red Line.
Dec. 6, 1907	Agreement between Britain and Ethiopia relative to the frontiers between British East Africa, Uganda, and Ethiopia signed at Addis Ababa. Most of Lake Rudolf is given to Britain, and the Omo River delta remains in Ethiopia.
Sept. 1908	Captain Chauncey Hugh Stigand arrives on the eastern shore of Lake Rudolf after trekking up from Gilgil in British East Africa
Feb. 22, 1909	Major Charles William Gwynn arrives at the northern end of Lake Rudolf as head of the Abyssinian–East African Boundary Commission and makes adjustments in the Butter-Maud line. The modified border becomes known as the Blue Line.
Dec. 12, 1913	Menelik II of Ethiopia dies.

Notes

Introduction

1. During the historical period covered in this book, Ethiopia was generally known to Europeans as Abyssinia. However, the name Ethiopia is more encompassing both historically and geographically. It is also the one preferred by modern Ethiopians, who officially discarded the name Abyssinia in 1923.

2. Patrick Brantlinger, *Rule of Darkness: British Literature and Imperialism, 1830–1914*, Ithaca: Cornell University Press, 1988, pp. 180–181.

3. Tim Youngs, *Travellers in Africa: British Travelogues, 1850–1900*, Manchester and New York: Manchester University Press, 1994, pp. 39–50.

4. Mary Louise Pratt, *Imperial Eyes: Travel Writing and Transculturation*, London and New York: Routledge, 1992, p. 202.

Chapter One

1. For a fuller description of Ptolemy's writings and map, see William Desborough Cooley, *Claudius Ptolemy and the Nile*, London: J.N. Parker and Son, 1854; and Harry Johnston, *The Nile Quest: A Record of the Exploration of the Nile and Its Basin*, New York: Frederick A. Stokes, 1903, pp. 14–29.

2. Johann Rebmann, "Narrative of a Journey to Jagga, the Snow Country of Eastern Africa," *Church Missionary Intelligencer* 1849; 1:12–23.

3. William Desborough Cooley, *Inner Africa Laid Open*, London: Longman, Brown, Green and Longmans, 1852 (reprint ed., Westport, Conn.: Negro Universities Press, 1969), p. 126.

4. MacQueen's name is alternatively spelled McQueen and M'Queen in various publications. Born in 1778 in Scotland, he died in 1870 at the age of ninety-two.

5. James MacQueen, *A Geographical and Commercial View of Northern Central Africa, Containing a Particular Account of the Course of the Great River*, Edinburgh: William Blackwood, 1821.

6. Karl Wilhelm Isenberg, *Journals of the Rev. Messrs. Isenberg and Krapf, Missionaries of the Church Missionary Society, Detailing Their Proceedings in the Kingdom of Shoa, and Journeys in Other Parts of Abyssinia, in the*

Years 1839, 1840, 1841, and 1842, London: Seeley, 1843 (microfiche ed., Leiden: IDC, 1985).

7. Charles Tilstone Beke, "Communications Respecting the Geography of Southern Abyssinia," *Journal of the Royal Geographical Society* 1843; 12:84–102. Also see Charles Tilstone Beke, "On the Nile and Its Tributaries," *Journal of the Royal Geographical Society* 1847; 17:1–84.

8. Beke described his theories about the Nile sources and this expedition in his book *The Sources of the Nile: Being a General Survey of That River and of Its Headstreams: With a History of Nilotic Slavery*, London: Taylor and Francis, 1860.

9. Krapf, who was born in 1810, died on November 25, 1881, in Württemberg; Rebmann was born in 1820 and died in October 1876 in Württemberg; Jacob Erhardt left East Africa in 1856 and worked as a missionary for thirty-five years in India, from where he retired to Stuttgart. He died there in August 1901, at the age of seventy-eight. For details about the lives and careers of Krapf, Rebmann, and Erhardt, see Roy C. Bridges, "Introduction to the Second Edition," J. Lewis Krapf, *Travels, Researches, and Missionary Labours During an Eighteen Years' Residence in Eastern Africa*, London: Frank Cass, 1968.

10. Bridges, "Introduction," p. 63.

11. Jacob Erhardt, "On an Inland Sea in Africa," *Proceedings of the Royal Geographical Society* 1856; 1:8–13.

12. Richard F. Burton, *The Lake Regions of Central Africa: A Picture of Exploration*, New York: Harper and Brothers, 1860, p. 22.

13. John Hanning Speke, *What Led to the Discovery of the Source of the Nile*, Edinburgh and London: William Blackwood and Sons, 1864, pp. 305, 307.

14. Burton, *The Lake Regions*, p. 409.

15. Christopher Hibbert, *Africa Explored: Europeans in the Dark Continent, 1769–1889*, New York: W.W. Norton, 1982, pp. 212–213.

16. Alan Moorehead, *The White Nile*, New York: Harper and Row, 1960, p. 42.

17. The Royal Geographical Society presented Burton with its gold medal for his Lake Tanganyika explorations, and he was also later knighted by Queen Victoria.

18. Burton, *The Lake Regions*, p. viii.

19. The expedition was described by Speke and Grant in their respective books. See John Hanning Speke, *Journal of the Discovery of the Source of the Nile*, Edinburgh and London: William Blackwood and Sons, 1863; and James Augustus Grant, *A Walk Across Africa; or Domestic Scenes from the Nile Journey*, Edinburgh: William Blackwood and Sons, 1864. After Speke's death, Grant referred to the journey as the "Speke and Grant Expedition." See also James Augustus Grant, "Summary of Observations on the Geography, Climate, and Natural History of the Lake Regions of Equatorial Africa, Made by the Speke and Grant Expedition," *Proceedings of the Royal Geographical Society* 1872; 42:243–342.

20. For details concerning Speke and Grant's campaign against Petherick, see Moorehead, *The White Nile*, p. 65; Richard Hall, *Lovers on the Nile: The*

Incredible African Journeys of Sam and Florence Baker, New York: Random House, 1980, pp. 127–132; and Johnston, *The Nile Quest*, p. 168.

21. Petherick and his wife presented their version of Speke and Grant's arrival at Gondokoro in their 1869 book. See John Petherick and Katharine Petherick, *Travels in Central Africa*, London: Tinsley Brothers, 1869.

22. Samuel Baker, *The Albert Nyanza*, London: Macmillan, 1866.

23. Hall, *Lovers on the Nile*, p. 129.

24. For details of the Speke-Burton controversy, see Zoë Marsh, *East Africa Through Contemporary Records*, Cambridge: Cambridge University Press, 1961, pp. 68–75.

25. Burton and MacQueen laid out their views about the sources of the Nile in an 1864 book that they jointly authored. See Richard F. Burton and James MacQueen, *The Nile Basin, Part 1, Showing Tanganyika to Be Ptolemy's Western Lake Reservoir: A Memoir Read Before the Royal Geographical Society, November 14, 1864, with Prefatory Remarks* (by Richard F. Burton), and Part 2, *Captain Speke's Discovery of the Source of the Nile: A Review* (by James McQueen), London: Tinsley Brothers, 1864.

26. For Burton's reactions to Speke's death, see Richard Rice, *Captain Sir Richard Francis Burton: The Secret Agent Who Made the Pilgrimage to Mecca, Discovered the Kama Sutra, and Brought the Arabian Nights to the West*, New York: Charles Scribner's Sons, 1990, pp. 382–385.

27. Henry Morton Stanley, *How I Found Livingstone*, London: Sampson Low, 1872.

28. Henry Morton Stanley, *Through the Dark Continent, or the Sources of the Nile Around the Great Lakes of Equatorial Africa and Down the Livingstone River to the Atlantic Ocean*, London: Sampson Low, Marston, Searle and Rivington, 1878.

29. Charles Chaillé-Long, *Naked Truths of Naked People*, London: Sampson Low, 1876. Also see Charles Chaillé-Long, *My Life in Four Continents*, London: Hutchinson, 1912; Romolo Gessi, *Seven Years in the Sudan: Being a Record of Explorations, Adventures, and Campaigns Against the Arab Slave Hunters*, London: Sampson Low, Marston, 1892 (microfilm ed., Watertown, Mass.: Erasmus Press, 1985).

30. The travels of the seventeenth-century Portuguese missionaries Father Pedro Paez and Father Jeronimo Lobo are described by Johnston in *The Nile Quest*, pp. 51–58, and by Moorehead in *The White Nile*, pp. 24–28.

31. James Bruce, *Travels to Discover the Source of the Nile in the Years 1768, 1769, 1770, 1771, 1772 and 1773*, London: Longman and Rees, 1804.

Chapter Two

1. Johann Ludwig Krapf, *Reisen in Ost-Afrika: Ausgefuhrt in den Jahren 1837–1855*, Kornthal, Germany: Johann Ludwig Krapf, 1858.

2. Léon des Avanchers, "Esquisse géographique des Pays Oromo ou Galla, des Pays Soomali, et de la Côte Orientale d'Afrique," *Bulletin de la Société de Géographie*, Series 4, 1859; 17:153–170.

3. Ibid., pp. 163–164.

4. Ibid., p. 154.

5. C.F. Beckingham and G.W.B. Huntingford, *Some Records of Ethiopia, 1593–1646*, London: Hakluyt Society, 1954, pp. 29, 155, 157.

6. Antoine Thomson d'Abbadie, *Note sur le Haut Fleuve Blanc*, Paris: Martinet, 1849.

7. For further details concerning this controversy, see "Charles Tilstone Beke (1800–1874)" in *The Dictionary of National Biography*, edited by Sir Leslie Stephen and Sir Sidney Lee, Volume 2, Oxford: Oxford University Press, 1921, pp. 138–139.

8. Charles Tilstone Beke, *An Enquiry into M. Antoine d'Abbadie's Journey to Kaffa in 1843–44 to Discover the Sources of the Nile*, London: James Madden, 1851.

9. Antoine Thomson d'Abbadie (1810–1897) and his brother Arnaud Michel d'Abbadie (1815–1893) were among Europe's leading geographers. Born in Ireland of a French father and an Irish mother, they quickly distinguished themselves in scientific exploration. The French Academy sent Antoine to Brazil and Arnaud to Algeria; both gathered much scientific information while abroad. A number of years elapsed following their return from Ethiopia before they published the wealth of information they had gathered on the country's natural history. For a description of their years in Ethiopia, see Arnaud d'Abbadie, *Douze ans de séjour dans la Haute Ethiopie*, Vatican City: Biblioteca Apostolica Vaticana, 1900.

10. J. Lewis Krapf, *Travels, Researches, and Missionary Labours During an Eighteen Years' Residence in Eastern Africa*, London: Trubner, 1860.

11. Ernst Georg Ravenstein (1839–1913) eventually became the cartographer for the Royal Geographical Society and completed the maps of a number of later travelers.

12. For Krapf's later career, see Roy C. Bridges, "Introduction to the Second Edition," J. Lewis Krapf, *Travels, Researches, and Missionary Labours During an Eighteen Years' Residence in Eastern Africa*, London: Frank Cass, 1968, pp. 7–75. Krapf used the name "Galla" for the people known today as the Oromo.

13. For Wakefield's life and work, see his wife's biography of him written shortly after his death in 1901: E.S. Wakefield, *Thomas Wakefield: Missionary and Geographical Pioneer in East Equatorial Africa*, London: Religious Tract Society, 1904.

14. Learning from Burton's then recent and bitter experience with Speke, von der Decken made Richard Thornton sign a contract stipulating that the latter could not publish anything about the trip except geology and then only a year after the conclusion of the expedition. In addition, Thornton, who died in Africa in 1863, had to surrender all papers and notes arising from the trip to von der Decken. Von der Decken was generous in his willingness to let Thornton publish. But after von der Decken's death in 1865, his brother Jules held Thornton's heirs to the conditions of the contract. As a result, their plans to publish Thornton's diaries came to nothing. For details of Thornton's life and accomplishments in Africa, see H.A. Fosbrooke, "Richard Thornton in East Africa," *Tanganyika Notes and Records* 1962; 58–59:43–63. Otto Kersten,

with the help of Jules von der Decken, compiled a six-volume work describing the explorer's accomplishments in Africa: See Otto Kersten, *Von der Decken's Reisen in Ost-Afrika in den Jahren 1859 bis 1865*, Leipzig: C.F. Winter, 1869–1871.

15. Charles New, *Life, Wanderings, and Labours in Eastern Africa: With an Account of the First Successful Ascent of the Equatorial Snow Mountain, Kilima Njaro and Remarks upon East African Slavery*, London: Hodder and Stroughton, 1874.

16. Ibid., pp. 286–287.

17. Joseph Thomson, *Through Masai Land: A Journey of Exploration Among the Snowclad Volcanic Mountains and Strange Tribes of Eastern Equatorial Africa*. London: Sampson Low, Marston, Searle, and Rivington, 1885, p. 4.

18. Ibid.

19. Ibid., p. 70.

20. For details concerning New's life and work, see Alison Smith, "Introduction to the Third Edition," Charles New, *Life, Wanderings, and Labours in Eastern Africa: With an Account of the First Successful Ascent of the Equatorial Snow Mountain, Kilima Njaro and Remarks upon East African Slavery*, London: Frank Cass, 1971, pp. 7–30.

21. Thomas Wakefield, "Routes of Native Caravans from the Coast to the Interior of Eastern Africa, Chiefly from Information Given by Sadi Bin Ahedi, a Native of a District near Gazi, in Udigo, a Little North of Zanzibar," *Journal of the Royal Geographical Society* 1870; 40:303–339.

22. Ibid., p. 322.

23. Jonathan Swift, "On Poetry: A Rhapsody," in *Jonathan Swift*, edited by Ross Argus and David Woolley, Oxford: Oxford University Press, 1984, p. 539.

Chapter Three

1. Verney Lovett Cameron, *Across Africa*, London: Daldy Isbister, 1877. Also see Henry Morton Stanley, *Through the Dark Continent, or the Sources of the Nile Around the Great Lakes of Equatorial Africa and Down the Livingstone River to the Atlantic Ocean*, London: Sampson Low, Marston, Searle, and Rivington, 1878.

2. For a discussion of the International African Association, see Auguste Rolykens, *Les débuts de l'oeuvre Africaine de Léopold II (1875–1879)*, Brussels: Academie Royale des Sciences Coloniales, 1955; for details about the African Exploration Fund, see Roy C. Bridges, "The Royal Geographical Society and the African Exploration Fund 1870–1880," *Geographical Journal* 1963; 129:25–35.

3. Bridges, "The Royal."

4. The fund's proposed exploration projects were described in *Proceedings of the Royal Geographical Society* 1877; 21:388–390.

5. Johann Maria Hildebrandt, "Uber seine Reisen in Ost-Afrika," *Verhandbingen der Gesellschaft für Erdkunde zu Berlin* 1877; 4:284–295. This article

was later translated by C.P. Rigby and published as "Travel in East Africa," *Proceedings of the Royal Geographical Society* 1878; 22:452–453.

6. Keith Johnston's life and career are summarized in "Obituary—Keith Johnston," *Proceedings of the Royal Geographical Society* 1879; 1:598–600.

7. For information on Thomson's early years and how he obtained a place on the Johnston expedition, see Robert I. Rotberg, *Joseph Thomson and the Exploration of Africa*, London: Chatto & Windus, 1971, pp. 13–32.

8. Keith Johnston, "Note of a Trip from Zanzibar to Usambara, in February and March, 1879," *Proceedings of the Royal Geographical Society* 1879; 1:546–547; and Joseph Thomson, "Notes on the Geology of Usambara," *Proceedings of the Royal Geographical Society* 1879; 1:558–564.

9. Rotberg, *Joseph Thomson*, p. 39.

10. Ibid.

11. Details on Johnston's death are presented in "The East African Expedition: Further Information Respecting the Death of Mr. Keith Johnston (Letters from Keith Johnston and Joseph Thomson to John Kirk)," *Proceedings of the Royal Geographical Society* 1879; 1:669–673.

12. Letter from John Kirk to Henry Walter Bates, Zanzibar, August 23, 1879, Royal Geographical Society Archives, London.

13. For a discussion of Thomson's character and accomplishments, see Rotberg, *Joseph Thomson*, pp. 298–304.

14. Thomson regularly kept the society informed of the expedition's progress. These progress notes were published in *Proceedings of the Royal Geographical Society* 1880; 2:209–212, 306–309, and 721–742.

15. A summary of the scientific results of the expedition is presented in Rotberg, *Joseph Thomson*, p. 107.

16. Ibid., p. 113.

17. Ibid., p. 111.

18. "Report of the Evening Meetings, Mr. Joseph Thomson, 8 November, 1880," *Proceedings of the Royal Geographical Society* 1880; 2:772.

19. Rotberg, *Joseph Thomson*, p. 112.

20. Bridges, "The Royal," pp. 25–35.

21. Joseph Thomson, *To the Central African Lakes and Back: The Narrative of the Royal Geographical Society's East Central African Expedition, 1878–1880*, London: Sampson Low, Marston, Searle, and Rivington, 1881.

22. An insightful analysis of Thomson's *To the Central African Lakes and Back* is found in Rotberg, *Joseph Thomson*, pp. 113 and 301.

23. For a fuller discussion of the creation of the fictional character Allan Quartermain, see H. Rider Haggard, *The Days of My Life: An Autobiography*, edited by C.J. Longman, London: Longmans, Green, 1926, pp. 7–8 (Volume 1), 85–86 (Volume 2); and Pascal James Imperato and Eleanor M. Imperato, *They Married Adventure: The Wandering Lives of Martin and Osa Johnson*, New Brunswick, N.J.: Rutgers University Press, 1992, pp. 95–96.

24. Joseph Thomson, "Notes on the Basin of the River Rovuma, East Africa," *Proceedings of the Royal Geographical Society* 1882; 4:65–79.

25. Rotberg, *Joseph Thomson*, p. 133.

26. Minutes of the Expedition Committee meeting of June 26, 1882, Royal Geographical Society Archives, London.

27. "Address by Henry Morton Stanley Before the Royal Geographical Society, 27 March, 1878," *Proceedings of the Royal Geographical Society* 1878; 22:149; James Augustus Grant, "Summary of Observations on the Geography, Climate, and Natural History of the Lake Region of Central Africa Made by the Speke and Grant Expedition," *Journal of the Royal Geographical Society* 1872; 42:243–342.

28. D.A. Low, "The Northern Interior," in *History of East Africa*, Volume 1, edited by Roland Oliver and Gervase Mathew, Oxford: Oxford University Press, 1963, pp. 303–308.

29. James Christie, *Cholera Epidemics in East Africa: An Account of the Several Diffusions of the Disease in That Country from 1821 till 1872, with an Outline of the Geography, Ethnology, and Trade Connections of the Regions Through Which the Epidemics Passed*, London: Macmillan, 1876, p. 207.

30. J.P. Farler, "Native Routes in East Africa from Pangani to the Masai Country and the Victoria Nyanza," *Proceedings of the Royal Geographical Society* 1882; 4:730–738.

31. Letter from Joseph Thomson to Henry Walter Bates, London, June 22, 1882, Royal Geographical Society Archives, London.

32. Joseph Thomson, *Through Masai Land: A Journey of Exploration Among the Snowclad Volcanic Mountains and Strange Tribes of Eastern Equatorial Africa*, London: Sampson Low, Marston, Searle, and Rivington, 1885, pp. 9–10.

33. Frederick Jackson, who served as governor of the Uganda Protectorate from 1907 to 1911, knew James Martin in later years. He said that when Thomson became seriously ill, Martin's "devoted attention and nursing pulled him through." After his trip with Thomson, Martin served under General (later Sir) Lloyd William Mathews, as second in command of the Zanzibari army. He later accompanied a number of expeditions of the Imperial British East Africa Association (later Company) and in 1890 climbed Mount Elgon with Frederick Jackson, Ernest Gedge, and Dr. Archibald D. Mackinnon. He became a district officer at the Ravine station for the Uganda Protectorate but was caught poaching ivory. He was then sent to Entebbe as a collector, and after leaving the services of the Uganda Protectorate, Martin managed a rubber estate there. With the outbreak of World War I, he served with the intelligence section of the British army and also with the Belgians. He later lived in Dar es Salaam, the capital of modern Tanzania, and died in Portugal in December 1924. See Frederick Jackson, *Early Days in East Africa*, London: Edward Arnold, 1930, pp. 66–72; see also Rosabel Walker, "Little Martin," *Kenya Weekly News*, September 20, 1957, pp. 24–25, and September 27, 1957, pp. 32 and 45.

34. Thomson, *Through Masai Land*, p. 340.

35. Gustav A. Fischer, *Reise in das Massai-Land*, Hamburg: L. Friederichsen, 1885.

36. Thomson, *Through Masai Land*, pp. 69–70.

37. In his *Early Days*, p. 193, Jackson characterized Kimemeta as "the great-est and the best of the caravan leaders whose spheres of operations were gener-ally referred to as Masailand, but really extended from Kilimanjaro as far as Lake Rudolf." His caravans were always large and well armed, and he had a re-markable knowledge of local languages. He had had smallpox earlier in his life, which had left his face badly scarred, and he was blind in one eye. Jackson thought that without Kimemeta's backing, Thomson could not have crossed Maasai country. Jackson met Kimemeta many years later at Ravine station when the old man, in ill health and almost blind, was leading what proved to be his last safari. Jackson helped make this final trip a success by giving Kimemeta material assistance. Kimemeta died in 1890 at Pangani, on the coast. For a fuller description of Kimemeta and his importance to Thomson's expedition, see Jackson, *Early Days*, pp. 193–196. Some authors refer to Kimemeta as Jumba Kimameta.

38. There has been much confusion about the precise date of Thomson's ar-rival at Rabai, primarily because he implied different dates in his writings. This was probably because of the severity of his illness, which had invalided him over the previous three months. Rotberg, *Joseph Thomson*, p. 193, con-cluded that Thomson arrived on June 2, 1884, based on this diary entry by Mrs. Thomas Wakefield. However, Mrs. Wakefield's diary entry itself was dated June 2, 1884, and in it, she stated that Thomson had arrived on Saturday afternoon. Since June 2, 1884, was a Monday, he must have arrived on May 31 or perhaps on the previous Saturday, May 24, as he himself suggested in his writings. See E.S. Wakefield, *Thomas Wakefield: Missionary and Geographi-cal Pioneer in East Equatorial Africa*, London: Religious Tract Society, 1904, p. 193.

39. Thomson, *Through Masai Land*, p. 338.

40. Robert I. Rotberg provided an insightful analysis of the book and the ex-pedition on which it was based in his "Introduction to the Third Edition," Joseph Thomson, *Through Masai Land: A Journey of Exploration Among the Snowclad Volcanic Mountains and Strange Tribes of Eastern Equatorial Africa*, London: Frank Cass., 1968, pp. VI–XIII.

41. Rotberg, *Joseph Thomson*, p. 304.

42. Thomson, *Through Masai Land*, p. 314.

Chapter Four

1. Roland Oliver and Gervase Mathew (editors), *History of East Africa*, Vol-ume 1, Oxford: Oxford University Press, 1963, pp. 266, 366.

2. Ibid., p. 369.

3. Ibid., p. 366.

4. Zoë Marsh and G.W. Kingsnorth, *An Introduction to the History of East Africa*, Cambridge: Cambridge University Press, 1963, p. 109.

5. Oliver and Mathew, *History*, p. 374.

6. M.F. Hill, *Permanent Way: The Story of the Kenya and Uganda Railway*, Nairobi: East African Railways and Harbours, 1961, p. 108.

7. Ibid., p. 10.

8. Laszlo Kadar, "The Man Whose Name the African Teleki Volcano Bears," *Communications of the Geographical Institute of Debrecen* 1966–1967; 12–13:181–184.

9. Oliver and Mathew, *History*, p. 378.

10. Ibid., pp. 383–384.

11. Marsh and Kingsnorth, *Introduction*, p. 114; see also Carl Peters, *New Light on Darkest Africa: Being A Narrative of the German Emin Pasha Expedition*, London: Ward, Lock, 1891.

12. Ibid., p. 114.

13. Hill, *Permanent Way*, p. 10.

14. Teleki Samuel grof in *Révai Nagy Lexikona Az Ismeretek Enciklopédioya XVIII*, Kotet, Budapest: Révai Testverek Irodalmi Intézet Reszeny Tarsaság, 1925, pp. 87–92; see also "Graf Samuel Teleki" (obituary), *Wiener Abendpost*, March 11, 1916, p. 3.

15. Ibid., p. 90.

16. "Romai Szentbirodalmi Széki Gróf Teleki Samuel" (death announcement), *Wiener Zeitung Jahrgang*, March 11, 1916.

17. Judith Listowell, *A Habsburg Tragedy: Crown Prince Rudolf*, New York: Dorset Press, 1978, p. 216.

18. Lajos Erdélyi, *Teleki Samu Afrikában: Az Afrika-Kutató Eredeti Fényképfelvételeivel*, Bucharest: Kriterion Könyvkiadó, 1977, pp. 5–10.

19. Joseph Thomson, *Durch Masai-Land Forschungsreise in Ostafrika zu den Schneebergen u. wilden Stämmen Zwischen den Kilima-Ndjaro u. Victoria-Njansa un den 1883–1884*, Leipzig: Brockgaus, 1885.

20. Ludwig Ritter von Höhnel, "Over Land and Sea in Earlier Times and More Recent Days (1857–1909): Being an Austrian Rear Admiral's Own Narrative of His Life" (unpublished), 1924, chapter 4, p. 49, William Astor Chanler Correspondence, Rokeby Papers, Rokeby, Barrytown, New York; at the time of this writing, this manuscript is scheduled to be published in 1998 by Holmes & Meier under the tentative title "Over Land and Sea: The Memoirs of Ludwig von Höhnel—Africa Explorer, Rear Admiral and Imperial Aide-de-Camp," edited by Ronald E. Coons, Pascal James Imperato, and John Winthrop Aldrich; all chapter and page references cited here refer to the unpublished manuscript. Also see "Ludwig Ritter von Höhnel: Admiral und Afrika forscher," in *Österreichisches Biographisches Lexikon 1815–1950*, edited by Leo Santifaller, Volume 2, Cologne: Graz-Hermann Böhlaus Nachf, 1959, p. 358.

21. Listowell, *Habsburg*, pp. 144–149.

22. Ibid., pp. 149–150.

23. Von Höhnel, "Over," chapter 4, p. 43; see chapter 4, p. 28, for von Höhnel's account of his youthful desire to travel in Africa.

24. Ibid., chapter, 4, p. 44.

25. Georg Schweinfurth (1836–1925) was a German botanist who traveled in the Upper Nile regions between 1868 and 1871. His book contains a rough map of East Africa that prominently depicts Lake Tanganyika and Lake Zamburu; see George Schweinfurth, *The Heart of Africa: Three Years' Travels and*

Adventures in the Unexplored Regions of Central Africa from 1868 to 1871, New York: Harper and Brothers, 1874.

26. Von Höhnel, "Over," chapter 4, p. 44.

27. The noble honorific "Ritter von" was bestowed on Ludwig's father in recognition of his government service.

28. Von Höhnel's early life is detailed in his as yet unpublished English-language autobiography, "Over Land and Sea," chapters 1 and 2, and in his published German-language autobiography, *Mein Leben zur See auf Forfchunosreifen und beihofe,* Berlin: Verlag von Reimar Hobbing, 1926; von Höhnel's "Over Land and Sea" was edited and prepared for publication in 1995–1997 by Ronald E. Coons, Ph.D., professor of history, University of Connecticut, and by Pascal James Imperato and John Winthrop Aldrich.

29. Von Höhnel, "Over," chapter 3, p. 61.

30. Count Samuel Teleki, "A Personal Diary of Explorations in East Africa, October 1886–October 1888, by Count Samuel Teleki (1845–1916), with Descriptions of His Pioneer Climbs on Mounts Kilimanjaro and Kenya in 1887, His Discoveries of Lakes Rudolf and Stefanie in 1888, and His Return Safari to Mount Kilimanjaro in 1895." Text translated from the handwritten Hungarian version into English by Charles and Vera Teleki, Warkworth, Ontario, Canada, 1961, entry of December 30, 1886, p. 2 (courtesy of Geza Teleki); Teleki's original handwritten Hungarian diaries of his two African journeys are in the Special Collections of Michigan State University Library, East Lansing, Michigan.

31. Teleki, "Personal Diary," December 30, 1886, p. 3.

32. Ibid., December 30, 1886, pp. 1–6.

33. Personal communication, Geza Teleki, Washington, D.C., August 13, 1996.

34. Von Höhnel, "Over," chapter 5, pp. 11–13.

35. Lloyd William Mathews (1850–1901) first arrived in East Africa in 1877 as a Royal Navy lieutenant aboard the HMS *London,* which was engaged in suppressing the slave trade. In 1877, he was asked to take charge of the sultan of Zanzibar's army, and in 1881, he was given the rank of brigadier general. He resigned from the Royal Navy the same year. Although he was in a sense a freelancer in the employ of the sultan, he strongly promoted British interests in East Africa, such that he was named consul general in 1891, a position he never assumed. The establishment of a British protectorate over Zanzibar on November 4, 1890, placed him in a key position to advance London's East African colonial policies. In October 1891, he was named prime minister of the sultan's government, a post he occupied until his death from malaria on October 11, 1901 (see Robert Nunez Lyne, *An Apostle of Empire: Being the Life of Sir Lloyd William Mathews, K.C.M.G.,* London: George Allen and Unwin, 1936).

36. Von Höhnel, "Over," chapter 5, p. 17.

37. Teleki, "Personal Diary," December 30, 1886, p.7.

38. Ibid., December 30, 1886, p. 9.

39. Von Höhnel, "Over," chapter 5, pp. 25–27; it is difficult to ascertain the precise number of men in Teleki's caravan because of varying figures given in the four existing accounts of the expedition. Although there were 495 loads at

the outset, some of these were transported by the 25 donkeys purchased by Kimemeta. Even allowing for the transport of several loads per donkey, there must have been in excess of 300 porters leaving Pangani. To their numbers must be added the askari (guards) and Kimemeta's men. Thus, the expedition must have numbered between 300 and 400 as it left the coast.

40. At the time of this expedition, Teleki was forty-one years old and von Höhnel twenty-nine. Both were in excellent health, but Teleki proved to be the sturdier of the two.

41. Joseph Thomson, *Through Masai Land: A Journey of Exploration Among the Snowclad Volcanic Mountains and Strange Tribes of Eastern Equatorial Africa*, London: Sampson Low, Marston, Searle, and Rivington, 1885, p. 57.

42. There are four firsthand accounts of this expedition. These include Teleki's personal, handwritten diary, the English translation of which contains 326 pages, and von Höhnel's three accounts, two of which were published. The latter include a chapter in *Mein Leben zur See*, which appeared in 1926, and the two-volume account of the expedition published in German in 1892 and in English in 1894 (see Ludwig von Höhnel, *Discovery of Lakes Rudolf and Stefanie: A Narrative of Count Samuel Teleki's Exploring and Hunting Expedition in Eastern Equatorial Africa in 1887 and 1888*, translated by Nancy Bell [N. D'Anvers], Volumes 1 and 2, London: Longmans, Green, 1894). Von Höhnel's soon to be published English-language autobiography, "Over Land and Sea," written at the urging of his American friend and benefactor William Astor Chanler in 1924, contains a 76-page, handwritten chapter about the expedition. To these four primary sources can be added Teleki's personal letters to Crown Prince Rudolf, written from Africa. These contain fuller descriptions of a number of experiences and events only tersely mentioned in his diary. The diary, which has not been extensively used to date by scholars and researchers, records a number of events, observations, analyses, and opinions not covered by von Höhnel in any of his writings.

43. Von Höhnel, "Over," chapter 5, p. 27.

44. Teleki, "Personal Diary," March 12, 1887, p. 30.

45. Ibid., February 8, 1887, p. 18.

46. Ibid., March 20, 1887, p. 34.

47. Ibid., March 30, 1887, p. 37.

48. Von Höhnel, *Discovery*, pp. 200–201; see also Sir Frederick Jackson, *Early Days in East Africa*, London: Edward Arnold, 1930, p. 143.

49. Ibid., p. 125–127.

50. Teleki, "Personal Diary," March 30, 1887, pp. 37–38.

51. Jackson, *Early Days*, p. 122.

52. Teleki, "Personal Diary," April 27, 1887, p. 44.

53. Von Höhnel, "Over," chapter 5, p. 27.

54. Teleki, "Personal Diary," April 12, 1887, p. 38.

55. Ibid., April 28, 1887, p. 46.

56. Ibid., May 4, 1887, pp. 50–50a.

57. Von Höhnel, "Over," chapter 5, pp. 23–24.

58. Ibid., chapter 5, p. 23.

59. Teleki secured the same four guides who had accompanied Harry Hamilton Johnston (1858–1927), who in 1884 had climbed the mountain while securing treaties for the Imperial British East Africa Company (see von Höhnel, *Discovery*, Volume 1, p. 183).

60. Teleki, "Personal Diary," June 19, 1887, p. 69; June 20, 1887, pp. 69a–70.

61. Ibid., June 27, 1887, pp. 74–74a.

62. Ibid., July 9, 1887, p. 76.

63. Teleki regularly sent letters about the expedition's progress to Crown Prince Rudolf via trading caravan leaders who then gave them to William Oswald in Zanzibar. Oswald also reported on the expedition to Count Kalnocky, the minister of the imperial house and foreign affairs. On June 6, 1887, for example, he reported in a letter that Teleki and von Höhnel had arrived at Mount Kilimanjaro (see Letter from William Oswald, Consul of Austria-Hungary, to Count Kalnocky, Zanzibar, June 6, 1887, Austrian State Archives, Vienna).

64. Teleki wrote in his diary that "Höhnel is sick again with his stomach. . . . His nose is swollen and I'm afraid he might have blood poisoning" (see Teleki, "Personal Diary," September 11, 1864, p. 114).

65. Von Höhnel provided a detailed account of the troubles the expedition encountered with the Kikuyu (see von Höhnel, *Discovery*, Volume 1, pp. 286–363).

66. Von Höhnel, "Over," chapter 5, p. 35.

67. Teleki, "Personal Diary," September 14, 1887, p. 119.

68. Von Höhnel, *Discovery*, Volume 1, p. 320.

69. Ibid., pp. 329–330.

70. Teleki, "Personal Diary," September 27, 1887, p. 130.

71. Von Höhnel, *Discovery*, Volume 1, p. 339.

72. Letter from Count Samuel Teleki to Crown Prince Rudolf, Leikipea, November 4, 1887, Crown Prince Rudolf Papers, Austrian State Archives, Vienna (in Hungarian).

73. Teleki, "Personal Diary," October 3, 1887, p. 134.

74. Von Höhnel, *Discovery*, Volume 1, p. 345; when the British geologist John Walter Gregory (1864–1932) visited this area several years later, the Kikuyu demonstrated that they were as adept at recounting revisionist history as they were at ambushing travelers. If Gregory had at first believed their story of having been the innocent victims of unprovoked attacks by Teleki, he soon changed his mind, for the Kikuyu tried to rob his camp soon after having gone through a blood-brotherhood ceremony. As a safeguard against further attacks, he held the chief's son captive and told him "that in case of treachery, he would be shot" (see J. W. Gregory, *The Great Rift Valley: Being the Narrative of a Journey to Mount Kenya and Lake Baringo*, London: John Murray, 1896, pp. 158–159).

75. Teleki, "Personal Diary," October 22, 1887, p. 143; the Teleki Valley, at 13,500 feet, commemorates this climb.

76. Ibid., November 3, 1887, p. 155; Teleki also had five of his askari severely flogged on this day for sexually molesting three Maasai women. The guards received from forty to fifty strokes with a stick. This once again

demonstrated that Teleki was a strong leader capable of maintaining strict discipline among his men.

77. Letter from Count Samuel Teleki, November 4, 1887.

78. Ibid.

79. Teleki, "Personal Diary," December 8, 1887, pp. 175–176; while von Höhnel was exploring the Guaso Nyiro, Teleki spent his time hunting in the rich game country around Lake Baringo.

80. Letter from Count Samuel Teleki to Crown Prince Rudolf, Baringo, December 16, 1887, Crown Prince Rudolf Papers, Austrian State Archives, Vienna (in Hungarian).

81. Ibid.

82. Von Höhnel, *Discovery*, Volume 2, pp. 49–50.

83. Teleki, "Personal Diary," February 20, 1888, p. 20.

84. Von Höhnel, *Discovery*, Volume 2, pp. 63–64.

85. Ibid., pp. 92, 95.

86. Teleki, "Personal Diary," March 5, 1888, p. 222.

87. Ibid., April 19, 1888, pp. 247–248.

88. Von Höhnel, *Discovery*, Volume 2, p. 163.

89. Teleki, "Personal Diary," January 24, 1888, p. 192.

90. Von Höhnel, "Over," chapter 5, p. 40.

91. Teleki ended his diary on October 3, 1888, after he had arrived in Taveta. On approaching Mount Kilimanjaro, they "fell in with a young, very tall American, Dr. Abbott" (von Höhnel, "Over," chapter 5, p. 41); William Louis Abbott, M.D. (1860–1936) was an independently wealthy naturalist who explored Mount Kilimanjaro in 1888–1889 with Otto Ehlers, the German explorer (see "William Louis Abbott," in *The National Cyclopedia of American Biography*, Volume 27, New York: James T. White, 1939, pp. 312–313; see also William Louis Abbott, *Descriptive Catalogue of the Abbott Collection of Ethnological Objects from Kilimanjaro, East Africa*, Washington, D.C.: U.S. Government Printing Office, 1891).

92. Teleki and von Höhnel met not only General Mathews in Mombasa but also George Mackenzie, the chairman of the Imperial British East Africa Company (IBEA). Mackenzie had recently arrived in Zanzibar in order to organize the Mombasa headquarters of the IBEA. The British government had assigned responsibility to the IBEA for administering its sphere of influence.

93. Ill health was not the only reason Teleki remained in Zanzibar. He auctioned off eighty-four elephant tusks on the local ivory market. The sale brought in $200,000, which in the late twentieth century would be the equivalent of $2 million. Teleki used the proceeds of the auction to help cover the costs of the expedition. Von Höhnel said that "Hindu merchants were in general the highest bidders" (von Höhnel, "Over," chapter 5, p. 44); Teleki also killed large numbers of other big game, including eighty-four buffaloes and eighty-two rhinoceroses (see Samuel Teleki, "Rifles for Big Game," *The Field, The Country Gentleman's Newspaper* 1894; 83[2145]:155). While stopping in Aden at the Hotel de l'Univers, Teleki and von Höhnel met Dr. Georg Schweinfurth, whose famous book *The Heart of Africa* "Count Teleki held in hand, when first he came on board the *Greif*." At the same hotel, they also

met the German explorer Dr. Carl Peters (1856–1918), who was about to embark on his fruitless marathon trip to secure what is now Kenya and Uganda for Germany. See Peters, *New Light;* von Höhnel, "Over," chapter 5, p. 51.

94. It was on their fourth march toward Harar that a messenger sent by the Austro-Hungarian consul in Aden brought them the news of Rudolf's death. Teleki was so devastated that "he did not want to hear of anything, and to all my comforting words he only answered that he wished to return at once to the coast." See von Höhnel, "Over," chapter 5, p. 55.

95. Letter from William Oswald, Consul of Austria-Hungary, to Count Kalnocky, Zanzibar, June 6, 1887, Austrian State Archives, Vienna.

96. Letter from William Oswald, Consul of Austria-Hungary, to the Ministry of the Imperial House and Foreign Affairs, Zanzibar, May 8, 1888, Austrian State Archives, Vienna.

97. Letter from Alfred Oswald, Consul of Austria-Hungary, to the Ministry of the Imperial House and Foreign Affairs, Zanzibar, October 22, 1888, Austrian State Archives, Vienna.

98. Jules Borelli, *Ethiopie Mériodionale: Journal de mon voyage aux Pays Amhara, Oromo et Sidama, Septembre 1885 à Novembre 1888*, Paris: Ancienne Maison Quantin, 1890.

99. Von Höhnel, "Over," chapter 5, p. 71.

100. Borelli, *Ethiopie*, p. 485.

101. Ibid., p. 484.

102. Ibid., p. 443.

103. Ludwig von Höhnel, "The Lake Rudolf Region: Its Discovery and Subsequent Exploration, 1888–1909," Part 1, *Journal of the Royal African Society* 1938; 37:21–45.

104. Von Höhnel, "Over," chapter 6, p. 3.

105. Ibid., chapter 5, p. 75.

106. Ibid., chapter 6, pp. 2–3.

107. Personal communication, Geza Teleki, Washington, D.C., August 13, 1996.

108. Pascal James Imperato and Geza Teleki, "Count Samuel Teleki's Second Voyage to East Africa," *SWARA* 1992; 15(2):23–25.

109. Count Samuel Teleki, "Diary of a Voyage to Africa, March 17 to April 11, 1895, by Count Samuel Teleki," text translated from the handwritten Hungarian version into English by Charles and Vera Teleki, Warkworth, Ontario, Canada, April 30, 1961.

110. Von Höhnel, "Over," chapter 6, p. 15.

111. Ibid., chapter 4, p. 45.

112. *Révai*, p. 92; "Romai."

113. Listowell, *Habsburg*, p. 3. The Soviets also vandalized Teleki's tomb in search of valuables (Personal communication from Lajos Erdélyi, New York City, May 12, 1997).

114. Personal communication from Lajos Erdélyi, New York City, May 12, 1997.

115. Erdélyi, *Teleki*.

116. Janos Kubassek, "Magyar Tudományos Afrika-Expedició 1987–1988," *Földrajzi Muzeumi Tanulmanyok* 1989; 6:45–54.

Chapter *Five*

1. For details concerning William Astor Chanler's early life and family, see Lately Thomas, *A Pride of Lions: The Astor Orphans—The Chanler Chronicle*, New York: William Morrow 1971.

2. See Lately Thomas, *Sam Ward: "King of the Lobby,"* Boston: Houghton Mifflin, 1965; Britain's Lord Rosebery called Ward the "uncle of the human race." His closest friends included Henry Wadsworth Longfellow, James A. Garfield, William H. Seward, and Lord Rosebery.

3. After the death of his wife, Emily Astor Ward, Sam Ward filled his life with the activities of high society, international travel, political lobbying, and venture capitalism. In 1875, he, Lord Rosebery, and William Henry Hurlbert, editor in chief of the *New York World*, formed "The Mendacious Club," of which Ward was president. Ward's successful lobbying of Congress on behalf of British interests won for him the admiration of Prime Minister William Gladstone and other powerful figures. When Ward died at Pegli, Italy, on May 19, 1884, Rosebery, Hurlbert, and Crawford erected a simple stone cross over his grave, on which were inscribed their names and the tribute "and God gave him largeness of heart even as the sands of the seashore." See Thomas, *Sam Ward*, pp. 490–491.

4. William Astor Chanler Jr., "William Astor Chanler," Camden, Maine, manuscript, pp. 1–2 (courtesy of William Astor Chanler Jr.); Chanler took a preliminary entrance examination for Harvard College in 1885 and passed in seven subjects. Although he did well in Greek, Latin, French, and English composition, he failed algebra and arithmetic (Harvard College, Preliminary Examination for W.A. Chanler, Cambridge, July 10, 1885, William Astor Chanler Correspondence, Rokeby Papers, Rokeby, Barrytown, New York).

5. Chanler, "William Astor Chanler," p. 1.

6. Ibid.

7. Maddie DeMott, "William Chanler," *Africana* 1967; 3, 1:15–19; Chanler's friend Theodore Roosevelt persuaded Harvard's president, Charles W. Eliot, to grant him an honorary M.A. degree. This enabled him to keep himself on the alumni rolls for the class of 1890 (Personal communication, William Astor Chanler Jr., January 6, 1988).

8. George E. Galvin (1872–1951) was born in Red Hook, New York, the son of a farmer, Patrick Galvin, who was from County Cork, Ireland, and Sarah Catherine Corbett, who was born in Rhinebeck, New York. In 1905, he married Helen Goldner, and they had seven children. In the early part of the century, he managed Chanler's horse breeding stables in Leesburg, Virginia. Chanler later set him up as a travel agent at the Vanderbilt Hotel in New York City, in which he held an interest. "He knew all the customs officials in New York, and would whisk people through in no time" (Personal communication, William Astor Chanler Jr., Camden, Maine, July 6, 1994). Galvin lived in Ja-

maica, New York, for many years, where he died on February 14, 1951, at the age of seventy-nine (Letter from George E. Galvin Jr. to John Winthrop Aldrich, Albuquerque, New Mexico, November 2, 1986, Rokeby Papers, Rokeby, Barrytown, New York).

9. George E. Galvin, *Diary of George E. Galvin, Chanler Expedition, Kenya (formerly British East Africa), 1888–1890*, compiled by George E. Galvin Jr., proofread and edited by Daniel Terry Galvin, original draft by Marilyn Corbett Galvin, additional information and moral support by David Warren Galvin, Marion Galvin-Beckers, Evelyn P. Galvin-Vogt, and Olive Pope-Galvin, Albuquerque, New Mexico, 1996.

10. Ibid., December 7, 1888, to March 3, 1889, pp. 1–4.

11. Ibid., May 18, 1889, p. 6.

12. Ibid., May 26, 1889, p. 8.

13. Ibid., May 29, 1889, p. 7.

14. Ibid., pp. 12–13, 19. In October 1889, Reverend Alexander Steggall of the Church Missionary Society, knowing of Chanler's imminent departure from Taveta, urged the society to take over the buildings and the two acres of land. The society finally agreed, and in March 1890, Steggall went to Taveta to discuss the matter with the elders (see Ann E. Frontera, *Persistence and Change: A History of Taveta*, Waltham, Mass.: Crossroads Press, 1978, p. 22). Steggall had considerable contacts with Chanler in 1889 and visited him at Abbott's camp on September 25, when he brought him a package that had arrived at Taveta containing a compass, boiling thermometers, and a camera (Galvin, *Diary*, September 25, 1889, p. 31).

15. William Louis Abbott, M.D. (1860–1936) was born in Philadelphia and received his medical degree from the University of Pennsylvania School of Medicine. He spent most of his life collecting natural history specimens and ethnographic materials in many different parts of the world for the Smithsonian Institution. His letters and papers are in the archives of the Smithsonian (see "William Louis Abbott Papers, 1887–1923," Webster, New York: Photographic Sciences Corporation, 1983, 3 microfilm reels). This collection consists of letters to his mother and sister and Smithsonian curators and other miscellaneous documents. His ethnographic collection is now held by the Smithsonian Institution's National Museum of Natural History (see William Louis Abbott, *Descriptive Catalogue of the Abbott Collection of Ethnological Objects from Kilimanjaro, East Africa*, Washington, D.C.: U.S. Government Printing Office, 1891; and Judith Boruchoff, *Register to the Papers of William Louis Abbott*, Washington, D.C.: National Anthropological Archives, 1986).

16. De Mott, "William Chanler," p. 16.

17. Hans Meyer, *Across East African Glaciers: An Account of the First Ascent of Kilimanjaro*, translated from the German by H.S. Calder, London: George Philip & Son, 1891, pp. 20, 120.

18. De Mott, "William Chanler," p. 16.

19. Chanler and the Africans clearly exposed themselves to a number of disease risks (e.g., hepatitis B infection) by participating in blood-brotherhood ceremonies. His son recently made the following cogent observation about this: "He and the chiefs drew blood in each other's arms and pressed the bleed-

ing parts together, mingling the blood. This today would be sure suicide, in view of the alarming spread of AIDS" (Letter from William Astor Chanler Jr. to Pascal James Imperato, Camden, Maine, May 7, 1993).

20. Galvin, *Diary*, October 27, 1889, p. 34.

21. Ibid., November 3, 1889, to May 27, 1890, pp. 34–36. Chanler later wrote an account of his African hunting experiences. See William Astor Chanler, "Hunting in East Africa," in *Hunting in Many Lands: The Book of the Boone and Crockett Club*, edited by Theodore Roosevelt and George Bird Grinnell, New York: Forest and Stream Publishing, 1895, pp. 13–54. In all, he shot 150 head of game.

22. Richard Harding Davis, "An American in Africa," *Harper's New Monthly Magazine*, 1893; 86:632–635.

23. De Mott, "William Chanler," p. 16.

24. Ludwig von Höhnel, "Reminiscences: An Interview with William Astor Chanler, Jr.," 1935, pp. 1, 8, William Astor Chanler Papers, New York Historical Society, New York City.

25. William Astor Chanler, *Through Jungle and Desert: Travels in Eastern Africa*, New York: Macmillan, 1896, p. 7.

26. Thomas, *A Pride*, p. 152.

27. Von Höhnel, "Reminiscences," p. 15.

28. Ibid.

29. Ibid., p. 16.

30. Chanler, *Through Jungle*, p. 7.

31. As von Höhnel noted in his autobiography, they hoped "to find the cradle of the Galla, a formerly powerful, but today scattered tribe." This fascination with the Galla on the part of Europeans was long-standing but was revived in the 1860s and 1870s by missionaries such as Ludwig Krapf, Charles New, and Thomas Wakefield.

32. Letter from William Astor Chanler to Margaret Chanler, off Port Said, June 18, 1892, William Astor Chanler Correspondence, Rokeby Papers, Rokeby, Barrytown, New York.

33. As he had done on Teleki's expedition, von Höhnel marched in the rear so that he could make careful observations necessary for drawing maps. Writing years later, he said that Chanler's worst weakness was his "great impulsiveness" but that one willingly overlooked this because he was always "a faithful and reliable friend." He spoke highly of Galvin, saying that he was "strong, very calm, cold-blooded, intelligent, and interested in everything." He also said that Galvin's "practical sense and calm reflection permitted him to solve every problem in a satisfactory manner" (see Ludwig von Höhnel, "Over Land and Sea: Being an Austrian Rear Admiral's Own Narrative of His Life," unpublished, 1924, chapter 7, pp. 22–23; and William Astor Chanler Correspondence, Rokeby Papers, Rokeby, Barrytown, New York).

34. Chanler, *Through Jungle*, p. 81.

35. Ibid., p. 140.

36. Ibid., p. 119.

37. Ibid., p. 139.

38. Ibid., p. 202.

39. Letter from William Astor Chanler to Margaret and Alida Chanler, Hameye on Tana, March 6, 1893, William Astor Chanler Correspondence, Rokeby Papers, Rokeby, Barrytown, New York.

40. Von Höhnel, "Over," chapter 8, p. 36.

41. Letter from William Astor Chanler to Ludwig von Höhnel, Daitcho, East Africa, October 19, 1893, William Astor Chanler Correspondence, Rokeby Papers, Rokeby, Barrytown, New York.

42. Letter from William Astor Chanler to Ludwig von Höhnel, Daitcho, East Africa, December 16, 1893, William Astor Chanler Correspondence, Rokeby Papers, Rokeby, Barrytown, New York.

43. Chanler, *Through Jungle*, p. 456.

44. Ibid., p. 462.

45. Ibid.

46. Ibid., p. 466.

47. Von Höhnel, "Reminiscences," p. 28.

48. Ibid., p. 30.

49. Chanler, *Through Jungle*, p. 500.

50. James White Allen, Acting U.S. Consul, Dispatch to Walter Quintin Gresham, Secretary of State, Zanzibar, April 2, 1894, Dispatch Files, Zanzibar, British Africa, 1836–1906, Record Group 59, The National Archives, Washington, D.C.

51. Ibid.

52. Ibid.

53. Ibid.

54. Lloyd Mathews, Memorandum on Zanzibar Porters, Zanzibar, March 16, 1894, Foreign Office File 107/19, Public Record Office, Richmond, England.

55. Zoë Marsh and G.W. Kingsnorth, *An Introduction to the History of East Africa*, Cambridge: Cambridge University Press, 1963, p. 145.

56. Ibid., p. 145.

57. Roland Oliver and Gervase Mathew (editors), *History of East Africa*, Volume 1, Oxford: Oxford University Press, p. 385.

58. Ibid., p. 388.

59. Ibid.

60. Marsh and Kingsnorth, *Introduction*, p. 148.

61. Oliver and Mathew, *History*, p. 388.

62. James Rennell Rodd, *Social and Diplomatic Memories, 1884–1893*, Volume 1, London: Edward Arnold, 1922, p. 275.

63. Chanler, *Through Jungle*, p. 7.

64. Marsh and Kingsnorth, *Introduction*, p. 148.

65. Oliver and Mathew, *History*, pp. 387–389.

66. Rodd, *Social*, pp. 299–300.

67. Ibid., pp. 304–305.

68. Ibid., p. 317.

69. Ibid., pp. 323–324.

70. Ibid., pp. 337–339.

71. Chanler, *Through Jungle*, p. 402.

72. Ibid., p. 423.

73. Ibid., p. 419.

74. Ibid.

75. Marsh and Kingsnorth, *Introduction*, p. 148.

76. Chanler, *Through Jungle*, p. 462.

77. Letter from Ludwig von Höhnel to William Astor Chanler, Vienna, December 8, 1923, William Astor Chanler Correspondence, Rokeby Papers, Rokeby, Barrytown, New York.

78. Chanler, *Through Jungle*, p. 462.

79. M. Cracknall, Acting British Agent and Consul General, Dispatch to Lord Rosebery, Zanzibar, January 29, 1894, Foreign Office File 107/18, Public Record Office, Richmond, England.

80. Although Sam Ward had died in 1884, it is unlikely that Rosebery's fond memories of his unusually close friendship with him would have waned over the ensuing decade.

81. M. Cracknall, Acting British Agent and Consul General, Dispatch to Lord Rosebery, Zanzibar, March 15, 1894, Foreign Office File 107/19, Public Record Office, Richmond, England.

82. Chanler, *Through Jungle*, p. 508.

83. Ibid., p. 509.

84. Dispatch to M. Cracknall, London, April 16, 1894, Foreign Office File 107/16, Public Record Office, Richmond, England.

85. Ibid.

86. Allen, Dispatch to Walter Quintin Gresham, pp. 7–8.

87. Lord Rosebery, Memorandum, London, April 20, 1894, Foreign Office File 107/16, Public Record Office, Richmond, England.

88. Minute from Lord Rosebery to M. Cracknall, London, April 10, 1894, Foreign Office File 107/19, Public Record Office, Richmond, England.

89. Chanler, *Through Jungle*, p. 500.

90. Letter from William Chamberlain Chanler to Pascal James Imperato, New York, May 8, 1978, author's files.

91. Chanler, *Through Jungle*, p. 462; Chanler showed great discretion in not openly accusing Mathews of treachery in his book. This was driven not only by his upbringing but also by practical considerations. He wrote his book for both British and American audiences and had not ruled out a third trip to British East Africa. A public denunciation of Mathews would have alienated his British publisher and readers and made a return trip impossible.

92. For an independent assessment of the then customary treatment of deserting porters, see Letter from J. Robinson to William Waite Allen, Zanzibar, March 30, 1894, Dispatch Files, Zanzibar, British Africa, 1836–1906, Record Group 59, The National Archives, Washington, D.C.

93. For the details of Mathews's life, see Robert Nunez Lyne, *An Apostle of Empire: Being the Life of Sir Lloyd William Mathews K.C.M.G.*, London: George Allen and Unwin, 1936. This complimentary biography, as its title implies, extols Mathews's life and career and presents him as a heroic figure in the history of the British Empire. It is devoid of any critical observations and does not mention Chanler.

94. Rodd, *Social*, p. 348.

95. Von Höhnel, "Reminiscences," p. 18.

96. Chanler, *Through Jungle*, pp. 517–519; as with most expeditions of the time, the photographic results were modest. Chanler had used a new type of plate, but it did not hold up well under tropical heat and humidity.

97. Letter from William Astor Chanler to Ludwig von Höhnel, December 16, 1893.

98. Ibid.

99. Beatrice later became a prominent philanthropist and raised funds for a French sanitarium and for relief efforts during both world wars. On July 6, 1994, I visited with William Astor Jr. and Ashley in Camden, Maine. Ashley, who was extremely ill at the time and living in a retirement home, asked me to help him walk down the hall toward a clock twenty feet away. He held onto my arm, but we had only gotten a few feet when he stopped and said: "I really can't go any farther. And to think that my father walked thousands of miles across Africa." Ashley died on November 14, 1994.

100. John Brent, *A Man's Game*, New York: Century, 1921; Richard Hart, *The Sacrifice*, London: Boswell, 1925.

101. Personal communication from John Winthrop Aldrich, Barrytown, New York, August 30, 1996. Chanler successfully used Mannlicher and Winchester rifles, which are light weapons, to kill big game. This was an important empirical observation since prior to Chanler's report of his success with light weapons, big-game hunters firmly believed that large animals could only be killed with larger-bore rifles (see William Astor Chanler, "Rifles and Big Game in East Equatorial Africa," *The Field, The Country Gentleman's Newspaper* 1893; 82[2135]:826).

102. For the details of von Höhnel's departure from the navy, see Erwin F. Sieche, "Austria-Hungary's Last Naval Visit to the USA," *Warship International* 1990; 2:142–164; additional information about von Höhnel's career is contained in Ildikó Cazan-Simányi, "Ludwig Ritter von Hoehnel (1857–1942) Leben und werk," Ph.D. dissertation, University of Vienna, March 1988, 225 pp. A copy of this dissertation is in the collection at the Universitats Bibliothek, Vienna. It contains five pages describing the ethnographic objects von Höhnel gave to the Museum fur Volkerkunde in Vienna. Cazan-Simányi stated (p. 13) that Valeska was of Jewish origin, based on secondhand information that came from Rosa Zündel, the wife of von Höhnel's nephew. This information has not been independently corroborated by any other source.

103. Ludwig Ritter von Höhnel, *Mein Leben zur See auf Forfchunosreifen und beihofe*, Berlin: Verlag von Reimar Hobbing, 1926.

104. In 1992, Aldrich loaned the manuscript to me, and I in turn had several photocopies made. He also suggested I contact Professor Ronald E. Coons of the University of Connecticut, who had been his preceptor at Harvard. Professor Coons, a published historian of the Habsburg Monarchy and a leading authority on the maritime and administrative history of Austria, and I undertook the editing of the manuscript in 1995–1997. The manuscript is scheduled to be published in 1998 by Holmes & Meier, as: Ludwig von Höhnel, "Over Land and Sea: The Memoirs of Ludwig von Höhnel—Africa Explorer, Rear Ad-

miral and Imperial Aide-de-Camp," edited by Ronald E. Coons, Pascal James Imperato, and John Winthrop Aldrich, with a foreword by Sir Vivian Fuchs.

105. Von Höhnel, "Reminiscences," p. 16; to date, this manuscript has not been found.

106. Ludwig von Höhnel, "Zur Karte des Nordostlechen Kenia-Gebrets," *Petermann's Mitteilungen* 1894; 40:193–199.

107. Letter from The Bankers Trust Company to William Astor Chanler, Paris, October 21, 1931, William Astor Chanler Correspondence, Rokeby Papers, Rokeby, Barrytown, New York.

108. Letter from William Astor Chanler to Ludwig von Höhnel, Paris, February 12, 1929, William Astor Chanler Correspondence, Rokeby Papers, Rokeby, Barrytown, New York.

109. Letter from Ludwig von Höhnel to Margaret Aldrich, Vienna, March 12, 1934, William Astor Chanler Correspondence, Rokeby Papers, Rokeby, Barrytown, New York; von Höhnel was in such dire financial straits that he asked if he could have two of Chanler's suits, as his were threadbare.

110. Cazan-Simányi, "Ludwig Ritter von Höhnel," and Sieche, "Austria," p. 160. In 1996, the Afrika Museum collection was moved to a hunting museum at Schloss Marchegg near the Czech border.

Chapter Six

1. A. Donaldson Smith, *Through Unknown African Countries: The First Expedition from Somaliland to Lake Lamu*, London and New York: Edward Arnold, 1897, p. 289.

2. Ibid., p. 290.

3. Registry of Baptism, All Saints Episcopal Church, Philadelphia, Pennsylvania, September 10, 1866; Certificate of Death, Commonwealth of Pennsylvania, Department of Health, Division of Vital Statistics, New Castle, Pa., Arthur Donaldson Smith, File No. 13166, filed February 21, 1939.

4. Affidavit in support of application for membership and application for membership of Arthur Donaldson Smith in the Pennsylvania Society of the Sons of the Revolution, May 1 and May 2, 1890, Archives of the General Society of the Sons of the Revolution, Ruxton, Maryland.

5. For details of Smith's early life and education, see Pascal James Imperato, *Arthur Donaldson Smith and the Exploration of Lake Rudolf*, Lake Success, N.Y.: Medical Society of the State of New York, 1987, pp. 1–6.

6. Personal communication, H. Spencer Potter, Ph.D., Manhasset, New York, July 7, 1986.

7. Smith, *Through*, p. 359.

8. Death Certificate, Jesse Smith, No. 089222, City of Philadelphia, Department of Records, City Archives, November 24, 1892; Death Notice, Jesse Evans Smith, *Philadelphia Inquirer*, November 27, 1892; Estate of Jesse E. Smith, Letters of Administration, granted December 1, A.D. 1892, No. 1505, Register of Wills and ex-officio Clerk of the Orphans' Court for the City and County of Philadelphia, in the Commonwealth of Pennsylvania.

9. Smith, *Through*, p. 1.

10. Errol Trzebinski, *The Kenya Pioneers*, New York: W.W. Norton, 1986, pp. 137–138.

11. Philip Graves, *The Life of Sir Percy Cox*, London: Hutchinson, 1941, p. 34.

12. *British and Foreign State Papers*, London: William Ridgway, Volume 77, 1885–1886, pp. 1263–1269; *British and Foreign State Papers*, London: Her Majesty's Stationery Office, Volume 81, 1888–1889, p. 936; for the colonial history of Somaliland, see Saadia Touval, *Somali Nationalism, International Politics and the Drive for Unity in the Horn of Africa*, Cambridge, Mass.: Harvard University Press, 1963, and Robert L. Hess, *Italian Colonialism in Somalia*, Chicago: University of Chicago Press, 1966.

13. Percy Z. Cox, in *The Dictionary of National Biography, 1931–1940*, edited by L.G. Wickham Legg, London: Oxford University Press, 1949, pp. 196–199.

14. Smith, *Through*, p. 2. For an account of the two Smiths' hunting trip, see William Lord Smith, "An African Shooting Trip," in *Trail and Camp-Fire: The Book of the Boone and Crockett Club*, edited by George Bird Grinnell and Theodore Roosevelt, New York: Forest and Stream Publishing, 1897.

15. Vittorio Bottego, *Il Giuba esplorato: Viaggio di scoperta nel cuore dell'Africa—Sotto gli auspici della Società Geografica Italiana*, Rome: Loescher, 1895 (reprint ed. edited by Nicola Labanca, Parma: Ugo Guanda Editore, 1997).

16. Smith, *Through*, pp. 3–4.

17. Ibid., p. 5.

18. Ibid., pp. 8–9.

19. Letter from A. Donaldson Smith to John Coles, Hargeisa, Somaliland, July 19, 1894, A. Donaldson Smith Correspondence File, Royal Geographical Society Archives, London.

20. Smith, *Through*, pp. 20–22.

21. Ibid., p. 43.

22. Ibid., p. 99.

23. Ibid., pp. 135–136.

24. Letter from A. Donaldson Smith to J. Scott Keltie, Philadelphia, Pennsylvania, February 27, 1896, A. Donaldson Smith Correspondence File, Royal Geographical Society Archives, London.

25. A. Donaldson Smith, "Expedition Through Somaliland to Lake Rudolf," Part 2, *Geographical Journal* 1896; 8:221–239.

26. Smith, *Through*, p. 193. The hostility of the Boran was due to their mistaking Smith and his men for Ethiopians who had recently raided them.

27. Ibid., p. 199.

28. Ibid., pp. 264–265.

29. The several small ethnic groups that live to the north of Lake Rudolf have been extensively studied in the twentieth century by several scholars, including Uri Almagor, M. Lionel Bender, Ernesta Cerulli, Katsuyoshi Fukui, Peter Garretson, Serge Tornay, and David Turton, some of whose works are listed in the bibliography.

30. Smith, "Through," p. 289.

31. Arthur H. Neumann, *Elephant Hunting in East Equatorial Africa*, London: Rowland Ward, 1898, p. 259.

32. Imperato, *Arthur Donaldson Smith*, pp. 39–40.

33. Smith, *Through*, p. 352.

34. Ibid. The crater lake that Smith saw on Marsabit was later named Lake Paradise by the American wildlife photographers Martin and Osa Johnson, who chose it for their base for a few years in the 1920s (see Osa Johnson, *Four Years in Paradise*, Philadelphia: J.B. Lippincott, 1941). In 1913, Geoffrey Archer, the first British administrator to survey what is now northern Kenya, praised the accuracy of Smith's original survey of Mount Marsabit (see Geoffrey Archer, "British East Africa: I—Recent Exploration and Journey in the North of British East Africa," *Geographical Journal* 1913; 42:421–435).

35. Smith, *Through*, p. 354. On September 10, 1995, the Reverend Paolo Tablino of the Marsabit Catholic Mission and Brother Martin of the Catholic Secondary School at Marsabit organized a commemorative celebration of the centenary of Smith's visit to Marsabit. Father Tablino officiated at a mass in honor of Smith and all his traveling companions, during which he spoke of their visit to Marsabit. The celebration was attended by a large number of Boran students (Letter from Paolo Tablino to Pascal James Imperato, Marsabit, Kenya, September 14, 1995).

36. Smith, *Through*, pp. 363–364.

37. Ibid., p. 364.

38. "A Successful Explorer: Dr. Donaldson Smith Accomplished His Mission in Africa," *New York Times*, November 6, 1896, p. 6.

39. There are now 276 of Smith's ethnographic objects in the museum's collection. In 1896, the museum opened an exhibition of Smith's collection of ethnographic objects and animal trophies curated by Stewart Culin, who described it in detail (see Stewart Culin, "Trophies of Somaliland: Collection Presented by Explorer Smith to the University," *Philadelphia Times*, October 25, 1896, p. 3). In 1989, I and Dr. Dilys Winegrad, then assistant to the president of the University of Pennsylvania, examined this collection and, along with the museum's curatorial staff, selected 91 items for a commemorative centenary exhibition, "A Nineteenth-Century Traveler in the Horn of Africa—The Arthur Donaldson Smith Collection." Although two years of effort went into planning this exhibition for the Arthur Ross Gallery of the then recently refurbished Furness Building, it was never mounted because of a lack of sufficient funding. During the process of preparing this exhibition, I arranged for Grayel Tauscher of Tioga, Pennsylvania, to donate to the university archives the telescope Smith had carried with him on his African travels. Smith had given it to Tauscher in Roulette, Pennsylvania, in the early 1930s.

40. Smith, "Expedition," p. 233.

41. Ibid., pp. 238–239.

42. Letter from A. Donaldson Smith to J. Scott Keltie, February 27, 1896.

43. Henry Pleasants Jr., M.D., "Some Horses Are Lucky: Biographical Sketch of Arthur Donaldson Smith, M.D.," *The General Magazine and Historical Chronicle*, University of Pennsylvania General Alumni Society 1946; 48, 4:254–261 (courtesy of the late H. Spencer Potter, Ph.D.).

44. Letter from A. Donaldson Smith to J. Scott Keltie, February 27, 1896.

45. Letter from J. Scott Keltie to A. Donaldson Smith, London, March 9, 1896, A. Donaldson Smith Correspondence File, Royal Geographical Society Archives, London.

46. Letter from A. Donaldson Smith to J. Scott Keltie, Philadelphia, Pennsylvania, April 2, 1896, A. Donaldson Smith Correspondence File, Royal Geographical Society Archives, London.

47. Letter from A. Donaldson Smith to J. Scott Keltie, Philadelphia, Pennsylvania, June 17, 1896, A. Donaldson Smith Correspondence File, Royal Geographical Society Archives, London.

48. "Exploring Eastern Africa: Dr. Donaldson Smith, an American Traveler Encounters Queer People to the Northward of Abyssinia," *New York Times,* December 24, 1895, p. 13.

49. Pleasants, "Some," p. 256.

50. Letter from A. Donaldson Smith to J. Scott Keltie, June 17, 1896; for a detailed account of Smith's suspicions that the Royal Geographical Society was purposely delaying publication, see Imperato, *Arthur Donaldson Smith,* pp. 43–44.

51. Letter from A. Donaldson Smith to J. Scott Keltie, Kaolin, Pennsylvania, June 21, 1896, A. Donaldson Smith Correspondence File, Royal Geographical Society Archives, London.

52. Letter from J. Scott Keltie to A. Donaldson Smith, London, June 26, 1896, A. Donaldson Smith Correspondence File, Royal Geographical Society Archives, London.

53. Ibid.

54. A. Donaldson Smith, "Expedition Through Somaliland to Lake Rudolf" Part 1, *Geographical Journal* 1896; 8:120–137; Part 2, 1896; 8:221–239; Smith's book, *Through Unknown African Countries,* was published in 1897, when he was in Manchuria.

55. Letter from A. Donaldson Smith to J. Scott Keltie, DeBruce, Pennsylvania, August 20, 1896, A. Donaldson Smith Correspondence File, Royal Geographical Society Archives, London.

56. Letter from J. Scott Keltie to A. Donaldson Smith, London, February 2, 1897, A. Donaldson Smith Correspondence File, Royal Geographical Society Archives, London.

57. Letter from A. Donaldson Smith to J. Scott Keltie, San Francisco, California, March 2, 1897, A. Donaldson Smith Correspondence File, Royal Geographical Society Archives, London.

Chapter Seven

1. Arthur H. Neumann, *Elephant Hunting in East Equatorial Africa,* London: Rowland Ward, 1898, pp. VIII, IX.

2. Ibid., p. VIII.

3. For the details of Neumann's life and career, see J.G. Millais, *Wanderings and Memories,* London: Longmans, Green, 1919, pp. 138–168; and Monty

Brown, *Hunter Away: The Life and Times of Arthur Henry Neumann 1850–1907*, London: MJB, 1993.

4. Margery Perham and Mary Bull (editors), *The Diaries of Lord Lugard*, Volume 1, *East Africa, November 1889 to December 1890*, Evanston, Ill.: Northwestern University Press, 1959, pp. 222, 262–263; despite his generally low opinion of Neumann, Lugard admired him as an accomplished sportsman (p. 264).

5. Lugard told Neumann that he had "no orders whatsoever for him (for he kept pressing me as to what he was to do)." However, Neumann also had no kit or boots and thus was unable to make the trip (Perham and Bull, *Diaries*, p. 264).

6. Ludwig Ritter von Höhnel, "Over Land and Sea in Earlier Times and More Recent Days (1857–1909), Being an Austrian Rear Admiral's Own Narrative of His Life" (unpublished), 1924, chapter 7, p. 44, William Astor Chanler Correspondence, Rokeby Papers, Rokeby, Barrytown, New York.

7. William Astor Chanler, *Through Jungle and Desert: Travels in Eastern Africa*, New York: Macmillan, 1896, p. 491.

8. Neumann, *Elephant*, p. 257.

9. Ibid., p. 310.

10. Ibid., p. 321.

11. Ibid., p. 326.

12. Millais, *Wanderings*, pp. 143–144.

13. Ibid., p. 147.

14. Ibid., p. 155.

15. Ibid., p. 155–156.

16. Ibid., p. 156.

17. Ibid.; Brown, *Hunter*, pp. 313–316.

18. There is some evidence that Neumann may have been unscrupulous in obtaining ivory from local Africans (see Errol Trzebinski, *The Kenya Pioneers*, New York: W.W. Norton, 1986, p. 55).

19. For a detailed description of the indiscriminate killing of African elephants to satisfy the world ivory market of Neumann's time, see Derek Wilson and Peter Ayerst, *White Gold: The Story of African Ivory*, New York: Taplinger Publishing, 1976.

20. Peter Townend (editor), *Burke's Genealogical and Heraldic History of the Peerage, Baronetage and Knightage*, 103rd edition, London: Burke's Peerage Limited, 1963, pp. 2517–2518.

21. H.S.H. Cavendish, "Through Somaliland and Around the South of Lake Rudolf," *Geographical Journal* 1898; 11:372–396.

22. Letter from A. Donaldson Smith to Percy Z. Cox, Rittenhouse Club, Philadelphia, September 2, 1898, A. Donaldson Smith Correspondence File, Royal Geographical Society Archives, London; Eliot was curator of the Department of Zoology at the Field Museum in Chicago, and Akeley, who worked under him, would later become a renowned naturalist, sculptor, inventor, and taxidermist (see Penelope Bodry-Sanders, *Carl Akeley: Africa's Collector, Africa's Savior*, New York: Paragon House, 1991, pp. 48–67).

23. Cavendish, "Through," p. 373.

24. See Uri Almagor, "Institutionalizing a Fringe Periphery: Dassanetch-Amhara Relations," in *The Southern Marches of Imperial Ethiopia: Essays in History and Social Anthropology*, edited by Donald Donham and Wendy James, Cambridge: Cambridge University Press, 1986, pp. 96–115; in the same volume, also see David Turton, "A Problem of Domination at the Periphery: The Kwegu and The Mursi," pp. 148–171.

25. Cavendish, "Through," pp. 375–376.

26. Herbert Henry Austin, personal diary, September 2, 1898, as cited by A.T. Matson in "Introduction," Herbert H. Austin, *With Macdonald in Uganda*, Folkestone and London: Dawson's, 1973, p. xv.

27. Cavendish, "Through," p. 382.

28. Ibid., p. 390.

29. Austin, personal diary, October 2, 1898, as cited by A.T. Matson in "Introduction," *With Macdonald*, p. xv.

30. Trzebinski, *Kenya*, p. 24.

31. David Turton, "Exploration in the Lower Omo Valley of Southwestern Ethiopia Between 1890 and 1910," in *L'Africa ai tempi di Daniele Comboni*, edited by Maria Genoino Caravaglios, Rome: Instituto Italo-Africano e Missionari Comboniani, 1981.

32. Cavendish, "Through," p. 394.

33. Turton, "Exploration."

34. Cavendish did make a few original observations about the Omo delta and the northern end of Lake Rudolf (see Karl W. Butzer, *Recent History of an Ethiopian Delta: The Omo River and the Level of Lake Rudolf*, Chicago: University of Chicago Department of Geography, 1971, p. 113).

35. Cavendish, "Through," pp. 395–396.

36. Townend, *Burke's*, p. 2518.

37. L.G. Pine (editor), *Burke's Genealogical and Heraldic History of the Peerage, Baronetage and Knightage*, 102nd edition, London: Burke's Peerage Limited, 1959, pp. 635–636.

38. Elspeth Huxley, *White Man's Country: Lord Delamere and the Making of Kenya*, Volume 1, *1870–1914*, London: Chatto & Windus, 1935, pp. 5–22.

39. Ibid., pp. 23–26.

40. Ibid., pp. 31–32; Trzebinski, *Kenya*, p. 27.

41. Huxley, *White*, p. 47.

42. Frederick Jackson, *Early Days in East Africa*, London: Edward Arnold, 1930, pp. 70–72.

43. Huxley, *White*, p. 56.

44. The late Elspeth Huxley pieced together this account while doing research for her biography of Lord Delamere, *White Man's Country* (Personal communications from Elspeth Huxley to Pascal James Imperato, 1990).

45. The photographic collection from Delamere's expedition is now in the archives of the Rhodes House Library of the University of Oxford. It is modest in size, consisting of one album. "The vast majority of the photos are of dead animals, but others show landscapes and Africans with whom Delamere was traveling" (Letter from Amanda Hill, archivist, to Pascal James Imperato, Rhodes House Library, Oxford, January 27, 1997).

46. Huxley, *White*, Volume 2, p. 320.

47. One of the white hunters in Atkinson's employ was A. Arkell-Hardwick, who left a detailed account of his ivory hunting (see A. Arkell-Hardwick, *An Ivory Trader in North Kenia: The Record of an Expedition Through Kikuyu to Galla-Land in East Equatorial Africa*, London: Longmans, Green, 1903).

48. Trzebinski, *Kenya*, p. 54.

49. H.R. Tate, "Journey to the Rendile Country, British East Africa," *Geographical Journal* 1904; 23, 2:220–228, 280.

50. Trzebinski, *Kenya*, pp. 54–55.

51. Mary Gillett, "Dr. Eustace Atkinson," *Tribute to Pioneers*, Oxford: J.M. Considine, 1986.

Chapter Eight

1. Chris Prouty, *Empress Taytu and Menelik II: Ethiopia 1883–1910*, Trenton, N.J.: Red Sea Press, 1986, pp. 46–48.

2. Ibid., pp. 59–61; Harold G. Marcus, *A History of Ethiopia*, Berkeley: University of California Press, 1994, pp. 86–89; Harold G. Marcus, *The Life and Times of Menelik II: Ethiopia 1844–1913*, Lawrenceville, N.J.: Red Sea Press, 1995, pp. 104, 111–112.

3. Prouty, *Empress*, pp. 61–62.

4. G.N. Sanderson, *England, Europe and the Upper Nile, 1882–1899*, Edinburgh: University Press, 1965, p. 69; for a detailed discussion of the Treaty of Wuchale, see Marcus, *The Life*, pp. 114–188; for the problem of Mengasha's submission, see Marcus, *The Life*, p. 120.

5. Prouty, *Empress*, pp. 50–51.

6. Ibid., p. 90.

7. Marcus, *The Life*, p. 120.

8. For a detailed discussion of Crispi's grandiose colonial schemes and his reckless plans for achieving them, see Denis Mack Smith, *Italy and Its Monarchy*, New Haven and London: Yale University Press, 1989, pp. 93–96.

9. During the nineteenth century, the Bottego family added a grave accent to their name to distinguish it from the Italian word *bottega* (shop). During the twentieth century, they dropped the accent. However, the name is still pronounced as if the accent were present (Letter from Manlio Bonati to Pascal James Imperato, Parma, March 12, 1997). Bottego's life and career were described in authoritative and comprehensive detail by his biographer, Manlio Bonati (see Manlio Bonati, *Vittorio Bottego: Un ambizioso eroe in Africa*, Parma: Silva Editore, 1997). Earlier volumes on Bottego's life include: Rinaldo De Benedetti, *Vittorio Bottego e l'esplorazione del Giuba*, Turin: G.B. Paravia, 1931; Rinaldo De Benedetti, *Vittorio Bottego e l'esplorazione dell'Omo*, Turin: G.B. Paravia, 1933; Silvio Campioni, *I Giam Giam: Sulle orme di Vittorio Bottego*, Parma: Casa Editrice Luigi Battei, 1960; Maria Sanguini, *Vittorio Bottego*, Turin: Paravia, 1946 and 1971. For a detailed bibliography of previously published works related to Bottego, see Bonati, *Vittorio*, pp. 415–427.

10. Manlio Bonati, "Vittorio Bottego, un Parmigiano in Africa," *Forza Rapid*, pp. 14–16, 1992; for the development of Italian Somaliland, see Robert L. Hess, *Italian Colonialism in Somalia*, Chicago: University of Chicago Press, 1966.

11. Hess, *Italian*, p. 32.

12. A.C. McEwen, *International Boundaries of East Africa*, Oxford: Clarendon Press, 1971, p. 105.

13. For a full account of Grixoni's desertion, see Manlio Bonati, "Il dissidio tra Matteo Grixoni e Vittorio Bottego, Esploratorii Africani," in *Miscellanea di storia delle esplorazioni* 1989; 14:175–229; for an account of the expedition, see Vittorio Bottego, *Il Giuba esplorato: Viaggi di scoperta nel cuore dell'Africa—Sotto gli auspici della Società Geografica Italiana*, Rome: E. Loescher, 1895 (reprint ed. edited by Nicola Labanca, Parma: Ugo Guanda Editore, 1997), and Bonati, *Vittorio*, pp. 139–245.

14. Prouty, *Empress*, p. 131.

15. Hess, *Italian*, p. 57.

16. Sanderson, *England*, p. 25.

17. Hess, *Italian*, p. 57.

18. Ibid., p. 32.

19. "Eugenio Ruspoli," *Enciclopedia Italiana*, Rome: Enciclopedia Italiana, Volume 28, 1936, p. 262; Bonati, *Vittorio*, p. 247.

20. Bonati, "Vittorio Bottego."

21. L. Vannutelli and C. Citerni, *Seconda spedizione Bottego: L'Omo—Viaggio d'esplorazione nell'Africa Orientale*, Milan: Ulrico Hoepli Editore, 1899, p. 59.

22. Ibid., pp. 81–111; Bonati, *Vittorio*, p. 328.

23. For a detailed account of the Battle of Adowa, see G. F-H. Berkeley, *The Campaign of Adowa and the Rise of Menelik*, London: Archibald Constable, 1902; Italian casualties were heavy: 4,000 European men and officers and 2,000 Eritrean soldiers died, and 1,428 European and Eritrean men were wounded (see Marcus, *The Life*, p. 173). The Ethiopians' custom of emasculating their dead victims rapidly became known in Italy. My great-aunt, Maria Libera Insante Verde, who was twenty-eight years old at the time and living on the island of Ischia in the Bay of Naples, vividly recalled the mutilation of the Italian dead: "Menelik and the Abyssinians cut out their intestines and severed their genitals. They attached them to the tops of their spears and poles, and carried them aloft while celebrating" (Personal communication, Ozone Park, New York, 1953). Menelik's wife, Taytu, received special condemnation such that a half century later in Italy, her name was still used in a common saying rebuking pretentious people. This expression—"Who do you think you are, the Princess Taytu?"—was charged with negative connotations. Implicit in it was a rebuke and a downgrading of Taytu's status from empress to princess, a title below that of Italy's queen (Personal communication, Carmela Pescione Maiella, Naples, Italy, 1989).

24. Smith, *Italy*, pp. 119–122.

25. Prouty, *Empress*, p. 186.

26. Vannutelli and Citerni, *Seconda*, pp. 206–207, 234.

27. Von Höhnel, who met Borelli in Egypt, assessed his map as thoroughly inaccurate. He said the following: "It was very fortunate for Mr. Borelli to meet us . . . according to this map, Mr. Borelli had penetrated south, right across the country in which Lake Rudolf is lying without seeing it. . . . I advised him not to show this map to anybody, and promised to make it harmonious with our discoveries and to set it right. This was no easy task on which I had to work hard three days reducing his latitudes by several degrees (see Ludwig Ritter von Höhnel, "Over Land and Sea in Earlier Times and More Recent Days [1857–1909]: Being an Austrian Rear Admiral's Own Narrative of His Life," [unpublished], 1924, chapter 5, p. 71, William Astor Chanler Correspondence, Rokeby Papers, Rokeby, Barrytown, New York).

28. Vannutelli and Citerni, *Seconda*, p. 283.

29. Ibid., p. 330.

30. Ibid., p. 331. Bottego's expedition was the most scientifically proficient of those that visited the Omo, and it contributed the most to an understanding of the river's course and its relationship to Lake Rudolf. Turton accurately characterized Bottego as "the giant among explorers of the Omo Valley. . . . This was by far the most ambitious, systematic and successful of the expeditions which visited the Lower Omo during this period. It was also the only one to traverse the territory of the Mursi, and Bottego has a secure place in their history" (see David Turton, "Exploration in the Lower Omo Valley of Southwestern Ethiopia Between 1890 and 1910, in *L'Africa ai tempi di Daniele Comboni*, edited by Maria Genoino Caravaglios, Rome: Istituto Italo-Africano e Missionari Combiniani, 1981).

31. Vannutelli and Citerni, *Seconda*, p. 335. They were amused to find an English-language newspaper left behind by Smith in a hut at the campsite.

32. Bonati, "Vittorio Bottego," p. 16; Bonati, *Vittorio*, p. 352.

33. Prouty, *Taytu*, pp. 196–197. In her extremely pro-Ethiopian volume, Prouty characterized Bottego as "unscrupulous" without providing any documentation for such harsh criticism (p. 196).

34. Vannutelli and Citerni, *Seconda*, p. 416.

35. Ibid., p. 417. It is reasonable that Giote, having received orders from Addis Ababa to bring the Italians there, was not intent on killing them. Bottego, however, would never have submitted to being a prisoner. "The word surrender was not in his vocabulary" (Personal communication, Manlio Bonati, Parma, February 23, 1997).

36. Bottego's remains were mutilated according to Ethiopian custom and left to the elements and scavengers (Personal Communication, Manlio Bonati, Parma, February 23, 1997). See Bonati, *Vittorio*, p. 366.

37. Vannutelli and Citerni, *Seconda*, pp. 475–477.

38. Turton, "Exploration."

39. The museum is part of the Museo di Storia Naturale dell'Università di Parma (Personal communication, Manlio Bonati, Parma, February 23, 1997).

40. Manlio Bonati, "Carlo Citerni," *La Rivista del Trekking*, 82:83–85, January-February 1995.

41. Manlio Bonati, "Lamberto Vannutelli," *La Rivista del Trekking*, 23:340–341, July-August 1988.

42. In 1940, some Italians stationed in western Ethiopia erected a large stone monument to Bottego at Daga Roba. This, however, was later demolished by the Ethiopians. In 1987, an Italian-led expedition retraced Bottego's travels through eastern Africa beginning in Massawa and ending at Daga Roba (see Piero Amighetti and Antonio Mascolo, "Bottego e l'Etiopia cent'anni dopo," *La Rivista del Trekking*, Prima Parte, 4, 21:112–127, March-April 1988; see also Piero Amighetti, Leandro Lucchetti, and Antonio Mascolo, "Bottego e l'Etiopia cent'anni dopo," *La Rivista del Trekking*, Seconda Parte, 4, 22:212–227, May 1988). This expedition placed a bronze plaque in honor of Bottego at Daga Roba on behalf of the city of Parma. In 1995, an expedition marking the centenary of Bottego's Omo voyage visited Ethiopia and descended the river (see Fabrizio Pompily and Carlo Cavanna, *La spedizione maremmana in Etiopia 100 anni dopo Vittorio Bottego*, Grosseto: Scripta Manent Editore, 1996). In 1996, the Comitato per le Celebrazioni del Centenario Della Morte di Vittorio Bottego was organized in Parma to mark the centennial of his death. The commemorative activities began with a conference on March 7, 1997, in Piacenza, where the Bottego family now resides. The theme of this conference was "Il Capitano Bottego: Un ambizioso eroe in Africa," and it coincided with the release of Manlio Bonati's centenary biography. A second centennial celebration marking Bottego's death was held in Parma from October 24 to November 29, 1997. This celebration included a conference, "Vittorio Bottego e le esplorazioni in Africa 1897–1997," held on October 24 and 25.

Chapter Nine

1. Robert Arthur Talbort Gascoyne Cecil, third marquess of Salisbury (1830–1903), served as prime minister on three occasions, 1885–1886, 1886–1892, and 1895–1902. He also simultaneously acted as foreign secretary, and as such, he was a principal architect of Great Britain's imperial expansion.

2. G.N. Sanderson, *England, Europe and the Upper Nile, 1882–1899*, Edinburgh: University Press, 1965, pp. 14–15.

3. Ibid., p. 13.

4. Richard Hall, *Lovers on the Nile: The Incredible African Journeys of Sam and Florence Baker*, New York: Random House, 1980, pp. 185–202.

5. Robert O. Collins, *The Southern Sudan, 1883–1898: A Struggle for Control*, New Haven and London: Yale University Press, 1962, pp. 15–17.

6. Robert O. Collins, "History of the Nilotic Sudan," *Encyclopaedia Britannica*, Chicago: Encyclopaedia Britannica, 1973, Volume 12, pp. 108–116.

7. Alan Moorehead, *The White Nile*, New York: Harper and Row, 1960, p. 206.

8. Collins, "History."

9. Sanderson, *England*, p. 13.

10. Robert O. Collins, *Land Beyond the Rivers: The Southern Sudan, 1898–1918*, New Haven and London: Yale University Press, 1971, p. 107.

11. Marc Michel, *La mission Marchand 1895–1899*, Paris: Mouton, 1972, pp. 19–20.

12. Ibid.

13. Sanderson, *England*, pp. 67–79.

14. Ibid., pp. 162–187.

15. Michel, *La mission*, p. 20.

16. Lord Rosebery was prime minister at the time Grey made his statement in Parliament and apparently told him exactly what to say (see Sanderson, *England*, p. 214).

17. Errol Trzebinski, *The Kenya Pioneers*, New York: W.W. Norton, 1986, p. 205.

18. For the details of Marchand's travel, see Michel, *La mission*, pp. 81–212.

19. For a detailed analysis of Menelik's foreign policy strategy during these years, see G.M. Sanderson, "The Foreign Policy of the Negus Menelik, 1896–1898," *Journal of African History* 1964; 5:87–97.

20. James Rennell Rodd, *Social and Diplomatic Memories*, Volume 2, *1894–1901: Egypt and Abyssinia*, London: Edward Arnold, 1923, pp. 111–191.

21. Sanderson, "The Foreign," pp. 89–91.

22. Ibid.

23. Charles Michel, *Mission de Bonchamps vers Fachoda: A la rencontre de la mission Marchand à travers l'Etiopie*, Paris: Librairie Plon, 1900, pp. 204–205.

24. Michel, *La mission*, p. 144.

25. Ibid., p. 145; Michel, *Mission de Bonchamps*, pp. 93–94; Sanderson, *England*, p. 294.

26. As Sanderson noted, Menelik apologized to the French but showed continued ingenuity in sabotaging their expedition (see Sanderson, "The Foreign," p. 88).

27. Michel, *Mission de Bonchamps*, pp. 254, 276–334.

28. Ibid., pp. 431–444.

29. Ibid., pp. 445, 454–455.

30. Ibid., pp. 456–460.

31. Charles Michel, "Resultats géographiques de la mission de Bonchamps," *La Géographie* 1900; 2:25–34.

32. Sanderson, "The Foreign," p. 94.

33. Sanderson, *England*, p. 256.

34. For a summary of Macdonald's life and career, see "James Ronald Leslie Macdonald (1862–1927)," in *The Dictionary of National Biography, 1922–1930*, edited by J.R.H. Weaver, London: Oxford University Press, 1937, pp. 528–530. For Macdonald's first years in East Africa, see J.R.L. Macdonald, *Soldiering and Surveying in British East Africa, 1891–1894*, London and New York: Edward Arnold, 1897.

35. Sanderson, *England*, pp. 256–257.

36. For details concerning Austin's early life and career, see A.T. Matson, "Introduction," Herbert H. Austin, *With Macdonald in Uganda*, Folkestone

and London: Dawson's, 1973, pp. v–vi; and Monty Brown, *Where Giants Trod: The Saga of Kenya's Desert Lake*, London: Quiller Press, 1989, pp. 232–233.

37. Herbert H. Austin, "Ted and Billy," in "African Shades," unpublished, p. 2 (courtesy of Simon F. Austin); the ruse of exploring the sources of the Juba River was convincing to some because Ludwig von Höhnel and Arthur Donaldson Smith had incorrectly assumed they were in the Omo River valley and thus closer to the Nile.

38. Herbert H. Austin, *With Macdonald in Uganda: A Narrative Account of the Uganda Mutiny and Macdonald Expedition in the Uganda Protectorate and the Territories to the North*, London: Edward Arnold, 1903, pp. 7–10; Austin met Cavendish and Andrew at Bondoni in August on their way to the coast from their visit to Lake Rudolf (p. 20). In his diaries, Austin was extremely critical of the manner in which Cavendish had "looted and plundered the Turkana" (see Matson, "Introduction," p. xv). Austin's four African diaries were deposited by his son, Major Rudolf Edmund Austin, on long-term loan at the McMillan Memorial Library in Nairobi, from where they were later stolen (Letters from Simon F. Austin to Pascal James Imperato, Dorchester, England, May 5, 1996, and September 15, 1997).

39. Austin, *With Macdonald*, pp. 36–54; D.A. Low, "Uganda": The Establishment of the Protectorate 1894–1919," in Vincent Harlow and E.M. Chilver (editors), assisted by Alison Smith, *History of East Africa*, Volume 2, Oxford: Clarendon Press, 1965, pp. 72–77. The Sudanese had arrived in Uganda in 1889, after being safely evacuated from the Sudan by Henry Morton Stanley. They had been members of the army of Emin Pasha (Edward Schnitzer), the Silesian governor of Equatoria Province, who had been isolated by the Mahdist uprising (see Roger Jones, *The Rescue of Emin Pasha: The Story of Henry Morton Stanley and the Emin Pasha Relief Expedition, 1887–1889*, New York: St. Martin's Press, 1972).

40. Sanderson, "The Foreign," p. 94.

41. Ibid.

42. H.H. Austin, "Journeys to the North of Uganda. 2. Lake Rudolf," *Geographical Journal* 1899; 14:148–155.

43. Austin, *With Macdonald*, p. 184.

44. Ibid., p. 185.

45. For a description of Austin's treaty-making activities around Lake Rudolf, see Matson, "Introduction," pp. vi–vii.

46. Austin, *With Macdonald*, p. 196.

47. Carlo Zaghi, *I Russi in Etiopia. 2. Menelik e la Battaglia di Adua*, Naples: Guida Editori, 1972, p. 249.

48. Austin, *With Macdonald*, p. 220.

49. Matson, "Introduction," pp. vii–viii.

50. Ibid., p. viii.

51. Ibid., p. vii.

52. Herbert H. Austin, *Among Swamps and Giants in Equatorial Africa: An Account of Surveys and Adventures in the Southern Sudan and British East Africa*, London: C. Arthur Pearson, 1902.

53. See Matson, "Introduction," p. VII; J.R.L. Macdonald, "Journeys to the North of Uganda," *Geographical Journal* 1899; 14:129–148; *Report by Lieutenant-Colonel Macdonald, R.E. of His Expedition from the Uganda Protectorate, May 3, 1898 to March 5, 1899,* London: Her Majesty's Stationery Office, 1899.

54. Matson, "Introduction," pp. VIII–IX.

55. Sanderson, *England,* p. 333.

56. Ibid.

57. Although their encounters were cordial, Kitchener and Marchand each stood their ground. Kitchener forcefully argued not for British rights in the Upper Nile but for those of Egypt, which France had historically supported. For descriptions of their encounter at Fashoda, see Sanderson, *England,* pp. 333–343; David Levering Lewis, *The Race to Fashoda: European Colonialism and African Resistance in the Scramble for Africa,* New York: Weidenfeld and Nicolson, 1987, pp. 222–228; and Philip Warner, *Kitchener: The Man Behind the Legend,* New York: Atheneum, 1986, pp. 101–104.

58. Sanderson, *England,* p. 345.

59. Michel, *La mission,* p. 222.

60. Ibid., pp. 233–234.

61. Ibid., pp. 233–239.

62. Sanderson, *England,* p. 371; Michel, *La mission,* p. 247.

Chapter Ten

1. Teshale Tibebu, *The Making of Modern Ethiopia 1896–1974,* Lawrenceville, N.J.: Red Sea Press, 1995, p. 32; Zwede Bahru, *A History of Modern Ethiopia, 1855–1974,* Athens: Ohio University Press, 1991.

2. Circular Letter from Menelik II, April 1891, Foreign Office File 403/155, Public Record Office, Richmond, England.

3. Tibebu, *The Making,* p. 41.

4. Ibid., p. 33.

5. Ibid., p. 39.

6. Richard Pankhurst, *Economic History of Ethiopia 1800–1935,* Addis Ababa: Haile Selassie University Press, 1968, p. 563.

7. Richard A. Caulk, "Armies as Predators: Soldiers and Peasants in Ethiopia Circa 1850–1935," *International Journal of African Historical Studies* 1978; 11, 3:457–493.

8. Richard Pankhurst, *An Introduction to the Medical History of Ethiopia,* Trenton, N.J.: Red Sea Press, 1991.

9. Gebru Tareke, *Ethiopia: Power and Protest—Peasant Revolts in the Twentieth Century,* Cambridge: Cambridge University Press, 1991, p. 71.

10. Tibebu, *The Making,* pp. 44–45.

11. For a detailed historical analysis of the Russian agenda in late-nineteenth-century Ethiopia, see Carlo Zaghi, *I Russi in Etiopia,* Volume 1, *Il Protettorato Italiano sull'Etiopia,* Volume 2, *Menelik e la Battaglia di Adua,* Naples: Guida Editore, 1972.

12. Ibid., Volume 1, pp. 245–246.

13. Ibid., pp. 237–266.

14. The most authoritative and comprehensive account of the Ethiopian mission to Russia was provided by Zaghi. See *I Russi*, Volume 2, pp. 111–178.

15. Ibid., Volume 2, p. 167.

16. The most detailed account of Leontiev's remarkably bold attempts to serve as a mediator between Ethiopia and Italy was provided by Zaghi. See *I Russi*, Volume 2, pp. 179–235.

17. Leontiev provided this rationale. See Nicholas Leontiev, "Exploration des provinces Equitoriales d'Abyssinie," *La géographie, Bulletin de la Société de Géographie* 1900; 2:105–118. Since Menelik's own generals had performed well in the field, it is more likely, as Marcus suggested, that the emperor intended to "use him as a catspaw and disavow him when necessary." Menelik reasoned that Leontiev's entourage of Frenchmen and Russians could more successfully push his border well into British-claimed territory than an Ethiopian general since Britain was unlikely to raise a challenge that would involve it with France and Russia. See Harold G. Marcus, "A History of the Negotiations Concerning the Border Between Ethiopia and British East Africa, 1897–1914," in *Boston University Papers on Africa*, Volume 2, *African History*, edited by Jeffrey Butler, Boston: Boston University Press, 1966, pp. 239–265.

18. See Zaghi, *I Russi*, Volume 2, pp. 294–308.

19. Ibid., pp. 247–256.

20. Bulatovich wrote two books about his travels in Ethiopia. See Alexander K. Bulatovich, *Ot Entotto do Reki Baro*, St. Petersburg: V. Kirshbaum, 1897, and *S. Voyskami Menelika II*, St. Petersburg: Artistic Press Publishing House, 1900. These volumes were republished together in 1971 by Science Publishing House in Moscow, under the editorship of the late Isidor Savvich Katsnelson (1910–1981), who was then a professor at the Institute of Oriental Studies of the Academy of Sciences of the Union of Soviet Socialist Republics. In 1993, Richard Seltzer translated both books into English and grouped them together, along with Katsnelson's introduction to the 1971 edition. This English-language translation is available at Seltzer's web site on the Internet, http://www.samizdat.com. See Richard Seltzer (editor), "Ethiopia Through Russian Eyes: An Eyewitness Account of the End of an Era, 1896–98, Consisting of Two Books by Alexander Bulatovich: From Entoto to the River Baro— An Account of a Trip to the Southwestern Regions of the Ethiopian Empire, 1896–97; With the Armies of Menelik II—Journal of an Expedition from Ethiopia to Lake Rudolf," 681 pp. At the time of this writing, the Seltzer manuscript had not yet been published in hardcopy form. Unless otherwise noted, the information cited here on Bulatovich is drawn from the Seltzer translation.

21. The information on Bulatovich's early life and career is drawn from Seltzer's translation of Katsnelson's introduction to the 1971 edition, pp. 659–664, and from personal communications from Prince André and Princess Irene Orbeliani, 1997. Bulatovich's middle name, Xavier, is rendered in Rus-

sian by various sources as either Xavieryevich or Ksaveryevich. As a result, his middle initial appears as either an X or a K.

22. Seltzer, "Ethiopia," p. 668.

23. Ibid., pp. 13–288.

24. Ibid., p. 299.

25. Ibid., pp. 294–296.

26. Ibid., p. 390.

27. Ibid., p. 393.

28. Ibid., p. 413.

29. Ibid., p. 396.

30. Ibid., p. 433.

31. Ibid., p. 435.

32. Ibid., p. 437.

33. Ibid., p. 438.

34. Later, when he arrived in the Omo River valley and at the northern end of Lake Rudolf, Bulatovich accurately recorded the names of a number of ethnic groups.

35. Seltzer, "Ethiopia," p. 497.

36. Ibid.

37. Ibid., p. 480.

38. Ibid.

39. Ibid., pp. 480, 496–497.

40. Giorgis had been given clear instructions from Menelik to assist any scientific caravans he encountered and to firmly but diplomatically stand up to any European military force. He himself fully appreciated the value of geographic observations and took great interest in Bulatovich's solar observations, which he characterized as "to screw up the sun." See Seltzer, "Ethiopia," p. 466.

41. Traders would have quickly fled from the Ethiopians out of fear that they would be looted of their ivory.

42. Seltzer, "Ethiopia," p. 532.

43. Ibid., p. 560.

44. Ibid., p. 561.

45. Ibid., p. 574.

46. Ibid., p. 567.

47. Ibid., pp. 629–631. Bulatovich donated the arms that Menelik gave him to the Military Museum in St. Petersburg, where they are now on display (Letter from Princess Irene Orbeliani to Pascal James Imperato, Nelson, British Columbia, June 23, 1997).

48. Alexander K. Bulatovich, "Dall'Abissinia al Lago Rodolfo per il Caffa: Letta nell'adunanza generale della Imperiale Società Geografica Russa il 13(25) gennaio 1899, con note di G. Roncagli," *Bolletino della Società Geografica Italiana* 1900; Series 4, 37:121–142.

49. Ibid. See Karl W. Butzer, *Recent History of an Ethiopian Delta: The Omo River and the Level of Lake Rudolf*, Chicago: University of Chicago, 1971, p. 112.

50. Bulatovich's book about his Lake Rudolf trip, *S Voyskami Menelik II* (*With the Armies of Menelik II*), was published in Russian in 1900.

51. Bulatovich never wrote an account of this third trip. However, an account was later pieced together from dispatches found in the Soviet state archives by Isidor Saavich Katsnelson and finally published in book form in 1987 under the editorship of A.B. Davidson (see Alexander K. Bulatovich, *Tretye: Puteshestiviye po Efiopii*, edited by A.B. Davidson, Moscow: Isdatelstvo "Nauka," 1987).

52. For a fictionalized account of Bulatovich's time in Manchuria, with flashbacks to his early years and life in Ethiopia, see Richard Seltzer, *The Name of Hero*, Boston: Houghton Mifflin, 1981.

53. Seltzer, "Ethiopia," pp. 671–672. The information presented is derived from Seltzer's translation of Katsnelson's introduction to the 1971 Russian edition of Bulatovich's two books.

54. Bulatovich's theological teaching, known in Russian as "Imeslowzev" (praisers of the name), was rehabilitated by the exiled Russian Orthodox hierarchy in Yugoslavia in the early 1920s. Although he was only forty-nine years old when he died, he was in generally poor health as a result of diseases contracted during his years in Africa. In 1911, when he was living with his sister, Princess Mary Orbeliani, in St. Petersburg, he already had difficulty with his eyesight. His nephew, Prince André Orbeliani, who was then eleven years old, remembered that his Uncle Sacha used a typewriter as he could not read his own handwriting. He also recalled that his uncle preferred sitting in a dark room and wore a visor, indicating that he was suffering from severe photophobia, most probably due to onchocerciasis, which he contracted in Africa. Bulatovich himself thought that he was suffering from inflammation of the tear ducts and sought treatment from a number of physicians, one of whom produced a salve that proved useless. André Orbeliani was fascinated by his uncle's African adventures, which inspired him to go to Africa himself, where he spent nine years (Letter from Princess Irene Orbeliani to Pascal James Imperato, Nelson, British Columbia, June 23, 1997).

55. G.V. Pantano, *Ventitrè anni di vita Africana*, Firenze, 1923, p. 126.

56. Despite this change in policy, Menelik was still willing to push his southern border as far as he could. See Marcus, "A History," pp. 243–245; and G.N. Sanderson, "The Foreign Policy of the Negus Menelik, 1896–1898," *Journal of African History* 1964; 5:87–97.

57. Czeslaw Jesman, *The Russians in Ethiopia: An Essay in Futility*, London: Chatto & Windus, 1958, p. 116.

58. James Rennell Rodd, *Social and Diplomatic Memories, 1894–1901*, Volume 2, London: Edward Arnold, 1923, p. 152.

59. Jesman, *The Russians*, pp. 115–116.

60. Alfred Ilg (1854–1916) was a Swiss engineer who served Menelik from 1879 until 1908 in a variety of capacities, including builder, trader, architect, and foreign affairs adviser. He left Ethiopia in 1908 and retired to Zurich, Switzerland (see Conrad Keller, *Alfred Ilg: Sein Leben und Seine Wirken als Schweizerischer Kulturbote in Abessinien*, Frauenfeld, Leipzig: Huber, 1918).

61. The Russians retaliated against Menelik's treatment of Vlassov by not sending an ambassador to replace him for almost four years. This action coincided with their growing recognition that they had no vital political interests in Africa (see Jesman, *The Russians*, p. 118).

62. Zaghi, *I Russi*, Volume 2, p. 306.

63. Leontiev, "Exploration," p. 114.

64. Jesman, *The Russians*, p. 121.

65. Ibid.

66. Leontiev, "Exploration," p. 116.

67. Leontiev renamed Sanderson's Gulf Taytu Bay in honor of the empress. The naming of geographical features in honor of people was quite alien to Ethiopian custom, and the name did not survive Leontiev's trip.

68. Butzer, *Recent History*, p. 114.

69. As late as May 1899, a month before Leontiev left Addis Ababa for Lake Rudolf, Menelik had offered to settle his southern border with the British. His map, however, clearly showed Lake Rudolf inside of Ethiopia (see Marcus, "A History," p. 245).

70. Zaghi, *I Russi*, Volume 2, p. 303; Jesman, *The Russians*, p. 122.

71. P.H.G. Powell-Cotton, *A Sporting Trip Through Abyssinia*, London: Rowland Ward, 1902, p. 72.

72. Leontiev tried to reinstate himself with Menelik but to no avail. He later claimed that the British agent, John Lane Harrington, and some of the Ethiopian princes influenced by him were responsible for his dismissal (see Jesman, *The Russians*, p. 123).

73. Zaghi, *I Russi*, Volume 2, p. 309.

74. Jesman, *The Russians*, p. 125.

75. Leontiev died at the same age as Bulatovich but eight years later. Zaghi established 1910 as the year of his death, based on an examination of Alfred Ilg's papers. Among them, he found a letter written by Ilg from Zurich to Countess Leontiev on July 22, 1910, offering condolences (see Zaghi, *I Russi*, Volume 2, p. 312).

Chapter *Eleven*

1. G.N. Sanderson, *England, Europe and the Upper Nile, 1882–1899*, Edinburgh: University Press, 1965, p. 258.

2. "Sir John Lane Harrington," in *Who Was Who, 1916–1928*, London: Adam and Charles Black, 1929, p. 462.

3. See Harold G. Marcus, "A History of the Negotiations Concerning the Border Between Ethiopia and British East Africa, 1897–1914," in *Boston University Papers on Africa*, Volume 2, *African History*, edited by Jeffrey Butler, Boston: Boston University Press, 1966, pp. 239–265.

4. "Obituary—Captain M.S. Wellby, 18th Hussars," *Geographical Journal* 1900; 26:358–359. Wellby was born on October 10, 1866, in London, where his father was a member of the family's jewelry firm, D. and J. Wellby of Garrick Street, London, which had been established in 1820. The firm later became di-

amond purveyors and silversmiths to several members of the British Royal Family, including King George VI and Queen Elizabeth.

5. Ibid., p. 359.

6. See Montagu Sinclair Wellby, *Through Unknown Tibet*, London: T. Fisher Unwin, 1898.

7. Letter from Montagu Sinclair Wellby to J. Scott Keltie, Lucknow, India, December 15, 1896, Correspondence File 1881–1910, Royal Geographical Society Archives, London.

8. Captain M.S. Wellby, *'Twixt Sirdar and Menelik: An Account of a Year's Expedition from Zeila to Cairo Through Unknown Abyssinia*, London: Harper and Brothers, 1901, pp. 1–2.

9. Letter from A. Donaldson Smith to Percy Z. Cox, London, October 26, 1898, A. Donaldson Smith Correspondence File, Royal Geographical Society Archives, London.

10. Letter from Montagu Sinclair Wellby to J. Scott Keltie, Lucknow, India, July 20, 1898, Correspondence File 1881–1910, Royal Geographical Society Archives, London.

11. Wellby, *'Twixt*, p. 6.

12. Ibid., p. 9.

13. Ibid., p. 13.

14. Ibid.

15. Ibid., pp. 76–77.

16. Ibid., p. 88.

17. Letter from Montagu Sinclair Wellby to J. Scott Keltie, Addis Ababa, Abyssinia, December 16, 1898, Correspondence File 1881–1910, Royal Geographical Society Archives, London.

18. Wellby, *'Twixt*, pp. 103–105, 119, 121–122.

19. Ibid., p. 180.

20. Ibid., p. 173.

21. Ibid., pp. 179–180.

22. Ibid., p. 194; it is impossible to determine with precision when Wellby arrived at the lake since his published accounts contain few dates.

23. Ibid., p. 196; from the hillock on which his camp was situated, Wellby was able to "view the country for many miles around, and easily distinguish the various herds of antelope." Among them, he saw a snow-white hartebeest, which he unsuccessfully tried to shoot (pp. 196–197).

24. Wellby eventually lost half his original transport animals to this disease. Although he described it in his book as anthrax, he wrote to Keltie from Omdurman saying it was glanders (see Letter from Montagu Sinclair Wellby to J. Scott Keltie, Omdurman, Sudan, July 15, 1899, Correspondence File 1881–1910, Royal Geographical Society Archives, London).

25. Wellby, *'Twixt*, p. 199.

26. Ibid., p. 213.

27. Ibid., p. VIII.

28. Ibid., p. 225.

29. Ibid., p. 227.

30. Ibid., pp. 225–226.

31. Ibid., pp. 255–256.

32. Ibid., pp. 382–383.

33. Wellby, Letter, Omdurman, July 15, 1899.

34. David Turton, "Exploration in the Lower Omo Valley of Southwestern Ethiopia Between 1890 and 1910," in *L'Africa ai tempi di Daniele Comboni*, edited by Maria Genoino Caravaglios, Rome: Instituto Italo-Africano e Missionari Comboniani, 1981, pp. 11–12.

35. Ludwig von Höhnel, "The Lake Rudolf Region: Its Discovery and Subsequent Exploration, 1888–1909," Part 1, *Journal of the Royal African Society* 1938; 37:32.

36. Ibid.

37. Letter from Montagu Sinclair Wellby to J. Scott Keltie, Omdurman, Sudan, August 9, 1899, Correspondence File 1881–1910, Royal Geographical Society Archives, London.

38. Wellby, *Twixt*, p. VIII.

39. Ibid., p. 330.

40. Ibid.

41. Letter from Montagu Sinclair Wellby to J. Scott Keltie, London, September 29, 1899, Correspondence File 1881–1910, Royal Geographical Society Archives, London.

42. "Obituary," p. 359.

43. Wellby, *'Twixt*, p. XIX.

44. Montagu Sinclair Wellby, "King Menelek's Dominions and the Country Between Lake Gallop (Rudolf) and the Nile Valley," *Geographical Journal* 1900; 21:292–306.

45. Letter from Nancy Marples to Pascal James Imperato, Cullompton, Devon, August 14, 1996.

46. Letter from Nancy Marples to Pascal James Imperato, Cullompton, Devon, November 11, 1996.

Chapter Twelve

1. Letter from A. Donaldson Smith to Sir Clements Markham, London, July 29, 1898, A. Donaldson Smith Correspondence File, Royal Geographical Society Archives, London.

2. Letter from A. Donaldson Smith to J. Scott Keltie, Shanghai, China, A. Donaldson Smith Correspondence File, Royal Geographical Society Archives, London. For details of Smith's travels in Asia, see A. Donaldson Smith, "A Journey Through the Khingan Mountains," *Geographical Journal* 1898; 11:498–509.

3. Montagu Sinclair Wellby, who visited Lake Rudolf in 1899, also participated in the Tirah Campaign.

4. Philip Graves, *The Life of Sir Percy Cox*, London: Hutchinson, 1941, p. 51.

5. Letter from Percy Z. Cox to Colonel Martelli, Baroda, India, December 29, 1897, Sir Percy Z. Cox Papers, Royal Geographical Society Archives, London.

6. Letter from the office of the gaekwar of Baroda to Percy Z. Cox, Baroda, India, May 29, 1898, Sir Percy Z. Cox Papers, Royal Geographical Society Archives, London.

7. Letter from A. Donaldson Smith to Percy Z. Cox, Bombay, India, May 31, 1898, A. Donaldson Smith Correspondence File, Royal Geographical Society Archives, London.

8. Letter from A. Donaldson Smith to Percy Z. Cox, Aden, July 3, 1896, A. Donaldson Smith Correspondence File, Royal Geographical Society Archives, London.

9. Letter from Percy Z. Cox to George Curzon, Baroda, India, June 21, 1898, Percy Z. Cox Papers, Royal Geographical Society Archives, London.

10. Smith was referring to the negative comments made by Henry Cavendish and Frederick Lugard about his armed conflicts with the Boran when the former addressed the Royal Geographical Society on January 31, 1898. See Letter from A. Donaldson Smith to Percy Z. Cox, London, August 6, 1898, A. Donaldson Smith Correspondence File, Royal Geographical Society Archives, London.

11. Letter from A. Donaldson Smith to Percy Z. Cox, Philadelphia, A. Donaldson Smith Correspondence File, Royal Geographical Society Archives, London.

12. Letter from A. Donaldson Smith to Percy Z. Cox, Philadelphia, September 16, 1898, A. Donaldson Smith Correspondence File, Royal Geographical Society Archives, London.

13. Letter from A. Donaldson Smith to Percy Z. Cox, London, October 26, 1898, A. Donaldson Smith Correspondence File, Royal Geographical Society Archives, London.

14. Ibid.

15. Percy Z. Cox, "Diary of an Expedition to Somaliland, December 1898," Sir Percy Z. Cox Papers, Royal Geographical Society Archives, London, p. 10.

16. Ibid.

17. Ibid., p. 11.

18. Ibid., p. 40. Sadler was concerned that Smith and Cox would make a surreptitious run for Lake Rudolf and thus made no secret that he wanted them to conclude their hunting trip as soon as possible.

19. Cox, "Diary," p. 88.

20. Ibid., pp. 92–93.

21. Ibid.

22. Ibid.

23. Ibid.

24. Sadler, who later became commissioner in Uganda (1901–1905), governor of the British East Africa Protectorate (1905–1909), and governor of the Windward Islands (1909–1914), had strict orders from the Foreign Office to prevent all expeditions from going to Lake Rudolf.

25. Cox, "Diary," p. 93.

26. Cox was ambitious and could not turn down such an important promotion. His wife, who was opposed to his trip with Smith, "felt an immense relief" when she became aware of the Muscat assignment (see Graves, *The Life*, p. 55).

27. For a fuller description of these collections, see Pascal James Imperato, *Arthur Donaldson Smith and the Exploration of Lake Rudolf*, Lake Success, N.Y.: Medical Society of the State of New York, 1987, pp. 63–66. It is of interest that the gaekwar's grandson, the late Lieutenant Colonel Fatesinghrao C. Gaekwad of Baroda, who was head of the World Wide Fund for Nature, was not familiar with the Smith-Cox Expedition (Letter from Lieutenant Colonel Fatesinghrao C. Gaekwad of Baroda to Pascal James Imperato, Bombay, India, January 5, 1988).

28. A. Donaldson Smith, "An Expedition Between Lake Rudolf and the Nile," *Geographical Journal* 1900; 16:600–625.

29. Ibid., p. 605.

30. Ibid., p. 607.

31. Ibid., p. 622.

32. Letter from A. Donaldson Smith to J. Scott Keltie, Fort Berkeley, Nile, March 21, 1900, A. Donaldson Smith Correspondence File, Royal Geographical Society Archives, London.

33. Ibid.

34. Ibid.

35. Ibid.

36. "The Monthly Record, Africa, Dr. Donaldson Smith's Expedition," *Geographic Journal* 1900; 16:102.

37. Smith, "An Expedition," pp. 624–625.

38. "Meetings of the Royal Geographical Society Session 1900–1901 Anniversary Meeting, May 20, 1901, Sir Clements Markham, KCB, FRS, in the Chair," *Geographical Journal* 1901; 18:98–100.

39. Personal communication, H. Spencer Potter, Ph.D., East Northport, New York, September 30, 1986.

40. *Diplomatic and Consular Service of the United States, Corrected to November 9, 1909*, Washington, D.C.: Department of State, 1910, p. 28.

41. For some details of Smith's later life, see Henry Pleasants Jr., "Some Horses Are Lucky: Biographical Sketch of Arthur Donaldson Smith, M.D., *The General Magazine and Historical Chronicle*, University of Pennsylvania General Alumni Society 1946; 67:254–261.

42. Personal communication, H. Spencer Potter, Ph.D.

43. For the details of Smith's last years, see Imperato, *Arthur Donaldson Smith*, pp. 88–93. Smith's grave in Philadelphia's Laurel Hill Cemetery remained unmarked until 1989, when his grandnephew, H. Spencer Potter, Ph.D., arranged for the Veterans' Administration to erect a stone inscribed with his name, dates, and the epitaph "Physician, Explorer, Naturalist, and Diplomat." The epitaph was derived from the subtitle of a four-part biographical series I wrote, published in 1987 in the *New York State Journal of Medicine* (see Imperato, *Arthur Donaldson Smith*; and Margaret A. Potter, "Tomb-

stone Erected on Grave of Arthur Donaldson Smith, M.D.," *New York State Journal of Medicine* 1989; 89:685).

Chapter Thirteen

1. James J. Harrison, "A Journey from Zeila to Lake Rudolf," *Geographical Journal* 1901; 18:258–275.
2. "Intrepid Hunter: Brandesburton Squire's Trophies of the Chase," *Daily Mail*, March 14, 1923, p. 5.
3. Letter from James J. Harrison to J. Scott Keltie, Hull, July 24, 1899, Correspondence Block 1881–1910, Royal Geographical Society Archives, London.
4. Ibid.
5. "W.F. Whitehouse, Newport Leader, Former State Senator Dies: Retired Broker Was on City Review Board," *New York Times*, May 28, 1955, p. 15.
6. "The Powell-Cotton Museum," illustrated guide, Quex Park, Birchington, Kent, pp. 3–4 (courtesy of Keith W. Nicklin, former curator).
7. Letter from John Butter to Pascal James Imperato, Nairobi, April 10, 1996.
8. P.H.G. Powell-Cotton, *A Sporting Trip Through Abyssinia*, London: Rowland Ward, 1902, pp. 50–51.
9. P.H.G. Powell-Cotton, "Diary," January 3, 1900, Archives, Powell-Cotton Museum, Quex Park, Birchington, Kent.
10. Powell-Cotton, *Sporting*, p. 145.
11. Ibid., p. 150.
12. Harrison, "A Journey," p. 271.
13. Ibid., p. 272.
14. Ibid., p. 271.
15. Ibid.
16. William F. Whitehouse, "To Lake Rudolf and Beyond," in *Hunting and Conservation: The Book of the Boone and Crockett Club*, edited by George Grinnell and Theodore Roosevelt, New Haven: Yale University Press, 1925, p. 327.
17. Ibid., p. 328.
18. Harrison, "A Journey," pp. 272–273.
19. Letter from James J. Harrison to J. Scott Keltie, Hull, undated, Correspondence Block 1881–1910, Royal Geographical Society Archives, London.
20. Personal communication from William F. Whitehouse, Palm Beach, Florida, March 8, 1996.
21. James J. Harrison, *Life Among the Pygmies of the Ituri Forest, Congo Free State*, London: Hutchinson, 1905. Harrison exhibited the Mbuti people in London. A short time later, an eccentric American missionary, Samuel Phillips Verner, exhibited a pygmy named Ota Benga in a cage with an orangutan and several chimpanzees at the New York Zoological Society Gardens. Even at the time, there were strong protests and outrage at these attempts to demonstrate human evolution by exhibiting an alleged "missing link" (see

Phillips Verner Bradford and Harvey Blume, *OTA: The Pygmy in the Zoo*, New York: St. Martin's Press, 1992).

22. "J.J. Harrison Archive Collection," Wood End Museum of Natural History, Scarborough Borough Council, Scarborough.

23. "The Powell-Cotton Museum," pp. 3–28.

24. William F. Whitehouse, "Through the Country of the King of Kings," *Scribners Magazine* 1902; 32:286–296.

25. Whitehouse, "To Lake Rudolf," pp. 258–339.

26. Lord Hindlip, *Sport and Travel: Abyssinia and British East Africa*, London: T. Fisher Unwin, 1906, pp. 7–117.

27. "W.F. Whitehouse, Newport Leader."

28. Letter from William F. Whitehouse to Pascal James Imperato, Palm Beach, Florida, May 30, 1990.

29. Personal communication from William F. Whitehouse, Palm Beach, Florida, May 10, 1996.

Chapter Fourteen

1. Harold G. Marcus, "Ethio-British Negotiations Concerning the Western Border with the Sudan," *Journal of African History* 1963; 4:81–94.

2. For an account of these expeditions, see Charles W. Gwynn, "The Frontiers of Abyssinia: A Retrospect," *Journal of the Royal African Society* 1937; 36:150–161; Herbert H. Austin, *Among Swamps and Giants in Equatorial Africa: An Account of Surveys and Adventures in the Southern Sudan and British East Africa*, London: C. Arthur Pearson, 1902, pp. 3–54; and Austin, "Major Austin, R.E., to Director of Surveys, Egyptian Army," Confidential Memorandum Printed for the Use of the Foreign Office, London, August 1900, 13 pp.

3. For details of the expedition's travels, see Austin, *Among*, pp. 57–334; and Herbert H. Austin, "A Journey from Omdurman to Mombasa via Lake Rudolf," *Geographical Journal* 1902; 19:669–690.

4. Austin, *Among*, p. 155.

5. Austin, "A Journey," p. 677.

6. The expedition's fruitless efforts to find both food and the relief column were given in detail by Austin in his three accounts of the trip. See Austin, *Among*, pp. 157–174; Austin, "A Journey," pp. 677–679; and Herbert H. Austin, "North-East Africa and Soudan," Confidential Document from Major Austin to the Marquess of Lansdowne, London, November 30, 1901, 28 pp. This official report to the then foreign secretary, who had assumed office a year before, was later adapted by Austin for his 1902 article published in the *Geographical Journal*.

7. Austin, "A Journey," p. 679.

8. Austin, *Among*, p. 188. The two soldiers killed were Abdil K'heir and Hasabo Adam (Herbert Henry Austin, "Role of Escort Xth Sudanese," Herbert Henry Austin Papers, courtesy of Simon F. Austin).

9. Austin, *Among*, p. 190.

10. Garner attributed Austin's illness to an excess consumption of tinned meat (see Dr. Garner to the Marquess of Lansdowne, Inclosure 2, in Austin, "North-East Africa," p. 17).

11. Austin, *Among*, p. 198.

12. Garner, in Austin, "North-East Africa," p. 17.

13. Austin, *Among*, pp. 229–230. This is an extremely important point since one might otherwise assume that the Jehadia received the least amount of food.

14. Austin, *Among*, p. 229.

15. Ibid., p. 235.

16. Ibid., pp. 238–239. Austin fully disclosed his decision to execute Abdul in his official report and book but not in his article published in the *Geographical Journal*. It is of more than passing interest that he chose not to execute any of the Sudanese soldiers for similar offenses. Despite his characterization of them as "sterling good fellows" (Austin, *Among*, p. 235), two deserted and another five left either to die or because they deserted. Austin probably refrained from meting out severe punishment to any of the soldiers since it might have provoked a mutiny. It is also of interest to note that William Astor Chanler, the American explorer, had been severely criticized in 1894 by Sir Lloyd William Mathews, the prime minister of Zanzibar, for his decision to execute a porter in equally distressed circumstances. The fact that Austin's decision was not publicly questioned by British officials is additional proof of the political motives behind Mathews's expression of selective moral indignation against Chanler.

17. In his published accounts, Austin claimed that twelve men associated with the Tenth Sudanese Battalion who died were either killed or else succumbed to starvation. In his personal listing, however, he recorded that of the original twenty-three, five were missing (had either deserted or wandered off and died), two had deserted, two were killed, one had died, and two were sent back early in the trip because of illness (Austin, "Role").

18. Garner, in Austin, "North-East Africa," p. 17.

19. Ancel Keys, Josef Brozek, Austin Henschel, Olaf Mickelsen, Henry Longstreet Taylor et al., *The Biology of Human Starvation*, Volume 2, Minneapolis: University of Minnesota Press, 1950, pp. 921–923.

20. P.E.C. Manson-Bahr and D.R. Bell, *Manson's Tropical Diseases*, London: Ballière Tindall, 1987, pp. 439–446.

21. Severe trichinosis is generally associated with vomiting and diarrhea. Garner did not comment on the former but did clearly state: "Never once during the expedition was there a case of dysentery or even severe diarrhea" (Garner, in Austin, "North-East Africa," p. 18). The absence of diarrhea greatly lessens but does not absolutely exclude the possibility that the men were also suffering from acute trichinosis.

22. Based on Garner's detailed description, it appears Austin developed a severe case of scurvy with extensive hemorrhaging into his muscles, bones, and other bodily tissues (see Garner, in Austin, "North-East Africa," pp. 17–18). In addition to the severe pain caused by this bleeding, he must have also developed a profound anemia that was life-threatening (see Jean D. Wilson, "Vita-

min C Deficiency and Excess," in *Harrison's Principles of Internal Medicine,* 12th ed., edited by Jean D. Wilson et al., New York: McGraw-Hill, 1991, pp. 438–440).

23. Austin later wrote brief, unpublished tributes to two of his African companions, Bakhir Ahmed, his interpreter, and Mabruk Effendi Faki, who commanded the men of the Tenth Sudanese Battalion. See Herbert H. Austin, "Bakhir Ahmed," in "African Shades," pp. 11–13, and "Mabruk Effendi Faki," in "African Shades," pp. 17–20 (Herbert Henry Austin Papers, courtesy of Simon F. Austin).

24. "The Abyssinian-Frontier Expeditions," *Geographical Journal* 1901; 18:533.

25. For details of Austin's later life and career, see "Brigadier-General Herbert Henry Austin," in *Who Was Who, 1929–1940,* 2d ed., London: Adam and Charles Black, 1967, pp. 45–46.

26. Herbert H. Austin, *Some Rambles of a Sapper,* London: Edward Arnold, 1928.

Chapter Fifteen

1. Eduard Wickenburg, *Wanderungen in Ost-Afrika,* Vienna: Gerold, 1899. For details concerning Wickenburg's life and travels, see Bairu Tafla, *Ethiopia and Austria: A History of Their Relations,* Wiesbaden: Harrassowitz Verlag, 1994, pp. 283–285.

2. "Count Wickenburg's Journey from Jibuti to Lamu," *Geographical Journal* 1902; 19:216. In the 1980s, Wickenburg's daughter retraced portions of his original journey with the assistance of Monty Brown, a leading authority on northern Kenya. See Marietheres Waldbott, *Es steht ein Berg in Afrika: Reisen auf den Spuren meines Vaters,* Vienna: Ueberreuter, 1988.

3. Eduard Wickenburg, "Von Dschibuti bis Lamu," *Petermann's Mitteilungen* 1903; 49:193–199.

4. "Eduard Graf Wickenburg," in *Abenteuer Ostafrika: Der Anteil Osterreich-ungarns an der Erforschung Ostafrikas.* Hornsetin: Repro-Studio Danek, 1988, pp. 285–286.

5. *Mission scientifique du Bourg de Bozas: De la Mer Rouge à l'Atlantique à travers l'Afrique Tropical, October 1900—Mai 1902,* Paris: F.R. de Rudeval, 1906, p. 295.

6. Ibid., p. 307.

7. Ibid., p. 413. De Bozas was buried on the grounds of the Amadi Catholic Mission, but his remains were later exhumed and returned to France in 1905.

8. For an analysis of Menelik's political strategy during these years, see Harold G. Marcus, "A History of the Negotiations Concerning the Border Between Ethiopia and British East Africa, 1897–1914," in *Boston University Papers of Africa,* Volume 2, *African History,* edited by Jeffrey Butler, Boston: Boston University Press, 1966.

9. A.C. McEwen, *International Boundaries of Africa,* Oxford: Clarendon Press, 1971, p. 106.

10. Instructions from John Lane Harrington to Archibald E. Butter, 1902, Foreign Office File 403/323, Public Record Office, Richmond, England.

11. Philip Maud, "Exploration in the Southern Borderland of Abyssinia," *Geographical Journal* 1904; 23:552–579.

12. Correspondence from Archibald E. Butter and John L. Baird to Sir John Lane Harrington, 1903, Foreign Office File 403/334, Public Record Office, Richmond, England.

13. Philip Maud, "Personal Diary, 6 November 1902–21 January 1903," Philip Maud Papers, Royal Geographical Society Archives, London.

14. Letter from John L. Baird to Philip Maud, January 13, 1903, Philip Maud Papers, Royal Geographical Society Archives, London.

15. Maud, "Exploration," pp. 574–575.

16. Shortly after Butter and Maud left Lake Rudolf, the East African Syndicate's expedition arrived there from Mount Elgon in the west. Led by J.W. Brooke, this expedition was without either political or geographic significance. Its members concluded that the lake's chief economic asset was ivory (see J.W. Brooke, "A Journey West and North of Lake Rudolf," *Geographical Journal* 1905; 25:525–531).

17. *Report by Mr. A.E. Butter on the Survey of the Proposed Frontier Between British East Africa and Abyssinia*, Africa No. 13, London: Colonial Department, 1904. Butter returned to his 3,000-acre estate, Faskally, which he eventually sold in 1910. For many years, he raised thoroughbred sheepdogs, and he became keenly interested in farming. He died in 1928 at the age of fifty-four (Letter from John Butter to Pascal James Imperato, Nairobi, Kenya, April 10, 1996). Maud never returned to Africa and retired from the army in 1910. He then became chief officer of the Department of Parks and Open Spaces of the London County Council and continued in this post for many years, except for a period of army service during World War I. In 1918, he was given the rank of brigadier general. He died on February 28, 1947, at the age of seventy-six (see *Who Was Who, 1911–1950*, fourth edition, London: Adam and Charles Black, 1907, pp. 776–777).

18. Marcus, "A History," pp. 251–252.

19. Monty Brown, *Where Giants Trod: The Saga of Kenya's Desert Lake*, London: Quiller Press, 1989, p. 305.

20. E. Hertslet, *The Map of Africa by Treaty*, Volume 2, third edition, London: His Majesty's Stationery Office, 1909, p. 445.

21. Gwynn, who was born on February 4, 1870, in County Donegal, Ireland, was thirty-eight years old when he accepted the assignment to demarcate the Ethiopian border with British East Africa.

22. Charles W. Gwynn, "A Journey in Southern Abyssinia," *Geographical Journal* 1911; 38:113–135.

23. Gwynn never returned to sub-Saharan Africa, but he served in a number of posts in Britain and abroad. He distinguished himself in World War I, and in 1923, he was appointed aide-de-camp to King George V. In 1925, he was promoted to major general and the following year became commandant of the Staff College at Camberley. Following his retirement in 1931, he continued to be active in military affairs, and from 1938 to 1941, he served as president of

the Institution of Royal Engineers. He wrote on military matters during his retirement, including a book entitled *Imperial Policing*, London: Macmillan, 1934, and served as military editor of the nine volumes of *The Second World War*, edited by Sir J. Hammerton. He died a widower in Dublin on February 12, 1963, at the age of ninety-three (see "Major-General Sir Charles Gwynn, KCB, CMG, DSO," *Royal Engineers Journal* 1963; 77:191–193).

24. By any measure, the Ethiopians ended up with the better stretch of territory. John Boyes, an early trader and buccaneer in Kenya, made this observation when he crossed the border in 1906: "On the British side of the boundary, the country is low-lying arid waste covered with thick scrub. It appeared that the Abyssinians had got everything that was worth having in that part of the country—all the land of value being on their side of the frontier" (John Boyes, *The Company of Adventurers*, London: East Africa, 1928, p. 286).

Epilogue

1. A.C. McEwen, *International Boundaries of East Africa*, Oxford: Clarendon Press, 1971, pp. 103–112.

2. Georg Escherich, *Im Lande des Negus*, second edition, Berlin: G. Stilke, 1921.

3. Chauncey H. Stigand, *To Abyssinia Through an Unknown Land: An Account of a Journey Through Unexplored Regions of British East Africa by Lake Rudolf to the Kingdom of Menelik*, Philadelphia: J.B. Lippincott, 1910. Stigand's discovery of tsetse in the Omo River forest galleries was of great importance for both public health and veterinary officials in East Africa. The presence of these flies meant that trypanosomiasis would soon become a major disease problem for humans and domestic cattle at the northern end of the lake.

4. Pamela Gulliver and P.H. Gulliver, *The Central Nilo-Hamites*, London: International African Institute, 1953, p. 54.

5. Karl W. Butzer, *Recent History of an Ethiopian Delta: The Omo River and the Level of Lake Rudolf*, Chicago: University of Chicago Department of Geography, 1971, p. 116.

6. L.F.I. Athill, "Through Southwestern Abyssinia to the Nile," *Geographical Journal* 1920; 56:347–370.

7. Camille Arambourg, *Mission scientifique de l'Omo (1932–1933): Géologie-anthropologie*, Paris: Musée Nationale d'Histoire Naturelle, Fascicule 1 (1935), pp. 1–59; Fascicule 2 (1944), pp. 60–230; Fascicule 3 (1948), pp. 231–562.

8. Vivian E. Fuchs, "The Lake Rudolf Rift Valley Expedition (1934)," *Geographical Journal* 1935; 86:114–142.

9. Osa Johnson, *I Married Adventure*, Philadelphia: J.B. Lippincott, 1940, pp. 350–353.

10. Richard Leakey and Roger Lewin, *People of the Lake: Mankind and Its Beginnings*, Garden City, N.Y.: Anchor Press/Doubleday, 1978.

11. Alistair Graham and Peter Beard, *Eyelids of Morning: The Mingled Destinies of Crocodiles and Men*, Greenwich, Conn.: New York Graphic Society, 1973.

12. Letter from Reverend Paolo Tablino to Pascal James Imperato, Marsabit, Kenya, March 30, 1997; see also Gregory Jaynes, "Kenyan Region Gives Comfort Only to Bandits," *New York Times*, May 13, 1981, p. 10.

13. John Hillaby, *Journey to the Jade Sea*, London: Paladin, 1973; see also Holcomb B. Noble, "John Hillaby, 79, a Naturalist; Took Readers on Exotic Treks," *New York Times*, October 23, 1996, p. B20.

14. Stephen Pern, *Another Land, Another Sea: Walking Round Lake Rudolph*, London: Victor Gollancz, 1979.

15. Mohamed Amin, *Cradle of Mankind*, London: Chatto & Windus, 1981.

Selected Bibliography

Amin, Mohamed. *Cradle of Mankind*. London: Chatto & Windus, 1981.

Austin, Herbert H. "A Journey from Omdurman to Mombasa via Lake Rudolf." *Geographical Journal* 1902; 19:669–690.

_____. *Among Swamps and Giants in Equatorial Africa: An Account of Surveys and Adventures in the Southern Sudan and British East Africa*. London: C. Arthur Pearson, 1902.

_____. "Journeys to the North of Uganda. 2. Lake Rudolf." *Geographical Journal* 1899; 14:148–155.

_____. *Some Rambles of a Sapper*. London: Edward Arnold, 1928.

_____. *With Macdonald in Uganda: A Narrative Account of the Uganda Mutiny and Macdonald Expedition in the Uganda Protectorate and the Territories to the North*. London: Edward Arnold, 1903 (reprint ed., Folkestone and London: Dawson's; 1973).

Baxter, P.T.W. "Social Organization of the Boran of Northern Kenya." Shortened version of a D. Phil. thesis. Oxford, Lincoln College, 1954.

Baxter, P.T.W., and Uri Almagor (editors). *Age, Generation and Time: Some Features of East African Age Organizations*. London: C. Hurst, 1978.

Baxter, P.T.W., Jan Hultin, and Alessandro Triulzi. *Being and Becoming Oromo: Historical and Anthropological Enquiries*. Uppsala: Nordiska Afrikainstitutet, 1996.

Bodry-Sanders, Penelope. *Carl Akeley—Africa's Collector, Africa's Savior*. New York: Paragon House, 1991.

Bonati, Manlio. "Carlo Citerni." *La Rivista del Trekking* 1995; 82:83–85.

_____. "Lamberto Vannutelli." *La Rivista del Trekking* 1988; 23:340–341.

_____. *Vittorio Bottego: Un ambizioso eroe in Africa*. Parma: Silva Editore, 1997.

Borelli, Jules. *Ethiopie-Mériodionale: Journal de mon voyage aux Pays Amhara, Oromo et Sidama, Septembre 1885 à Novembre 1888*. Paris: Ancienne Maison Quantin, 1890.

Bottego, Vittorio. *Il Guiba esplorato: Viaggio di scoperta nel cuore dell'Africa—Sotto gli auspici della Società Geografica Italiana*. Rome: Loescher, 1895 (reprint ed. edited by Nicola Labanca, Parma: Ugo Guanda Editore, 1997).

Brantlinger, Patrick. *Rule of Darkness: British Literature and Imperialism, 1830–1914*. Ithaca: Cornell University Press, 1988.

Brooke, J.W. "A Journey West and North of Lake Rudolf." *Geographical Journal* 1905; 25:525–531.

Brown, Monty. *Hunter Away: The Life and Times of Arthur Henry Neumann 1850–1907*. London: MJB, 1993.

_____. *Where Giants Trod: The Saga of Kenya's Desert Lake*. London: Quiller Press, 1989.

Bulatovich, Alexander K. "Dall'Abissinia al Lago Rodolfo per il Caffa: Letta nell'adunanza generale della Imperiale Società Geografica Russa il 13(25) gennaio 1899, con note di G. Roncagli." *Bolletino della Società Geografica Italiana* 1900; Series 4, 37:121–142.

_____. *Ot Entotto do Reki Baro*. St. Petersburg: V. Kirshbaum, 1897.

_____. *S. Voyskami Menelika II*. St. Petersburg: Artistic Press Publishing House, 1900.

Bulla, Stefano. *Animali Africani a Parma: Nel centenario della morte di Vittorio Bottego*. Parma: Università degli Studi di Parma, 1997.

Burton, Richard F. *The Lake Regions of Central Africa: A Picture of Exploration*. New York: Harper and Brothers, 1860.

Butzer, Karl W. "Geological Interpretation of Two Pleistocene Hominid Sites in the Lower Omo Basin." *Nature* 1969; 222:1133–1135.

_____. *Recent History of an Ethiopian Delta: The Omo River and the Level of Lake Rudolf*. Chicago: University of Chicago Department of Geography, 1971.

Campioni, Silvio. *I Giam Giam: Sulle orme di Vittorio Bottego*. Parma: Casa Editrice Luigi Battei, 1960.

Castellani, C. *Vers le Nil français avec la mission Marchand*. Paris: Ernest Flammarion, 1898.

Cavendish, H.S.H. "Through Somaliland and Around the South of Lake Rudolf." *Geographical Journal* 1898; 11:372–396.

Cerulli, Ernesta. *Peoples of South-West Ethiopia and Its Borderland*. London: International African Institute, 1956.

Chanler, William Astor. "Hunting in East Africa." In *Hunting in Many Lands: The Book of the Boone and Crockett Club*, edited by Theodore Roosevelt and George Bird Grinnell. New York: Forest and Stream Publishing, 1895, pp. 13–54.

_____. "Rifles and Big Game in East Equatorial Africa." *The Field, The Country Gentleman's Newspaper* 1893; 82(2135):825.

_____. *Through Jungle and Desert: Travels in Eastern Africa*. New York: Macmillan, 1896 (reprint ed., Detroit: Negro History Press, 1970).

Collins, Robert O. *Land Beyond the Rivers: The Southern Sudan, 1898–1918*. New Haven and London: Yale University Press, 1971.

_____. *The Southern Sudan, 1883–1898: A Struggle for Control*. New Haven and London: Yale University Press, 1962.

Cooley, William Desborough. *Inner Africa Laid Open*. London: Longman, Brown, Green and Longmans, 1852 (reprint ed., Westport, Conn.: Negro Universities Press, 1969).

d'Abbadie, Antoine Thomson. *Note sur le Haut Fleuve Blanc*. Paris: Martinet, 1849.

DeBenedetti, Rinaldo. *Vittorio Bottego e l'esplorazione dell'Omo*. Turin: G.B. Paravia, 1933.

DeCaix, Robert. *Fachoda: La France et L'Angleterre*. Paris: Librairie Africaine et Coloniale, 1899.

DeMott, Maddie. "William Chanler." *Africana* 1967; 3(1):15–19.

Donham, Donald, and Wendy James (editors). *The Southern Marches of Imperial Ethiopia: Essays in History and Social Anthropology*. Cambridge: Cambridge University Press, 1986.

d'Orléans, Prince Henri. *Une visite à l'Empereur Ménélick*. Paris: Librairie Dentu, 1898.

Erdélyi, Lajos. *Teleki Samu Afrikában: Az Afrika-Kutató Eredeti Fényképfelvételeivel*. Bucharest: Kriterion Könyvkiadó, 1977.

Fuchs, Vivian E. "The Lake Rudolf Rift Valley Expedition (1934)." *Geographical Journal* 1935; 86:114–142.

Galvin, George E. *Diary of George E. Galvin, Chanler Expedition, Kenya (Formerly British East Africa), 1888–1890*, compiled by George E. Galvin Jr. Albuquerque, N.M., 1996.

Gillett, Mary. *Tribute to Pioneers*. Oxford: J.M. Considine, 1986.

Graham, Alistair, and Peter Beard. *Eyelids of Morning: The Mingled Destinies of Crocodiles and Men*. Greenwich, Conn.: New York Graphic Society, 1973.

Grant, James Augustus. *A Walk Across Africa; or Domestic Scenes from the Nile Journey*. Edinburgh: William Blackwood and Sons, 1864.

Graves, Philip. *The Life of Sir Percy Cox*. London: Hutchinson, 1941.

Gwynn, Charles W. "The Frontiers of Abyssinia: A Retrospect." *Journal of the Royal African Society* 1937; 36:50–161.

_____. "A Journey in Southern Abyssinia." *Geographical Journal* 1911; 38:133–135.

Hall, Richard. *Lovers on the Nile: The Incredible African Journeys of Sam and Florence Baker*. New York: Random House, 1980.

Harrison, James J. "A Journey from Zeila to Lake Rudolf." *Geographical Journal* 1901; 18:258–275.

Heaton, Tom. *In Teleki's Footsteps: An East African Journey*. London: Macmillan, 1989.

Hemsing, Jan. *Encounters with Lions*. Agoura, Calif.: Trophy Room Books, 1994.

_____. *Then and Now: Nairobi's Norfolk Hotel*. Nairobi: Sealpoint Publicity and Public Relations, 1982.

Hess, Robert L. *Italian Colonialism in Somalia*. Chicago: University of Chicago Press, 1966.

Hill, M.F. *Permanent Way: The Story of the Kenya and Uganda Railway*. Nairobi: East African Railways and Harbours, 1961.

Hillaby, John. *Journey to the Jade Sea*. London: Paladin, 1973.

Huxley, Elspeth. *White Man's Country: Lord Delamere and the Making of Kenya*. Volumes 1 and 2. London: Chatto & Windus, 1935.

Imperato, Pascal James. *Arthur Donaldson Smith and the Exploration of Lake Rudolf*. Lake Success, N.Y.: Medical Society of the State of New York, 1987.

_____. "Count Samuel Teleki's 1888 Expedition to Lake Turkana." *SWARA* 1988; 11(2):31–33.

Imperato, Pascal James, and Eleanor M. Imperato. *They Married Adventure: The Wandering Lives of Martin and Osa Johnson*. New Brunswick, N.J.: Rutgers University Press, 1992.

Imperato, Pascal James, and Geza Teleki. "Count Samuel Teleki's Second Voyage to East Africa." *SWARA* 1992; 15(2):23–25.

Jackson, Frederick. *Early Days in East Africa*. London: Edward Arnold, 1930.

Jesman, Czeslaw. *The Russians in Ethiopia: An Essay in Futility*. London: Chatto & Windus, 1958.

Johnston, Harry. *The Nile Quest: A Record of the Exploration of the Nile and Its Basin*. New York: Frederick A. Stokes, 1903.

Keefer, Edward Coltrin. "The Career of Sir John L. Harrington: Empire and Ethiopia, 1884–1918." Ph.D. diss., University Microfilms, Ann Arbor, Mich., 1974.

Krapf, J. Lewis. *Travels, Researches, and Missionary Labours During an Eighteen Years' Residence in Eastern Africa*. London: Trubner, 1860 (reprint ed., London: Frank Cass, 1968).

Leakey, Richard, and Roger Lewin. *People of the Lake: Mankind and Its Beginnings*. Garden City, N.Y.: Anchor Press/Doubleday, 1978.

Leontiev, Nicholas. "Exploration des provinces Equitoriales d'Abyssinie." *La géographie, Bulletin de la Société de Géographie* 1900; 2:105–118.

Lewis, David Levering. *The Race to Fashoda: European Colonialism and African Resistance in the Scramble for Africa*. New York: Weidenfeld and Nicolson, 1987.

Lyne, Robert Nunez. *An Apostle of Empire: Being the Life of Sir Lloyd William Mathews, K.C.M.G.*. London: George Allen and Unwin, 1936.

Macdonald, J.R.L. "Journeys to the North of Uganda." *Geographical Journal* 1899; 14:129–148.

Marcus, Harold G. "A History of the Negotiations Concerning the Border Between Ethiopia and British East Africa, 1897–1914" In *Boston University Papers on Africa*. Volume 2. *African History*. Edited by Jeffrey Butler. Boston: Boston University Press, 1966, pp. 239–265.

_____. *The Life and Times of Menelik II: Ethiopia 1844–1913*. Lawrenceville, N.J.: Red Sea Press, 1995.

Marsh, Zoë. *East Africa Through Contemporary Records*. Cambridge: Cambridge University Press, 1961.

Marsh, Zoë, and G.W. Kingsnorth. *An Introduction to the History of East Africa*. Cambridge: Cambridge University Press, 1963.

Maud, Philip. "Exploration in the Southern Borderland of Abyssinia." *Geographical Journal* 1904; 23:552–579.

Meyer, Hans. *Across East African Glaciers: An Account of the First Ascent of Kilimanjaro*. Translated from the German by H.S. Calder. London: George Philip & Son, 1891.

Michel, Charles. *Mission de Bonchamps vers Fachoda: A la rencontre de la mission Marchand à travers l'Etiopie*. Paris: Librairie Plon, 1900.

Michel, Marc. *La mission Marchand 1895–1899*. Paris: Mouton, 1972.

Millais, J.G. *Wanderings and Memories*. London: Longmans, Green, 1919.

Mission scientifique du Bourg de Bozas: De la Mer Rouge à l'Atlantique à travers l'Afrique Tropicale, Octobre 1900-Mai 1902. Paris: F.R. de Rudeval, 1906.

Moorehead, Alan. *The White Nile*. New York: Harper and Row, 1960.

Neumann, Arthur H. *Elephant Hunting in East Equatorial Africa*. London: Rowland Ward, 1898 (reprint ed., New York: Abercrombie & Fitch, 1966).

New, Charles. *Life, Wanderings, and Labours in Eastern Africa: With an Account of the First Successful Ascent of the Equatorial Snow Mountain, Kilima Njaro and Remarks upon East African Slavery*. London: Hodder and Stroughton, 1874 (reprint ed., London: Frank Cass, 1971).

Oliver, Roland, and Gervase Mathew (editors). *History of East Africa*. Volume 1. Oxford: Oxford University Press, 1963.

Pankhurst, Richard. *Economic History of Ethiopia 1800–1935*. Addis Ababa: Haile Selassie University Press, 1968.

_____. *An Introduction to the Medical History of Ethiopia*. Trenton, N.J.: Red Sea Press, 1991.

_____. *Travellers in Ethiopia*. London: Oxford University Press, 1965.

Perham, Margery, and Mary Bull (editors). *The Diaries of Lord Lugard*. Volume 1. *East Africa, November 1889 to December 1890*. Evanston, Ill.: Northwestern University Press, 1959.

Pern, Stephen. *Another Land, Another Sea: Walking Round Lake Rudolph*. London: Victor Gollancz, 1979.

Pompily, Fabrizio, and Carlo Cavanna. *La spedizione maremmana in Etiopia 100 anni dopo Vittorio Bottego*. Grosseto: Scripta Manent Editore, 1996.

Powell-Cotton, P.H.G. *A Sporting Trip Through Abyssinia*. London: Rowland Ward, 1902.

Pratt, Mary Louise. *Imperial Eyes: Travel Writing and Transculturation*. London and New York: Routledge, 1992.

Prouty, Chris. *Empress Taytu and Menelik II: Ethiopia 1883–1910*. Trenton, N.J.: Red Sea Press, 1986.

Prouty, Chris, and Eugene Rosenfeld. *Historical Dictionary of Ethiopia and Eritrea*. Metuchen, N.J., and London: Scarecrow Press, 1994.

Rice, Richard. *Captain Sir Richard Francis Burton: The Secret Agent Who Made the Pilgrimage to Mecca, Discovered the Kama Sutra, and Brought the Arabian Nights to the West*. New York: Charles Scribner's Sons, 1990.

Rodd, James Rennell. *Social and Diplomatic Memories*. Volumes 1, 2, and 3. London: Edward Arnold, 1922, 1923, 1925.

Rotberg, Robert I. *Joseph Thomson and the Exploration of Africa*. London: Chatto & Windus, 1971.

Sanderson, G.N. *England, Europe and the Upper Nile, 1882–1899*. Edinburgh: University Press, 1965.

_____. "The Foreign Policy of the Negus Menelik, 1896–1898." *Journal of African History* 1964; 5:87–97.

Schweinfurth, Georg. *The Heart of Africa: Three Years' Travels and Adventures in the Unexplored Regions of Central Africa from 1868 to 1871*. New York: Harper and Brothers, 1874.

Seltzer, Richard (editor). "Ethiopia Through Russian Eyes: An Eyewitness Account of the End of an Era, 1896–98, Consisting of Two Books by Alexander Bulatovich: From Entoto to the River Baro—An Account of a Trip to the Southwestern Regions of the Ethiopian Empire, 1896–97; With the Armies of Menelik II—Journal of an Expedition from Ethiopia to Lake Rudolf." Internet, http://www.samizdat.com, 1993.

_____. *The Name of Hero.* Boston: Houghton Mifflin, 1981.

Sieche, Erwin F. "Austria-Hungary's Last Naval Visit to the USA." *Warship International* 1990; 2:142–164.

Smith, A. Donaldson. "An Expedition Between Lake Rudolf and the Nile." *Geographical Journal* 1900; 16:600–625.

_____. "Expedition Through Somaliland to Lake Rudolf." Parts 1 and 2. *Geographical Journal* 1896; 8:120–137, 221–229.

_____. *Through Unknown African Countries: The First Expedition from Somaliland to Lake Lamu.* London and New York: Edward Arnold, 1897 (reprint ed., New York: Greenwood Publishers, 1969).

Speke, John Hanning. *Journal of the Discovery of the Source of the Nile.* Edinburgh and London: William Blackwood and Sons, 1863.

_____. *What Led to the Discovery of the Source of the Nile.* Edinburgh and London: William Blackwood and Sons, 1864.

Spencer, Paul. *Nomads in Alliance: Symbiosis and Growth Among the Rendille of Kenya.* London: Oxford University Press, 1973.

Stanley, Henry Morton. *Through the Dark Continent, or the Sources of the Nile Around the Great Lakes of Equatorial Africa and Down the Livingstone River to the Atlantic Ocean.* London: Sampson Low, Marston, Searle, and Rivington, 1878.

Stigand, Chauncey H. *To Abyssinia Through an Unknown Land: An Account of a Journey Through Unexplored Regions of British East Africa by Lake Rudolf to the Kingdom of Menelik.* Philadelphia: J.B. Lippincott, 1910 (reprint ed., New York: Negro Universities Press, 1969).

Tablino, Paolo. *African Traditional Religion: Time and Religion Among the Gabra Pastoralists of Northern Kenya.* Marsabit, Kenya: Marsabit Catholic Parish, 1989.

_____. *The Diocese of Marsabit: Some Historical Notes.* Marsabit, Kenya: Catholic Diocese of Marsabit, 1989.

_____. *I Gabbra del Kenya.* Bologna: E.M.I., 1980.

_____. "'Jila Galana,' La Massina Festività dei Gabra." *Rassegna di Studi Etiopia* 1988; 31:199–211.

Tate, H.R. "Journey to the Rendille Country, British East Africa." *Geographical Journal* 1904; 23:220–228, 280.

Teleki, Count Samuel. "Rifles for Big Game." *The Field, The Country Gentleman's Newspaper* 1894; 83(2145):155.

_____. "A Personal Diary of Explorations in East Africa, October 1886–October 1888, by Count Samuel Teleki (1845–1916), with Descriptions of His Pioneer Climbs on Mounts Kilimanjaro and Kenya in 1887, His Discoveries of Lakes Rudolf and Stefanie in 1888, and His Return Safari to Mount Kilimanjaro in 1895." Text translated from the handwritten Hungarian version into English by Charles and Vera Teleki, Warkworth, Ontario, Canada, 1961 (Geza Teleki Papers, Washington, D.C.).

Thomas, Lately. *A Pride of Lions: The Astor Orphans—The Chanler Chronicle*. New York: William Morrow, 1971.

_____. *Sam Ward: "King of the Lobby."* Boston: Houghton Mifflin Company, 1965.

Thomson, Joseph. *Through Masai Land: A Journey of Exploration Among the Snowclad Volcanic Mountains and Strange Tribes of Eastern Equatorial Africa*. London: Sampson Low, Marston, Searle, and Rivington, 1885 (reprint ed., London: Frank Cass, 1968).

Tibebu, Teshale. *The Making of Modern Ethiopia 1896–1974*. Lawrenceville, N.J.: Red Sea Press, 1995.

Trzebinski, Errol. *The Kenya Pioneers*. New York: W.W. Norton, 1986.

Turton, David. "Exploration in the Lower Omo Valley of Southwestern Ethiopia Between 1890 and 1910." In *L'Africa ai tempi di Daniele Comboni*, edited by Maria Genoino Caravaglios. Rome: Instituto Italo-Africano e Missionari Comboniani, 1981.

_____. "Looking for a Cool Place: The Mursi, 1890s–1990s." In *The Ecology of Survival: Case Studies from Northeast African History*, edited by D. Anderson and D. Johnson. London and Boulder: Lester Crook Academic Publishing/Westview Press, 1988, pp. 261–282.

_____. "Movement, Warfare, and Ethnicity in the Lower Omo Valley." In *Herders, Warriors, and Traders: Pastoralism in Africa*, edited by John G. Galaty and Pierre Bonte. Boulder: Westview Press, 1991, pp. 145–169.

_____. "Mursi Response to Drought: Some Lessons for Relief and Rehabilitation." *African Affairs* 1985; 84:331–346.

Vannutelli, L., and C. Citerni. *Seconda spedizione Bottego: L'Omo—Viaggio d'esplorazione nell'Africa Orientale*. Milan: Ulrico Hoepli Editore, 1899.

von Höhnel, Ludwig. *Discovery of Lakes Rudolf and Stefanie: A Narrative of Count Samuel Teleki's Exploring and Hunting Expedition in Eastern Equatorial Africa in 1887 and 1888*. Translated by Nancy Bell (N. D'Anvers). Volumes 1 and 2. London: Longmans, Green, 1894 (reprint ed., London: Frank Cass, 1968).

_____. "The Lake Rudolf Region: Its Discovery and Subsequent Exploration, 1888–1909." Parts 1 and 2. *Journal of the Royal African Society* 1938; 37:21–45, 206–226.

_____. *Mein Leben zur See auf Forfchunosreifen und beihofe*. Berlin: Verlag von Reimar Hobbing, 1926.

_____. "Over Land and Sea: The Memoirs of Ludwig von Höhnel—Africa Explorer, Rear Admiral and Imperial Aide-de-Camp," edited by Ronald E. Coons, Pascal James Imperato, and John Winthrop Aldrich, with a foreword by Sir Vivian Fuchs, scheduled to be published in 1998 under this tentative title by Holmes & Meier, New York.

_____. "Zur Karte des Nordostlechen Kenia-Gebrets." *Petermann's Mitteilungen* 1894; 40:193–199.

Wakefield, E.S. *Thomas Wakefield: Missionary and Geographical Pioneer in East Equatorial Africa*. London: Religious Tract Society, 1904.

Warner, Philip. *Kitchener: The Man Behind the Legend*. New York: Atheneum, 1986.

Wellby, Montagu Sinclair. "King Menelek's Dominions and the Country Between Lake Gallop (Rudolf) and the Nile Valley." *Geographical Journal* 1900; 21:292–306.

_____. *Through Unknown Tibet*. London: T. Fisher Unwin, 1898.

_____. *'Twixt Sirdar and Menelik: An Account of a Year's Expedition from Zeila to Cairo Through Unknown Abyssinia*. London: Harper and Brothers, 1901 (reprint ed., New York: Negro Universities Press, 1969).

Whitehouse, William F. "Through the Country of the King of Kings." *Scribners Magazine* 1902; 32:286–296.

_____. "To Lake Rudolf and Beyond." In *Hunting and Conservation: The Book of the Boone and Crockett Club*, edited by George Grinnell and Theodore Roosevelt. New Haven: Yale University Press, 1925, pp. 257–340.

Wickenburg, Eduard. "Von Dschibuti bis Lamu." *Petermann's Mitteilungen* 1903; 49:193–199.

_____. *Wanderungen in Ost-Afrika*. Vienna: Gerold, 1899.

Youngs, Tim. *Travellers in Africa: British Travelogues, 1850–1900*. Manchester and New York: Manchester University Press, 1994.

Zaghi, Carlo. *I Russi in Etiopia*. Volume 1. *Il Protettorato Italiano sull' Etiopia*. Volume 2. *Menelik e la Battaglia di Adua*. Naples: Guida Editori, 1972.

Index